THE IDEA OF THE PAST

PSYCHOANALYTIC CROSSCURRENTS
General Editor: Leo Goldberger

THE DEATH OF DESIRE: A STUDY IN PSYCHOPATHOLOGY
by M. Guy Thompson

THE TALKING CURE: LITERARY REPRESENTATIONS OF
PSYCHOANALYSIS
by Jeffrey Berman

NARCISSISM AND THE TEXT: STUDIES IN LITERATURE AND
THE PSYCHOLOGY OF SELF
by Lynne Layton and Barbara Ann Schapiro, Editors

THE LANGUAGE OF PSYCHOSIS
by Bent Rosenbaum and Harly Sonne

SEXUALITY AND MIND: THE ROLE OF THE FATHER AND THE
MOTHER IN THE PSYCHE
by Janine Chasseguet-Smirgel

ART AND LIFE: ASPECTS OF MICHELANGELO
by Nathan Leites

PATHOLOGIES OF THE MODERN SELF: POSTMODERN STUDIES
ON NARCISSISM, SCHIZOPHRENIA, AND DEPRESSION
by David Michael Levin, Editor

FREUD'S THEORY OF PSYCHOANALYSIS
by Ole Andkjær Olsen and Simo Køppe

THE UNCONSCIOUS AND THE THEORY OF PSYCHONEUROSES
by Zvi Giora

CHANGING MIND-SETS: THE POTENTIAL UNCONSCIOUS
by Maria Carmen Gear, Ernesto César Liendo, and Lila Lee Scott

LANGUAGE AND THE DISTORTION OF MEANING
by Patrick de Gramont

PSYCHOANALYTIC ROOTS OF PATRIARCHY: THE NEUROTIC
FOUNDATIONS OF SOCIAL ORDER
by J. C. Smith

SELF AND OTHER: OBJECT RELATIONS IN PSYCHOANALYSIS
AND LITERATURE
by Robert Rogers

SUBJECT AND AGENCY IN PSYCHOANALYSIS: WHICH IS TO BE
MASTER?
by Frances M. Moran

THE IDEA OF THE PAST: HISTORY, SCIENCE, AND PRACTICE IN
AMERICAN PSYCHOANALYSIS
by Leonard Jonathan Lamm

THE IDEA OF THE PAST

History, Science, and Practice in American Psychoanalysis

Leonard Jonathan Lamm

NEW YORK UNIVERSITY PRESS
New York and London

NEW YORK UNIVERSITY PRESS
New York and London

Library of Congress Cataloging-in-Publication Data
Lamm, Leonard Jonathan, 1945
The idea of the past : history, science, and practice in American
psychoanalysis / Leonard Jonathan Lamm.
p. cm.—(Psychoanalytic crosscurrents)
Includes bibliographical references and index.
ISBN 0-8147-5073-7
1. Psychoanalysis—United States—History. I. Title.
II. Series.
BF173.L226 1993
150.19′5′0973—dc20   92-44651
CIP

New York University Press books are printed on acid-free paper,
and their binding materials are chosen for strength and durability.

Manufactured in the United States of America

10 9 8 7 6 5 4 3 2 1

In Memory of My Father
ELIAS LAMM, 1910–1993

CONTENTS

FIGURES

FOREWORD

The *Psychoanalytic Crosscurrents* series presents selected books and monographs that reveal the growing intellectual ferment within and across the boundaries of psychoanalysis.

Freud's theories and grand-scale speculative leaps have been found wanting, if not disturbing, from the very beginning and have led to a succession of derisive attacks, shifts in emphasis, revisions, modifications, and extensions. Despite the chronic and, at times, fierce debate that has characterized psychoanalysis, not only as a movement but also as a science, Freud's genius and transformational impact on the twentieth century have never been seriously questioned. Recent psychoanalytic thought has been subjected to dramatic reassessments under the sway of contemporary currents in the history of ideas, philosophy of science, epistemology, structuralism, critical theory, semantics, and semiology as well as in sociobiology, ethology, and neurocognitive science. Not only is Freud's place in intellectual history being meticulously scrutinized, but his texts, too, are being carefully read, explicated, and debated within a variety of conceptual frameworks and sociopolitical contexts.

The legacy of Freud is perhaps most notably evident within the narrow confines of psychoanalysis itself, the "impossible profession" that has served as the central platform for the promulgation of official orthodoxy. But Freud's contributions—his original radical thrust—reach far beyond the parochial concerns of the clinician psychoanalyst as clinician. His writings touch on a wealth of issues, crossing traditional boundaries—be they situated in the biological, social, or humanistic spheres—that have profoundly altered our conception of the individual and society.

A rich and flowering literature, falling under the rubric of "applied psychoanalysis," came into being, reached its zenith many decades ago, and then almost vanished. Early contributors to this literature, in addition to Freud himself, came from a wide range of backgrounds both within and outside the medical/psychiatric field, and many later became psychoanalysts themselves. These early efforts were characteristically reductionist in their attempt to extrapolate from psychoanalytic theory (often the purely clinical theory) to explanation of phenomena lying at some distance from the clinical. Over the years, academic psychologists, educators, anthropologists, sociologists, political scientists, philosophers, jurists, literary critics, art historians, artists, and writers, among others (with or without formal psychoanalytic training), have joined in the proliferation of this literature.

The intent of the *Psychoanalytic Crosscurrents* series is to apply psychoanalytic ideas to topics that may lie beyond the narrowly clinical, but its essential conception and scope are quite different. The present series eschews the reductionist tendency to be found in much traditional "applied psychoanalysis." It acknowledges not only the complexity of psychological phenomena but also the way in which they are embedded in social and scientific contexts that are constantly changing. It calls for a dialectical relationship to earlier theoretical views and conceptions rather than a mechanical repetition of Freud's dated thoughts. The series affirms the fact that contributions to and about psychoanalysis have come from many directions. It is designed as a forum for the multidisciplinary studies that intersect with psychoanalytic thought but without the requirement that psychoanalysis necessarily be the starting point or, indeed, the center focus. The criteria for inclusion in the series are that the work be significantly informed by psychoanalytic thought or that it be aimed at furthering our understanding of psychoanalysis in its broadest meaning as theory, practice, and sociocultural phenomenon; that it be of current topical interest and that it provide the critical reader with contemporary insights; and, above all, that it be high-quality scholarship, free of absolute dogma, banalization, and empty jargon. The author's professional identity and particular theoretical orientation matter only to the extent that such facts may serve to frame the work for the reader, alerting him or her to inevitable biases of the author.

The *Psychoanalytic Crosscurrents* series presents an array of works from the multidisciplinary domain in an attempt to capture the ferment of scholarly activities at the core as well as at the boundaries of psychoanalysis. The books and monographs are from a variety of sources: authors will be psychoanalysts—traditional, neo- and post-Freudian, existential, object relational, Kohutian, Lacanian, etc.—social scientists with quantitative or qualitative orientations to psychoanalytic data, and scholars from the vast diversity of approaches and interests that make up the humanities. The series entertains works on critical comparisons of psychoanalytic theories and concepts as well as philosophical examinations of fundamental assumptions and epistemic claims that furnish the base for psychoanalytic hypotheses. It includes studies of psychoanalysis as literature (discourse and narrative theory) as well as the application of psychoanalytic concepts to literary criticism. It will serve as an outlet for psychoanalytic studies of creativity and the arts. Works in both the cognitive and neurosciences will be included to the extent that they address some fundamental psychoanalytic tenet, such as the role of dreaming and other forms of unconscious mental processes.

It should be obvious that an exhaustive enumeration of the types of works that might fit into the *Psychoanalytic Crosscurrents* series is pointless. The studies comprise a lively and growing literature as a unique domain; books of this sort are frequently difficult to classify or catalog. Suffice it to say that the overriding aim of the editor of this series is to serve as a conduit for the identification of the outstanding yield of that emergent literature and to foster its further unhampered growth.

LEO GOLDBERGER
Professor of Psychology
New York University

PREFACE AND ACKNOWLEDGMENTS

All the clever thoughts have long since been thought. What matters is to think them anew.

—Goethe

I came to my subject when I began to wonder, like many analysts and therapists before me, whether theory had anything much to do with practice, or practice anything much to do with theory. Most of us, I think, work from the seat of our pants, moment to moment, in a "cloud of unknowing." We pay homage to science, theory, and research—but if truth be known, we rely, as we must, on a potpourri of techniques, intuitions, and "approaches" acquired through the chain of supervision and apprenticeship, through academic study, and through the experiences of our personal histories.

Yet this cannot quite be the *complete* story. As responsible and reflective clinicians, we still wish to believe that good practice is derived from sound theory and that theory, in the best of all worlds, should properly prescribe the conduct of practice. Indeed, if Edith Kurzweil (1989) is at all correct in supposing that every country creates the psychoanalysis it needs (although it does so unconsciously), then America has assuredly given birth to a psychoanalytic outlook marked by a buoyant and optimistic belief in the utility of its theories and in the practical applicability of its technical recommendations and empirical findings. This is no less than an article of faith, but in the course of writing this book I have come to question it. Led by a chain of argument, I arrived at the disquieting conclusions that practice is not just another form of theory, that psychoanalytical theory of *any* sort bears no obvious relationship to the practical knowledge of psychotherapy, and that its claims of clinical relevance are therefore doubtful at best.

Given such skeptical conclusions, I might well have chosen to abandon theory. Instead I choose to stay with it. Thus, in the end, this is a book which aspires to make sense of theory in psychoanalysis, to inquire anew into its nature, uses, and aims. More exactly, this is a book which lays bare the dream of American psychoanalysis, the dream of a common language which might somehow bridge the great divide between self and other, body and mind, science and history, theory and practice. Of course, the dream of a common language (or common discourse) can never be more than a dream. But it is a dream which nonetheless animates the analytic enterprise and lends credence to the aim of psychoanalytic understanding in general, which is thought itself.

Thus in this book I defend a paradox—that psychoanalytic understanding is at once both radically practical and radically theoretical in character. I do this even though I recognize that there is and can be no "common language," no unified theory, no single or all-encompassing discourse. Psychoanalysis speaks instead in many voices and engenders a plurality of psychoanalytic pasts. Moreover, each mode of discourse (history, science, practice), in endeavoring to make sense of garbled versions of people's childhood pasts, implies or elaborates its own canonical construction of the psychoanalytic past. This, after all, is part of what I mean by the pluralist principle, a key corollary of which is that universes of discourse (history, science, and practice) may differ without disagreeing. The principle of pluralism in psychoanalysis is my lodestar. It is, so to speak, the root metaphor of this project and my own considered response to the dream of a common language for psychoanalysis—precisely because I recognize that the idea of a common language cannot be more than a dream, perhaps because it emerges from a memory trace that predates language and therefore can never be realized in words (Wexler 1991; Lacan 1977).

I was offered the unusual opportunity to begin work on this book while still a doctoral candidate in clinical psychology at the Graduate Faculty of the New School for Social Research. I owe an extraordinary debt to my advisors, Dr. Morris Eagle of the University of Toronto, and Professors Arnold Wilson and Henri Zukier of the New School. I regard their support as all the more generous since it need not imply agreement with my approach to psychoanalytic studies.

This project has been years in the making. It reflects my apprenticeship as a psychotherapist and also bears the imprint of my past and my education. For these reasons, I am grateful to my teachers, colleagues, supervisors, and patients, past and present. I owe more than I can say to my parents and, above all, to Marianne, a companion throughout. I would like to believe that she still dances between the lines of these pages.

Finally, I have been fortunate in the steadfast support of my editor, Jason Renker, and in the imaginative understanding of Dr. Leo Goldberger, general editor of the *Psychoanalytic Crosscurrents* series of New York University Press. In the technical preparation of this manuscript, I was expertly assisted by Alice Thomas and Judy Lubin.

I
THE PLURALIST PROPOSAL

1

Introduction: Method, Context, and Approach

The fact that there cannot be a guaranteed method of discovering what is true about some matter does not imply that nothing *is* true about that matter.

—John Dunn

This book offers an account of the conceptualization of the past in American psychoanalytic thought. The idea of the past is the alpha and the omega of psychoanalysis as a theoretical discourse. In the traditional idiom of Freudian psychology, this past is "where we live," where we start from, and where we end. It is the original traumatic situation along with its supposed residues in the here and now. Yet the meaning of the psychoanalytic past—the past which obtrudes into the present, interferes with it, and is interwoven with it—remains opaque and obscure, "as scientifically elusive as the edges of space" (Havens 1989 60) and the beginnings of time. Does it really refer to:

- an individual's history, consciously and unconsciously remembered, or to the facts, events, and actions of a person's past, whether remembered or not;
- the fantasies of occurrences which never took place, or to the traumatic experiences of infancy and childhood and the scars they leave in later life and in the "inner world"; or
- the biopsychical processes of development which only the scientific observer has inferred (and of which the patient is unaware), or to the changing narrative perspectives from which the story

3

of one's past is told and retold, or might have been told and retold?

The psychoanalytic idea of the past, then, is neither simple nor self-evident. It may even be legitimate to assert that the "past"—in at least one important sense—is just an epiphenomenon or product of present circumstances. Thus, the expectation with which I begin is that the idea of the past must first be unraveled or disambiguated if we are to make sense of the current state of psychoanalytical theory, and of those peculiar and durable controversies that define the intellectual world of American psychoanalysis. This is the task which I have set for myself in this book. The account which I offer is necessarily interpretive, local, and contextual. It does not pretend to final truth and must be judged, in the end, by its relative fruitfulness, by its ability to open up new avenues of inquiry, practice, and self-understanding.

The Theme and Plan of This Book

It is one hundred years since Freud's early work on the "neuro-psychoses." Psychoanalysis is no longer (if it ever was) a monotonic or monological discourse. I mean by this that present-day psychoanalysis is not only divided into numerous "schools" or "approaches" (e.g., Ego Psychology, Object Relations, Self Theory, Interpersonal Theory, Lacanianism, Freudian Feminism, etc.), but is also expressed and refracted through every conceivable form of cultural utterance. One hundred years after Freud, psychoanalysis speaks to us in many voices and each announces its own version of the psychoanalytic past. This is the "pluralist principle," and the elaboration of its implications for theory and practice forms the substance of this book. In the chapters to follow, I argue that the past is constructed in a variety of theoretical and practical contexts and that

- there is therefore a plurality of "pasts" in psychoanalysis,
- and each may be said to exhibit distinctive and, on occasion, divergent rationalities.[1]

Indeed, much confusion in contemporary psychoanalytic argument flows from the failure to recognize the *conceptual* complexity of the past, particularly the complexity that is engendered by the scientific, historical, and practical constructions of the past.

This book is loosely divided into two parts, the first of which (Chapters 1–3) introduces a pluralist model of a psychoanalytic understanding, mainly by showing how the idea of the past actually figures in the various strata and contexts of psychoanalytic discourse. In Chapters 4–6, which form the second part of this book, I apply, illustrate, and test the pluralist model within the distinctive world of American psychoanalysis.

• Chapter 1 lays the groundwork and answers such questions as these: what kind of book is this; what is its method or approach, and what does it presuppose; what is the "core controversy" in American psychoanalysis and why does it matter; what is meant by "pluralism in psychoanalysis" and how can I argue for it?

• Chapter 2 hones in on the argument between the "traditionalists" and "revisionists" over the nature and role of the past in theory and therapy (e.g., is what happens in analysis really related to what happened in the past?). I shift freely from the original "developmental" concepts of Freud to the contemporary thinking of such theorists as Schafer, Spence, Schimek, Stern, and Zukier. I conclude by providing a first formulation of the contrast between the "scientific" (orthogenetic) and "historical" (narrative-retrospective) constructions of the psychoanalytic past.

• In Chapter 3, I attend closely to the historical mode of discourse and contrast its version of the psychoanalytic past with the "practical" construction of the past. With this distinction in hand, I argue that historical self-understanding is acquired and transmitted through therapeutic engagements and may even be implicated in the processes of therapeutic action. By the end of Chapter 3, I have outlined the ways in which the psychoanalytic past is constructed scientifically, historically, and practically. The pluralist model is now essentially specified, and I propose that what is really required is not the unification of psychoanalysis into a homogeneous discourse, but rather the recognition of where, when, and how each mode of discourse is applicable and appropriate.

• In Chapter 4, I construct an exemplary version of *historical psychoanalysis*. I rely heavily on proposals advanced by Roy Schafer (1976, 1978, 1982, 1983), but also make use of the contributions of Edelson (1984, 1985, 1986), Spence (1982), and others. I argue that the historical approach to psychoanalytic understanding, particularly as articulated on the American scene, finds its necessary rationale in the European tradition of philosophical hermeneutics (Gadamer 1975, 1976). I suggest that historical psychoanalysis has as its paramount object or aim the construction of a "narrative past." It is this "inexistent" past which is now said to define the nature and uses of psychoanalysis as theory and as therapy.

• Chapter 5 presents an exemplary version of *scientific psychoanalysis,* based largely on proposals advanced by Gedo (1979, 1981, 1984, 1986, 1988), Noy (1969, 1977, 1979), Basch (1973, 1976a, 1976b, 1981, 1983, 1988), and Weiss and Sampson (1986), among others.[2] I am now concerned with the *logic* of scientific argument in psychoanalysis, and with the kind of psychoanalytic past that this logic stipulates. I call this past the "developmental past" and examine its relationship to the "narrative past" of historical psychoanalysis. I proceed to assess the relevance of psycho-analytic theorizing as such (scientific *or* historical) for therapeutic practice. Is psychoanalytic theory of any benefit to the clinician? Is experience in practice of any real use in the enterprise of theory? In asking and answer-ing such questions, I am led to acknowledge the autonomy and legitimacy of *practical psychoanalysis.* I argue that practice (praxis) is not just another form of theory, and for that reason alone, is not to be assimilated to either psychic engineering ("science") or hermeneutic interpretation ("his-tory").

• In Chapter 6, I recapitulate the argument for pluralism in psycho-analysis, review objections to it, and indicate directions for further in-quiry. My topic in this book has indeed been large and general, and my "reading" of the literature unabashedly speculative. I believe, nonetheless, that I succeed in showing some of the interesting ways in which psycho-analytic thinking is multivalent, how its various universes of discourse may differ without disagreeing. Yet, as I finally conclude, I have the obligation to wrestle with these last (and possibly unanswerable) ques-tions. If psychoanalytic theorizing (scientific or historical) lacks direct clinical relevance, what, then, is it for, and for whom? And if this book ends in such a question, what is its use, and for whom have I written it?

The Plurality of Ends

The question of method must be addressed in any scholarly or systematic investigation. In one sense, my method is quite simple: it is the method of reflection. "The improvement of thought always requires reflection, the formation of ideas of ideas, and a critical self-consciousness; there is no other method" (Hampshire 1977 16). And yet, in another sense, "reflection," the method of this study, is absolutely problematical and requires a certain justification.[3]

Isaiah Berlin (1981), in the context of political philosophy, has brought forward one such justification. He asks us, in a kind of thought experiment, to imagine a society dominated by a single goal or end, in which all argument is about means and is therefore scientific, empirical, or technical in character. In such a society, dominated by a single goal, all serious discussion can

> at least in principle be reduced to positive sciences. . . . It follows that the only society in which political philosophy in its traditional sense, that is, an inquiry concerned not solely with the elucidation of concepts, but with the critical examination of presuppositions and assumptions . . . is possible, is a society in which there is no total acceptance of any single end. (149–50)

According to Berlin's argument, then, reflection—or the critical examination of presuppositions and assumptions—can only make sense (not seem superfluous, subversive, or nonsensical) in a society "in which there is not total acceptance of any single end." There is thus a political or rhetorical condition attached to this study. Only if psychoanalysis, and more broadly, the human sciences,[4] are still seen to constitute an intellectual community characterized by a "plurality of ends," is the present undertaking defensible and legitimate. If the community of psychoanalysis were successfully to enact some single, exclusive, and superordinate goal (e.g., effectiveness of clinical intervention, natural scientific canons of investigation and theorizing, the primacy of the hermeneutic circle, etc.), there could be no *point* to a reflective inquiry into the conceptualization of the past in psychoanalytic thought—just as there is no point, or virtually no point, to such an inquiry in the relatively settled psychological fields of perception and psychophysics. The intelligibility of this book, then, depends at least on the initial "negative capability" of its potential readers: their capability, as the poet Keats described it, to contain competing truths, tolerate ambiguity, and above all, resist the call to certainty and closure.

Are we entitled, and if so, on what grounds, to understand psychoanalysis, and more broadly, the human sciences, as characterized by a plurality of ends?

Jürgen Habermas (1971) has proposed that there is, both analytically and in fact, a plurality of ends characteristic of the human sciences. Three such ends or cognitive interests are stipulated, each corresponding to an aspect of human society. For example, since all societies must exist in a material environment bound to nature, this condition necessitates labor, and labor is said to promote an interest in the prediction and control of events. It is this interest which Habermas holds to be categorically constitutive of what he calls the *empirical-analytic sciences.* And it cannot be denied that the natural and behavioral sciences have given us greatly extended capacities for intervening in biological, social, and psychological processes: they have given us more power. Indeed it is the reality of this power (the power of impersonal law and statistical probability), at least as much as the promise of understanding, which has sustained and invigorated the empirical-analytic vision of a science of man and society; and it is thus this interest—in the prediction and control of events—which positivism, as an ideology, is always prone to generalize to all knowledge and activity. In the words of one of Habermas' more astute commentators (McCarthy 1978):

> The real problem . . . is not technical reason as such, but its universalization, the forfeiture of a more comprehensive concept of reason in favor of the exclusive validity of scientific and technological thought, the reduction of *praxis* to *techne,* and the extension of purposive-rational action to all spheres of life. (22)

Habermas, however, adhering to "a more comprehensive concept of reason," proposes the two additional interests of (a) understanding of meaning, and (b) emancipation. The former is said to arise out of symbolic interaction and the interpretability of human communication. Hermeneutics and, more generally, the historical sciences, become the reflective and cultural articulations of this interest. Finally, the third (and most problematic) cognitive interest, emancipation, is said to stem from the human inclination toward autonomy or freedom from domination. Critical theory is advanced as being that form of knowledge or reason distinctively shaped by the imperative (shaped normatively, logically, psychologically?) for emancipation from systems of domination.

Although Habermas never explains why there are only three knowledge-constitutive interests, or the precise nature of their connection to conditions of social life and to underlying psychological processes, he has at least advanced a preliminary model of the "plurality of ends," which has also been applied and illustrated in his influential interpretation of clinical psychoanalysis as involving hermeneutic, empirical-analytic, and critical theoretic concepts and procedures (Apel 1977; Thoma and Kachele 1975).

The Controversy Introduced

While this model will not govern my analysis of the conceptualization of the past in psychoanalysis, nor my specific treatment of the various modes of psychoanalytic understanding, it nevertheless helps to focus attention on what may be the primary tension or core controversy in American psychoanalytic thought: namely, the debate between (a) those who hold that psychoanalysis is nothing like a natural science, and that its proper analogue is (or ought to be) historical interpretation rather than scientific and causal explanation, versus (b) those who reject the "retreat to hermeneutics" (Blight 1981), and who would continue to adhere to some version of traditional scientific norms and methods in their research, theory, and investigations. In short, this is the debate between (a) the "dichotomists" who (echoing the nineteenth-century distinction between the *Geisteswissenschaften* and *Naturwissenschaften*) argue that nature and culture are sufficiently distinguishable as objects of knowledge that they require different methods and modes of explanation, and (b) the "unitarians" who maintain the essential unity of inquiry across all domains and subject matters, notwithstanding marginal and secondary variations of method and approach (e.g., Popper 1972). It is noteworthy that the founder of psychoanalysis believed himself to be a "unitarian" and explicitly rejected the "dichotomist" position in the following summary statement:

> As a specialist science . . . it is quite unfit to construct a *Weltanschauung* of its own; it must accept the scientific one . . . the *uniformity* of the explanation of the universe . . . the intellect and the mind are objects for scientific research in exactly the same way as any non-human beings. (Freud 1933 158–59)

Although the debate is usually couched in the terms presented above, it may also be construed in such a manner as to avoid any *dualistic* (Kantian and Cartesian) commitments. Von Wright (1971), for example, has argued that there are two competing traditions concerned with the "conditions an explanation has to satisfy in order to be scientifically respectable": the Aristotelian and the Galilean. And thus he writes (while accounting for the importance of Hegel) that:

> it seems to me true to say that Hegel is the great renewer—after the Middle Ages and therefore in opposition to the platonizing spirit of Renaissance and Baroque science—of an aristotelian tradition in the philosophy of method. For Hegel, as for Aristotle, the idea of a law is primarily that of an intrinsic connection to be grasped through reflective understanding, not that of an inductive generalization established by experiment. . . . For both philosophers, explanation consists in making phenomena teleologically intelligible rather than predictable from knowledge of their efficient causes. (8)

However this controversy is understood, and whatever its philosophical pedigree, it is clear that it is currently dividing the American psychoanalytic community. Simply put, there is now a clash of paradigms which pits the (historical-hermeneutic-Aristotelian) research program of a Roy Schafer (1978, 1983) against the (empirical-analytic-Galilean) research program of a Joseph Weiss and a Harold Sampson (1986). It is obvious that different cognitive or "knowledge-constitutive interests" govern such psychoanalytic research programs, but it is far from obvious how we are to go about the job of "reflecting" upon this seeming conflict of interests. Is there even agreement on the very domain of psychoanalytic inquiry, i.e., on what psychoanalysis aims to explain or understand? And if not, is there really a debate or controversy to elucidate, or conflicting claims to adjudicate?

In order that we may begin to understand, in a general way, what is actually at issue in the apparent argument between the hermeneuts and scientists in psychoanalysis, it will be useful to return to Berlin's analysis of disputation in political philosophy (1981), his endeavor to legitimate "reflection" as a rational form of discourse. Berlin is now trying to establish how we are to construe Rousseau's disagreement with Hobbes. Surely it wasn't the case that Hobbes had missed certain psychological facts, or had argued wrongly from what he had seen. Rather, in Berlin's view, it is *implicit* in Rousseau's position that it

> is not that the facts used to construct Hobbes' model had gaps in them, but that the model was inadequate in principle; it was inadequate not because this or that psychological or sociological correlation had been missed out,

but because it was based on a failure to understand what we mean by motive, purpose, value, personality and the like. (163–64)

Is Rousseau correct in his critique? Is Hobbes' model (even though it may be said to underlie the empirical-analytic science of human nature and society) "inadequate in principle?" This controversy, after two hundred or more years, is by no means dead (or resolved). Thus Louch (1966 235) can argue, for example, that "the idea of a science of man or society is untenable," because its method and conception of science are "borrowed from physics," while its *conception* of its subject matter "is borrowed from moral action." Moreover, if we agree with Berlin's interpretation, *empirical research* will not help to resolve and settle such controversies as Hobbes versus Rousseau (and Louch et al.), since the very terms of such controversies are likely to be presupposed by (or imported into) empirical research, rendering the results of such research equally ambiguous, and liable to self-confirming interpretations.

So following Berlin's proposal, we look, instead, to reflection or philosophical discourse, *not* because it can definitively settle such controversies as Hobbes versus Rousseau (or scientist versus hermeneut in psychoanalysis), but because it (a) recognizes the pervertibility of our metaphors and the contestability of our concepts, and (b) specializes in getting clearer about our concepts, their limits, and their implications. In brief, what reflection can do is at least to offer an explication of our competing and disputable understandings such that their innermost presuppositions are finally exposed, and we may begin to appreciate what is actually at stake in the apparent argument. Perhaps there is the hope, too, that a kind of simultaneous contemplation[5] of what is right in each view (or mode of psychoanalytic understanding) might lead toward a new synthesis, or at least, a perspicuous overview of why we are torn between the two positions. This, I suggest, would represent a legitimate and credible increment in our understanding, as would equally the expectation of many philosophers since Austin and Wittgenstein that such an overview might even release us from the controversy itself—by showing how conceptual confusion and "false pictures" have interfered with substantive work on some genuine practical or theoretical problem.

Two Propositions

The core controversy (reduced to its barest essentials) has now been introduced. We have also taken the initial step toward understanding how philosophical discourse—reflection upon fundamental, contested, and disputable concepts and categories—can generate the kind of *synoptic overview* that may shed some light on traditions of argument now current in psychoanalysis and the human sciences in general.

Let me proceed to illustrate through a consideration of the following two "propositions":

1. "The actual world is independent of our descriptions or knowledge of it, our values, preferences and emotional responses to it, and our attempts to understand or explain it" (Edelson 1985 572).
2. "All knowledge . . . is a set of conventions governed by a central paradigm. It is derived and informed by that paradigm and does not refer to anything other than the paradigm it is informed by" (Munz 1985 132).

The first proposition may be regarded as a fundamental presupposition of empirical-analytic science. What is implied is a conception of knowledge, the content of which "is recognized to have a condition independent of mind" (Lewis 1956 189–92). Knowledge is necessarily *relational:* the knower (the organism) is somehow related to something (an environment) outside and independent of himself. It is in this sense that there are non-negotiable "brute facts," or at least the presumption of objectivity: the postulate of a universe of objects with independent existences and careers. From within this horizon, the cognitive task of the knower (qua scientist) is to reveal or uncover reality *in its objectivity,* "to obtain evidence relevant to evaluating the truth of a sentence asserting that such-and-such a state of affairs does obtain *in the actual world*" (Edelson 1985 573, my emphasis).

Consider, now, the second proposition. What is implied in the present case is that knowledge is not reducible to a relationship between knower and known, but is rather a self-constituting (or socially constituted) activity, carried on *inside* the circle of a particular, authoritative speech community. Both knower and known (subject and object of knowledge) are thus "functions" of some local and non-universal semiotic system. Objectivity is therefore inconceivable, at least in the ontological sense noted above. Paradigms and epistemic circles are recognized as incommensurable; and the idea of meaning and truth as "negotiable" sense would seem to displace the idea of meaning and truth as reference, since there is now no foundational reality (outside the circle) to be mirrored or referred to. This is surely the view (however oversimplified my depiction of it) of many prominent post-Wittgensteinian philosophers. Peter Winch (1958, 1964), for example, has argued extensively that terms such as reality, world, nature, and God have no sense apart from the language games in which they are used; even the meaning of the concept of truth can vary, depending on in which of many possible language games (theoretical and practical contexts) it is used. From the standpoint of Proposition 1, such an argument seems hopelessly relativistic and non-objective since it is indeed the case that standards for what is rational and intelligible vary among language games and speech communities. But from within its own epistemic horizon, the issue of "foundations" is moot, and investigation and reflection are seen to involve a dialectical process in which the rationality of one game is brought into relationship with the rationality of another, so that a new unity for the concept of rationality can be established. Such a Proposition 2 point of view has also been advanced by Goodman (1978) and Rorty (1979), the latter arguing against the traditional (Hobbesian-Cartesian) conception of knowledge (one of whose paradigmatic expressions is empirical-analytic science), in which mind is compared to a mirror that reflects or represents nature or reality.

Clearly these two propositions underlie discrete, if not antithetical, conceptions of knowledge and inquiry in American psychoanalysis. According to the first proposition, theoretical knowledge in psychoanalysis is relational, entails reference to an "outside," and implies, at least in principle, an unchanging reality (psychic reality?) which can be broken down (analytically abstracted) into unambiguous terms. It is committed, in addition, to the generation of data derived, ultimately, from non-negotiable brute fact (mental or physical), and finally, to the explanation of the behavior of "objects" in terms of the replicable and reliable analysis of regularities and causal processes. Edelson (1986) has offered a qualified defense of such an objectivist paradigm, even in the context of the narratively constructed single case study, still the most common context for the sharing of "knowledge" in the American community of clinical psychoanalysis; Weiss and Sampson (1986) presuppose such a paradigm in their more elaborate and scientifically credible research program, aimed at testing what they interpret to be crucial psychoanalytic hypotheses. But both Edelson and Weiss appear to agree, and rightly so, given their common commitment to Proposition 1, that the domain of psychoanalytic study is properly comprised of such potentially *objective* psychological entities as "pathogenic beliefs," as well as other alleged mental events along with certain of their properties and relations, including their hypothetical relations and linkages to behavior and action.

The Methodological Circle

If the analysis I have just offered is correct, then it would appear that fundamental presuppositions of an epistemological and ontological kind do indeed constrain the choice and characterization of domain in psychoanalysis, especially insofar as it is conducted as an empirical-analytic science. However, it is probably more accurate to say that, in actual research practice, it is the assumptions and presuppositions inherent in methodology (e.g., in statistical inference) which directly determine, or are the efficient causes of, such basic theoretical decisions as choice and characterization of domain. Danziger (1985), for example, addressing American academic psychology in general, has argued for the possibility of a vicious "methodological circle," where methods based on assumptions about the nature of the subject matter only produce observations which confirm these assumptions. "The point is that methods used to test a theory may presuppose the truth (or falsity) of the theory to be tested" (1).

More specifically, he goes on, academic psychology—while notoriously lacking in theoretical coherence—is nonetheless unified methodologically, especially in prescribing the use of the techniques of statistical inference. But since this requires the imposition of numerical systems on some data source, and hence the likelihood of tacitly equating the *structure* of the numerical system with the *structure* of the empirical system, it becomes expedient to conform the domain to the requirements of a specific methodology. For example, elements of a given domain (e.g., pathogenic beliefs) must be construed as independently identifiable, and as insertable or resolvable into very particular sorts of relationships. The dominant methodology thus requires that the world of any given domain be a world of *parts* and their abstracted external relations, rather than a world of *wholes* and their intrinsic relations. And so Danziger goes on to state:

> Moreover, for these relations to operate it is also necessary for each variable to be defined independently of any other and to remain identical with itself irrespective of changing circumstances. In other words, intrinsic relations and qualitative changes are excluded. They could only enter the system by undergoing an appropriate transformation. (9)

The dominant methodology, as Danziger describes it, is of course a Galilean methodology; as such, it delegitimates Aristotelian explanation (the idea of a law "as an intrinsic connection grasped through reflective understanding"). It also excludes historical and hermeneutic understandings, which usually involve narrative organizations of experience or evidence, as well as phenomenological systems of understanding which focus on the structures of experience prior to any judgment about the factual or illusory status of what appears. In Danziger's view, moreover, influential and important theories (or models) like Piagetian psychology, Gestalt psychology and, of course, classical psychoanalysis, were generated *outside* the now dominant methodology, and none of them "would or could endorse the assumptions on which statistical theory testing methodology is based. The act of subjecting such theories to this kind of testing already presupposes that the theories are mistaken in some of their assumptions" (7).

Whether or not Edelson or Weiss and Sampson can agree with Danziger's assessment is debatable; but what is not disputed is that their respective research programs construct or *reconstruct* the domain of psychoanalytic inquiry to conform to the presuppositions and implicit (questionable) assumptions underlying both the dominant methodology *and* the traditional epistemology and ontology of the empirical-analytic sciences. Edelson (1984) has almost conceded as much in stating:

> Questions about the choice of a kind of domain for study or the choice of a way to characterize entities in a domain are not questions that can be decided by collecting evidence. (120)

But if such questions are not decided on the basis of evidence, on what basis, then, are they decided? In this section, I have argued that such decisions as the choice and characterization of domain are determined, directly or indirectly, by fundamental presuppositions and implicit (often unstated) assumptions. And I have earlier described "reflection," the method of this study, as the critical examination of presuppositions and assumptions.

An Unscientific Postscript

Recall my assertion that Propositions 1 and 2 underlie discrete, if not antithetical, conceptions of knowledge and inquiry in psychoanalysis. Upon closer inspection, however, it appears that this claim is not quite borne out. For it is a fact that Proposition 2 is perfectly compatible with the picture of empirical-analytic inquiry I have just sketched in the preceding pages. To endorse Proposition 2 is, indeed, to alter nothing in the "internal" affairs and practices of that particular "speech community" involved in the language game of science.[6] What difference, then, does it make to endorse Proposition 2?

My claim is now just this: to endorse Proposition 2 is to commit oneself to a view of empirical-analytic science (and empirical-analytic psychoanalysis) which radically modifies its place on the "map" of inquiry. No longer can it be presumed (as Proposition 1 implies) that empirical-analytic science has a monopoly on rationality or truth (or even on its reliable and valid acquisition and transmission). A plurality of theoretical and practical "speech communities" is now postulated, and it thus becomes possible to conceive of historical and hermeneutic "language games" (among others), which are capable of eliciting and establishing "rationalities" of their own, uninhibited by the specific presuppositions and assumptions of the empirical-analytic approach. It follows that to require of such non–empirical-analytic inquiries that they "achieve some explicable form of objectivity and explanatory power" (Russell 1988 131) is only reasonable if such "requisites" are not construed solely in terms of the assumptive framework native to empirical-analytic science.

The importance of Proposition 2, then, is that it allows for a plurality of modes of inquiry, along with the "rationalities" which are their objective correlates. In sum, Proposition 2 legitimates the pluralist program of this book. For this book, taken as a whole, aims to describe (as well as deconstruct) the psychoanalytic idea of the past as it is diversely conceptualized in a variety of speech communities practicing distinct and disparate (if sometimes overlapping) language games, and regulated by autonomous, but possibly complementary, canons of rationality.

Now my particular focus, as indicated at the outset, is on the scientific, historical, and practical constructions of the past, and on the roles these constructions play in the scheme of psychoanalytic understanding. Having already provided a brief and summary sketch of the scientific approach (oriented by Proposition 1), it should now be possible to move on and consider the character of non–empirical-analytic approaches (e.g., history, hermeneutics, etc.). But such a move is not easily achieved. Prevailing opinion inhibits reflection, claiming that history is either mere chronicle, or at best, a weak and defective variant of (social and behavioral) science; to paraphrase the philosopher Bosanquet, history is nothing but a "tissue of conjunctions," and the "doubtful story of successive events." A full account of history as a rational mode of inquiry, as well as of its legitimate role and function in the scheme of psychoanalytic understanding, will therefore have to be postponed until Chapters 3 and 4. What can be offered now is just a *prolegomenon* to that account. And the first step toward this goal will be to build up a "model" of what psychological studies, in general, might look like, when not governed by Proposition 1 (the "scientific" or objectivist proposition), and when not constrained by Danziger's "methodological circle." So the initial question becomes the following: what might the *domain* of psychological or psychoanalytic study look like, released from the presuppositions, assumptions, and considerations of empirical-analytic science?

Prolegomenon

An interesting answer to that question is proposed by the phenomenological psychologist Romanyshyn (1982). The appropriate domain (psychological experience) is apprehended

> as a metaphorical reality which is neither a thing nor a thought . . . neither material nor a mental activity . . . it is a way of seeing things which opens up a world which matters and must be understood. A metaphor establishes a world and one understands a metaphor by participating in its vision. Psychological experience inclines one toward a view of the world. Taking up that inclination, one is able to explore the boundaries and limits of that world . . . (173)

Before proceeding further, let us bear in mind that as a phenomenologist, Romanyshyn's purpose is not (as is sometimes thought) to reproduce lived experience, but rather to explicate it by taking the appearance of what appears prior to any judgment about the factual or illusory status of what appears. In other words, what phenomenology uncovers is not some aboriginal realm of "concrete experience," but simply experience as *abstracted* (explicated) from a certain point of view. This means that in bracketing or suspending those commitments specific to science and theory, Romanyshyn's approach is not so much anti-scientific as it is non-scientific (or extrascientific) in character or aim. It thus becomes possible, in principle, to envision such undertakings as subpersonal, scientific models of mental functioning (e.g., Rubenstein 1977), which are nevertheless consistent with the phenomenological structure of psychological experience, as explicated, perhaps, by Romanyshyn himself. A phenomenological account, in short, does not necessarily compete with a scientific, explanatory, or empirical-analytic account.

Let us now assess the relevance of Romanyshyn's proposal that the appropriate domain of study is psychological experience "as a metaphorical reality." As such, psychological experience does not come prepackaged in material or mental form; nor does it normally appear as an object, thing, or process. Rather it is recognized as a *way of seeing* things. The domain, so viewed, is not so much a reproduction of lived experience as it is a perspective on it. It is from within such a view of the appropriate domain of psychological studies that Romanyshyn can now suggest that "it is not the empirical events of one's biography that are psychological, but the way in which those events are gathered together to weave a tale" (16). Phenomenologically, then, what is distinctively psychological is not the empirical or experienced event as such ("fact"), nor the mere memory or recall of it, nor, certainly, the processes hypothesized to underlie (or explain) such experience and recall. What is distinctively psychological is rather the *weaving* of memory, or more aptly, the work of recollection and remembrance—as enacted (in stories and self-narratives, for example) prior to any judgment about its "real" or underlying nature. And it is inherent in such a perspective that the psychological past appears neither as fixed fact nor as false illusion—for it is only from the non-phenomenological vantage points of science (and everyday life) that such judgments are possible. The past, then, is neither real nor unreal, but that which becomes accessible and available through the "weaving" of memory, the work of remembrance, and the vicissitudes of narration. The phenomenologist is open both to the pliability of the past and to the recalcitrance of the past, and recognizes that though life is finite, a remembered event is infinite "because it is only a key to everything that happened before it and after it" (Benjamin 1968 204).

In summary, Romanyshyn has interwoven his notion of "psychological experience as metaphorical reality" with the individual's life history, and has proposed that what is distinctively psychological are not the empirical events of anyone's biography, but the *way in which* those events are gathered together to tell a story. Thus what may be called the "narrative organization of events," rather than the events themselves, becomes the appropriate object of psychological and psychoanalytic understanding. Furthermore, narrative organization or narrativity ("the way in which those events are gathered together . . .") does not refer just to temporal or causal relations: the psychological subject (or self) is not essentially a naive chronicler or proto-scientist. It is rather that narrative organization (narrativity) refers, more fundamentally, to the ways in which events are (a) distinguished and demarcated, (b) recognized as wholes or parts of wholes, (c) seen to combine into larger events (and vice versa). And so high narrativity—related to what Bruner (1986 26) calls "subjunctivity" —may be derived, in part, from totalizing and detotalizing events, from constructing and deconstructing, from making sums and unmaking sums. "Narrative is usually not a simple concatenation of events in time, but a hierarchical one" (Prince 1982 151–52).

Many specific features of discourse seem to contribute to narrativity or subjunctivity (the "storiness" or interpretability of stories), including: the triggering of presupposition; the subjectification of experience; the simultaneity of multiple perspectives; the deployment of metaphor. The upshot is that phenomenal reality itself is rendered subjunctive through the language and discourse of narrative—for "how one *talks* comes eventually to be how one *represents* what one talks about" (Bruner 1986 131). To be in the subjunctive mode is thus to constitute and reconstitute experience as narrative: it is to recognize that human plights and pasts (including one's own) are by their very nature *intended* to be rewritten and be otherwise. Again in Bruner's words, "To be in the subjunctive mode is . . . to be trafficking in human possibilities rather than in settled certainties" (26), and is in this respect to be sharply distinguished from the stance of "science," which engages the world in its *objectivity*—as a world which remains invariant across human intentions and human plights.

Bringing this perspective to bear on Romanyshyn's presentation, it follows that we live (ordinarily and pretheoretically) in a more or less *subjunctivized reality*. This means that through the prism of metaphorized language and metaphorized conceptual systems (Lakoff and Johnson 1980), experience and conduct appear to us as configured *narratives,* long before and long after we dismember them analytically (scientifically). Metaphor, moreover, moves or energizes narrative, and opens up possibilities for the development of new categories and self-understandings (even as it may sometimes entrap us in old ones). Lastly, self-narratives or recollected life histories (those potentially rewritable personal pasts) may eventually be understood as "metaphorical realities" themselves, in that real-life-as-experienced comes to appear as a product of one's narrative, rather than the other way around. The narrative comes to stand for the life. Walter Benjamin seems to have captured a clinically relevant dimension of this phenomenon when he observes:

> A man . . . who died at thirty-five will appear to *remembrance* at every point in his life as a man who dies at the age of thirty-five. In other words, the statement that makes no sense for real life becomes indisputable for remembered life. (1968 100)

In phenomenological terms, then, the "clinical" problem comes into view when the remembered life somehow supplants the real life, when life is lived as if it were remembered (or narrated), when it is one and the same man who lives as if he had died at the age of thirty-five. For Romanyshyn, the phenomenological psychologist, this is exactly the sort of metaphor that defines the *domain* of psychological inquiry—when that domain is allowed to appear unobstructed by the presuppositions and assumptions of empirical-analytic science. And so in the chapters to follow —as the historical construction of the past is examined in detail—we will begin to discover that the *psychoanalytic narrative* (the "history" of psychic reality) claims a legitimate place in theory and practice, precisely because it purports to loosen the hold on us of such (unconscious) stories as Benjamin's "man who died at thirty-five," by convincing us that they are "just stories," and not the way things are or must be.

The Narrative Turn

Although Romanyshyn is not in the mainstream, the "narrative turn" he proposes has, in recent years, engaged the interest of many American researchers and theorists in cognitive, social, developmental, and clinical psychology (Sarbin 1986; Bruner 1986; Cohler 1981; Freeman 1984; Mandler 1984); and it has intersected, as well, with the enduring debate between scientists and hermeneuts in the human sciences and in psychoanalysis (Ricoeur 1970, 1974, 1985; Habermas 1971; Spence 1982; Grunbaum 1984; Schafer 1983; Eagle 1984a). One might go as far as to assert that the decision to regard "narrative phenomena" as necessary constituents of the *domain* of psychological and psychoanalytic studies marks the beginning of a potentially significant, if inherently risky, research program[7] in the human sciences as such.

Let me begin by first citing the risks associated with the "narrative turn." The first risk concerns the cultural context that surrounds the current upsurge of academic interest in narrative, while the second is directly connected to recent developments in theoretical and clinical psychoanalysis.

1. It has been observed that the art of storytelling (as well as story-making and story-listening) has been on the decline (Benjamin 1968), and that this decline is associated with the waning of oral traditions and the rise of mass communications in the postindustrial bourgeois societies of Western Europe and North America. Moreover, the emergence of the modern novel in the nineteenth century, far from affording evidence of the health of storytelling, may be regarded as an early symptom of the process of its decline. For, as Benjamin has put it, what distinguishes the novel from other forms of narrative "is that it neither comes from oral tradition nor goes into it" (87). Benjamin further observes that as the art or craft of (communal) storytelling has become more rare, the dissemination of mass-produced information ("news") has accelerated.

> And so it now appears that no event any longer comes to us without already being shot through with explanation. . . . Actually, it is half the art of storytelling to keep a story free from explanation as one reproduces it. (89)

If Benjamin's cryptic diagnosis is at all on target, then it would appear that psychology and the human sciences have chosen to thematize a vanishing phenomenon. Of course, this is not to deny that our ordinary thinking is inescapably narrative (Zukier and Pepitone 1984), but only that our social and cultural systems discourage the "amplitude" (or sub-junctivity) that narrative expression requires, and which "information" lacks. Perhaps this situation helps explain the current popularity of narra-tive in American psychotherapy (cognitive as well as psychodynamic). Psychotherapy is once again performing a remedial public function, in seeking to overcome "deficits" in narrative competence, and in assisting patients to recover or develop the ability to generate a believable self-narrative.

2. The second risk associated with the "narrative turn" directly con-cerns psychoanalysis. In recent years, psychoanalytic researchers and clini-cians (Gedo 1979, 1984; Wilson 1986; Stern 1985) have argued that any narrative or purely linguistic focus will lead psychoanalytic theory and practice astray. In Gedo's view, for example:

> the most essential of our therapeutic activities pertain to preverbal and presymbolic issues, including optimal tension regulation and the establish-ment of a stable hierarchy of biological aims and patterns, especially in the affective realm. (1984 165)

Gedo further maintains that such presymbolic, prerepresentational "ar-chaic dispositions" may manifest themselves as "archaic transferences" (and hence, as pathological diagnostic signs) in the clinical situation. Since such biological-affective repetitions of early infant-caretaker rela-tionships are presumably not coded and stored in mental images or language, they do not enter, as such, into the patient's psychodynamic narrative, and are "beyond interpretation." Intervention, in such a clinical context, becomes pedagogical, managerial, and empathic, essentially aimed at assisting the patient to learn how better to regulate him- or herself.

In some respects, this "biological" position (which derives support from both clinical and developmental observations) serves to refocus attention on what has always been the basic task of psychoanalytic *meta-psychology:* namely, the explanation of human intentionality in terms of its relation to biological finalities—the Freudian attempt to forge a bridge between the biological and the psychological. Consideration of the me-tapsychological question will have to be postponed till later chapters (especially Chapter 5), but it should here suffice to observe that any version of historical or hermeneutic psychoanalysis, focused on the domain of narrative phenomena, will still have to take into account the "biological past." The problem (theoretically and clinically) would appear to lie not only in recognizing a prelinguistic world, but also in discerning how language (or narrative discourse) can appropriate it.

Notwithstanding these real risks, the narrative research program remains a significant venture. What is being wagered is that the elucidation and explanation of narrative, whether through mainly historical-hermeneutic or empirical-analytic strategies, will somehow lead to fundamental insights into the *actual workings* and *natural organization* of mind. Yet it must also be conceded that the meanings of the italicized terms are not at all self-evident. For the actual workings or natural organization of mind may be alternatively construed as (a) causally explicable inner mental (or neural) processes, imbedded in the biological substrate of the brain or as (b) processes of social transaction and *praxis,* imbedded in the cultural-linguistic medium of communication and tradition. The coordination of these two constructions or discourses remains problematic (and points, again, to the enduring task of metapsychology). However, in such an assessment, the emerging research program on narrative can be seen as aiming not merely at the elucidation and explanation of mind, but also, in a certain sense, at the ascertainment of its "location" in nature and culture. And this last objective, insofar as it is a valid one, cannot be met through empirical investigation alone. Philosophy, or what I have here preferred to term "reflection," will once again have to play a role in psychology and psychoanalysis—if only to help avert likely confusions over what is involved in mental concepts (McGinn 1982); for it is only *through* such concepts that we have any access at all to the postulated (or hypothesized) mental phenomena, wherever in the world we "find" them.[8]

The Unity of Inquiry (The Core Controversy Revisited)

The proposal advanced in the preceding pages that "narrative phenomena" move to the forefront of psychological and psychoanalytic studies has not, however, met with universal or unqualified approval—especially when joined to the view that historical-hermeneutic methods are peculiarly adapted to elucidate such phenomena.[9]

Most notably, Morris Eagle, in his major study on recent developments in psychoanalysis (1984a) and in an essay on the theorist Benjamin

Rubenstein (Reppen 1985 83 108), has couched his objections in terms of an argument for the unity of inquiry and method (Popper 1972, 1976), and in terms of a critique of the classic *Geisteswissenchaften-Natur-wissenschaften* dichotomy.

That dichotomy, as Eagle interprets it, is the view in which "human beings are seen as either *nothing* but mechanisms *or* immune from the laws of nature . . ." (Reppen 1985 84). From this a dichotomous "either-or approach" to explanation is seen to follow: science *or* hermeneutics, with one method "trading in verifiable, empirically meaningful, induc-tively-derived knowledge, and the other occupying the domain of unveri-fiable, nonempirical, intuitively derived knowledge" (Blight 1981 186). In his critique of this neo-Kantian dichotomy, Eagle follows Rubenstein in adopting the latter's "ontological insight" that we are, from one per-spective, persons, and from another, organisms—and that there is thus conceptual space for a certain *complementarity* of explanation in psycho-analysis, which is at the same time consistent with the unity of all inquiry as conjectural, hypothetical, and objectively significant.[10] But in the Ea-gle-Rubenstein position, complementarity is *not* construed in either of the following familiar ways: (a) as implying that the same occurrence in the world may submit to alternative explanations, causalistic or intentionalis-tic, though not in the same inferential schema; (b) as implying an inter-play of causes and purposes (or reasons), such that causes bring about situations which, given a set of purposes, lead agents to act in ways that cause new situations and so trigger other sets of purposes, etc.

It is rather that, in the Eagle-Rubenstein position, complementarity (or unity of inquiry) is achieved through the construction of a "neutral language" model of mental functioning, "faithful to the worlds of both persons and organism" (Reppen 1985 105). While such a model must necessarily depersonify the narrative discourse of ordinary language and psychoanalytic dialogue, it will nevertheless reflect the *phenomenological structure* of the specific experience at issue (e.g., the intentionality of wishing). Such a model is also required to be consistent with what is known about neurophysiology. Two implications immediately follow from this perspective on unity and complementarity in psychoanalytic theory: (a) historical-hermeneutic interpretations, couched in the personal lan-guage and narrative discourse of wishes, aims, and feelings, are ill suited for, or misconceived as, *theoretical* understandings in psychoanalysis, be-cause "there is no good reason that a theoretical explanation of these wishes, aims, etc. needs to use the same kinds of concepts" (Eagle 1984a 152); (b) psychoanalytic interpretations (whether or not construed as narrative constructions) must be consistent with what is known about the structure of neural processes; thus Rubenstein states:

> No matter how apt an interpretation of a symbol in terms of its meaning, if the processes by which symbol formation is explained are improbable, we have no alternative but to discard the interpretation. (Quoted in Reppen 1985 105)

In other words, in the position just summarized, the "narrative truth" of psychoanalytic interpretation—if it aspires to be explanatory—must at least answer to "neural truth" if not, necessarily, to "historical truth" (see also Spence 1982).

The Eagle-Rubenstein model assures a formal continuity between the explanatory principles of psychoanalysis and those of such sciences as physics and biology. There is no ontological split between psychology and biology; and the metapsychological program of psychoanalysis has thus been specified through the proposal of a "neutral language" model of mental functioning. Let me now proceed to examine the import or relevance of this model for explanation and understanding within the clinical setting. How is the unity of inquiry articulated in clinical psychoanalysis and what difference does it actually make?

Eagle would not, I believe, object to the empirical investigation of narrative phenomena, or of the processes hypothesized to underlie narrative thought and expression. For example, one might imagine—in the context of psychotherapy—testing the hypothesis that subjunctivity-enhancing interpretations are therapeutic for some particular subset of patients, or that such interpretations are more effective than some set of relevant alternative interventions. But the point, for Eagle, is that narrative interpretations, whatever their meaningful nature, and however negotiated or evaluated, are always *interventions:*

> Furthermore, in the clinical context, it is the response of the subject of one's interpretations to one's interpretations that defines issues of accountability and effectiveness. This consideration makes it immediately apparent that, in contrast to historical inquiry, in the clinical context, interpretations are above all *interventions*. (Eagle 1984a 169)

What is highlighted above is the disjuncture between clinical interpretation (the activity of being a psychotherapist) and historical interpretation (the activity of being a historian). For it is surely evident that, unlike the patient, the "text" does not (a) *change* as the result of interpretation, (b) *respond* to interpretation, (c) *co-constitute* a *moral field* with the historian. Yet, the argument will be made, in Chapter 4, that on one interpretation of hermeneutic understanding (Gadamer 1975, 1976), all three conditions cited above are actually fulfilled in historical inquiry. The possibility, therefore, of an analogy between the psychotherapist and the historian is not immediately to be dismissed.

Curiously, Eagle's argument is more effective in distinguishing the theory of therapy (intervention) from the other spheres and strata of psychoanalytic discourse (e.g., psychopathology, development, metapsychology). For it would appear that even when inquiry is conducted experimentally in these latter areas, it cannot quite meet the conditions cited above, which specify the clinical situation as at once a *moral* and *practical* situation. It is in this sense that the theory of therapy is autonomous, and thus decisively distinguishable from other departments of psychoanalytic thought, if not, necessarily, from historical inquiry.

Returning, now, to Eagle's immediate argument, just as the hermeneuticists have been criticized for illegitimately extending interpretative "explanations" from the clinical context where they may at least seem *pragmatically* appropriate to extraclinical contexts where they are not (1984a 151–52, 202), so too is it now suggested that even in clinical settings, narrative understandings are not relevant understandings[11]—and are themselves to be explained as interventions which are more or less effective:

> While interpretations may be like historical or hermeneutic activities in certain respects, the measure of their effectiveness, as well as theoretical explanations of whatever degree of effectiveness is achieved, are not at all like historical accounts or hermeneutic activities. Rather they are like other theoretical accounts in the natural and social sciences. (1984a 170)

It is important that we now register the significance of Eagle's *implicit* argument. Because psychotherapy is construed as a practical (technical?) activity, its formal end cannot but be "effectiveness." Given the priority of this single and exclusive end, all further inquiry, insofar as it pertains to clinical outcome, must be about means, and so be scientific, empirical, or technical in character. Such an argument assumes that whatever the manifold *meanings* circulating in the clinical situation, they may be presumed to be irrelevant for establishing the lawfulness of certain occurrences: namely, the conditions under which specific interventions are effective. Thus, any historical or hermeneutic investigation[12] into how meanings are constituted, negotiated, and shared in psychotherapy (Goldberg 1987) becomes subordinate and peripheral to the "separate" practical and empirical task of accounting for the lawfulness of certain events.

In summary: there is no question that therapeutic interpretations, as well as other clinical practices and transactions, *can* be conceptualized as narratives, and that these, themselves, can in turn be elucidated and explicated along historical and hermeneutic lines (e.g., Schafer's "action language" proposal). But Eagle does not appear to believe that "theoretical" understanding of this type has any significant value or function in the economy of psychoanalytic knowledge. It surely cannot be central to an autonomous theory of therapy, because it is not governed by the end or "cognitive interest" of effectiveness—and hence cannot contribute to "theoretical explanations of whatever degree of effectiveness is achieved." For it is assumed that effectiveness is best assessed, as well as conceptualized and defined, through empirical-analytic (and *not* historical-hermeneutic) investigation and negotiation. In short, such knowledge claims (as those arising from the historical-hermeneutic explication of the narrative phenomena of the clinical situation) are not, in Eagle's usage, clinical or *practical* in character. At the same time, we recall, such knowledge is ill-suited for, or misconceived as, *theoretical* understanding in psychoanalysis. In Eagle's words:

> While interpretative explanations in the clinical context may use the personal language of wishes, aims and feelings, there is no good reason to expect that a theoretical explanation of these wishes, aims, etc. needs to use the same kinds of concepts. (1984a 152)

The Price of the "Unity of Inquiry"

It thus turns out that the Eagle-Rubenstein model of the unity of inquiry does not allow much scope for a historical or hermeneutical psychoanalysis. It is neither possible nor fruitful for me to attempt to refute such a model. What can be done, however, in this introductory chapter, is to estimate the price exacted by this particular version of the unity of inquiry. My specific concern is with the price exacted by the apparent extrusion of history and hermeneutics from the *idea* of an autonomous theory of therapy; and my thesis will be that the empirical-analytic conception of a theory of therapy, as advanced by Eagle, is an insufficient and partial conception, and certainly a one-sided one. It is an insufficient conception because it fails to appreciate that analysis or explication of an activity (e.g., psychoanalysis) can advance our understanding of that activity as *practical* activity even when such analysis or explication is unregulated by the "end" of effectiveness or the presuppositions of the empirical-analytic approach.

That there are non–empirical-analytic *conceptions* of the theory of therapy is clear enough. Consider the contributions of Schafer (1976, 1983). His version of a "theory of therapy," though couched in part in "action language," is really a second-order narrative (or historical-hermeneutic treatment) of the narrative possibilities of the psychoanalytic encounter. And while Schafer's project is not, of course, empirical-analytic (it doesn't rely on controlled observation, experiment, or statistical methodology), it nevertheless purports to provide a faithful representation (or ideal type) of the normative therapeutic experience (see Chapter 4 of this book for an extended discussion). But in sharp contrast to most "process research" (Greenberg and Pinsoff 1986), Schafer's representation is not achieved through the analytic abstraction of structures or patterns of relations, which are then virtually reified, as if these now constituted the reality or significance of events, actions, and discourse. For Schafer the events, actions, and circumstances of the clinical situation are not to be reduced to the abstracted patterns of their external relationships. He will not meet the *price* exacted by the "unity of inquiry," by the empirical-analytic approach. Instead, he chooses to identify the concrete "goings-on" of psychoanalytic therapy primarily as exhibitions of intelligence, subscriptions to practices, or narrative expressions, and *not* (as science appears to require) as causally explicable processes understood in terms of laws which are not themselves exhibitions of understanding, and which do not have to be learned to be operative.

Schafer is not alone in advocating and illustrating an alternative conception of the "theory of therapy." Atwood and Stolorow (1984), for example, have sought to articulate a clinical psychoanalytic phenomenology, which also aims to avoid or minimize the abstractions (and presuppositions) of the empirical-analytic approach. Furthermore, numerous and diverse clinicians and researchers have found it useful to attend to what might be called the "clinical epistemology" of the therapeutic situation. Here the endeavor has been to explicate the assumptive frameworks (regarding human knowledge and cognition) of both patient and therapist within the shifting contexts of treatment. Burrell (1987) has argued that such conceptual analyses can help us to appreciate the role of tacit knowledge (Polanyi 1958) in both articulating and applying treatment plans and interventions.

Having demonstrated the existence of non–empirical-analytic conceptions of the theory of therapy, what, then, is their *point* in the present argument? Their point is just this: that they counteract those aspects of Eagle's model of the theory of therapy which inhibit a fuller understanding of what is genuinely *practical* in any activity, including the practice of psychoanalysis or psychotherapy.[13] But the question immediately arises: how can a model so indebted to "effectiveness," to the cognitive interest of prediction and control, inhibit our understanding of what is genuinely *practical* in psychotherapy?

It is in exactly this connection that the philosopher Michael Oakeshott (1962) has argued that every science, every art, and every practical activity involves knowledge of two sorts: technical knowledge and practical knowledge, the latter *existing only in use* (and hence, unlike the products of science, according to Popper [1972], which "exist" independent of use), and resistant to formulation into rules. This is the sort of knowledge of which we always know (and see) more than we can ever say. Possible synonyms and cognate terms for practical knowledge include know-how, bricolage, tacit or procedural knowledge, social judgment, and perhaps what Aristotle called *phronesis,* the art of applying theory or understanding in a variety of contexts and situations. Surely it is reasonable to suppose that one important task for a historical-hermeneutic treatment of "psychotherapy as practice" is to explicate the nature-in-use of such practical knowledge,[14] which is not only part of the therapist's art, but also part of any patient's skill (or lack thereof) in *responding* to so-called interventions, and in modifying his or her conduct and self-understandings.

It is noteworthy that the explicit *empirical* investigation of practical knowledge, of its hypothetical components, of its antecedents and consequents, is of relatively recent vintage, as Sternberg and Wagner (1986), editors of a valuable collection on the subject, concede. Why is this so? One answer certainly has to do with the degree of specialization in the behavioral sciences, such that the work of a Cicourel (1982) on expert medical systems, and of a Rumelhart (1981) on the interplay of declarative and procedural knowledge, does not easily or rapidly filter into clinical psychology, psychiatry, and psychoanalysis. However, the answer I find even more convincing might run as follows: the phenomena of practical knowledge seem so constituted that they escape or elude the net of empirical-analytic inquiry, and are barely recognizable through the prism of empirical-analytic assumptions and presuppositions. This is probably why it has been philosophers (Polanyi 1958; Oakeshott 1962; Schutz 1966), ethnomethodologists (e.g., Garfinkel 1967), anthropologists (Geertz 1983), hermeneutic psychoanalysts (e.g., Schafer 1983), and other non-scientific workers who have initially identified and conceptualized the domain of practical knowledge in a variety of contexts, including that of psychoanalysis. It has been further suggested (Argyris et al. 1985) that the empirical-analytic approach to *practical knowledge*—once that domain has been "discovered" by the hermeneuticists—is handicapped by the fact that its explanations must conform to an ideal of non-pragmatic explanation (e.g., the covering law model), or are otherwise depragmaticized by the assumptions underlying both the epistemology and the methodologies of empirical-analytic science.

If I have been belaboring the non-practical character of science, it is because this issue is so often muddled. For what is sometimes thought to be the practical payoff of science (via prediction and control of events) is essentially a spinoff of technique or technical knowledge. But, as we have already seen, technical knowledge (which an empirical-analytic theory of therapy can indeed engender) is just *one* of two modes of knowledge and skill inherent in any activity, including, in fact, science itself. This proposition is beautifully (and perhaps inadvertently) endorsed by Weiss and Sampson (1986), our aforementioned empirical-analytic psychoanalytic investigators. Referring to a key aspect of their research approach, they state:

> The assessment of the patient's plan is a crucial step in studies involving hypotheses about plans, tests, and the analyst's interventions. We cannot fully communicate here how to go about formulating a patient's plan. This is because it is not possible to communicate from books or manuals the application of *any* theory to clinical material, especially if that application requires inference. (152)

The conclusion that must be reached, then, is this: the "unity of inquiry," in the version now under consideration, exacts too high a price, especially to the degree that it prescribes and governs our explanation and understanding of the activities, practices, and processes of clinical psychoanalysis. More specifically, the empirical-analytic model of the "theory of therapy," by systematically subordinating the historical-hermeneutic explication of narrative phenomena to the explanation of such phenomena in terms of "effectiveness of intervention," appears unable to recognize and disclose the strategic and necessary role of *practical knowledge*. This is a major defect in the empirical-analytic approach, and in the idea of the "unity of inquiry" that undergirds it. For the so-called technical recommendations of clinical psychoanalysis (which are presumably the result of theoretical argument and empirical investigation), require for their reasonable application some *perspective* on practical knowledge; this (it will be argued) can be supplied, principally, if not exclusively, through historical and hermeneutic accounts of the narrative character and rhetorical functions of therapeutic discourse. I thus conclude that the empirical-analytic model affords an incomplete and, therefore, an inadequate understanding:

> For to understand an activity is to know it as a concrete whole; it is to recognize the activity as having the source of its movement within itself. And understanding which leaves the activity in debt to something outside is, for that reason, an inadequate understanding. (Oakeshott 1962 113)

Final Objections, Future Directions

In the preceding section, the focus has been on the extrusion of history and hermeneutics from the idea of an autonomous theory of therapy. However it is also true that the Eagle-Rubenstein model allows narrative an even smaller theoretical role in non-clinical contexts. For it is hard for such a model to perceive the *point* of such second-order narrative accounts (e.g., historical-hermeneutic accounts) in a "theoretical" understanding of human development, personality, psychopathology, and in general, those unconscious aspects of human experience which, in some widely accepted sense, are the special province of psychoanalysis as a theoretical enterprise.

My objections to this viewpoint are twofold. First, from within the parameters of the Eagle-Rubenstein model itself, it would seem that historical and hermeneutic analysis helps to elicit the "phenomenological structure of experience," knowledge of which is required, in principle, for the model's *own* elaboration and implementation. This is necessarily so, unless it is assumed that phenomenological understanding is self-evident, and arrives unsolicited without any intellectual labor. Relatedly, I have argued, such historical and hermeneutic interpretation also helps to identify and conceptualize such crucial (but elusive) domains as those of practical knowledge. These are often the very domains which, without hermeneutic interpretation, would remain ignored or marginalized in mainstream empirical-analytic science. Finally, historical and hermeneutic inquiry can challenge the characterization of those elusive domains, once they have been "reconformed" to suit the methodological and epistemological requirements of empirical-analytic science. So challenged and interrogated, inquiry is less liable to be caught up in a kind of *anti-hermeneutic* circle, in which all further intellectual activities are assimilated to a preestablished and indubitable set of categories, hence nullifying the development of genuinely new categories in the course of inquiry, argument, and dialogue.

My second objection is metatheoretical and reflects my doubt that the Eagle-Rubenstein model (the "neutral language" model) has, in fact, actually overcome the traditional dichotomy posed by the *Geisteswissenschaften-Naturwissenschaften* distinction. I, too, question the necessity for such a "Great Divide" (Blight 1981), and reject the notion that human beings must be seen as "either nothing but mechanisms *or* immune from the laws of nature." Of course human beings are not immune from the laws of nature; of course there is no ontological divide between nature and spirit; of course there is nothing that is in principle unpredictable. The problem is rather, to paraphrase Rorty (1979 355), that we are able to predict what noises will come from someone's mouth, without knowing what they mean. There *is* a truth to be known, but no guaranteed method for discovering (or predicting) it. As Rorty puts it, the language (or language game) suitable for coping with *neurons* may well be different from the one suitable for coping with *people*. This, in short, is the native conundrum of psychology and psychoanalysis: they are necessarily caught up in two (or more) language games, often unreflectively so, and the task, I think, becomes one of self-conscious coordination rather than one of linguistic neutrality.

Thus the particular direction I have set for myself in this book. Taking cognizance of the very real disparity between (a) the competing traditions of Aristotelian and Galilean explanation and (b) the two propositions introduced earlier in this chapter, I shall have to traverse a rather different path toward the sought-after "unity of inquiry." Therefore, in the chapters to follow, my task is to argue for a version of coherence or complementarity which is sharply at odds with the one advanced by Eagle and Rubenstein. And this I propose to do by undertaking *inter alia* an interpretative analysis of the conceptualization of the past in American psychoanalytic thought.

Summation and Conclusion

Chapter 1 has defined the method, context, and approach of this study. The method is reflective and non-empirical; the approach is synoptic and speculative; and the context is specified by the principle of "pluralism in psychoanalysis."

In introducing the argument, plan, and theme of this book, I have had to concede that the character of American psychoanalysis is decisively shaped by its "core controversy": namely, the perennial contest between scientists and hermeneuts over the intellectual identity of psychoanalytical theory. My strategy in this book is, quite frankly, to circumvent ("make a circuit around") this contest. This I have already begun to do by taking the first steps toward framing a *pluralist model* of psychoanalytic discourse. Such a model is one which:

- repudiates the exclusivist and totalist claims of both scientific (unitarian) and hermeneutic (dichotomist) psychoanalysis; and
- proposes that what is required is not the unification of psychoanalysis into a homogeneous discourse, but rather the recognition of where, when, and how each *mode* of discourse is applicable and appropriate.

As I proceed to examine the implications of the pluralist model for the theory and practice of psychoanalysis, I am guided throughout by the hypothesis that such a model, and only such a model, furthers the recognition that different "pasts" and different universes of discourse (e.g., science, history, and practice) "enjoy an oblique relationship which neither requires nor forecasts their being assimilated to one another" (Oakeshott 1962 199).

NOTES

1. The concept of "divergent rationalities" is borrowed from Shweder (1986 180–82). He distinguishes rational from non-rational and irrational processes, and then hypothesizes that some rational processes are universally distributed across the human species, whereas others are not. "The version of reality we construct is a product of both universal and the nonuniversal rational processes, but it is because not all rational processes are universal that we need a concept of divergent rationality" (181). In terms of my argument, this means that historical, scientific, and practical constructions of the past share certain relatively universal rational processes, but are also distinguished from one another by the presence of other non-universal and particularistic rational processes. For example, what *counts* as good evidence will vary among the three constructions or modes of understanding; similarly, the metaphors, models, and analogies used for generating explanations will be dissimilar, as will the classifications used for demarcating events and partitioning objects.

2. Scientific psychoanalysis is not necessarily equivalent to empirical psychoanalysis. There are numerous *non-empirical* activities which are indispensable to the advancement of psychoanalysis as a science (Kukla 1989), and which even help to define it as a scientific and theoretical discourse. In this book, such indispensable (but non-empirical) activities are brought together under the rubric of "problems and issues of scientific conceptualization in psychoanalysis." When, in Chapter 5, I construct an exemplary version of "scientific psychoanalysis," I am thus concerned primarily with problems of scientific and theoretical conceptualization, and only secondarily with problems of empirical research and methodology. This emphasis helps to explain and justify the selection of that particular group of theorists upon whose contributions I rely. While I do not deny a certain arbitrariness in my selection, I suggest, nonetheless, that my choices are amply justified by the argument expounded in Chapter 5, and by my overall objective in that chapter—which is to identify what is *distinctively* scientific (not historical or practical) in psychoanalytic discourse.

3. In describing the method of this study as "reflection," I am not asserting that there is something called a *philosophical* method or technique through which I am able to know something about knowing which nobody else (e.g., the non-philosopher) is able to know. Reflection is a more or less universally available stance, from which a person may think about his or her thoughts or deliberate about his or her desires. Phenomenologically, it is as if reason has *stepped back* from a thought or experienced desire, and has carried out its evaluation from a second-order position.

4. The term "human sciences" probably has its origins in J. S. Mill's "moral sciences," i.e., the sciences of human nature, whose progress, Mill believed, depended on the adoption of the methods employed in the physical sciences. When Mill's *System of Logic* was translated into German in 1849, "moral sciences" was rendered as *Geisteswissenschaften* (virtually the earliest such usage of that term).

Dilthey extended the meaning of *Geisteswissenschaften* to include such disciplines as philology and aesthetics, as well as psychology, anthropology, law, and history, and urged (in opposition to Mill) that these human sciences should not be modeled on the natural sciences. In current usage, "behavioral" or "social" science characteristically implies a commitment to a unified science based on methods developed for exploration of physical and biological processes; in contrast, the intent of the "human sciences" is to bracket such a commitment, and to approach the human realm with "an openness to its special characteristics and a willingness to let questions inform which methods are appropriate" (Polkinghorne 1983 289).

5. The idea of a "simultaneous contemplation of what is right in each view" can be regarded as an epistemic analogue of Piaget's psychological concept of cognitive or perspectival *decentering*. Decentering is the developmental process through which an individual becomes increasingly able to coordinate another person's viewpoint with his own (infer the other's point of view while decentering one's own). It has been argued that only in *simultaneous* (not successive) decentering are distortions most effectively corrected. Being able to take into account a number of facets of a situation at one time (and in relation to another) is thus viewed as socially adaptive.

6. The "language game" of science is examined in some detail in Chapters 2 and 3 of this book. It is important to realize that the concept of language game discourages the search for "essences." Indeed, the last half century of debate in the history of science suggests the futility of any attempt to establish a diacritical marker for scientificity. Thus, in this book, the usage of such terms as "science" and "history" does not imply any commitment to essentialism in their definitions. At the same time, it seems both useful and necessary to explore the manner in which history and science (as activities, as intellectual constructions) may be distinguished from one another.

7. The term "research program" is used to suggest the specific conception of the growth of knowledge advanced by Lakatos (1970). Lakatos believes that there is a kind of rational pattern that leads scientists to make problem shifts to more "progressive" research programs. A program is more progressive if it (a) is more comprehensive, (b) predicts and explains "new facts," (c) resolves inconsistencies or lacunae in the old program it replaces. The key, for Lakatos, is that the reasoning pattern used to create change in science is at the level of a *research program* rather than at the level of an individual hypothesis.

8. Wittgenstein (1968) reminds us that we needn't assume that, when a man tells us "Now I understand," that he is reporting an event or process within himself.

> It would be quite misleading . . . to call the words a "description of a mental state." One might rather call them a "signal"; and we judge whether it was rightly employed by what he goes on to do. (180)

In this view, the ordinary language (narrative and rhetoric) through which we ascribe and convey wishes, wants, understanding, and insight is *not* necessarily a metaphorical description of (or evidence for) someone's "real," occurrent, and inner mental processes; rather, argues Wittgenstein, understanding means "knowing how to go on"—it is a commitment about performance to come. Where, then, is mind?

9. It appears that Bruner (1986, 1990) has endorsed the view that historical-hermeneutic methods are peculiarly adapted to elucidate narrative phenomena. Referring to the problem of subjunctivity in narrative, he thus writes (1986):

> One cannot hope to "explain" the processes involved in such rewriting in any but an interpretative way, surely no more precisely, say, than an anthropologist "explains" what the Balinese cockfight means to those who bet on it (to take an example from Clifford Geertz's classic paper on that subject). (35)

10. I am proposing that the Eagle-Rubenstein model of the "unity of inquiry" is actually a Popperian model. Popper (1976) has attacked the "myth of the framework," which contends that, even in science, we are prisoners of intellectual frameworks (paradigms) and can make only an irrational leap from one framework to another. In contrast, Popper holds that we can eliminate errors and make cognitive progress by participating in other "language games," and by subjecting our own to rational criticism. There is, in his view, a universal, evolutionarily grounded praxis of rationality. The unity of inquiry (science) is thus founded in the fact that our concepts and knowledge claims are conjectures about reality which are submitted (metaphorically?) to some sort of evolutionary test. The intuition behind this view is that if there had not been a *real* world to select us for survival by providing selective pressures, we would not be here to wonder about it (generate and test our conjectures).

11. Narrative interpretations would of course be *relevant* if their veridicality were closely related to their therapeutic effectiveness. But this Eagle does not appear to presume (he endorses Grunbaum's critique of Freud's "tally argument"). It follows that since the "truth" of psychoanalytic narrative interpretations need not be established (e.g., through historical-hermeneutic investigation), all that remains for a "theory of therapy" is to assess their *effectiveness* as interventions, and this is most efficiently achieved through empirical-analytic methods and approaches. It seems, however, that the crucial problem, here overlooked, concerns discriminating between psychoanalytic interpretations which are true and "enactive" (capable of bringing about some change), and those which are enactive and false. Such a formulation admits the possibility of therapeutic "truth" in interpretation (even if evidence from the clinical situation is too tainted to be of probative value). Wisdom (in Wollheim 1974 346–48) has explored this issue.

12. Thus far in this chapter, I have not yet distinguished between "historical" and "hermeneutical" psychoanalytic approaches. Historical discourse may be more or less hermeneutic, and the issue is further complicated by the fact that there are several distinct models of hermeneutic method and understanding. For example, the objectivist, "positivist" hermeneutics of Dilthey (see Blight 1981) operates at an altogether different level of abstraction and analysis than does the philosophical or ontological hermeneutics of Gadamer (1975, 1976). Consideration of this

important distinction will have to postponed till Chapter 4 of this book, when the "historical construction of the psychoanalytic past" is examined in detail.

13. Psychotherapy is used in a broad sense to include all types of therapy by psychological means, under which psychoanalysis is included. In other words, psychotherapy is generic and psychoanalysis is a subset. I further follow Oremland (1991) in assuming that the central distinction between psychoanalysis in particular and psychotherapy in general is that the former consists of interaction *with* analysis of the interaction, while the latter consists of interaction without analysis of the interaction. Psychoanalysis (when construed as a therapy) is thus that subset of psychotherapy which *requires* "interaction with analysis of the interaction."

14. Practical knowledge (however acquired or transmitted) is what enables the therapist to "apply" technical recommendations. Without the former, the latter are useless and of no practical value. Hermeneutic or historical representations of practical knowledge may thus be helpful in assisting the therapist to exploit technique, without, however, affording a "crib" or rule book that magically supplies judgment or *phronesis:* the ability to apply theories and principles in the diverse and shifting contexts of therapy. Hence, in this account, some form of historical-hermeneutic analysis is necessary, in principle, to account fully for the genuine effectiveness of any particular intervention.

2

An Overview: Conceptualizing the Psychoanalytic Past

Seldom, very seldom, does complete truth belong to any human disclosure; seldom can it happen that something is not a little disguised, or a little mistaken.

—Jane Austen

Introduction: Two Points of View

We are born with a past and that past shapes us as we seek to shape the present. This is not a proposition of psychoanalysis but a conviction of common sense. The enduring appeal and power of psychoanalysis are surely related to the fact that it gives content and form to that conviction and promises a method for understanding (and coping with) the influence of the past.[1]

Specifically, psychoanalysis—in presupposing the influence of the past on present experience—requires not only some account of how that influence survives in and acts on the present, but also some account of its *substantive* or *constitutive* features. Hence the *traditional* or received view that the psychoanalytically relevant past is "carried" as unconscious mental representations (images, fantasies, wishes, etc.), and that these mental contents (meanings) are permanently stored in the unconscious from where they keep manifesting themselves to consciousness in various transformed or disguised ways. It was because he possessed such a picture of the persistence, activity, and efficacy of the past that Freud, in the case of the "Rat Man," could report the following:

38

> I pointed out to him that he ought logically to consider himself in no way responsible for any of these traits in his character; for all of these reprehensible impulses originated from his infancy, and were only derivatives of his infantile character surviving in his unconscious. (1909a 185)

Moreover, the traditional or received view implies not only that present-day desires, fears, and fantasies originated in certain *past* conditions and continue to be bound to the living representations of these conditions, but also that psychoanalysis, as a therapeutic practice, may be characterized as a kind of interpretative recovery of the past, the "process" of which is actually explanatory (i.e., really does describe a *prior* psychological reality in the mind of the patient, or actually retraces a *genetic* process in time, starting with an actual past event or state as cause of the present conditions).

So summarily stated is the traditional position (a) according to which the past remains preserved and intact in the present and can therefore act as a causal agent of present conditions, and (b) according to which the reconstruction of the past is tantamount, in principle, to the search for underlying motives and causes of present behavior. And it may be safely concluded that in this received point of view, few ideas figure as prominently, at all levels and in all genres of psychoanalytic discourse, as the idea of the past.

However, there is also a contrary trend of opinion. Increasingly it is doubted that there is any genuine relation between what happens *in analysis* and what happened *in the past*. The past, at least insofar as it can be detached from the present and objectively inspected, recedes in psychoanalytic significance. The past is no longer explanatory. And so it can now be argued from this, the *revisionary* point of view, that clinical narratives are instruments for change, not candidates for historical (or scientific) truth; that analytic constructions in the clinical setting thus

> refer to relations and regularities between present phenomena and can alter the meaning and influence of the present on future behavior; their validity need not rest on the claim that the past and its transformations once occurred as now conceptualized. (Schimek 1975a 861, 1975b)

This critique of the traditional archaeological position (really a critique of Freud's cognitive psychology which assumes, as already noted, the permanent storage of mental contents in the unconscious) has been complemented by somewhat different arguments which effectively question whether conditions can ever exist for an interpretative (and mutative) recovery of the past (Spence 1982). Finally, the transference itself is no longer construed by some psychoanalytic writers as involving, in any obvious sense, a recapitulation or reenactment of the past. Consequently, all references to the past are now to be interpreted as indirect, resistant allusions to the here and now (Gill 1983, 1984; Schafer 1983), and there is nothing, strictly speaking, to be unearthed, excavated, or reconstructed in clinical psychoanalysis that antedates the interactions that comprise the "here and now" of the therapeutic encounter.

Let us consider briefly what is actually at stake in the argument between the traditional and revisionary points of view. It appears of course that they offer rival evaluations of the *role* of the "past" in psychoanalytic theory and clinical practice—with the traditional position holding that its role is fundamental, and with the revisionary position holding that its role is negligible. But is this really so? What I maintain in this chapter, and throughout this book, is that the real dispute is not so much over the role of the past in psychoanalysis, as it is over the nature of the past; and this dispute in turn reflects divergent approaches to the *conceptualization* of the past in psychoanalytic discourse. It is quite possible, for example, that the traditional point of view is a "Proposition 1" point of view (see Chapter 1), committed to a realist view of the objectivity and reality of the past, wherein past events and experiences are presumed to possess an inherent structure and force, independent of the imaginative activity of mind. In such an understanding, the past and its transformations are indeed real, occurrent, and highly relevant for any psychoanalytic model of human development and clinical process. For example, transference interpretations can now be understood either as veridical reports of past mental contents, or as veridical reports dealing with structures and patterns of experience identical with, or isomorphic to, those once experienced by the patient.

It is likewise possible, however, that the revisionary point of view is a "Proposition 2" point of view (see Chapter 1), committed to an antirealist view of the reality of the past, in which the past is not reconstructed, and certainly not described, but is rather recognized as a product or artifact of present constructions. In such an understanding, the "past" is a *thought* to which one is committed by virtue of past-tensed assertions which present circumstances entitle one to make, according to the rules of a particular speech community or language game. There is no "objective past"—even in principle—against which to check the veridicality of one's constructions. The past is simply not the kind of thing one can look at. And it follows that in psychoanalysis, the past (so construed) cannot be "separated" from the present. In Schafer's words: "the so-called past and present may not be regarded as independent variables that are testable against one another" (1983 196). It is therefore eminently reasonable, in this characteristically American statement, that transference references "to the past" are properly interpretable as allusions to the "here and now," for the past is only known and real (efficacious) through *current* interpretations of it.

The decisive argument between the traditionalists and the revisionists is not, therefore, about the role of the past in psychoanalysis, but about the nature of the past, and hence, about the manner and mode of its conceptualization. This is an important argument, and one to which I will return periodically.[2] It is an argument which overlaps with the core controversy between scientists and hermeneuts in American psychoanalysis, and it is also an argument which intersects with the related clinical theory-metapsychology debate.[3] However, for now it is sufficient that the focus for the present chapter has been established.

My plan is therefore to offer an overview of some of the problems attendant to the conceptualization of the past in psychoanalysis. This I propose to do by shifting from the "top-down" analysis sketched above to a "bottom-up" treatment of the *equivocality* of the idea of the past. Such a shift is warranted by the fact that the "psychoanalytic past" is complicated not only by the epistemological and ontological controversies already alluded to, but also by the ambiguities of usage that are imported from the contexts of everyday life. Hence the need for a brief explication of the equivocality of the past in the ordinary language and rhetoric of psychoanalytic discourse. After specifying the equivocality of the idea of the past, I then proceed to explore how it is articulated in the classical psychoanalytic construct of development. The classical or traditional model of psychoanalytic development is a *mixed* and hence an equivocal model of development. Its obvious vulnerabilities will be duly considered. This chapter concludes, however, with a provisional justification for retaining the mixed model, since psychoanalytic discourse is recognized as a "hybrid discourse," and the psychoanalytic past as a "composite past."

In Chapter 3, I seek to develop the categorical distinction between the "past" as scientifically constructed and the "past" as historically constructed. This distinction overlaps with, but is not identical to, the distinction between Proposition 1 and Proposition 2 (between the traditional and the revisionary points of view, as interpreted above). And thus, by the end of Part I of this book, I will have begun to outline an approach (or model) through which the *plurality* of psychoanalytic "pasts" can be identified, distinguished, and disambiguated.

The Equivocality of the "Past"

The "past" is an equivocal concept in psychoanalytic as in everyday discourse; its usage and meaning are not at all uniform, invariant, or determinate. Let me illustrate through a consideration of the following familiar truism: *analysis leaves its scars; it cannot cure the past, but only lay it to rest in a forgivable way.*

This is a typical example of psychoanalytic rhetoric. Though not a theoretical statement, it might be found almost anywhere in the theoretical literature; though not a clinical interpretation or construction, it is surely at home in the therapeutic and colloquial discourse of the clinical setting. As a piece of psychoanalytic rhetoric, we thus view it as a hybrid utterance, with one foot in the world of everyday life, and with another foot in the world of psychoanalytic ideas. And its efficacy, as an example of psychoanalytic rhetoric, depends, therefore, not only on the specialized erudition and expertise of those to whom it is addressed, but also on the ordinary "background knowledge" they possess and bring to bear.

Now the truism under consideration is not just an example of psychoanalytic rhetoric, but also an exhibition of metaphor. A metaphor is said to work when it helps us to understand an aspect (or diverse aspects) of a concept (Lakoff and Johnson 1980 97). And it appears that in the statement above, "analysis" (or therapeutic action) is treated metaphorically, in such a way as to illuminate aspects of the *conceptualization of the past.* Let us see how through the following gloss:

1. The therapeutic action of psychoanalysis cannot help the patient to undo or redo the past, though the patient may wish that this were otherwise; the past is like a thing, resistant to alteration, dead, fixed, and finished;

2. The past is active and effective in the present; the past continues to be preserved within the depths of the mental; the past makes things happen; it is something active and alive, immaterial but enduring;

3. The past is that which carries the present disease; the past carries something forward into the present or revives something in the present; the past won't leave the present; the past pulls the present backward;

4. Psychoanalytic understanding aims to establish "how the disturbed past has continued to be, unconsciously, the disturbing present" (Schafer 1978 16); the past pushes the present forward and pulls the present backward; the past takes over or occupies the present;

5. Effectiveness in psychoanalytic therapy, while requiring a certain (painful) reflection on the past, implies neither (a) its recovery, reliving, or recollection, nor (b) its negation, undoing, or suppression; the past is something we feel, interpret, and decipher; the past is that which we weave and fabricate, as well as that which we recall, recollect, misremember, and reenact;

6. Successful treatment involves the acquisition of a new *relationship* to the past, such that the past can now become past and thus be laid to rest "in a forgivable way"; the past is understood not just as a container of events and experiences, but also in terms of one's (present) stance toward those events and experiences; human beings are capable of constituting a distance between the "here and now" and the "there and then"; the therapeutic process, though interminable, has a natural closure which is marked by the attainment of a more empathic perspective on one's own ineliminable past (Erikson 1963); the *mode* of an individual's relationship to his past may be of greater therapeutic import than the actual and fantasied events and experiences that comprise the *content* of that individual's past (Kierkegaard 1959).

What this gloss indicates is that the psychoanalytic idea of the past is not only an equivocal and ambiguous idea, but also one that is deeply imbedded in the conceptual infrastructure of psychoanalysis. Consider, for example, such fundamental clinical and metapsychological concepts as transference, resistance, neurosis, regression, return of the repressed, repetition-compulsion, working-through, etc. All have in common, at the very least, the intuitive and pretheoretical notion of the "past as present." It follows that psychoanalytic thinking, at all levels and in all contexts of inquiry (metapsychological, clinical, technical-practical), is most likely to be infected by the equivocality and ambiguity of the idea of the past.

The equivocality of the "past" is explicable once it is recognized that the idea of the "past as present" resolves into two seemingly distinct and discrepant notions: (a) the presentness of the past as potentially intelligible (if now distorted or unavailable) meaning, sign, and semiotic system; and (b) the presentness of the past as force, cause, and unintelligent (but lawful) process. Furthermore, the presentness of the past is manifested along at least two dimensions (or vectors): (a) the present "pulled backward by" (or interpretable in terms of) the past (the *past-directedness* of unconscious experience); or (b) the present "pushed forward by" (or the effect of) the past (the *prospective reference* of the unconscious past). This analysis is schematized in Figure 1, in which the four possibilities are represented.

In this chapter I am chiefly concerned with Boxes 1 and 3. These figure prominently in the psychoanalytic construct of development, and are related to what I call the historical and scientific constructions of the past. However, Boxes 2 and 4 merit mention as well. Box 2 conveys the teleological possibility: the notion of the future drawing (past) events toward it, as if the stream of history were flowing (by design) toward some designated and meaningful outcome. Teleological explanation is epistemically dubious, and psychoanalysis (we shall shortly see) has reacted strongly against its use. However it is also worth observing that it is not necessarily illegitimate for historical inquiry to ask how much a past period had in it the "seeds" of a specified future development. This teleological remnant is inherent in the *retrospective* viewpoint; and the retrospective viewpoint is not only part and parcel of historical inquiry, but also of psychoanalysis as well.

Box 4 conveys the notion of the present as being "pulled back" by some unintelligent (or unlearned) process. This is teleology in reverse, and is perhaps reflected in such Freudian (metapsychological) concepts as the death instinct and repetition-compulsion. Thus Freud writes in *Beyond the Pleasure Principle*:

> At this point we cannot escape the suspicion that we may have come upon the track of a universal attribute [the repetition-compulsion] of instincts

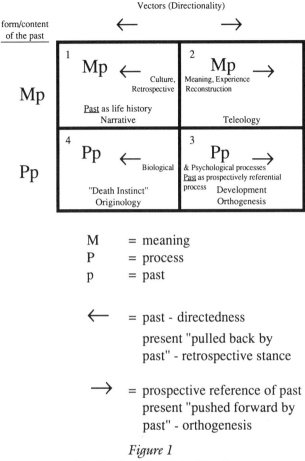

Figure 1
The Equivocality of the "Past"

and perhaps of organic life in general. . . . *It seems, then, that an instinct is an urge inherent in organic life to restore an earlier state of things . . .* the expression of the inertia inherent in organic life. (1920 36)

To the extent that such abstract conceptions as these control psychoanalytic understanding, it declines, inexorably, into some form of "originology" (Erikson 1962b 18–19), by which is meant the habit of thinking which reduces every human situation to its earliest, simplest, and most infantile precursor, and which is exclusively focused on repetition, regression, and perseveration in human life. Originology is anti-orthogenetic, and implies a biological-psychological tendency toward developmental entropy. Development is always being "pulled back" from a state of relative differentiation and hierarchic integration to one of increasing undifferentiatedness.[4]

However, it must be conceded that just as teleology is not entirely to be dismissed, so too with originology. For it is possible to conceive of certain biological processes (Box 3), such as those implicated in epilepsy, Alzheimer's disease, and perhaps manic depression, which entail the loss of developmental achievements and the disturbance of self-regulatory capacities. In this view, trauma (a causal process belonging to Box 3) may also be felt as an "organic tension," whose function in the biological-psychological system is retrogressive (Box 4), and which is finally interpreted and given retrospective *meaning* in terms of the psychodynamic "hermeneutics" of Box 1.

To summarize: on the one hand, human beings are viewed as so constituted that they are subject to the backward pull of the meaningful "past," and the task of psychoanalytic understanding is then to narrate, trace, or retrospectively reconstruct the particular history and detail (dynamics?) of this past-directed[5] movement; on the other hand, from what may be termed the genetic or orthogenetic point of view, human beings are seen as so constituted that they are always pushed forward by the "past," and the task of psychoanalytic understanding is now to abstract and infer the laws, processes, structures, and relationships inherent in such progressive movement and prospective (forward-looking) transformations.

This equivocality in the conceptualization of the past (the distinction, in particular, between Boxes 3 and 1) has elsewhere been interpreted in terms of "the ineradicable asymmetry between the knowledge that derives from looking forward in time and that which comes from looking back" (Freeman 1984 14). Whether or not this asymmetry is "ineradicable" or, for that matter, relevant or consequential for theoretical understanding and clinical practice in psychoanalysis, remains an open issue—and will duly be considered in the second part of this book. But for present purposes, it should be useful, first, to relocate the problem of the equivocality of the past into the context of the psychoanalytic construct of development. In so doing, a firmer link is forged between inquiry into the indeterminate status of the "past," and my concern in this book with problems of theoretical understanding (scientific and historical conceptualization) in psychoanalysis. For however construed, psychoanalytic inquiry is always about the *search* into the "past" which each adult carries within him- or herself and unconsciously repeats, reenacts, or revisions in his or her everyday life. In other words: (a) each of us comprises a "history," whether that history is articulated in a full narrative account or remains fragmentary and incomplete (Box 1 and perhaps Box 2); and (b) each human being is, equally, the outcome of a series of complex *processes* of development (Box 3 and perhaps Box 4). Such a search into both the "historical" and "genetic" pasts, the two modes of the presentness of the past, designates psychoanalysis as a developmental science, albeit (as we shall soon see) a most peculiar one.

The Mixed Construct of Psychoanalytic Development

In reviewing the scope of psychoanalytic theory, Freud, himself, observed:

> Not every analysis of psychological phenomena deserves the name of psychoanalysis. The latter implies more . . . from the very first, psychoanalysis was directed towards tracing the developmental processes. It . . . was led . . . to construct a genetic psychology. (1913 182–83)

And so Freud was led (but via his clinical work with adult patients who, he believed, exhibited "libidinal regressions,") to reconstruct a model of development, most fully elaborated in his *Three Essays on the Theory of Sexuality* (1905a). Here he begins, we recall, with "The Sexual Aberrations," and only after disassembling or decomposing the adult perversions is he able to recompose (or reconstruct) his famous model of infantile sexuality and the psychosexual stages of development. In thus conceptualizing the sequential reorganization of internal drive, and the organism's adaptation to it, Freud supplies, so to speak, a narrative grid through which certain periods and experiences of a person's remote past *(any* person's past) are given an extraordinary and privileged place in the psychoanalytic interpretation of the present (the concrete, individualized present of this or that particular patient).[6]

The further elaboration of this grid coincides with the intellectual and scientific history of psychoanalysis itself (e.g., Ego psychology, Object Relations, Self theory, etc.)—and has been marked in America, at least, by such notable emendations as Erikson's psychosocial approach (1959), as well as more recent efforts to accommodate, assimilate, or reformulate aspects of Piaget's non-psychoanalytic genetic epistemology (Basch 1977, 1981; Greenspan 1979). As we shall shortly see, such efforts as these to rectify psychoanalytic theory reflect increasing and accumulating doubt, especially among American analysts, about the logical status and coherence of the traditional Freudian model of development (Peterfreund 1978; Pine 1981). Moreover, such efforts seem to have set the stage for valuable and highly self-conscious projects aimed at coordinating, the "asymmetrical" constructions of the *observed* (genetic) and *clinical* (historical) infant (Stern 1985).

The significance for psychoanalysis of its developmental infrastructure cannot really be overstated. For it is reasonable to assert that a fundamental premise of psychoanalysis as a model or theory of psychopathology is the idea that all forms of psychoanalytically relevant psychopathology can

> in their essence be understood as manifestations of relative "primitivity"—
> as lower stages on a sort of developmental Great Chain of Being . . . toward
> the goals of self-monitoring and self-control of thought, action and the
> passions. (Sass 1987 26)

But the psychoanalytic construct of development is an odd and paradoxical construct, in that its domain or subject matter—(a) the past as meaningful content (as life history capable of more or less narrative articulation) and (b) the past as structure and process (as reducible to the pattern of relationships of its abstracted parts)—appears to coexist both in "actual" time and in "narrative" time. The past in "actual," linear or clock time is simply tantamount to the succession of moments which are reliably and externally observed (as in a typical longitudinal investigation); whereas the past in "narrative" time is the kind of past that changes in the act of narrating it, and as such, is therefore to be distinguished from (a) the so-called factual past, and (b) the processes, patterns, and structures that are alleged to underlie the "stream of personal history."[7]

The formulation I have just offered is of course only an alternative statement of the equivocality of the past, earlier expressed in terms of the contrasting vectors of the prospectively referential (genetic) past and the retrospectively constituted (meaningful) past. The former (the prospectively referential past situated in actual time) seems to underlie most *nonpsychoanalytic* developmental psychologies. It is the genetic or orthogenetic view that later configurations of a phenomenon are causally related to earlier ones. According to such a genetically or orthogenetically constrained model of development, the "past" is conceptualized wholly in actual time, is prospectively referential, and is the kind of "past" in which postulated biological, affective, cognitive, and behavioral structures (the "past" as analytically abstracted aspects of action and experience) can be shown, empirically, to be coordinated in a kind of evolutionary or adaptive process of directed growth (Cicchetti et al. 1988).

In marked contrast, we recall, the traditional psychoanalytic model of development is a *mixed model* in which the "past" is situated in narrative as well as in actual time; in which the "past" is recognized as a potentially meaningful semiotic system (an exhibition of human understanding and misunderstanding), as well as an analytically abstracted and causally explicable process understood in terms of laws which do not have to be learned to be operative; and in which development is past-directed or even circular in movement[8] (and retrospectively, narratively or historically conceptualized), as well as prospective in reference (and longitudinally or linearly conceptualized).

The Double-Edged Critique

Now there is no question that the traditional mixed model is a hybrid discourse which yields a composite image of the past. There is also no question that such a model is capable of generating serious confusions, especially when historical, retrospective or reconstructive conceptualizations of the past (appropriate in "narrative" time) are mechanically transposed into a genetic framework organized by "actual" time.[9] This is what Peterfreund (1978) has in mind when he speaks of "two fundamental conceptual fallacies, especially characteristic of psychoanalytic thought: the adultomorphization of infancy and the tendency to characterize early states of normal development in terms of hypotheses about later stages of psychopathology" (427). More generally, Schimek (1975a), in exposing a *third* fallacy (the genetic fallacy), has effectively questioned any expectation that analytic constructions in the clinical setting can provide a picture of the past rooted in actual reality. In Schimek's view, such narrative or interpretative transformations—while possibly of therapeutic benefit— do not yield knowledge either of a prior (past) psychological reality in the patient's mind, or of a genetic process in time, starting with some actual past event as the cause of present conditions. In short, clinical psychoanalysis (i.e., clinical interpretation) is unlikely to yield genuine developmental knowledge, if by this is meant knowledge of actual past genetic processes or knowledge of actual past psychic realities. It is worth recalling that in arriving at such a view, Schimek is also led to reject Freud's "rationalistic and non-developmental view of cognition" (1975b 186), namely the view that the "past" is carried as unconscious mental representations, and that these contents are permanently stored in the unconscious.

Schimek's conclusion—that the traditional mixed psychoanalytic construct of development is a paradoxical construct because it is in its cognitive assumptions non-developmental—is endorsed, from a very different perspective, by Zukier (1985). Now the paradox is understood as follows: while the premises of psychoanalysis (initial indeterminacy and structural variability) clearly require a developmental theory (to delineate the transformation of structures from initial polymorphism to the final integrated forms of sexuality and personality),

> a brief examination of the developmental parameters of psychoanalysis points to the absence of any theory of change or concepts of development in Freudian theory and therapy. (8)

The claim is made, for example, that while most developmental theories specify an end state, Freudian theory proposes instead primal events (e.g., the trauma associated with the death of the father). Or while most developmental theories describe a process of change in a *prospective* direction (recall Box 3), Freud's psychoanalysis insists that "the major mode of development is the repetitive mode, and the dominant characteristic of its concept of development is inertia" (12). Indeed, in Zukier's deconstructive reading, the narrative motion or direction of psychoanalytic "development" is, in truth, wholly *retrogressive* (recall Box 4), in the sense that psychic processes move in a backward direction whose *terminus ad quem* is death:

> Despite its repetitive and conservative nature, the compulsion to repeat does not seek to conserve an existing state of development. . . . The compulsion to repeat does not spell recurrence but change; it does not indicate the arrestment of development . . . but the demise of development, the dissolution of everything acquired so far. (19)

Change, then, is change backward—and this "backward pulsion" is articulated through such past-directed notions (processes?) as repetition, return of the repressed, and the *indestructibility*[10] of the individual's earliest experiences. Zukier thus concludes:

> Metaphorically, development can proceed backward; in effect it is always the earlier forces, preserved and uneroded by the passage of time, that erupt and come to dominate again. Hence timelessness characterizes the psychoanalytic conception of mind and its therapeutic practices. (22)

Such a conclusion is a remarkable one, for Zukier—through an internal metapsychology-driven critique—has refashioned psychoanalysis wholly as an "originology" (Box 4), and has implied that the psychoanalytic "past" is an atemporal construct, existing neither in "actual" time nor in narrative" time. Put paradoxically, Freud's *narrative* (his metapsychology) of development, by collapsing present and future into a timeless and indestructible past, is held to culminate in a repudiation of the narrative mode of thought.[11] Zukier thus portrays the traditional psychoanalytic construct of development as in essence *anti-historical* just as Schimek and Peterfreund expose its *anti-scientific* features. However, since "science" and "history" are viewed, in this book, as the primary avenues toward *theoretical* knowledge in psychoanalysis, any model of development (i.e., any strategy for the conceptualization of the past in psychoanalysis) must, at the very least, be consistent with the assumptions and presuppositions of either historical or scientific understanding, or possibly of both. And given the critiques cited above, the traditional psychoanalytic model of development is therefore found to be wanting on these counts.

Specifically: (a) Zukier has implied that, from the point of view of history, Freudian metapsychology is self-negating[12] in that it corrupts the historicality and narrativity of the psychoanalytic narrative; whereas (b) Schimek and Peterfreund have reasoned (but from the alternative perspective of empirical-analytic science) that Freud's underlying assumptions about perception and memory are untenable, and that a new *developmental* model of cognition or information processing is required to legitimate psychoanalysis as a scientific discourse.

The questions, then, that we are left with are these:

1. Given such a double-edged critique, is there really any place for the *mixed model* of psychoanalytic development? Is there any place for a hybrid discourse and a composite past?
2. Must "originology" (the backward pulsion of a biological-cum-

psychical past) *wholly displace* the historical-narrative stance implicit in Boxes 1 and 2?

3. Is the historical-narrative stance (Box 1) cognitively disqualified just because it counts as a retrospective and reconstructive stance, hopelessly caught up in the so-called genetic fallacy?

4. Is "knowledge of the past" at all accessible through the typically non-scientific practices of clinical psychoanalysis? And even if accessible, is such knowledge therapeutic? Or is *belief* in such knowledge therapeutic, or otherwise related to the effectiveness of intervention?

5. Finally, is there really any genuine relation between what once happened in the past and what is now happening in analysis?

We return, in short, to the argument which introduced this chapter, namely, the argument between the traditional and the revisionary points of view. We recall, however, that this is an argument about the nature of the past, about the manner and mode of its *conceptualization*. It is an argument that we are only just beginning to put in "synoptic" perspective. And it is an argument to which we must periodically return. But for now, it suffices to recapitulate the problem at hand: is there any role or function for a unitary model in which the "past" is conceptualized both in "actual" and in "narrative" time, and in which there is a genuine and legitimate reciprocity of influence between (a) observational-genetic and (b) reconstructive-clinical versions of development and therapy—in other words, between (a) the empirical-analytic (scientific) construction of the past, and (b) the narrative-hermeneutic (historical) construction of the past?

Saving the Mixed Model?

The clinical infant, writes Stern (1985), is:

> the joint creation of two people, the adult who grew up to become a psychiatric patient and the therapist, who has a theory about infant experience. This recreated infant is made up of memories, present reenactments in the transference, and theoretically guided interpretation. I call this creation the *clinical infant,* to be distinguished from the *observed infant,* whose behavior is examined at the very time of its occurrence. (14)

How is our understanding of the *clinical infant* (the narrative outcome of a joint act of retrospective abstraction) to be coordinated with our understanding of the *observed infant* (whose behavior is examined at the very time of its occurrence through empirical-analytic methods of replicable observation and experiment)? Stern's project offers a clue to how this question might be answered, and supplies, I suggest, a provisional justification for retaining the traditional mixed model of psychoanalytic development.

Stern's focus is on the subjective experience and intersubjective reality of the developing infant. Since the clinical situation appears to be similarly focused on the patient's (and therapist's) subjective and intersubjective realities, an interface of perspectives is both conceivable and perhaps fruitful. Such an interface is possible, however, only because Stern's mode of understanding is in considerable measure *phenomenological* and not purely empirical-analytic in character. This is evident when he comments:

> I am suggesting that the infant can experience the *process* of emerging organization as well as the result, and it is the experience of emerging organization that I call the *emergent sense of self.* (45)

What is now important is not just what Stern says (i.e., the domain of study conceptualized as the infant's *experience of* the process of emerging organization), but also what he does not. For the "processes" and "structures" of Stern's developmental psychology are not the analytically abstracted processes, patterns, and relationships characteristic of normal biological and behavioral science. Stern's processes and structures are conceptualized as "experiential integrations," as concrete or occurrent: they actually inhere in self-experience as such. That is to say, they are not intended or used as constructs (in the scientist's head) whose primary function is to generate "explanatory power," i.e., the prediction, extrapolation, and control of abstracted aspects of experience.

Thus, on the one hand, Stern's developmental psychology (insofar as it is phenomenological in the sense just described) is quite distinct from, but perhaps complementary to, such developmental psychologies as Cicchetti's (Cicchetti et al. 1988), Piaget's (1971), and Kagan's (1984). The latter, as instances of empirical-analytic science, are naturally focused on the organization and reorganization of analytically abstracted aspects of affect, cognition, and behavior (structures, patterns, processes), rather than on how *actual happenings* are transformed into subjective experience of various kinds and degrees of *(experienced)* integration and differentiation. On the other hand, Stern's approach, with its "experience-near" mode of conceptualization (Kohut 1971, 1977) clearly overlaps with the historical constructions of psychoanalytic narration, which likewise tend to minimize the analytically abstractive procedures of normal science. This contrast may be put metaphorically as follows: (a) empirical-analytic science unwinds the heterogeneous strands of experience, puts each strand into its analytically distinct box, and seeks to understand experience as a *function* of some paradigmatic pattern generated from the external relations of these abstracted strands; whereas (b) both the developmentalist, Stern, and the prototypical clinical psychoanalyst are alike in their concern, as reflective thinkers, with the problem of the "texture constituted by the interwoven strands" (Berlin 1981 131): they are concerned, that is, with the problem of knowing an experience or an activity as a concrete whole, significant in itself, "as having the source of its movement within itself" (Oakeshott 1962 113).

Given this common phenomenological ground, it becomes possible, in Stern's view, not only to look at the clinical infant through the eyes of the *observed infant,* but also to look at the observed infant through the eyes of the *clinical infant.* Such a "dialectical coordination" of the observed infant and the clinical infant yields a fuller account of the *content* of the former's subjective experience consistent with the *limits* of such experience as established by empirical-analytic science.

If, as I have just suggested in the preceding discussion, Stern's approach implies a strategy for preserving some version of the traditional mixed model of psychoanalytic development, how might it now help, specifically, in explicating the idea of the "past," the manner and mode of its conceptualization?

For Stern, the initial focus is on the *preverbal* development of the infant's sense of self, which includes the sense of enduring, the sense "of a continuity with one's own past so that one 'goes on being' and can even change while remaining the same" (1985 71). Moreover, the infant's subjective experience (of action, sensation, affect, and time) is always, in the phenomenological sense, an experience of the *real.* This means not only that the infant lacks a symbolizable concept of "external reality" against which to compare its "internal reality," but also that its subjective experiences suffer no conflictful distortion by virtue of wishes and defenses, and that the capacity for defensive—that is, psychodynamic—distortions of reality is a later developing capacity requiring more cognitive processes than are initially available. (255)

In sum, the beginnings of life are non-psychodynamic;[13] only with the later advent of symbolic thinking, verbal representations, and linguistic and narrative competence, is "fantasy distortion" and, hence "psychic reality," *conceivable* in any phenomenologically valid account of self-experience. It would appear to follow, then, that the "past" exists, initially, neither in "actual" nor in "narrative" time. Both "pasts" are *later* constructions (cognitive achievements) which—from this prospective vantage—emerge, from the experiential integration of continuity in change (the subjective reality of "lived time"), and which never wholly displace this preverbal component of core selfhood.

More precisely, the "past" as a parameter of psychic reality (and as located in narrative time) can only enter into subjective experience by very early childhood—that is, with the advent of symbolic thinking, linguistic competence, and the ability to narrate one's life story,[14] all of which, Stern argues, operate together to force a space between interpersonal experience (a) as lived and (b) as represented. The psychoanalytic significance of this phenomenological observation is that it is "exactly across this space that the connections and associations that constitute neurotic behavior may form" (182). In other words, the "Great Divide" (Blight 1981)—epistemologically and psychologically speaking—may not be between body and mind or science and hermeneutics, but rather, between experience and reflection. It is because of this "Great Divide" (the gap between interpersonal experience *as lived* and *as represented*)[15] that a distinctively psychoanalytic narrative can be constructed and perhaps prove therapeutic. It is also because of this "Great Divide" that psychic reality,[16] through the joint activities and transactions of analyst and analysand, can in fact be constituted out of the patient's enduring, active subjective experience. However, psychic reality (and the "past" as a dimension of it) only come into being through the retrospective, historical "reconstructions" of the clinical situation; yet the conditions for the appearance of psychic reality in general are knowable prospectively, in accord with the presuppositions and methods of empirical-analytic science. Once again, the psychoanalytic past is revealed as a *composite past:* in one sense, it exists "out there," given in the objective "connections and associations that constitute neurotic behavior"; in another sense, it exists only "as narrated," in the intersubjective practice of the psychoanalytic narrative.

When Stern proceeds to examine the implications of his developmental approach for the problem of practical intervention, he concludes that the essential task is to discover the *"narrative point of origin* of the pathology, regardless of when it occurred in actual developmental time" (1985 257). This can only mean that the therapeutically relevant "past" exists, by definition, in narrative time; and that this is therefore (a) the kind of past that is created as it is being spoken, (b) the kind of past that can change in the very act of narrating it, (c) the kind of past that incorporates the modifying influence of the analyst to whom it is addressed, (d) the kind of past that is (equivocally) the "past as such" and/or the story told about it. The *metaphor* that encapsulates this enigmatic past will be more or less effective to the extent that it taps the remembered or recollected experience (of the patient's self-narrative) which is *phenomenologically congruent*[17] with those domains of "self-experience" held to be implicated in the etiology of the pathological process. Again it is *not* the actual point of origin of pathology which is held to be therapeutically relevant, but rather the narrative or psychical point of origin. All that is required of this "past" (located anywhere in narrative time) is that it be phenomenologically isomorphic to the affected domains of self-experience. Stern, as a genetic developmentalist (recall Box 3), may indeed be able, through empirical-analytic methods, to identify or diagnose the "affected" domains of self-experience, and to infer the antecedents and consequents of such pathological self-experience. But he must change hats and become a clinical-historical developmentalist (recall Box 1) in order to conceptualize, formulate, and hence "discover" the narrative point of origin ("past") which is actually therapeutically effective. The developmentalist thus wears two hats; the psychoanalytic model of development remains, one hundred years after Freud, a mixed model, and the psychoanalytic past is still a composite past. Stern in fact appears to believe that his particular perspective on development—his dialectical coordination of the observed and clinical infant—may be most useful not in the prediction and control of behavior and psychopathology, but rather in the distinct clinical-practical task of "suggesting search strategies to aid in the construction of therapeutically effective life narratives" (1985 273).

We conclude this section with the observation that although Stern's approach has not quite saved the mixed model of psychoanalytic development, it has at least made a case for its continuing utility. We have seen, moreover, that the viability of any version of the mixed model depends upon the phenomenological grounding of *both* its genetic (empirical-analytic) and clinical (narrative-historical) components. Only such common grounding can counter or mitigate the obvious fact that statements (discourse) based on the interactive experience of therapy and statements based on the observation of infants are on different epistemological levels: in the former instance, the therapist is a participant observer whose stance codetermines the nature of interactions, the constitution of meanings and, indeed, the very form of the discourse; whereas in the latter case, the infant researcher is independent of (and irrelevant to) his domain of inquiry, and is obligated to observe and report in a reliable, replicable, and standardized mode of discourse. While there may be ways in which these different epistemological levels or discrete discourses can be joined or bridged, there is surely no shortcut to "commonality," and we cannot help recalling, in this context, the "Great Divide" between the two propositions discussed in Chapter 1.

Recapitulation and Conclusion

Before proceeding further, it will be useful to review what has been achieved so far. In the spirit of the "plurality of ends" espoused in Chapter 1, and in light of the tension between the so-called scientific and hermeneutic trends in American psychoanalysis, I have sought to provide a brief and schematic overview of the conceptualization of the past. Beginning with the argument between the traditionalists and the revisionists, I have wished to underline the *equivocality* of the "past" in psychoanalytic thinking, but without prematurely joining or settling the issue. That equivocality is captured and explicated through such formulas as: the past as backward-looking versus the past as prospectively referential; the past recognized as potentially meaningful conduct versus the past recognized as structure and process; the past as narrated versus the past as analytically abstracted; the past as life history versus the past as outcome of a series of developmental or orthogenetic processes.

Moreover, the equivocality of the "past," as here presented, clearly points back to the "conflict of interpretations" explored in Chapter 1.

There I cited two competing traditions in the philosophy of method and explanation, the Aristotelian and the Galilean, and suggested that the former was concerned with the idea of a law as "an intrinsic connection to be grasped through reflective understanding," while the latter was concerned with the idea of a law as "an inductive generalization established by experiment." This distinction is surely not alien or unrelated to the equivocality implicit in the conceptualization of the past. Also in Chapter 1, I introduced the two propositions which may be said to underlie the empirical-analytic and hermeneutic conceptions of inquiry, understanding, and experience. The first proposition, the *objectivist* proposition, leads us to presume that the "past" possesses an inherent structure or force, as well as sufficient independence from the present, so that it is susceptible to some form of scientific (Galilean) analysis and explanation. The second proposition, the *conventionalist* or closed circle proposition, presumes that the meaning of the "past" (as well as the manner and mode of its conceptualization) will vary, depending on the many possible language games in which it is used. According to this second proposition, the empirical-analytic (or scientific) language game is only one of many possible language games; it holds no monopoly on rationality, and the past may be intelligibly constructed in a variety of other language games, including those characteristic of historical inquiry as well as of practical life in general. In such a view, it is by no means clear that science is a superordinate language game entitled to explain (or explain away) the "past" already constructed by (or accounted for) through historical or hermeneutic inquiries.

The equivocality of the "past" is thus built into our very presuppositional horizon. It is therefore not at all surprising that it is also displayed in the various departments of psychoanalysis, including most notably, developmental theory and clinical theory. Lastly, the equivocality of the "past" may be said to infect all *levels* of psychoanalytic understanding, ranging from metapsychological speculation to the most casual, low-level inference in the clinical setting. Now, in offering my overview, I have also noted certain important proposals for cleansing or "curing" psychoanalysis of this equivocality, and for reorganizing theory and practice on a more logically sound basis. But my approach so far has not been to endorse such proposals and arguments (e.g., those of Schimek, Peterfreund, Eagle, etc.). To do so, I believe, would involve presupposing the epistemological (and methodological) assumptions of those arguments.

Instead, I have opted to circumvent (or bracket) such commitments, at least for the moment, in the hope that this would enable me to "contemplate simultaneously what is right in each view," which I cited in Chapter 1 as an essential ingredient of my approach and method.

The philosopher Nelson Goodman (1978, 1984) has recognized the issue at hand when he writes:

> The physicist flits back and forth between a world of waves and a world of particles as suits his purpose. We usually think and work within one world-version at a time—hence Hilary Putnam's term "internal realism"—but we shift from one to the other often. When we undertake to relate different versions, we introduce multiple worlds. When that becomes awkward we drop the worlds for the time being and consider only the versions. We are monists, pluralists, and nihilists . . . as befits the context. (1984 278)

In this book, then, I undertake "to relate different versions" and "introduce multiple realities." My interest is in the plurality of psychoanalytic pasts, and how these pasts may be recognized, distinguished, and placed, eventually, in some coherent relation. So far I have focused on the equivocality of the psychoanalytic past, and on how this equivocality appears to resolve into what may now be termed the historical and scientific versions of the past. It becomes necessary, at this point, to provide a more explicit account of what is involved in historical understanding, and how such understanding is distinguished from (as well as coordinated with) scientific explanation. The following chapter offers such an account. By placing "history" and "science" in the context of the plurality of psychoanalytic "pasts," I thus aim to establish the approach or model which will guide inquiry throughout the remainder of this book.

NOTES

1. Whether the psychoanalytic method is really derivable from a scientific theory, or whether it can actually contribute to the development or validation of such a theory, remains in dispute even today. Indeed Freud, himself, once commented: "psychoanalysis is not an impartial scientific investigation, but a therapeutic measure. Its essence is not to prove anything, but merely to alter something" (1909b 104). Observe that Freud's position (at least in this particular statement of the aim of psychoanalysis) is compatible with Eagle's proposal for an autonomous theory of therapy, whose focus is on "effectiveness of intervention," and whose scope encompasses a variety of therapeutic measures, including those known as "psychoanalytic."

2. The argument between the revisionists and the traditionalists is recapitulated in Chapters 4 and 5. In Chapter 4, I present the revisionist position and explore the paradox that it is *historical* psychoanalysis which undermines the reality and objectivity of the past. Chapter 5 ("The Scientific Construction of the Psychoanalytic Past") expounds a traditionalist position, and assumes, in contrast, that the past is hypothetically real and putatively objective: such a past (the "developmental past") is also held to underlie the "narrativity" of the historically constructed psychoanalytic past.

3. The clinical theory-metapsychology debate is between: (a) those who would jettison traditional metapsychology and totally reconfigure clinical theory as a hermeneutical or historical discipline (e.g., Schafer 1976, 1978; Klein 1976; Gill 1976); and (b) those who would argue that whatever the inadequacies of Freud's instinct theory or hydraulic and energic model, it remains vital to search for "a deeper level of explanation in the substrate and processes underlying the behavior we carry out and the goals we pursue" (Eagle 1984a 149). According to this latter view, it is possible to envisage (i) an explanatory metapsychology *and* a hermeneutic-historical clinical "theory," the two, however, being essentially unrelated, or (ii) an explanatory metapsychology logically joined to an empirical-analytic theory of therapy, with each theory or model operating at a different level of abstraction and comprehensiveness.

4. The *orthogenetic* principle is a heuristic principle that has helped to define and direct developmental inquiry. It states:

> Insofar as development occurs in a process under consideration, there is a progression from a state of relative undifferentiatedness to one of increasing differentiation and hierarchic integration. (Kaplan 1966 661)

In this book, the scientific psychoanalytic past is understood as an orthogenetically constituted past, whereas the historical psychoanalytic past is understood as a narratively constructed past. See also in Chapter 5, "The Idea of Development: Orthogenesis, Epigenesis, and Repetition."

5. The term "past-directed" is a convenient simplification. In truth, analytic work is *temporally circular,* rather than unidirectionally retrospective. In terms of the four-way scheme presented in Figure 1, clinical analysis therefore involves Box 2 (teleology) as well as Box 1 (past-directedness). Schafer (1983) has aptly evoked the dimension of temporal circularity in the following remarks:

> It soon becomes evident that, interpretatively, one is working in a temporal circle. One works backward from what is told about the autobiographical present in order to define, refine, correct, organize, and complete an analytically coherent and useful account of the past, and one works forward from various tellings of the past to constitute that present and that anticipated future which are most important to explain. (238)

6. Freud's conceptualization of the psychoanalytic past is explored throughout this book. Often his position is identified indirectly (e.g., as a "traditionalist" position), and becomes a foil for various "revisionists," ranging from Schafer and

Spence, on the one hand, to Gedo, Basch, and Noy on the other. However, it is probably more accurate to note that *both* traditionalist and revisionary points of view are represented in Freud's theorizing. Thus Freud propounds not only a "science of psychical history" (a developmental metapsychology), but also a "clinical historiography" (a clinical hermeneutic). It follows then, that Freud's conceptualization of the psychoanalytic past varies according to the "divergent rationalities" of (a) metapsychology (biopsychical development) (b) and clinical discourse (the therapeutic narrative). One might say that the "past" is objective, preformed, and preexistent in the former context, while it is intersubjective, constructed, and alterable in the latter context.

7. The narrative or meaningful past must be distinguished not only from the "past" as structure and process, but also from the "past" as fact or happening. The past-as-fact is therefore not necessarily equivalent to the meaning that fact (or happening) has assumed in a person's history or self-narrative. Thus, the *fact* that Dora was kissed by Herr K. is distinguishable from the *meaning* that fact assumed in Dora's self-narrative. Freud failed Dora, not in dismissing the fact of the kiss, but in failing rightly to credit Dora's understanding of the significance of this experience (Erikson 1962a). What Freud did was to marginalize Dora's conscious and preconscious self-understanding, in favor of his own genetic-dynamic rereading of the meaning of Dora's experience.

8. See Note 5.

9. The problem is *also* one of transposing genetic (empirical-analytic) conceptualizations of the past into historical-hermeneutic contexts organized by "narrative time." The problem, in short, concerns the relationship of scientific developmental formulations to the practical requirements of the psychoanalytic dialogue. Does developmental theory yield "technical recommendations," "practical knowledge," neither, or both? For further discussion, see in Chapter 5 of this book, "Development, Pathology, and Therapeutic Action"; "Scientific Psychoanalysis: Evaluation and Critique"; and "Science, History, and Practice: Pluralism in Psychoanalysis."

10. Zukier's reference to the *indestructibility* of the infant's earliest experiences recalls Schimek's critique of Freud's non-developmental cognitive assumptions (which imply that mental *contents* are permanently stored in the unconscious). A more developmentally oriented revision of Freud's theory must focus, of course, on the role of "schemata" in remodeling the data of experience (Horowitz 1988), and on the role of later experience in altering earlier schemata. Such a revisionary approach assumes, further, that only schemata, not mental contents, are actually stored in the "unconscious." It follows that if there is anything "indestructible" in anyone's psychological past, it cannot be "mental contents" (or even early "experience" or "trauma"); only the *schemata of experience* can lay claim to indestructibility, since only these are "stored," and even these schemata are apparently altered by later experience.

11. Bruner (1986) has argued that the narrative mode of thought and the logico-scientific (paradigmatic) mode of thought are two irreducible forms of cognitive functioning, each meriting the status of "natural kind." The paradig-

matic mode aims at context-free, universal explications, establishing truth through formal verification procedures and empirical proof. The narrative mode, however, entails particularistic, context-sensitive explications—and in the words of Ricoeur (1983), "temporality" belongs to its very linguistic structure. What Zukier has depicted, then, is the *detemporalization* of Freud's metapsychological narrative— its collapse (or *reductio ad absurdum*) into the "timeless" bedrock of a biological past. Zukier's account thus demonstrates how Freud's quasi-paradigmatic aspirations have seized control of the psychoanalytic narrative and divested it of all traces of historicality, temporality, and contextual particularity.

12. Freudian metapsychology is questionable from the point of view of history (or narrative) because it violates the historical presumption that the identity of any phenomenon is most effectively elicited through an account of continuity in change. As Note 11 suggests, Freudian metapsychology nullifies "change," and implies a timeless conceptualization of "identity."

13. Recall that John Gedo (1984), along with Daniel Stern, are among the few clinical psychoanalysts to focus attention on those preverbal and presymbolic issues (including optimum tension regulation) which originate in the *prepsychodynamic* (or non-psychodynamic) strata of development, but which nevertheless manifest themselves as "archaic transferences" (and as pathological diagnostic signs) in the clinical situation.

14. The emergence of narrative competence can of course be assessed empirically. I assume that some recognizable "ability to narrate one's life story" emerges in early childhood. Until recently, however, there has been little systematic empirical inquiry into the early development of narrative competence. Likewise, little is known (empirically) about the developmental transformations of narrative thinking over the life span (Bruner 1990).

15. The "gap" between experience as lived and experience as represented is normally bridged by language, and by such properties of language as metaphor (Lakoff and Johnson 1980). Language, however, sometimes fails to bridge this gap, and this failure may bear the imprint of neurotic conflict. Alternatively, such failure may have a non-conflictual basis. Consider the pathology of *alexithymia*. This disorder describes some deep difficulty in expressing or verbalizing feelings (Nemiah 1977; Krystal 1979). Feelings are presumably felt (there is emotional arousal), but they cannot be put into words—or if they can, the words seem disconnected from the apparent affective experience. Alexithymia, then, points to a condition in which there is an enduring and unbridgeable "divide" between experience as lived and experience as represented. See also Lane and Schwartz (1987) who attempt to explain alexithymic pathology in terms of a cognitive-developmental model of emotional awareness.

16. The concept of psychic reality is examined in greater detail in Chapters 4 and 5, where the historical and scientific versions of its construction are explicated. In the passage now under consideration, the term "psychic reality" is used narratively; it signifies a not-yet-well-formed *story* which is, in effect, a potential history of the relation of the expressed (present) to the unexpressed (past). The hermeneutic explication that generates this history is a double hermeneutic. It is both an

explication of (a) the unexpressed subjective reality of the individual, and an explication of (b) the unexpressed but dynamically unconscious reality of the individual. According to this formulation, then, "psychic reality" emerges as a complex artifact of historical inquiry where such inquiry is undertaken and practiced (to a greater or lesser degree) by analyst and analysand in the interactive setting of the clinical situation (see in Chapter 3, "Clinical Psychoanalysis and the Model of History").

17. The idea of "phenomenological congruence" is my own and it cannot easily be given a useful, empirical, or operational definition. As I understand it, however, the therapist must make a *practical* judgment that some piece of the patient's self-narration is correlated to (or congruent with) those domains of self-experience hypothesized to be implicated in the patient's presenting pathology (if known). The therapist's narrative-clinical task is now to come up with the metaphor—a salient way of elaborating that piece of the patient's remembered past— that incorporates a reflection on the transference and countertransference. I assume, of course, that the patient has been narrating (or constructing) a past under the modifying influence of the therapist to whom it is ostensibly addressed.

In referring to the patient's "remembered past," it is evident that neither the veridicality nor the actual chronological origin of the remembered event or experience is crucial. I assume that the patient interprets, remodels, and refashions his own history (the story of his past); that his changing memories, fantasies, beliefs, and desires bear the mark of the changing "phases" or stages of development, knowledge of which may well be available to the therapist. Thus, the analyst or therapist—in searching for the "narrative point of origin"—is always engaged in some sort of second-order elaboration of the patient's already much-elaborated retelling or reconstruction of his past experience (Freud 1909a 206).

It is interesting to note that Stern's dialectical methodology complements the revisionary point of view: the view that the psychoanalytic past is quite literally a construction or epiphenomenon of the present, and that transferential references "to the past" are appropriately interpretable as allusions to the here and now. Stern's "mixed model" permits those allusions to be coordinated with the developmental psychopathology hypothesized to be applicable to the patient. Stern's model thus places the "narrative past" in a kind of dialectical relation to the "developmental past." Yet it is also evident that Stern offers no formula or technique to "compute" this relationship, and the search for the "narrative point of origin" still belongs to the *practical knowledge* of the psychotherapist.

3

History, Science, and the
Plurality of Pasts

The past is a foreign country; they do things differently there.

—L. P. Hartley

One would expect people to remember the past and to imagine the future. But in fact, when discoursing . . . about history, they imagine it in terms of their own experiences, and when trying to gauge the future they cite supposed analogies from the past: till by a double process of repetition they imagine the past and remember the future.

—Lewis Namier

Is it possible that the antonym of "forgetting" is not "remembering," but *justice?*

—Yosef Hayim Yerushalmi

Introduction: History and the Natural Attitude

Why is anybody interested in the past? Surely not to perceive the past in its differentness, surely not to know it as an alien and "foreign country." On the contrary, for most of us, interest in the past is sustained by the feeling, more or less intense, that things could have happened otherwise, and could have taken a different turn. *If* Hitler had won the war, *if* Kennedy had lived, *if* my father hadn't run off, *if* I had married X . . . at each moment, one imagines a next (future) moment unlike the one that actually followed, so that one ends up, finally, with the fantasy of another, less unsatisfactory life; more exactly, one arrives at an alternative self-narrative, which though entirely impossible, is nonetheless perfectly co-

64

herent and intelligible. "If" is thus the secret of the link between life here and now, and the past there and then. "If" imparts to history (the past and our interest in it) the anxiety and expectation that define the present.

It is fair to conclude, then, that this *natural attitude*[1] toward the past (and especially toward one's own) is shaped and conditioned by present-day hopes, fears, passions, and preoccupations, and that the past is ordinarily imagined, narrated, and constructed in view of the felt needs of the present. But if this is the case, what in fact can we expect to learn from history, from the past so constituted? To which the reply must be: precisely what we wish to learn. But such an answer, if true, must mean that history (as construed above) does not easily or naturally move "beyond the information given," except in the narrative directions of (a) fantasy or fiction, and (b) repetition and reproduction of the present in the past. In either case, the "past," a mental thing comprised of images and beliefs, becomes hostage to, or a fulfillment of, the present wish.[2] In such an account, how can "history" be of use in clinical psychoanalysis; what role can it possibly play in the scheme of psychoanalytic understanding? It would seem, instead, that historical consciousness (insofar as it expresses a natural attitude toward the past) is actually *symptomatic,* itself requiring diagnosis, treatment, and (non-historical) explanation.

Concern on this score is especially pertinent now that leading American psychoanalysts (e.g., Schafer 1983; Spence 1982) propose to reinterpret clinical psychoanalysis as a *life historical* discipline, in which the crucial therapeutic task is said to consist in the creation of a meaningful life history integrating the "past" and "present" of the analysand, so fostering, for example, the ability to contemplate changes in self without fear of dissolution and fragmentation. Clearly, some account is now required which depicts "history" as also departing from the natural attitude, and as therefore distinguishable from the "presentistic" construction of the past described above. "History," in the new account, needs to imply an "unnatural" attitude toward the past, and it must be argued that it is indeed possible to learn from the "past," and through one's encounter or engagement with it.

The principal objective of this chapter is therefore to supply such an account—to sketch the outline of a view of history as inquiry, in terms of which the *historical past* can now be recognized as a "foreign country," and hence, as a potential source of understanding "beyond the information given." From such a perspective, it should be possible to demonstrate that the "acquisition of a more empathic perspective on one's own ineliminable past" (cited in Chapter 2, as a desired outcome of analytic treatment) necessarily entails a form of historical self-understanding and the therapeutic construction of a distinctively historical past. And such self-understanding, whether relatively explicit and reflective or relatively implicit and enactive, should be radically distinguished from the kind of "understanding" involved in the natural attitude toward the past.

However, prior to undertaking the principal task of this chapter, it will be useful to turn briefly to the following excerpt from a conversation in a psychotherapeutic session.[3] In so doing, I believe, we lend credence to the intuitive conviction (a) that historical self-understanding is indeed acquired and transmitted through therapeutic engagements, and (b) that historical inquiry and interpretation may help to explain how this is so.

1. PSYCHOTHERAPIST: It is exactly the way it was when you were 12 years old.
2. PATIENT: Of course. Now, all of a sudden, it becomes clear to me that it was exactly the same.
3. PSYCHOTHERAPIST: You've forgotten this connection, which you already knew about, and I have restored it to you.
4. PATIENT: Yes, now it occurs to me that I recently told you about it.
5. PSYCHOTHERAPIST: Well, then, if I restore it to you, you can recognize it once again as your own.

The therapeutic conversation divides into two phases, each of which is enacted at a distinct level. In the first phase (Statements 1 and 2), it proceeds in the "natural attitude," and is therefore focused on the informational *contents* of the conversation. There is little distance from the "anxiety and expectation which define the present" and which are accordingly read back into the past. This is a normal conversation (Grice 1975), proceeding so far within the conventional parameters. The therapist, however, is surprised since he had assumed that "he was merely indicating something that had long been known to the patient" (Argelander 1976 30). Were the conversation to continue in the natural attitude, the therapist and patient might now begin to discuss (argue) the question of who is mistaken or confused. Instead, the therapist realizes that the patient is treating his remark as though it were an entirely new idea. Thus, in its second phase (Statements 3–5), the conversation departs from the natural attitude and turns into a *reflection* upon itself. Both patient and therapist are now somewhat distanced from the conversational contents (from the anxiety and expectation that define the present and distort access to the past); and the therapist, by attending to his role as historian of the conversational encounter, is properly situated to aid the patient in under-standing the significance of the communication he had unconsciously introduced, that is, the fact that the patient is unable to recognize a thing as his own—and only if another person restores it to him can he identify it anew as his own.

The therapist, through his historical reading of the situation (evi-dence), has been able to "diagnose" the *discontinuity* in the interaction; he is also in a position, now, to diagnose the patient's problem, namely, the "identification disorder" which has been enacted and divulged through this conversational (and transferential) interaction. Of more importance, the patient, himself, has learned (or begun to learn) something. Guided by the therapist, he too has departed safely from the natural attitude; in doing so, he is no longer quite as rigidly locked into an "imagined" and presentistic past. The patient begins to recognize the present influence of *disenfranchised* aspects of his past, and learns to respond (not merely react) to them. He comes to see his past as "foreign" or unfamiliar country, and for that very reason, as a possible source of hope and insight.

This, then, is what I mean when I want to claim that historical self-understanding is acquired and transmitted through therapeutic engage-ments, and that historical inquiry may help to explain how this is so. The substantiation and validation of this claim are high on this book's agenda. But for now, the immediate task requires that "history" be displayed as a distinctive mode of discourse, and it is to that task that I now turn.

History and the Science of History

First, some very elementary distinctions. While the subject matter of history is said to be the "past" (or what human beings have done or suffered, according to Aristotle), history is ambiguous in referring both to the "actual course of events" and to inquiry about them. This parallels the distinction known to historians since antiquity between the "past" as the totality of events that ever happened *(res gestae)* and the "past" as stories told about the past *(historiae rerum gestarum)*. History as an inquiry therefore concerns stories that are told about the past. But it has always also been clear that the truth or validity of such stories cannot be assessed or established by a simple look at *res gestae,* "because *res gestae,* the past as totality, is not the sort of thing one can simply look at" (Munz 1985 91). This leads, on the one hand, to an understandable anxiety concerning the possibility of "historical truth" (e.g., is history just story-telling, just fiction?), and on the other hand, to an understandable (and compensatory) craving for a natural science of history.

Let us consider, first, the compensatory craving for a natural science of history. Historical stories are unsatisfactory because they are uncertain and piecemeal. Progress therefore lies in the "scientific" pursuit of certainty and totality. The idea of a natural science of history thus emerges as a science of the past as historical process: the attempt to represent "the past as totality," as a kind of lawful and linear *process* of development and growth, and/or one of disintegration and decline. Moreover, as Isaiah Berlin (1981) has observed, the appeal of this idea has been buttressed by one of our most powerful metaphors for "time."[4]

> We speak of the youth, the maturity, and the decay of peoples and cultures, of the ebb and flow of social movements, of the rise and fall of nations. Such language serves to convey the idea of an inexorably fixed time order —the "river of time" on which we float, and which we must willy-nilly accept; a moving stair which we have not created, but on which we are borne, obeying . . . some natural law governing the order and shape of events. . . . Metaphorical and misleading though such uses of words can be, they are pointers to categories and concepts in terms of which we conceive the "stream of history," namely as something possessing an objective pattern that we ignore at our peril . . . (108)

Thus the plausible metaphor of the "river of time" (birth, maturity, death) slides into the more dubious metaphor of the "stream of history" (lawful stages of development), and via a reification of the "past," terminates in the idea of a natural science of history. Now the past as totality *(res gestae)* is held to signify directly (unmediated by narrative or historical self-consciousness) the reality of pattern, law, and inherent structure; and any particular or concrete event is intelligible only as a function of that general pattern or law. Nothing is meaningful in and of itself, only by virtue of the part it plays in some lawful and objectively real "historical process." Such a project, aimed at comprehending and controlling the movement of history, was surely the dream of the great nineteenth-century philosophers of history (e.g., Comte, Spencer, Marx, et al.), and may be said, perhaps, to have decisively shaped the ideals and aims of the emerging social and behavioral sciences. It is important to realize that the idea of a science of history is offered as a substitute for history itself. For insofar as the latter merely involves the patient and detailed exploration of a period, or the endeavor to elucidate continuity in change, it is thought to be *atheoretical* and hence useless, except as a source of "facts" and "data" which illustrate the reality of objectively existent processes.

In this century, controversy has largely appeared to shift from *res gestae* (or history as the course of events) to *historiae rerum gestarum* (history as inquiry, as stories told about the past). The crucial question now becomes: is there a distinctively historical way of looking at the past, or is historical inquiry, insofar as it is rational, explanatory, or theoretical, best specified in terms of the well-established norms of natural science? The latter, of course, is the position of such twentieth-century positivist philosophers of science as Hempel (1942) who maintain that the concept of explanation is neutral with respect to subject matter, and that, therefore, history must be assessed and evaluated in light of that concept:

> Historical explanation, too, aims at showing that the event in question was not "a matter of chance," but was to be expected in view of certain antecedent or simultaneous conditions. The expectation referred to is ... [a] rational scientific anticipation which rests on the assumption of general laws. (1942 348–49)

It is important to appreciate that Hempel's deductive-nomological model is a *prescriptivist* model. The logic of explanation that is thought to prevail in physics is stipulated to be normative for the biological, behavioral, and historical sciences. As such, this model has had incalculable influence, for example, on the aims and ambitions of sociology (Giddens 1979), where "the logical empiricist philosophy of science came to be seen as what natural science 'is,' and as showing what sociology should become" (238). The situation has hardly been different in American academic psychology, where Clark Hull (to cite the obvious example) sought to develop a theory of learning based entirely on such a logical positivist approach, in which all empirical laws would be deductively linked through an axiomatic system (Leahey 1980).

When superimposed on historical inquiry, the positivist model of explanation *prescribes* that the historical event be conceptualized as nothing but the function of some general pattern, law, or regularity. True enough, the general pattern now in question is, strictly speaking, an analytic construct (in the scientist's head), and not, literally, a piece of objective reality (as it was for the aforementioned nineteenth-century philosophers of history). Yet the result is virtually identical. For the event as such is dissolved into a system of abstracted relations, and it is this system which is then taken to "stand for" (or constitute) reality. In other words, what is being prescribed is that the (reified?) reality of relations be systematically embraced at the expense of the actuality of objects, events, and experiences (Kuzminski 1986).

Unlike most of their colleagues in the behavioral sciences and psychology, historians have generally been reluctant to reconstruct their principles and practices along the lines recommended by the positivist and logical empiricist program. Admittedly, certain important practitioners such as Furet (1975)[5] have argued that *narrative* history achieves only the illusion of explanation, and should be replaced by "analysis" (e.g., the comparison of the productivity of slave labor and free labor in the United States before the Civil War); but most historians have remained skeptical and continue to ply their craft in the accustomed manner. Yet the positivist challenge posed by Hempel and his colleagues nevertheless calls for a response. Such a rejoinder has indeed been forthcoming, in the form of the reemergence in the past generation of the *critical philosophy of history,* a tradition that had been largely dormant since Collingwood's contributions (1946) earlier in the century. Thus it has been argued by such philosophers as Oakeshott (1962, 1975), Gallie (1964, 1968), Mink (1970, 1978), White (1981, 1984), Dray (1964, 1985), Danto (1965, 1985), and others that a perspicuous philosophical analysis of history is obliged to take into account the self-conceptions of those who actually practice history and that viewed from such a perspective, history is by no means a weak and defective variant of natural or behavioral science.

There are many important differences among those I have just assembled under the banner of the critical philosophy of history. But what unifies them into a school of thought, and what lends coherence to their various viewpoints, is their common rejection of a principal tenet of positivism, namely, the view that

> the exact natural sciences, in particular mathematical physics, set a methodological ideal or standard which measures the degree of development and perfection of all the other sciences, including the humanities. (von Wright 1971 121)

It is this rejection of the *prescriptivist* premise that defines the commonality and identity of the critical philosophy of history. It follows that such philosophers concur in the view that an examination of the concepts, categories, and procedures of historical inquiry will lead to a more or less coherent understanding of the type of knowledge they elicit. The premise, then, of the critical philosophy of history is that an *internal* analysis of a given activity yields knowledge of the principles that define and distinguish it; yields knowledge, that is, of the logical and normative structure of the activity under consideration. Note that this is a position (or premise) consistent with Proposition 2 (see Chapter 1), just as the prescriptivist premise is consistent with Proposition 1. Note, too, that the "internalist" premise of the critical philosophy of history is exactly the premise which informs such projects as Schafer's elucidation of the structure of psychoanalytic discourse and practice (see Chapter 1, "The Price of the 'Unity of Inquiry' "; and Chapter 4).

The specific contributions of the critical philosophy of history will be considered in context throughout this book, and especially in the two chapters which follow. It is obvious that this is a tradition of argumentation which has a special (if not privileged) role to play in explicating the conceptualization of the past in psychoanalytic thought, and in specifying the nature and function of historical self-understanding in therapeutic practice. It should be useful, then, to devote the next section to a brief resume of three interrelated themes (core issues) which have been highlighted by the critical philosophy of history, and which I deem particularly relevant to the argument I advance in this book.

Three Core Issues

In this section, I cite three interrelated themes: (1) retrospection and empathy; (2) narrative as inquiry; and (3) historical truth. As already suggested, the detailed elaboration of these themes or issues is pursued in context throughout this book. The treatment which follows therefore constitutes only a heuristic introduction.

1. *Retrospection and Empathy.* This issue, in its most general form, pertains to the tension or interplay between the concepts and categories of the investigator (historian) and those of the actual historical actors. The

historian (or interpretative social scientist) wants to reconstruct the "past," not only in terms of his or her own categories, but also in terms of how such past events and experiences must have looked to those who participated in them or who were affected by them. At the same time, historical inquiry cannot (literally) mean the replacement of the interpreter's "horizon" (Gadamer 1975) by that of the object of study. Historical inquiry is not re-enactment. And historical understanding is not just a reproductive attitude, but a productive attitude as well.

Part of the historian's "productivity" is implicit in his *retrospective* stance; he is the hindsighted observer who knows what happened after, as well as before, and on that account alone, knows more than any participant can ever know. This leads, of course, to considerations concerning to what extent an agent's intentional characterization of his action should be supplemented (or even replaced) by the historian's causal characterization. In this connection, certain psychoanalysts such as Leavy (1980 49–50) have insisted on the extreme hermeneutic position that to invoke causal or hypothetical factors is to depart "from any continuous sequence of historical interpretations . . ." For Leavy, then, there can be no question of causal supplementation in clinical psychoanalytic understanding. In opposition to this, it must suffice to assert that while historical inquiry probably precludes replacement, it is by no means incompatible with causal *supplementation* of the agent's intentional characterizations of his conduct. This is fortunate since psychoanalytic discourse—insofar as it refers to the "unconscious"—must necessarily supplement the agent's self-understanding (or self-misunderstanding). And this is accomplished not only through historical accounts of unconscious reasons, motives, and "disclaimed" actions (e.g., Schafer 1976), but also through historical accounts which invoke "causal factors" (Edelson 1986).[6]

The tension or interplay between retrospection and empathy, which is inherent in historical inquiry, is also fundamental to the therapeutic stance in clinical psychoanalysis. One may say, paradoxically, that an essential component of the therapist's empathy consists in his or her awareness (or practical knowledge) of when it is unhelpful to make his or her concern (or "empathy") explicit or known to the patient (Havens 1986). The patient may want and even solicit such concern, but the therapist *knows* that this conscious desire expresses and enacts the patient's self-misunderstanding.

There is no truth that, in passing through awareness, does not lie. (Lacan 1977 vii)

The hindsighted therapist is "ahead" of the patient. He knows what he knows, not only because he possesses a theory (e.g., Lacan, above), but also because he has retrospectively abstracted from his ongoing experience of the transference and countertransference. Such *knowledge* is historically structured: it exhibits and reflects the tension (or dialogue) between empathy and retrospection.

2. *Narrative as Inquiry.* The view is widespread, even among some historians (e.g., Furet), that narrative is not inquiry. The real task, so it goes, is to establish the facts; their narrative arrangement is just a matter of literary and rhetorical embellishment. This view, however, is untenable. It is untenable because it fails to notice that an essential cognitive role of narrative is to delineate configurations (wholes) which are, themselves, historical facts to be established. Narrative is always building larger wholes out of smaller wholes, bringing the former "into view," and placing any particular thing in its given temporal or cross-sectional context (Mink 1970). The point is that narrative is *productive.* It produces configurations (wholes), entire systems of relations which are, in fact, the arguable conclusions of historical inquiry. But these "conclusions" are not detachable from the inquiry; they *are* the inquiry. It is rare that genuine historical argument hinges on a disputable, abstractable fact. It is far more likely that such argument concerns the appropriateness of narrative configurations (the "conclusions" referred to above). And historical inquiry progresses, in the main, through the *reconfiguration* of preexistent narrative wholes. This is what we mean by argument in history and historiography.[7]

To regard narrative as inquiry is to concede that narrative is not merely something to be explained (see Chapter 1, "The Unity of Inquiry" and "The Price of the 'Unity of Inquiry'"), but is itself explanatory. Of course, like any cognitive function (e.g., formal reasoning), it is susceptible to empirical or psychological analysis; it may even be possible to model or infer the psychoanalytic *processes* that underlie its expression (see, for example, Chapter 5). But the fact remains that narrative (at least insofar as it belongs to historical discourse) preserves its intellectual and logical autonomy. For just as it is possible to envisage empirical-analytic explanations of narrative, so, too, is it possible to imagine narrative-historical accounts of empirical-analytic science. Both endeavors are legitimate; neither is privileged, and each is explanatory. They just pertain to different worlds (Goodman 1984).

3. *Historical Truth*. In an important sense, the problem of historical truth has already been treated in the previous discussion of "narrative as inquiry." It was there suggested that historical truth pertains to the *conclusions* of inquiry, namely, the configurations or wholes which are not detachable from the inquiry that bodies them forth. In other words, historical truth does not pertain to the "facts" upon which narrative configurations are ostensibly built. Factual truth is not the same as historical truth. This is not at all to demean the former since the systematic violation of "factual truth" is always a hallmark of political terrorism and totalitarianism (Arendt 1968). Thus, I do not dismiss the importance of "fact," and I offer no apologia for Orwell's "memory hole." I am only suggesting that the ascertainment of historical truth is a matter of negotiation and argument, according to the rules, traditions, and procedures of the authoritative "speech community" of historians, past and present.

Yet it cannot be denied that "historical truth" has emerged as an important and contentious issue in recent American psychoanalytic thought (Spence 1982). Can the critical philosophy of history shed any useful light on this development? To find out, let us consider—though only briefly—Spence's seminal work on the subject.

We recall that much of the rhetorical force of his argument depends upon a certain contrast between "narrative truth" and "historical truth." The former is pragmatically effective, and the latter is objective and factual. But Spence's conception of historical truth turns out to be a positivist, or else, prephilosophic and commonsensical conception of truth:

> Historical truth is time-bound and is dedicated to the strict observance of correspondence rules; our aim is to come as close as possible to what "really" happened. (32)

But such a view of historical truth-as-correspondence, if taken literally, seems to require a present or currently existing world against which to assess any candidate for "historical truth." Can this possibly be? Hence the conclusion of one philosopher of history that the realist's view of the reality of the past can be described, with only the mildest caricature, as the idea of another place, in which past events are *still occurring,* watched, perhaps, by God. (McDowell 1978 143–44)

Thus Spence's view of historical truth may perhaps be judged as somewhat naive. It is a view which fails to take seriously the implications of a distinctively historical approach to the past. It does not take seriously the fact that the "historical past" is something dead, fixed, and finished (at least logically and epistemologically, if not psychologically). Any coherent treatment of historical truth will therefore have to acknowledge the *pastness* of the past, and thus relinquish the nineteenth- and twentieth-century positivist dream of mirroring or reflecting *"eigentlich Gewesenes"* (how exactly it was, in Ranke's sense). The legitimate problems of validity and objectivity in historical knowledge will have to be reconceptualized in terms of what is actually *present:* namely, the evidence and the historical stories woven from it. To recall an earlier observation, the "past" is simply not the kind of thing one can look at. All we have are stories told about the past; and the problem now becomes one of comparison: of ascertaining (arguing) which of several possible narratives is most valid or least unsatisfactory.[8] In summary, the historian (analyst?) is not called upon to remember (or reenact) the past: to do so would be to succumb to the "natural attitude" described earlier in this chapter; the historian must, instead, come to terms with "historical truth" from within the parameters of an *unnatural attitude* toward the past, such as is evoked by Oakeshott (1962) in the passage below:

> It would appear that the task of the "historian" cannot be properly described as that of recalling or reenacting the past; that, in an important sense, an "historical" event is something that never happened and an "historical" action something never performed; that an "historical" character is one that never lived. (164)

Observe that Oakeshott is not denying that there can be knowledge of the past. He is only reminding us that historical inquiry does not describe the past; it constructs it. And historical constructions can never be "tested" against the past, because that past is dead, fixed, and finished. It is absent and unavailable. All we have (here and now) is the evidence, and what the evidence obliges us to believe. But this is only to say that the specifically historical past (paradoxically) belongs to the historian's (analyst's?) *present* world of experience, which means that it is not (and can never be) the past at all. This, then, begins to express what I want to describe as an unnatural attitude toward the past—the past recognized in *both* its absence and in its presence. And it is this attitude which is not captured or conveyed in Spence's treatment of the role and function of historical understanding in psychoanalysis.

My purpose in this subsection has not been to offer a critique of Spence's important study. His valuable project (devoted largely, in fact, to problems of historiography, narrativity, and historical consciousness) will actually be examined in some detail in Chapter 4. My present purpose has only been to suggest that Spence's interpretation might have been a richer and subtler one had it been more deeply informed by the insights and arguments of the critical philosophy of history.[9] More precisely, the gap between "narrative truth" and "historical truth" might have narrowed considerably (if not absolutely), and the "Great Divide" (if there is one) might now be between a kind of "historical-narrative" truth on the one hand, and a kind of "scientific" truth on the other. In other words, the relevant and fruitful contrast would now be between the *historical* and *scientific* constructions of the past in American psychoanalysis.

The Practical Past

Early in this chapter I put forth the requirement that "history" be displayed as a distinctive mode of understanding. We have now taken the first steps toward satisfying this requirement, and we have done so by focusing on how historical construction actually proceeds, and by eschewing the prescriptivist premise of the positivist philosophy of science. In the course of this discussion, we have begun to realize that a historical approach to the past should be distinguished not only from a scientific approach to the past (see also Chapter 2), but also from a "natural" approach to the past. Clearly, there are many ways in which we may be concerned with "the past." In short, historical understanding is a specific, unlikely, and unnatural form of understanding; yet the claim has been made not only that historical self-understanding is acquired and transmitted through therapeutic engagements, but also that historical inquiry may help to explain how this is so. In order to begin to substantiate such claims, it is now necessary to return to the theme which introduced this chapter, namely, the *natural attitude* toward the past. We recall that this is the normal and everyday approach to the past, in which the past is seen, always, as something which exists in relation to the present. Let us rename this past the "practical past."

By way of recapitulation: the practical past emerges or comes into view when the past is approached or acknowledged only insofar as it is felt to affect the purposes and interests of the present; accordingly, the preoccupations and passions of the present (including longings and anxieties about the future) cannot but be read back into the past. Here the past is "present-directed" or presentistic, in complete contrast to the "past-directedness" of the psychoanalytic life history depicted in Chapter 2. In other words, the construction of the practical past is a conscious (and preconscious) construction whose object is the future and whose direction (vector) is "ahead." The practical past is constructed with an eye on a more habitable and liveable future. This is the convenient past, the past from which we learn lessons (or regret not doing so), the past which we use to defend, justify, enhance (or diminish) ourselves by *persuasively* appealing to "illustrations" drawn from it. It appears, then, that there is even an internal dialogue within the practical past—a *rhetoric* of belief and self-persuasion which may actually become the object of diagnosis and treatment by certain psychotherapies, such as cognitive therapy. Treatment, in this instance, would involve the correction of such maladaptive "cognitive distortions" as all-or-nothing thinking, catastrophizing, mislabeling, personalization, etc. (Beck 1976; Freeman and Greenwood 1987). In this interpretation, cognitive therapy assists in the more "efficient" construction of the practical past, but operates wholly within the conscious and preconscious horizon of the practical past. It is, itself, a form of rhetoric designed to combat maladaptive rhetoric, and it need not involve (as we shall see) the exhibition or transmission of a distinctively historical form of self-understanding.[10] In conclusion, the practical past is the past that "by design" leads up to our particular problematic present, and from which, in turn, we forge whatever private (and public) myths are best suited to meet our felt needs—foremost among which is always the alteration of whatever we find unsatisfactory or objectionable in our present situation as we have understood or diagnosed it. Unhistorical therapies, such as cognitive therapy, simply help us to rediagnose or reframe our situations, or to acquire better coping strategies for managing and structuring our practical pasts. Unlike psychoanalysis, these therapies presuppose the parameters of the practical past.

The practical stance toward the past is therefore the primordial, pre-theoretical and everyday stance, perhaps reflecting the very basic structure of "remembering" (Bartlett 1932). But though pretheoretical, it is of course preinterpreted and subjunctivized. This means that when we ex-plain ourselves and our pasts (and those of others), we normally do so, not as proto-scientists, but as storytellers and folk psychologists (Zukier and Pepitone 1984). Now the contents (and cognitive styles) of any folk psychology will surely vary across cultures and subcultures, as well as over generational and life historical time. Thus, one person may say she's angry and out of sorts today because the ancestral demons are upset, another because her husband was selfish in bed last night, and a third (in the next century) because her limbic system has been hyperactive. None of these accounts (as I shall later argue) really belongs to science, and no single one can unequivocally lay claim to being more "rational" (from the *practical* point of view) than the other. It must be presumed, that is, that all such accounts are "reasonable" strategies to "remember" (imagine) the past with a view toward a more liveable future. And from the vantage of science, all such accounts must be seen as being based on insufficient and indefinite evidence.

Yet we know, as psychologists, that it is perfectly possible to undertake an empirical-analytic investigation which purports to reveal the *processes* underlying such folk beliefs and narrative reasonings, as well as the *func-tions* these serve in adaptation, etc. (e.g., Kahneman, Slovic, and Twersky 1982); and we know, as hermeneuticists, that it is equally reasonable to attempt distinctively historical inquiries into how such beliefs and man-ners of thinking have *come to be,* and what *rules* govern their construction and use in a given cultural setting or speech community. But such theo-retical accounts as these, drawn from psychology, anthropology, history and so forth—though they may be taken over and in some sense "used" by laymen as elements of their practical conduct—never quite replace or supersede the forms and contents of narrative discourse and folk psychol-ogy. My point is simply this: whenever bits and pieces of science or theory penetrate into ordinary life, they do so (by and large) by being used, by becoming parts of *practices* which are not "applied" (like tech-niques), but are enacted and expressed (precisely as languages are). These practices are always pursued in the context of ongoing traditions of continuity in change, just as they articulate present-day values, interests, expectations, and prejudices. Moreover, conduct and policy within these practices are necessarily controlled by such non-scientific considerations as the necessity to act, even though information or agreement about the aforementioned values and interests is always insufficient and indefinite. In short, though some people may actually lead more "rational" lives than others, nobody actually lives a more "scientific" life. The problem is that science cannot dictate "rational practice," if for no other reason than that it is unable (in the last analysis) to adjudicate or resolve the interpersonal and intrapersonal conflict of interests and values.[11]

If my account is at all correct, it appears that the practical stance is a stance from which it is always difficult to detach oneself. People may engage in scientific and historical activities, but their lives are conducted, for the most part, as practical lives, within the parameters of what I have called the practical past. We have seen, too, that cognitive therapy is one mode of treatment which is prepared to capitalize on this fact: it operates wholly within the conscious and preconscious horizon of the practical past, and it displays itself as a therapeutic rhetoric compatible with the rhetorical assumptions of (the patient's) practical experience (Blumenberg 1987). Psychoanalysis, however—in the view I am now advancing—is not in such a fortunate position. As a clinical practice, it violates our practical assumptions. It involves the acquisition and transmission of an *unnatural* (historical) attitude toward the past; it introduces a *discontinuity* in the patient's (and therapist's) construction of the past, and implies that historical self-understanding can modify that past (or the mode of one's relationship to it). How can this be? Of course, psychoanalytic therapy, like cognitive therapy, is practiced as a form of rhetoric, and as such, conforms to, and makes contact with, the patient's preinterpreted and practical world. But psychoanalysis, in my view, is also a *historical* (as well as rhetorical) form of therapeutic discourse. And the idea of history, as expounded above, is the idea of the study or construction of the past for its own sake; it involves the ability to recognize or constitute the past as it is independent of ourselves, or at least independent of our felt need. The past, we recall, is recognized as dead, fixed and finished, and yet, the historical past still belongs to the historian's *present* world of experience. The past, in short, is recognized both in its absence and in its presence. How can such a stance be represented in the clinical setting? How can "history" be modeled onto the psychoanalytic situation?

A Footnote to "Freud and Dora": The Historical Model Introduced

It has been observed that "Freud chose to demonstrate the utility of psychoanalysis through descriptions of largely unsuccessful cases" (Fisher and Greenberg 1977 281). Let me therefore introduce the "historical model" through yet another consideration of that most unsuccessful of all cases, the case of Dora (Freud 1905b). As everyone recalls, treatment was not "effective," for Freud concludes: "I did not succeed in mastering the transference in good time" (118). Freud believes that he failed to discern that "unknown quality" in himself that reminded Dora of Herr K. (a primary villain in her practical past): this allowed Dora to retaliate against Freud as she wished she had done against Herr K., by deserting Freud "as she believed herself to have been deserted and deceived by him."

However, as Erikson (1962a) has noticed, Freud may have failed in yet another respect. He may have failed to do justice to young Dora's *felt need* for "factual truth." For the source of her embitterment (what Freud saw as her endless "reproachfulness") seems to have been not only the lies and deceptions of Herr K., but also her father's "readiness to consider the scene by the lake as a product of her imagination" (Freud 1905b 46). So it was that five months after "deserting" Freud, she used the occasion of a condolence call to force the "truth" out of Herr K., and to declare to his wife that she, Dora, knew that Frau K. had had an affair with her father. Finally, almost a year later, Dora returns for a last visit with Freud ("father"?), and reveals to him these "facts." Freud then proceeds to "forgive her" for having deprived him of the "satisfaction of affording her a far more radical cure for her troubles" (Freud 1905b 122).[12]

Something is radically wrong. In Erikson's view, it is not just that Freud has misidentified the transference, but that he has bypassed or devalued Dora's insight into the truth of her own history. Freud, in short, is accused of discrediting the phenomenological validity of Dora's *practical past*. This past was itself articulated in the form of a personal myth whose theme or storyline was betrayal, and whose hallmark was the felt need for factual truth. In Erikson's words (alluding to the stage-salient developmental tasks of adolescence):

> Patients such as Dora . . . may insist that the genetic meaning of their sickness find recognition within an assessment of the historical truth, which

at the same time clarifies the determination of what has become irreversible, and promises the freedom of what is yet undetermined. (1962a 458)

But Freud did not construct or transmit his psychoanalytic interpretation (the genetic-dynamic meaning of the illness) within such an assessment of the felt need for factual truth. He did not recognize the developmental salience of Dora's felt need to force the adults to admit that they were lying, and so "set straight the historical past so that she could envisage a sexual and social future of her choice . . ." (Erikson 1962a 460). This is not to say that Freud disbelieved Dora's story (her conscious and preconscious version of her practical past): on the contrary, he conceded that it did "correspond to the facts in every respect" (Freud 1905b 46). It is rather that these facts could legitimately be discounted as surface facts. They belong to Dora's folk psychology, and it is as if (at best) they comprise the meaning *of* the dream as opposed to the meaning *behind* the dream. Such facts (and Dora's desire to discover and expose them) merely disguise and conceal the "real" meaning and explanation of Dora's illness —which Freud proceeds to discover and transmit to the patient. But Dora characteristically remains unconvinced: "Why, has anything so remarkable come about?" (Freud 1905b 105).

What, then, has gone wrong? Let us begin by recognizing that Freud, in slighting Dora's practical past, in offending her sense of reality, has also disrupted the *historical structure* of the psychoanalytic situation. In the context of my earlier discussion of three core issues, the dialogue between empathy and retrospection has, for all practical purposes, ceased. But this only redescribes the problem: what we want to know is why Freud lost contact, why empathic awareness was displaced by retrospective abstraction. So let us continue by hypothesizing that Freud lost empathic contact (could no longer "listen historically") because he was unable, during the course of treatment, to disengage himself from his own practical past (just as Dora was unable to disengage herself from hers). For if the hunger for "factual truth" (and its validation by others) was the hallmark of Dora's practical past, then it must be said that the *daimon* of "science" (the hunger after "real truth") presided, at this juncture, over Freud's construction of his practical past. What he knew and what he needed to know became more urgent than whether he could stand to listen. The critic Marcus (1987) in effect argues this point through a literary explication of the narrative structure of the case history itself:

In fact, as the case advances, it becomes increasingly clear to the careful reader that Freud and not Dora has become the central character in the action. . . . We begin to sense that it is his history that is being written about and not hers that is being retold. . . . At the same time, as the account progresses, Freud has never been more inspired, more creative, more inventive; as the reader sees Dora gradually slipping further and further away from Freud, the power and complexity of the writing reach dizzying proportions. (76)

In this interpretation, Freud is no longer listening to Dora, but to himself. He is responding not to Dora's inner world, but to his own need to know, and is therefore in danger of not finding out anything but what he already knows. In short, the narrative center of gravity has appeared to shift, and Freud's practical past has come to displace Dora's. The analyst is *enacting* his practical past instead of deconstructing it, and the patient is consequently disempowered from appropriating her own story (or identity) through the acquisition of a distinctively historical attitude toward her personal past. Dora is blocked because Freud is blocked, and the actual clinical process has degenerated into a battle of practical pasts, in which both analyst and analysand use "reality" (or truth) as weapons in an unacknowledged power struggle.

With hindsight and arguing unhistorically, I can now assert that just as Freud was unprepared to face or "master" the transference, so too was he unable to confront (or conceptualize) his own negative countertransference. However, in the language of this chapter, this can only mean that Freud failed to progress to a distinctively historical attitude toward his practical past. To have done so would have required Freud to (a) go against the grain of "needing to know," and (b) listen to his own feelings, fantasies, and conduct toward Dora, these comprising, as it were, the *evidence* of the *historical* past that belongs to the *present* world of the analyst (or historian).[13] But instead of listening and attending to such evidence from the here and now, Freud remained trapped in the practical past, dominated by unconscious mental processes. Constrained by the unconscious "past-in-present," as well as by the conscious and preconscious "presentistic past," Freud could not really move beyond the information given. So it is scarcely surprising that his brilliant interpretations (Marcus 1987) were perceived as assaults or counterassaults, and that we may even choose to regard them as driven by the compulsion to repeat.

To summarize: Freud apparently became what Dora (unconsciously) tried to make him become. That is to say, he remained trapped in his unanalyzed (and untreated) countertransference, thus perpetuating the "pathological" organization of Dora's self and object world. In the grip of his own conscious and preconscious myth, Freud "disliked" Dora, but failed to diagnose his feeling as evidence of an unknown historical past. We may further surmise that he disliked Dora, perhaps above all, because she refused to submit (mirroring Freud's refusal to submit to "not knowing"). Dora refused to yield to Freud's authoritative and masculine ("scientific") conception of her psychic reality, and obstinately resisted with what Erikson calls an appeal to "actuality" (1962a 463)—this taking the form of an implacable insistence on the recognition of historical fact as necessary for her own adolescent sense of justice, fidelity, and integrity. The clinical problem was of course systemic. On the one hand, Dora closed herself off to the possibility that her "reality" was not sufficiently defined by her subjectivity; on the other hand, Freud forgot that, in the clinical context of the analytic encounter, psychic reality is not a thing-in-itself, objectively there to be discovered, but is rather negotiated and constituted through the historically structured psychoanalytic dialogue. In the end, however, the clinical responsibility is Freud's. It would seem that in clinging to the natural attitude, in *enacting* his practical past, Freud has also reenacted (acted out?) the old positivist imperative that the "reality" and "objectivity" of external relations be embraced at the expense of the intrinsic (phenomenal) significance of objects and events—hence his demanding of Dora that she alienate herself from the *actuality* of these selfsame objects, events, and experiences. In this instance, at least, the scientist held sway over the clinician (or historian): and Freud, in 1900, has apparently not yet attained the wisdom of his own (later) words:

> the most successful cases are those in which one proceeds, as it were, without any purpose in view, and allows oneself to be taken by surprise by any new turn in them, and always meets them with an open mind, free from any presuppositions. (1912b 114)

We thus conclude with the following observation: although "Fragment of an Analysis of a Case of Hysteria" is an obvious hermeneutic and explanatory tour de force, the actual course of clinical treatment was psychoanalytically and therapeutically flawed. It was flawed, in my view, because it was insufficiently "historical," in the distinctive sense introduced in this chapter (and to be elucidated further in the pages to follow).

The specifically clinical problem, in other words, is not that Freud, in 1900, was still in need of more science, more theory, more facts. Clearly, Freud's work with Dora actually suffered from a surfeit of "knowledge." The problem, then, resides not in what Freud did not yet know, but in the historical consciousness he could not yet achieve. Freud's difficulty was not one of knowing, but one of imagining. He could not yet imagine that the psychoanalytic narrative is only intelligible as a historical inquiry; he could not quite imagine that clinical psychoanalysis can itself appear as a historical discourse conducted within the relatedness of care. What he could not imagine, and what (to quote Heidegger) he may therefore have forgotten is that

> there is the possibility of a kind of solicitude that does not so much displace the Other as anticipate him in his essential potentiality for Being—not in order to take "care" away from him but in order to restore it to him in a genuine fashion. (Dallmayr 1981 68–69)

Clinical Psychoanalysis and the Model of History

My object in reviewing the case of Dora has not been to shed new light on the hermetic world of Freud's Vienna, but to introduce the historical model, and to suggest how it figures in the processes and practices of clinical psychoanalysis. The thesis I am arguing may appear paradoxical. For it holds that the model of history is relevant precisely because psychoanalysis is a therapy, precisely because it consists of interpersonal interactions and interventions. In other words, psychohistory (extraclinical psychoanalytic narratives dependent on second-hand testimony, texts, artifacts, and so forth) [14] is not only less cogent as psychoanalysis, but also less successful as history, precisely because it lacks access to such evidence as the "data" of transference and countertransference. Let me now attempt, by way of summary, to specify this position in detail—with the understanding that Chapter 4 of this book is wholly devoted to the "historical construction of the psychoanalytic past."

1. The model of history maintains that the clinical situation is *historically structured* insofar as it is characterized by a kind of tension or dialogue between empathy and retrospection; thus the therapist is said to "listen historically," by virtue of his or her capacity to move to and fro between empathic awareness and retrospective abstraction.

2. The model of history maintains that the therapist conceptualizes and transmits his clinical understanding of the patient's psychic reality as a historical construction rather than as a scientific finding. So construed, psychic reality is recognized as a narrative configuration, negotiated and constituted through therapeutic transactions. Clinical psychoanalysis thus yields (co-authored) "histories" of psychic reality.

3. The model of history maintains that the evidence that contributes to such historical constructions and narrative configurations is always evidence from the here and now. Such evidence may include anything that occurs within the clinical setting, and especially the dreams, fantasies, feelings, enactments, and interactions ascribed to the transference and countertransference.

4. The model of history maintains that the "initial positions" of patient and therapist are symmetrical, in that each starts off in the natural attitude and brings some version(s) of the practical past to the clinical situation. The therapist, however, by virtue of training and practical knowledge, is presumably prepared to "not-know" (negate) his practical past, and to exploit the evidence of the "here and now" in order to construct a historical past. This may mean nothing more, for example, than that the therapist is attuned to his own countertransference reactions (the "tug of the patient"), and resists becoming what the patient wants to make of him. Accordingly, it is in *not* reenacting his practical past that the therapist first displays historical self-understanding; it is therefore the therapist's historical self-understanding which initiates interpersonal learning and which actually launches the process of therapeutic or mutative action.

5. The model of history maintains that as both patient and therapist move beyond the natural attitude, they also distance themselves from the *contents* of their practical pasts. Therapeutic conversation departs from the natural attitude and becomes a *reflection* upon itself. The evidence for narrative-historical constructions is drawn less and less from such conversational contents (folk psychologies), and more and more from the second-order "data" of interpersonal (and transferential) interactions.

6. The model of history maintains that insofar as therapy proves successful, the patient will achieve a certain detachment from, and perspective on, his or her practical past, such that it can be "laid to rest in a forgivable way." As the patient comes to acquire a distinctively historical attitude toward the past, he or she realizes that it no longer leads inexorably into the present (the presentistic or practical past), but can now be recognized

(a) as dead, fixed, and finished, and yet (b) as belonging to his or her *present* world of psychical experience. So reconfigured, the "past" (as construct, inference, abstraction) is now known as unstable, incomplete, and subject to change; such an attitude or stance toward the past is propadeutic to creating a future which can be connected to and continuous with the past, without being a repetition of it.

The model of history, as expounded above, assumes that psychoanalytic therapy involves the transmission and acquisition of *historical self-understanding*. Such self-understanding may be relatively explicit and reflective, or relatively implicit and enactive. But whatever its specific character, historical self-understanding is always contextualized by the psychoanalytic transference. Although the transference may seem to require the enactment of the past in the present, it does not (when successfully negotiated) bring the patient back to the past. What the transference does do is enable the patient, for the first time, to assess the *cost* of past solutions. For prior to the patient's experience of, and reflection upon, the transference, such "knowledge" (knowledge of the cost of past solutions) is unavailable or inaccessible, owing to the power of the practical past and the effects of unconscious mental processes. So when I now propose that historical self-understanding is acquired and conveyed through the practices of psychoanalytic therapy, I am also arguing that the *content* of such understanding pertains to the "cost" of past solutions.[15] This is what the analyzed patient "knows." Such knowledge is not about the past as it actually was *(eigentlich Gewesenes),* but is about the patterns of a factitious past constituted and constructed in the transferential present. Such knowledge, moreover, is not scientific; it offers nothing (in and of itself) toward the prediction and control of the future. Yet it may empower the patient to move toward a future, and to create or imagine a future. This "historical" (and non-scientific) view of clinical psychoanalysis is aptly rendered in the passage below:

> Psycho-analysis cannot propose anything for the future; it is concerned with the creation of a consciousness that *can negate*—that can move to a future based on an understanding of the past. To forget that ambivalence results from a conflict of desire is not to resolve the contradiction, the conflict. . . . To suppose that one can choose one of the conflicting desires without cost, without struggle, is to have learned nothing from Freud's study of the unconscious. Psychoanalysis is an attempt to uncover the meaning of the ambivalence, the cost of the resolution of the conflict. (Roth 1987 110–11)

To summarize and recapitulate: clinical psychoanalysis is redescribed as a historically structured practice which facilitates the transmission and acquisition of historical self-understanding. Such self-understanding is contextualized by the transference and the countertransference, and is articulated or enacted as (a) knowledge of the meaning of the ambivalences of the past, and (b) knowledge of the costs involved in the resolution of conflict and in the reinvestment in relatedness.

History, Science, and Practice

So far, discussion has concentrated on: (a) legitimating "history" as an autonomous mode of discourse; (b) distinguishing the historical construction of the past from the practical construction of the past; and (c) determining the role of historical self-understanding in clinical psychoanalysis. However, it is also true that an unmistakable emphasis has been placed on the contrast between scientific and historical thinking, between the scientific and historical constructions of the past. It is time now to return to this pivotal theme, and to review what has been achieved thus far.

We recall that in this inquiry, "history" and "science" are viewed as the primary avenues toward *theoretical* knowledge in psychoanalysis. A necessary (though not sufficient) condition for theoretical knowledge is that it represent a significant departure from commonsense experience and the naive interpretation of reality (Heider 1958). Historical discourse surely fulfills that condition. For even if (unlike science) it continues to adhere to ordinary language and the narrative organization of events, it nevertheless violates our pretheoretical and pragmatic expectations about the past, about our knowledge of it and our relationship (or stance) toward it. But these are precisely the expectations that normally coalesce in our naive, commonsensical, and practical view of the past. Here facts are facts, this or that event occurred, and the past "contains" meaning, value, and lessons to be learned. The practical past is therefore the "history" that we discover, reconstruct, and use in everyday life; as such, it is to be radically distinguished from the historical past. The historical past flies in the face of common sense, and this is nowhere more evident than in Oakeshott's claim cited earlier, "that, in an important sense, a 'historical' event is something that never happened and a 'historical' action something never performed."[16]

Science, in this respect, is no different from history. It, too, violates common sense and departs from the naive (practical) interpretation of reality. The world to which scientific discourse refers is concerned with abstract, general objects and not with particular objects. For example, a particular drop of water has scientific interest only as an *instance* of water. More precisely, the "practical" image of water has no meaning in a fully realized science, where it is replaced by "H_2O." The scientist does not first perceive water and then resolve it into H_2O: science begins only when water has been left behind. In other words, "water" and "H_2O" are not to be viewed as labels which refer to the same thing, but rather as signals employed in radically different language games. It should be obvious, then, that the discourse of science does not refer to the same world as the discourse of (practical) everyday life; nor, of course, does it refer to the same world as the discourse of history. But this truth is often obscured by the success of science in increasing our mastery and control over nature. Such success, however, cannot alter the truth that science is interested in the particular only insofar as it is an instance of the general. Whatever is peculiar to the particular is properly ignored by science. It thus belongs to the logic of scientific discourse that whatever turns out to falsify a given theory must imply, represent, or instantiate a competing theory, *not* just itself as a particular expression of concrete, practical, or commonsensical experience. Science, in short, does not recognize phenomenological particulars; it cannot address their internal relations or qualitative transformations. Hence, for example, it cannot recognize qualitative differentiations of temporality. Sequences of states of affairs can of course be described, but such sequences and the discourse referring to them are *ahistorical*. This means that "pasts," "presents," and "futures" are mere logical distinctions in a formal (general) pattern of succession, only in external relation to one another, and abstracted from the "concrete" phenomenon of becoming. From within such parameters, the future can no longer appear as that which is approaching the present, and the present can no longer be that which is falling back into a past. Science cannot elucidate or explicate such (practical) experiences. It can only "explain" them by describing the processes hypothesized to underlie them. But in so doing, it departs from the naive interpretation of reality, and in an important sense, never returns.

In the account just offered, both science and history are seen to depart from commonsense and the naive interpretation of reality. Both science and history are thus counterpoints to the practical world, and represent *theoretical* modifications of that world. At the same time (as argued throughout the first part of this book), science and history clearly *diverge* in their fundamental assumptions and presuppositions. By way of summary and recapitulation, this may be succinctly illustrated by first reviewing what I take to be certain basic (and interrelated) commitments of empirical-analytic science—commitments that are as applicable, in principle, to psychology and psychoanalysis, as they are to physics and molecular biology.

Science and History: Diverging Commitments

1. Empirical-analytic (or normal) science[17] assumes an objective universe which it endeavors to describe and explain. This means that empirical-analytic science is committed to the notion of knowledge as relational. The knower is related to something outside and independent of himself, and may thus presume the existence of a universe of objects with independent existences and careers. This is the commitment to *objectivity*.

2. Empirical-analytic science is logically and methodologically directed by the ideal of the quantitative and measurable formulation of its ideas, such that they can be ultimately inserted into mathematical relationships or subjected to statistical operations. "An ordinary object or event becomes finally a point, that is, an intersection of curves, a crossing of equations" (Kuzminski 1986 227). Science is characterized by an underlying tendency toward quantitative abstraction, since quantitative expression is presumed to be the most exact and most stable form of communication. Whatever cannot be construed quantitatively cannot belong, unproblematically, to scientific knowledge. This is the commitment to *quantitative abstraction*.

3. Empirical-analytic science is concerned with abstract, general objects, and not with concrete, particular objects. It is thus committed to the procedures of the analytic abstraction of aspects of objects, events, and actions, even though these aspects are concretely inseparable in the naive, pretheoretical experience of reality. All "wholes" are analytically abstracted into their parts, which are then recomposed into the abstract

patterns (or structures) of their external relationships. Intrinsic or internal relations, and the qualitative transformation of wholes, are inadmissible. This is the commitment to *analytic abstraction*.

These, then, are three commitments I take to be emblematic of empirical-analytic science[18] in general, and of the scientific construction of the past in particular. It is not of course to be expected that all sectors or samples of scientific discourse live up equally to each of these commitments. This will become clearer in the chapters to follow, when several *more* or *less* scientific (and historical) psychoanalytic inquiries are evaluated. In short, we are speaking of a continuum of "scientificity"; and it may be said that what has been constructed is, epistemologically, an ideal type (Weber 1964), and psychologically, a prototype (Rosch 1976).

Science and history, I have argued, diverge in their fundamental assumptions and presuppositions. This is readily borne out by history's inability to endorse the three basic commitments of empirical-analytic science.

1. History need not presume that things exist and act independently of our descriptions or that there is a universe of objects with independent existences. History is compatible with the contrary view of knowledge as self-constituting or socially constituted (see Proposition 2 in Chapter 1). An important implication is that the psychoanalytic idea of psychic reality need not refer to an objectivated thing-in-itself (Barratt 1984), and is not necessarily to be construed as an independent object, explained and described in terms of its abstracted aspects and postulated processes. Historical discourse thus grants that psychic reality is *explicable* as well as lawful. Historical discourse thus allows that psychic reality is intelligible as that which is constituted and constructed through the interpersonal transactions of the clinical situation; as such, psychic reality hasn't an objectivated or independent existence, but exists only in use, or as commitment to performance to come. It should be evident, though, that in bypassing science's commitment to objectivity, history does not condemn itself to an idiosyncratic or relativistic subjectivity. For one thing (as already noticed), historical discourse is always aiming to disengage itself from the presentistic (or subjectivist) grip of the practical past, and to reconstitute the past as independent of the felt need of the present. More generally, however, the traditional distinction between the "objective" and the "subjective" is probably misconceived (Rorty 1979 338–39), in that it presupposes that the mind is divided into a confused/imaginative/fantastical part

(which is mismatched to "what is out there") and a rational/intellectual part which is somehow able to mirror the external objects of nature. The assumptions underlying this distinction are untenable, and "rationality," in Rorty's view, is not endangered by abandoning the objectivist metaphor of the mind as the mirror of nature.[19]

2. History is not necessarily committed to the ideal of quantitative abstraction. Historical discourse remains imbedded in the inexact and semantically unstable contexts of ordinary language and the narrative organization of experience. Thus the "fact" that a student ranks third in academic performance out of a class of ten is recognized as a quantitative abstraction, but one which still must be interrogated historically (narratively) in terms of the full interaction and experience of a group of students in a classroom. This does not mean, of course, that statistical techniques (and mathematical concepts) cannot play a useful role in historical inquiries—only that the function of that role must be *ancillary,* since such techniques are often determined (or biased) by their particular models (Danziger 1985).

3. History is not committed to the analytic abstraction of aspects of events, actions, behaviors, and experiences. It is never sufficient that historical discourse analyze "narrative wholes" (or what Stern calls "experiential integrations") into their abstracted parts and external relations. It is rather that historical discourse presumes that: (a) all parts are perceivable in relation to wholes; (b) any particular part plays some role in a given whole; and (c) each event, action, or experience is understood, simultaneously, as both part and whole (e.g., as an episode within a story, and as a story containing episodes). History, in short, identifies the "goings-on" of experience as *parts* of stories and as *stories* with parts. It never mandates the one-sided analytic abstraction of narrative wholes.[20]

I have attempted, in this section, to characterize "history" by contrasting it with "science." Such a strategy was to be expected, since at least from the time of Hobbes and Descartes, science (empirical-analytic science) has been universally regarded as the paradigm of legitimate knowledge, the "mirror of nature"; whereas history (narrative history) has come increasingly to be seen as an "abnormal discourse" (Rorty 1979)—in Bosanquet's words, as nothing but a "tissue of conjunctions" and the "doubtful story of successive events."

Clearly, I hold to a contrary position: namely, that both science and history are equally authentic theoretical discourses, each involving a legitimate abstraction from experience, and neither constituting a mirror of nature or of the world. My task in this book is to examine the implications of such a position for the conceptualization of the psychoanalytic past. Specifically, I am arguing that the scientific and historical constructions of the past, though legitimate for their respective purposes, are *categorially distinct* constructions. This means that in the chapters to follow, as I proceed to interrogate a broad sample of psychoanalytic inquiries, my overall objective is twofold: (a) to disambiguate unreflective constructions of the past (those which neglect the categorial distinction between scientific and historical argument); and (b) to examine the possibility that scientific and historical constructions, though autonomous, can nonetheless be intelligibly coordinated in models, theories, research programs, and case studies.

The Plurality of Pasts

This book began with the observation that the "past" is not a simple or self-evident idea, either in pretheoretical everyday life, or in the various strata of reflection characteristic of psychoanalysis as a clinical, scientific, and philosophical enterprise. Thus far, three constructions of the past have been introduced and distinguished: the historical past, the scientific past, and the practical past. Let me now complete the presentation of the pluralist model by citing two collateral "pasts" which are also of psychological and psychoanalytic interest.[21]

1. The *poetic* or aesthetic version of the past constructs the past in terms of concepts and images whose value, utility, and veridicality are always subordinate to the contemplative delight that they afford. There is a sense in which poetic images are made, used, and enjoyed for themselves, and are not read as means to ulterior ends. Poetic images may reflect what Coleridge called "unthinkingness": that is, they are not necessarily expected to make (literal) sense, nor are they required to provoke moral approval or disapproval. To delight in Pound's *Cantos* and Picasso's *Guernica* poses no aesthetic or poetic conflict. In sum, to ask of poetic images of the past whether they are scientifically credible, or where they come from, or how they are made, or what consequences they involve, is to abandon the poetic stance and to shift to a scientific, historical, or practical one.[22]

It is typical of the poetic construction of the past that the "narrative organization" of the life-as-lived dissolves into the imagery of sight, sound, and touch (e.g., as in the *mémoire involuntaire* of Proust), or else is distilled into images of such compelling power that we see nothing but what is immediately before our eyes and are provoked to no "conclusions" whatsoever (e.g., as in the memoirs of a Nabokov or a Pasternak). The poetic past thus overcomes the mere pastness of the past, and in this respect may seem to evoke the "timelessness" of dreamtime, just as its "unthinkingness" will appear to suggest the automatism of "primary process." But the poetic past is not an intimation of biologically driven primary process; it is, instead, a complex expression of human intentionality and a form of sophisticated cultural utterance. In this book, it actually specifies a mode of psychoanalytic discourse. And while there are indeed psychoanalytic writers for whom the poetic mode of discourse is salient, of even greater interest, perhaps, are those patients who, on occasion, actually present their pasts as poetic constructions (and not only as practical self-narratives or as free associations). The empathic or skillful therapist, informed by the pluralist model of psychoanalytic discourse, will then be able to *recognize* such poetic constructions for what they are (prior to or beyond conventional interpretation); and the patient will, at least in this respect, feel supported and understood (Gedo 1979; Edelson 1975).

2. The *phenomenological* construction of the past has already been encountered in this study—initially through Romanyshyn's formulation which depicts phenomenology as that approach

> which allows us to take the appearance of what appears precisely as it appears, prior to any judgment about the factual or illusory status of what appears. (1982 136; see also Chapter 1, "Prolegomenon")

Phenomenology (like science, history, and practice) exemplifies a specific mode of abstraction from experience; in other words, it is not a privileged methodology which "reproduces" lived experience or reveals experience in its "aboriginal" or truest expression. Phenomenology is distinctive only because its approach aims to "bracket" those commitments and presuppositions specific to science, history, and practice. Phenomenology, in this sense, is a rigorous form of philosophical investigation, first elaborated and justified by Husserl (1962), Freud's contemporary.

The phenomenology of the past belongs to the more foundational phenomenological investigation of "lived time," of what the philosophers call "temporality" (Ricoeur 1983, 1985). *All* such treatments of temporality, including those which are clinically focused (e.g., Minkowski 1923; Binswanger 1945; Zaner 1981), are alike in at least the following respect: they all bracket or suspend the logical, atemporal construct of time, the very construct that is indispensable to the natural or empirical-analytic sciences, and to which Freudian theory appears, in part, to subscribe.[23] According to that construct (as we saw earlier in "History, Science, and Practice"), "pasts," "presents," and "futures" are mere logical distinctions in a formal pattern of succession, only in external relation to one another, and analytically abstracted from the pretheoretical phenomenon of "becoming." There are no privileged moments in scientific discourse. So, in an important sense, "beginnings" and "endings" (as in psychotherapy and psychoanalysis) thus possess no temporal significance. Clearly, then, phenomenology has a certain importance, if only as a necessary corrective to the "detemporalizing" thrust of scientific psychoanalysis—at least insofar as clinical practice and theoretical discourse are actually constrained by the empirical-analytic construct of time.

Given their sensitivity to the experience of "lived time," phenomenologists—both before and after Husserl—have often been successful in pointing to how we can go wrong in the ways we appropriate the past and anticipate the future. In *Either/Or* (1959), for example, Kierkegaard constructs a memorable phenomenological model of an imaginary figure, "The Unhappiest Man," who wants his past to be his future, and whose spiritual pathology therefore lies in his hoping what he ought to recollect and in his recollecting what he ought to hope. In other words, "The Unhappiest Man" is no simple depressive, bitter and regretful about his past and hopeless about his future, burdened by pathogenic beliefs and distorted cognitions. Our imaginary figure is more deeply confused than that, for the "normal" structure of his practical past (of his experience of temporality) has been radically disrupted. In the words of one astute commentator (Crites 1986): the recollective story has been confused with the projective scenario, and "in treating my own past as if it were as indeterminate as the future, my story will be so loose and fragmentary that I cannot recollect myself out of it" (172).[24]

Conclusion

Five constructions of the past have now been introduced and distinguished. Each, in my account, is a legitimate abstraction from experience; and each, by the same token, demarcates a specific modality of psychoanalytic discourse. It is therefore possible, in principle, to envision psychoanalysis as *science,* as *history,* as *phenomenology,* as *practice,* and as *poetics.*[25] There is a plurality of psychoanalytic pasts, and there is a plurality of psychoanalytic discourses. This is not a situation to be regretted or overcome, but one to be welcomed and reckoned with. For it is surely the case that no single discourse is so epistemically privileged as to offer *the* mirror of nature, reality, or the past; and no particular discourse is unconditionally entitled to replace or supersede the other. Thus the real task (and it is no easy one) is not to unify psychoanalysis into a homogeneous discourse, but to ascertain the conditions under which each mode of discourse is appropriate. The questions, therefore, which must be asked are where, when, and how each mode of discourse is applicable.

In principle, then, psychoanalysis comes into view as a plurality of distinct discourses. In practice, however, any specific psychoanalytic inquiry is a mixed discourse. This means that any given research program, any case study, any model, theory, or critical or clinical study almost surely articulates some combination or arrangement of scientific, historical, phenomenological, practical, or poetic elements. All inquiries are therefore mixed inquiries, and all psychoanalytic pasts are (at least to some degree) ambiguous or equivocal pasts.[26]

Throughout the remainder of this book (Chapters 4, 5, and 6), psychoanalytic inquiries of several sorts will be examined and interrogated in order to assess the actual and appropriate relations of the "plurality of pasts." My special concern, as indicated at the outset, is with the conceptual complexity engendered by the scientific, historical, and practical constructions of the past in American psychoanalysis. My focus, moreover, has been and will remain on *history* and *science* as the most theoretically relevant discourses. But if the "model" I have elaborated in the first part of this book is at all persuasive, then it must be clear by now that the real boundaries of interpretation are those which are circumscribed by the plurality of pasts.

NOTES

1. As introduced in this chapter, the *natural attitude* toward the past (Husserl 1962) presupposes the familiarity of the past. The past is not a "foreign country," but is taken for granted as a place where events occur, actions are performed, and persons exist, exactly as in the contemporary "life-world" (Schutz 1966). In other words, the past is not experienced as constructed, but rather as remembered and recalled. The natural attitude toward the past is thus one which has not yet been modified by psychoanalytic interpretation and explanation, nor (as we shall soon see) by the acquisition of a genuinely historical attitude toward the past.

2. From a psychodynamic perspective, the experience and representation of the past are distorted by the operations and effects of unconscious mental processes (e.g., defensive processes). This is what is meant when it's suggested that the "past" becomes hostage to the present (conflicted) wish.

3. Argelander (1976) is the source for this short conversational passage drawn from a psychotherapeutic session.

4. Lakoff and Johnson (1980 41–45) also offer a treatment of the metaphorical structure of "time," in which it is considered both as *moving object* and as *stationary medium through which we move.* Both senses are approximated in Berlin's references to the "river of time," and to the "moving stair of time." What the two treatments have in common is their focus on the *passage* of time, such that the "past" recedes behind us, while the "future" looms in front of us. Time is always passing, always being used, expended, or lost. In this connection, Munz (1985) has observed that the great obstacle to the acceptance of evolution has been the human tendency to equate the passage of time with the experience of loss. The more time passes, the more we feel impoverished.

In light of Munz's observation, we can now reframe the American debate between the traditional and revisionary points of view as a debate between evolutionary and anti-evolutionary approaches to psychoanalytic understanding. On the one hand, the traditionalists retain an "evolutionary" conception of the past as a vast hinterland "behind us" (which also forms and molds us); while on the other hand, the revisionists transpose that past into the transferential present, and in doing so, seek to overcome the experience of loss associated with the passage of time. For the revisionists, time neither proceeds in an irreversible line, nor is it irreversibly lost. Time is actually regained through the continuous reenactment of the past-in-the-transferential-present. The revisionists thus emerge as therapeutic optimists, in that they reject the proposition of the "scarcity of time," in that they are committed to a form of anti-evolutionary clinical "creationism." In this key respect, the psychoanalytic revisionists (e.g., Schafer, Gill, Schimek, etc.) also appear to espouse a characteristically American point of view. See also Chapter 4, Note 1.

5. Furet is one of the leading representatives of the influential French *Annales* school, long known for its hostility toward traditional narrative history.

6. Edelson's position on causal analysis in the context of the single case study is examined in Chapter 4.

7. It may appear paradoxical to assert that historical discourse does not pertain to the documentation and establishment of specific factual truths. That "Germany invaded Belgium in 1914" is one such "historical fact." But it is scarcely open to *argument;* it concerns events and circumstances in which many were involved; it has been established by witnesses and depends on testimony. Consequently, factual truth of this type, though recalcitrant to genuine historical argument, is nevertheless (typically) subject to distortion by the practice of lying; it thus belongs to political discourse, where power can "rewrite" history. But such practices, which involve the manipulation or obfuscation of factual truth, have little to do with genuinely historical argument.

8. The validity of a psychoanalytic narrative may also be viewed as a function of its "liveability" for the future. The point of such a narrative is not to reconstruct the past, but to facilitate a commitment to a future course of action (or indeed, to the very "actuality" of a future). In short, the validity of a psychoanalytic narrative resides in its power to bring about some change. Such narratives are, in Eagle's sense, *interventions* (or the sum of all interventions), and hence must be assessed in terms of their "effectiveness."

It is also true, however, that in clinical psychoanalysis (as in historical argument), there is always a plurality of possible (and plausible) narratives; the task in both contexts remains one of comparison. The historian (or community of historians), the patient and the therapist are alike in that they must each compare the available narratives. There is no "reality" (or objective past) against which to test the veridicality of any given narrative; nor is it ever unambiguously evident what will substantiate the *utility* (hence, "effectiveness") of narrative interventions.

9. Only one critical philosopher of history, W. H. Walsh, is cited among Spence's references.

10. Cognitive therapy presents itself as an application of scientific psychology. Whether or not this is an accurate self-presentation (especially in light of its origins with Ellis and Beck) is probably questionable. What I suggest, however, is that to the extent that cognitive therapy is *not* practiced as an applied science or behavioral technology, it may actually permit or facilitate historical understanding in the clinical situation. This is because cognitive therapy intersects with historical inquiry when it turns metacognitive or reflexive—that is, when it distances itself from conversational *contents* and proceeds to reflect on the conversational situation itself. But according to the "model of history," as expounded in this chapter, historical self-understanding is fully achieved only insofar as the evidence of patient-therapist interaction is subjected to historical interpretation. And because the clinical theory of psychoanalysis *requires* that the transference and countertransference become objects of reflection (Oremland 1991), it is (on its own internal logic) specifically conducive to the exhibition and transmission of historical self-understanding. By way of contrast, it appears that the principles and methods of cognitive therapy entail no similar requirement that the evidence of patient-therapist interaction move to the foreground of the clinical situation. In

short, the transmission and acquisition of historical self-understanding is "accidental" (but possible) in cognitive therapy, while theoretically necessitated (but not always actualized) in psychoanalytic therapy.

11. The problem of the relationship of "science" to everyday (or practical) life is vast and perplexing, with empirical, normative, and conceptual components. (a) Empirically, we wish to know how science impacts on everyday life, (b) Normatively, we want to ask how much science *should* inform our practical conduct, or how large its role *ought* to be, (c) Conceptually, we are perplexed by the question of *what* constitutes "scientific influence." Is that influence defined mainly by technologies or other alleged "applications" of science, or is it specified though so-called knowledge-claims or authenticated findings (e.g., smoking causes cancer)? Whatever one's position on these questions, I think it is evident that the "natural attitude" has not been displaced by the scientific attitude, and that science cannot prescribe practice—not only because science cannot resolve the inevitable conflict of values, but also because (as Gilbert Ryle has put it), efficient practice always precedes the theory or science of it (see also Chapter 5, "Science, History, and Practice: Pluralism in Psychoanalysis").

12. "Dora" never disengaged herself from her practical past and never achieved the "far more radical cure" of historical self-understanding. For what happened to Dora in later life, see Deutsch (1957).

It is a curious "literary fact" that the reader's sympathy toward Dora, as well as revulsion toward all the adults (including, perhaps, Freud himself), is an artifact of Freud's narrative account. It is as if Freud's unanalyzed countertransference (or more precisely, his struggle to recognize and reflect on it) is imbedded in the narrative structure of the case history itself.

13. The evidence of the historical past that belongs to the present world of the analyst (or historian) consists of nothing other than the transference and countertransference phenomena of the clinical situation. Countertransference experiences, in particular, seem to provide crucial evidence for the construction of a therapeutically effective psychoanalytic narrative. The key to the analysis of the patient may thus reside in the *analysis of the analyst* during the analysis. Consider, for example, the following possibility: for the analyst, the very act of interpreting may be an unwitting acting out of the need to get rid of unwanted projections, to attack the patient for what he or she is doing to the analyst; in short, the essence of psychoanalytic intervention (interpretation) may be driven by an unconscious impulse to attack and punish the patient. See Epstein and Feiner (1979) for several useful discussions of countertransference. It should be noted that Freud did not discuss the problem of countertransference (whether as an obstacle or tool in analysis) until the period 1910–12, over ten years after his work with Dora. See also Chapter 4, "The Analytic Encounter: Hermeneutics and Countertransference."

14. For a provocative if one-sided critique of psychohistory, see Stannard (1980).

15. I am employing the term "cost" metaphorically. There would appear to be no possibility of quantifying "the cost of past solutions" while within the clinical

context of the psychotherapeutic situation. It is conceivable, however, that extra-clinical empirical-analytic research might generate models depicting the costs and benefits of a variety of neurotic unconscious decisions. It would then be possible, in principle, to envisage psychoanalytic variants of political economy's theories of rational choice.

16. This again calls attention to the claim that historical inquiry *constructs* the past and does not describe or recover it. Historical consciousness requires that past events, actions, and persons be recognized as constructions of the "historian"; this implies, further, that one's "past self" is recognized as a construction of the present, just as one's present self will be so recognized in the future. In summary, *historical* selves, actions, and events are never viewed as unchanging "objects" in the (past) world, the descriptions of which are to be certified as true or false.

17. In using the term "normal science," I mean to bracket such proposals as Kuhn's and Feyerabend's, which offer a new interpretation of the nature of scientific discourse, and a revised view of the place of science in human experience.

18. Throughout this study, I have represented "science" through the prism of *empirical-analytic* methods and presuppositions. Quite apart from Freudian psychoanalysis, certain important scientific traditions and research programs cannot be satisfactorily located within the empirical-analytic (or hypothetico-deductive) paradigm. The work of Piaget, in psychology, immediately comes to mind. It is obvious that a structural-systems paradigm (as distinguished from an empirical-analytic paradigm) informs Piagetian psychology. This means that an event is not explained hypothetically deductively, but by describing its role in the system of which it is part. The aim of structural psychology is therefore a complete *description* of the structure behind the event. Although structural psychology also pursues strategies of analytic abstraction, it is more attuned to the possibility that human beings are not simply aggregates of independent parts.

19. Over and against the traditional (and misconceived) distinction between objectivity and subjectivity, Rorty (1979 338–39) proposes that "objectivity" is more intelligently viewed as a *property* of theories,

> which, having been thoroughly discussed, are chosen by a consensus of rational discussants. By contrast, a "subjective" consideration is one which has been, or would be, or should be, set aside by rational discussants—one which is seen to be . . . irrelevant to the subject matter of the theory . . .

20. Were historical inquiry to commit itself to the one-sided analytic abstraction of narrative wholes, it would turn into a positivist behavioral science. This is perhaps the hope of Furet and others of the *Annales* school (as well as many similarly inclined American social and economic historians): their goal is to redirect history from its pretheoretical affinity with events, experience, and conduct to those analytically abstracted aspects (e.g., birthrates) which are said to underlie them. It is evident, however, that even such a scientific history, which would involve the analytic dismemberment of narratively constructed wholes, nevertheless presupposes the existence of such wholes. In other words, scientific history is parasitic upon narrative history. It is not really that narrative history

provides the necessary "data base," but rather that it affords the occasion and rationale for an act of analytic abstraction. Without narrative history's narrative configurations, there is virtually nothing for scientific history to deconstruct.

21. There is no a priori limit on the number (or modes) of conceivable "pasts." Thus the five constructions which are cited here are simply those which have been deemed especially relevant to the various "language strata" (Waismann 1965) of psychoanalytic discourse.

22. My own sketch of poetry as an activity and of the poetic construction of the past is indebted to Michael Oakeshott's essay, "The Voice of Poetry in the Conversation of Mankind" (1962 197–247).

23. That Freudian theory subscribes (in part) to the atemporal construct of time should be evident from the discussions in Chapter 2 of both the scientific construction of the past (see Figure 1, Box 3), and the "timeless" psychoanalytic past as explicated by Zukier. The key point is that empirical-analytic science appears to take "time" as a given, or as a formal or empty variable with no intrinsic content. Time is just a container of events which are numerically ordered in terms of the unvarying sequence of past, present, and future. Occasionally, certain properties (e.g., primacy and recency effects) are attributed to the remote or immediate past, but "time" itself remains unrecognized as a differentiated phenomenon open to some form of explication. Accordingly, empirical-analytic science is still largely unable to "tap" psychological time, or even to acknowledge it as a theoretical problem. See Harré (1984) for an exploratory attempt to incorporate "lived time" in the metaphysics of psychology.

24. In any assessment of phenomenological inquiry, the question must finally be asked: what has it to offer, apart from interesting but unreliable *descriptive* accounts which still seem to call for "explanation"? In other words, even if Kierkegaard is able to explicate *how* we can go wrong in the ways we appropriate the past and anticipate the future, we still want to know *why* we go wrong, and *what can be done* to intervene and set things right. For answers (if any) to such questions, we turn to psychoanalysis, and certainly to cognitive and behavioral psychology, neuroscience, and biology. And we do so even though the logical relationship of a phenomenological account to a scientific (or explanatory) account remains obscure at best.

Lane and Schwartz (1987) are among the few contemporary empirical-analytic behavioral scientists to have explicitly addressed the phenomenology-science issue. Lane and Schwartz are concerned with the nature of emotional awareness, its structural development over time, and the cognitive processes which explain or account for the various stages and structures of emotional awareness and experience. What makes their particular model phenomenology-sensitive is its assumption that since both the representations of the emotional experience and the experience itself are hypothesized to arise from the same schemata, the structure of the representation should reflect the structure of the experience. In other words, what is experienced as an emotion is the actual structure; it is this structure—concrete and occurrent—which is *directly reflected* in the verbal representation of the experience. Lane and Schwartz thus propose a model which is able, in principle, to account for the intrinsic features of phenomenal emotional experience, and for the structures and processes associated with its development. Such a model and others like it (e.g., Vallacher and Wegner 1987) help to supply a coherent rationale for projects like Stern's (see in Chapter 2, "Saving the Mixed Model?") which seek to coordinate explanatory (empirical-analytic) and descriptive (phenomenological) modes of discourse.

25. Although any psychoanalytic inquiry is a *mixed* inquiry, it is nevertheless possible to cite works which specifically exemplify and emphasize one particular modality of psychoanalytic discourse:

1. Science: Weiss and Sampson, *The Psychoanalytic Process*
2. History: Schafer, *The Analytic Attitude*
3. Practice: Havens, *Making Contact* and *A Safe Place*
4. Phenomenology: Atwood and Stolorow, *Structures of Subjectivity*
5. Poetry: Lacan, *Ecrits*

26. In practice, any psychoanalytic inquiry is a mixed discourse, and all psychoanalytic "pasts" are therefore ambiguous or composite pasts. Ricoeur has elaborated a similar view of Freudian discourse as a *mixed,* if not equivocal discourse:

> The reading I presuppose considers Freudian discourse to be a mixed discourse. It mingles questions of meaning . . . and questions of force. . . . I allow here that this mixed discourse is not equivocal, but is appropriate to the reality which it wishes to take into account, namely the binding of force and meaning in a semantics of desire. (1974 160)

II

PLURALISM IN THEORY
AND PRACTICE

4

The Historical Construction of the Psychoanalytic Past

All past events are more remote from our senses than the stars of the remotest galaxies, whose own light at least still reaches the telescopes.

—George Kubler

And history cannot be more certain than when he who creates things describes them.

—Giambattista Vico

What kind of story are we in?

—John Dunn

According to the principle of pluralism, psychoanalysis speaks in many voices and each announces its own version of the psychoanalytic past. In the first part of this book (Chapters 1–3), I have outlined a pluralist model of psychoanalytic understanding—one which allows for a plurality of distinct discourses (history, science, practice), and for the psychoanalytic pasts which are their objective correlates. My task in Part II (Chapters 4–6) is to illustrate, apply, and test this model. I do so by redrawing the traditional map of American psychoanalytical inquiry, arguing that such inquiry is most successfully conducted not in terms of "schools" or "approaches," but in terms of discourses or modes of discourse. My strategy is to contrast ideal types or prototypes of historical, scientific, and practical psychoanalysis, and to show how each construction represents a distinct conceptual universe of psychoanalytic understanding. I begin in this chapter by setting forth an exemplary version of historical psycho-analysis and of the historically constructed past which is its objective correlate. That past is designated the "narrative past." It is the necessary postulate (or intentional object) of our self-awareness as makers of narrative meaning. As such, it stands as a key element in any comprehensive theory of psychoanalytic understanding.

The Analytic Encounter: Hermeneutics and Countertransference

The prototype of historical psychoanalysis derives largely from the contributions of the American psychoanalyst Roy Schafer (1976, 1978, 1983, 1984). We recall that Schafer's revisionary stance (see in Chapter 2, "Introduction: Two Points of View") deconstructs the autonomy and authority of the past. The past is actually viewed as an interpretable aspect of the here and now, as the product or epiphenomenon of present circumstances. Such a stance is exquisitely American in its faith in the "creationist" or constructivist power of the here and now, in its apparent contempt for the objectivity or fixity of the past, and in its buoyant and optimistic assertion of the superiority of the present. Yet the thesis I propound in this chapter upholds the paradox that this quintessentially American achievement[1] finds its rationale in the European tradition of philosophical hermeneutics, the most significant exponent of which is the German thinker Hans-Georg Gadamer (1975, 1976). Thus historical psychoanalysis (a typically American cultural expression) turns out to be nothing other than a specialized application of philosophical hermeneutics, and is logically (if not historically) indebted to an alien Continental tradition of philosophical discourse.[2]

The idea of historical psychoanalysis is actually an extension and refinement of the "historical model" already introduced in Chapter 3. According to that model, both patient and therapist are, wittingly or not, historians of their analytic encounter. The historical psychoanalyst, for example, is not looking for specific things: i.e., he or she is not intervening simply to fill in a missing memory, to correct a mistaken thought, or to diagnose a symptom. It is rather that the analyst is aiming to comprehend and influence the quiet and subtle realignment, the small shift in narrative perspective that somehow reorganizes figure and ground, yielding a "recognition" of what was always there (or almost always there), but not seen before.[3] Indeed, the therapeutic action of psychoanalysis may well depend on a kind of switching between two ways of seeing the past. Such a process—also described in terms of a loosening or disorganization of the practical past along with its reconstitution as a distinctively historical past —may even characterize the "good hour" in psychotherapy (Kris 1956). This, then, is part of what I mean when I claim that successful psychoanalytic therapy involves the acquisition and transmission of some form of historical self-understanding (see in Chapter 3, "Clinical Psychoanalysis and the Model of History").

However, the historical model by no means stipulates that it is only the patient or analysand who switches his narrative stance and reorganizes figure and ground. It is also, of course, the therapist or analyst who modifies his initial position (the practical past), and who thus renegotiates his relationship to both the patient's past and his own (Goldberg 1987). Moreover, if there is such a historical reorganization in the clinical situation, then it is evidently a *mutual* reorganization. The analytic encounter is now understood as a transactive, interactive, and transferential experience, in which the psychoanalytic narrative lies "in-between." Thus, the psychoanalytic narrative is not merely the history of one person's (the patient's) psychic reality, but is rather recognized as

> the product of two discourses playing against one another, often warring with one another, working toward recognitions mutually acknowledged but internalized in different ways. (Brooks 1984 283)

This, then, is the strong sense of the idea of mutuality. Implicit in it is the notion that both patient and therapist participate in a *productive* encounter, and that the analytic process is itself: (a) a dialogic process in which the mere presence of the analyst as narratee and potential narrator "dialogizes" the discourse of the analysand; and that (b) this process is constituted in the "transitional realm" of the transference which, by definition, is a realm in which discourse is always internalizing the presence of the other; and that (c) this is a process which makes it possible for the "past" to become the subject of imaginative reorderings and narrative revisions on the part of both analysand and analyst alike.

The movement toward mutuality and the emergence of a more transactional model of the analytic encounter can be discerned in the evolution of psychoanalytic teachings concerning countertransference. Freud first commented on countertransference in 1910, when he described it as arising "in the physician as a result of the patient's influence on his [the physician's] unconscious feelings" (1910 144). As with the concept of resistance and, indeed, the transference itself, countertransference was originally seen as only a hindrance or obstacle to therapy, not at all as a possible source of information and guidance for the therapist. In this traditional view, the analyst's countertransference is something to be recognized and overcome (e.g., through analysis), and is merely the mirror image of the patient's transference, accordingly defined by Greenson (1967) as follows:

> The analyst reacts to his patient as though the patient were a significant person in the analyst's early history. Countertransference is a transference reaction of an analyst to a patient. . . . Countertransference reactions can lead to persistent inappropriate behavior toward the patient. (348)

Over the past few decades, however, both the definition and the clinical impact of countertransference have been much debated (e.g., Orr 1954; Cohen 1952; Racker 1968)—with Marshall (1979) defining the concept most broadly through four subtypes, depending on whether the reaction is conscious or unconscious, and whether it is therapist-derived or patient-derived.[4] Focusing in particular on the subset of patient-induced reactions and upon the therapist's use of it, a consensus has gradually emerged that countertransference can be a useful way to understand oneself and one's patients, and that it may actually involve responses and feelings which are appropriate to, and give the therapist insight into, the real nature of the patient and his problems (Epstein and Feiner 1979).

Thus, what was once an obstacle in the path of psychoanalysis, a source of clinical misunderstanding, is now (typically) transformed into a diagnostic and therapeutic tool which facilitates the "psychoanalytic process." And so the analyst may ask herself, in the course of a session: "how is it that I'm having such and such a fantasy and feeling at this particular time?" The analyst's response, if analytic, will surely not be a "discharge of reciprocal emotion or a defense against it" (Feiner 1979), but rather a countercommunication about the patient himself or how he has been or is being experienced. Seen in this light, the processing of countertransference involves a reflective *response* to the patient's influence, not just a reaction caused by the patient's "processes" operating on the analyst's.

It follows that the therapist is now urged to attend to such "induced" feelings as clues to how the patient is feeling (or has felt in the past), and clues to how others feel or have felt about the patient (Spotnitz 1969). Such induced feelings (e.g., boredom, helplessness, jealousy, sexual longing, etc.) may also suggest how other people have been compelled to react to the patient, thereby providing the therapist with a rough index of the *wrong* response—that is, the "untreated" countertransference reaction most likely to perpetuate the pathological organization of the patient's self and object world (see also Sandler 1976).

In the contemporary position just reviewed, the analyst is required to reflect upon his or her countertransference experiences, and not just "be caused" to do something. Countertransference is therefore recognized as (a) an *interpretable* experience and (b) transformable into a form of rational or rule-governed conduct. It follows that countertransference "effects" are now viewed (a) not just as components of unintelligent and unlearned (causal) processes (b) not just as reflections of the analyst's inner emotional state or as unconscious reactions to the patient's monologue, but also (c) as intelligible signs (evidence) in the *hermeneutic* reading of an interpersonal and intrapsychic situation. It has even been proposed (in clinical work with the severely disturbed) that the analysis of countertransference effects may eventually enable the analyst to translate primitive and hitherto uninterpretable communication (verbal or preverbal) into "messages-in-action," and hence, into hermeneutical signs, in the psychic reality of the patient (McDougall 1979).

My point in the preceding discussion has been to underline the convergence between the contemporary view of countertransference and the movement toward a more transactive representation of the analytic encounter. According to this thesis, the (hermeneutic) interpretation of patient-induced countertransference experiences not only aids in the study or diagnosis of the patient's psychic reality (the internalized self-other relationships that he or she may be reenacting), but also in the formulation of therapeutic strategies of clinical intervention. It is important to keep in mind, however, that such therapeutic strategies, though *guided* by the interpretation of countertransference, need not themselves be overtly interpretative. The analyst need not convey or transmit his interpretations to the patient and the patient need have little "insight." For the transactive model of the analytic situation (though "hermeneutically driven" as suggested above) does not necessarily depend upon consciousness or awareness as much as learning. Indeed, it is because both patient and therapist are affected by one another and can learn from each other that psychoanalysis emerges as a transactive practice; and it is in this particular sense that "mutuality" depicts the interdependence of the analytic encounter.

For typically, therapeutic action (interpersonal learning) does not belong to the analyst (or analysand) alone: rather both participants—internalizing the presence of the other—contribute to organizing and constituting the mutative narrative. There is thus a dialogic structure to their *common understanding,* even if conscious insight, transferential awareness, and self-knowledge are not equally distributed.[5]

The Relevance of Philosophical Hermeneutics

The proposition has now been advanced that hermeneutic activities are at the basis of the clinical practice of psychoanalysis. The interpretation of countertransference *is* hermeneutics, and the specific form it assumes is conditioned and shaped by the transactive and transferential context that defines the psychoanalytic encounter. But the significance and relevance of this proposition are as yet unclear. Michael Basch (1976a, 1986), for example, has argued that hermeneutic activities (within and outside the clinical setting) must themselves be explained or represented in terms of theories of communication and models of information processing. In other words, it is readily conceded that hermeneutics figures prominently in psychoanalytic practice (and in elegant conceptualizations of such practice),[6] but it is always something which is cognitively insufficient and which therefore calls forth for "real explanation." This, of course, must proceed in terms of the empirical-analytic paradigm outlined in the first part of this book. Within the boundaries of such a paradigm, however, it remains unclear how hermeneutics actually contributes to our understanding of psychoanalysis as either a theory of mind or method of investigation, or as even a theory of therapy.

My present task, then, is to offer an account which argues that clinical hermeneutics (as introduced in the previous section) is not merely incidental to psychoanalytic understanding, but is of its very essence—at least insofar as psychoanalysis is construed as a cognitively significant historical enterprise. What is needed is a *rationale* for clinical hermeneutics, one which explicates its significance not only for our understanding of psychoanalysis as a theory of therapy, but also as a method of investigation and a theory of mind. Such a rationale is implicit in the philosophical hermeneutics advanced by Hans-Georg Gadamer (1975, 1976, 1981); and I argue below that it is this rationale which clarifies the nature and point of

Schafer's exemplary project to reshape Freudian psychology as a form of historical and hermeneutical psychoanalysis.[7]

Philosophical hermeneutics, as expounded by Gadamer, offers a critique of the traditional hermeneutic position currently associated with Betti (1962), Hirsch (1967), and Ricoeur (1974), and earlier with Dilthey (1906). Although traditional hermeneutics is typically dualistic, espousing the "Great Divide" (Blight 1981) between scientific knowledge of the physical world and interpretative knowledge of the human realm, it remains nonetheless committed to the pursuit of objective and reliable understandings of such "life-expressions" as textual meaning, authorial intention, and cultural forms and social practices. In this traditional position, objectivity in interpretation is assured through the application of empathic understanding. We are culturally so constituted that empathic understanding allows the interpreter to transcend his own historical situation and so relive the thought and action of the subjects under study (thereby "reproducing" it in an objective manner). In Dilthey's words (1906):

> Every word, every sentence, every gesture or form of politeness, every work of art and every political act is intelligible only because a commonality binds those who express themselves (through these forms) with those who understand (the forms). The individual experiences, thinks, and acts . . . only in such a sphere of commonality, and only in it does he understand. (175)

In short, the traditional hermeneutic position allows that life-expressions (conceptualized as objectivations of mind) may still be treated as preexistent *objects,* and that the task of the empathic interpreter is to reconstruct the ideas, messages, and intentions "carried" in them. For Betti (1962), then, hermeneutic understanding *is* the reconstruction of the intentions of the author (or actor), and objectivity or validity in this endeavor is perfectly feasible so long as the procedures of validation are seen to be closer to a logic of "qualitative probability" than to a logic of verification. As Ricoeur (1976) puts it:

> To show that an interpretation is more probable in the light of what we know is something other than showing that a conclusion is true. So, in the relevant sense, validation is not verification. It is an argumentative discipline comparable to the juridical procedures used in legal interpretation, a logic of uncertainty and qualitative probability. (78)

It would thus appear that traditional hermeneutics, though methodologically distinct from empirical-analytic science, shares with it the commitment to objectivity and may therefore be consistent with the requirements of Proposition 1, where what is implied is a conception of knowledge, the content of which is recognized to have a condition independent of mind. Within this, the traditional or objectivist hermeneutic paradigm, it is eminently reasonable for Freud (1937b) to claim (via the archaeological metaphor)[8] that he could make contact with—or validly reconstruct—pieces of the patient's actual past. For the past so constituted is simply the objectively knowable "precursor" to (and source of) present conditions, and not at all (as we shall see with Gadamer) a "partner" in dialogue, the meanings of which matter even as they are necessarily revised and integrated within a new and contemporary understanding. In short, Freud—the psychoanalytic archaeologist—was as much a traditional (objectivist) hermeneut as he was a natural scientist of mind. There is actually no contradiction between the two roles.

In his opus, *Truth and Method* (1975), Gadamer entirely rejects the objectivism common to both traditional hermeneutics and empirical-analytic science.[9] But in doing so, he does not substitute in its stead some new set of interpretative rules or some alternative method for the human sciences. Rather, operating at an altogether different level of analysis and abstraction, he offers an account of the conditions of understanding in general—conditions that, in his view, undermine rational belief in the ideas of both method and objectivity.

Two such conditions, in particular, seem essential to the hermeneutic rationale for Schafer's historical psychoanalysis, and are thus introduced below:

1. The first condition consists in the claim that what we understand, and the way in which we understand, are thoroughly conditioned by the past, or by what Gadamer calls "prejudice" or "effective history" (1975 267). We cannot escape the historically conditioned character (or "horizon") of our own understanding. The objectivity of our knowledge is therefore curtailed by its "situatedness," by its dependence on tradition, and this dependence is not one that method can in any way transcend. This is the condition of *effective history*.

2. The second condition consists in the claim that understanding occurs as a "fusion" of situations and cannot but appear as "coming to an understanding with others." This means that successful understanding involves neither adopting the "prejudices" of one's text or text-analogue,

nor imposing one's own upon it. Understanding rather involves a transformation of the initial positions of *both* text and interpreter—and with
it, the movement toward a "fusion of horizons" (Gadamer 1975 350) in
which our historically conditioned concerns are integrated with the object
of understanding such that this integration determines the content of the
object for us.[10] This, then, is the condition of the *dialogic structure of
understanding*.

These two conditions, properly elucidated, comprise the program of
philosophical hermeneutics. Together, they specify understanding as both
situated and *contextual*—a proposition which, in Gadamer's view, is perfectly general, as applicable in its way to the natural (and behavioral)
sciences as it is more obviously to historical inquiry and practical knowledge.[11] Let me now proceed, however, to spell out the implications of
this proposition for the discussion at hand.

To assert that understanding is *situated* is to recognize, for example,
that its aim can never be the recreation of an original creation (Gadamer
1975 149). For the interpreter cannot seek to recreate (or reexperience)
the original, past event (or experience) without depriving it of the meaning it has from the historian's perspective. The problem is this: how can
we conceive or understand an object or event as it is in itself, independently of the complex process by which we get access to it? Or, as the
philosopher Danto has put it:

> We could only witness the past "as it actually happened" if we somehow
> could forget just the sort of information which may have motivated us to
> make temporal journeys in reverse. (1965 159)

Furthermore, given the assumption that all understanding (including
psychoanalytic understanding) is situated in effective history, it follows
that even when we are concerned with an agent's (past or present) intentions, motives, or self-images, our description of these can represent no
more than one possible perspective on them. Yet, for Gadamer, this is not
a condition to be regretted, as if our access to "truth" or "reality" were
thereby diminished. On the contrary, it is exactly his view that the truth
value of any one of our understandings depends upon its object (a text,
an experience, an event) being understood in relation to our own "preju-
dicial" situation. It is just because there is no neutral (unsituated) vantage
point from which to assess the "real" meaning of a text, object, or event
that "truthful" understanding is at all possible.[12] In summary, what Gad-

amer calls our "effective history" (the horizon of our prejudices) is not, in the end, an obstacle to knowledge so much as a condition of it. The historical distance that is implicit in the situatedness of understanding is thus no mere methodological problem; it is rather an ontological "given" since it decisively affects the very nature of that which we seek to understand.

Philosophical hermeneutics not only proposes that all understanding is situated, but that it is contextual as well. The context in question is always dialogically structured. Just as the interpreter is inserted in a "vertical" historical horizon, so is he also imbedded in a "horizontal" and dialogical context. The interpreter does not approach the object (or other) as a blank page; armed with expectations of meaning (e.g., conscious and unconscious beliefs) he instead approaches the object (or other) with prejudgments about what will be found there. The interpreter thus *anticipates* or *projects* meaning in order to understand, while allowing that this initial projection may be corrected in subsequent encounters. It is Gadamer's view, moreover, that the hermeneutic circle [13] just sketched implies an *anticipation of completeness* in that there is a presumption that the object (or other) forms a potential intelligible unity or an internally consistent or self-coherent whole; it follows that one can therefore rely on a regulative ideal of unity to assess the adequacy of one's interpretations of its various parts. [14]

Seen in this light, interpretative understanding involves a "fusion of horizons," a specific form of interaction and transaction between the expectations (and anticipations) of the interpreter and the meaning-potential of the text (or text-analogue). For the "inert" text, no less than the embodied interpreter, is historically situated and already the result of interpretation by and through a tradition. [15] In this respect, the text and the interpreter are structurally isomorphic, and are functions of one another in a *dialogic* context. Each participant moves beyond its initial position toward a "consensus" that is (ideally) more differentiated and articulated than when the "conversation" began. It is for this reason that Gadamer can claim that our understanding even of a text (or of past actors and events) can *validly* change because of our historical experience. The validity of hermeneutic understanding depends, therefore, not on the original (fixed) positions of interpreter and text (or other), but on the retrospective consciousness of historically situated interpreters participating in an "interminable" dialogic encounter.

Philosophical hermeneutics proposes, in sum, that understanding in general is "vertically" or diachronically conditioned by its effective history, and "horizontally" or synchronically conditioned by its dialogic structure. The very content of whatever is to be understood is thus determined by these twin "vectors," or more exactly, by the manner in which the interpreter's historically conditioned concerns are integrated with the so-called object of understanding, which itself is hermeneutically active, historically situated, and open to the possibility of change.

The conclusion follows, then, that Gadamer's program of philosophical hermeneutics articulates a *transactive* model of understanding. Such a model implies a reciprocal integration of differing perspectives as well as a mutual reorganization of experience. Yet this model, though completely general and not conceived with psychoanalysis in mind, appears to be instantiated by the clinical hermeneutics of the analytical situation. For recalling that earlier discussion, I can now hypothesize that:

1. those preconceptions, prejudgments, and anticipations which make hermeneutic understanding possible in the first place are approximately equivalent to the "induced" countertransference experience recognized as essential to facilitating the psychoanalytic process;
2. such countertransference experience is always bound up with our potential awareness of the historical influence or "effectivity" of the analysand as other;
3. without such hermeneutic awareness, we neither understand the psychic reality of the patient, nor the true (narrative) character of our transactive and transferential encounter with him or her.

It seems likely, moreover, that Gadamer's philosophical hermeneutics is instantiated not only in psychoanalytic practice (as above), but also in the *conceptual design* of clinical psychoanalysis. That design appears to integrate the energic-dynamic model of *Beyond the Pleasure Principle* (Freud 1920) with Freud's transactive and transferential model of clinical process to be found in his papers on technique and in such case histories as that of the "Wolf Man" (1918).[16] Integration is purportedly realized in the role of repetition in the transference: wherein repetitive behaviors initially take the place of recall and remembrance; and in which the symbolic enactment of the past *as if* it were present puts the story of the past in such a form that it can then become the subject of dialogic reorderings and understandings on the part of both analysand and analyst alike. In other words, Gadamer's conditions of hermeneutic understanding in general are also the conditions of psychoanalytic understanding in particular, namely: (a) "effective history" (or the repetitive power of the past in the present); and (b) the "dialogic structure of understanding" (the collaborative reordering of the past, now as a narratively constructed object of hermeneutic understanding imbedded in a transactive and transferential context).

The generality of philosophical hermeneutics alerts us to the fact that its relevance need not be confined to a first-order treatment of the clinical hermeneutics of psychoanalytic practice. It is rather that Gadamer's conditions of hermeneutic understanding are more or less realized in *any* expression of psychoanalytic understanding, in whichever order of analysis and in whatever domain of study. This is why I can now propose that the program of philosophical hermeneutics is indeed capable of supplying the appropriate rationale for Schafer's project to reshape psychoanalysis as a historical and hermeneutic discipline: as at once a discipline which articulates a "theory of therapy," a method of clinical investigation, and an interpretative perspective on experience and psychic reality.

It is not, of course, that I claim that Schafer has actually "applied" philosophical hermeneutics in his formulation of a historical and hermeneutical psychoanalysis; my claim is rather that the point of Schafer's controversial project only becomes intelligible when *reinterpreted* in terms of philosophical hermeneutics. In proceeding at this juncture to introduce Schafer's exemplary project—understood below as a specialized expression of philosophical hermeneutics—it is well to keep in mind the possibility that not even historical psychoanalysis can be adequately or wholly construed as radically hermeneutic. For the thesis of "hermeneutic universality" is a problematic one, and needs to be recognized as such by philosophical hermeneutics itself. The real problem is that, as Habermas puts it:

> Hermeneutic consciousness remains incomplete as long as it does not include a reflection upon the *limits* of hermeneutic understanding. (1980 190, my emphasis)

Accordingly, it will become apparent, as this chapter proceeds, that the boundaries of Schafer's historical psychoanalysis and hence, of his version of the historically constructed psychoanalytic past, are defined precisely and exactly by the so-called "limits of hermeneutic understanding."

Schafer's Linguistic Psychoanalysis: An Interpretative Overview

There is a traditional and compelling picture of psychoanalytic knowledge which has endured and persisted almost since the time of Freud's original discoveries. According to that picture of psychoanalytic knowledge, human beings are observed and understood from the "inside" via empathy, while the observations and insights so gathered are then organized from the "outside" via empirical-analytic science. There is thus a *hermeneutic* inside (within which psychic reality and meaningful experience are objectively reconstructed), and a *scientific* outside where "clinical observations" are subjected to empirical test, ordered into explanatory structures, and instantiated by or represented through abstract models. Such, for example, is the position endorsed by Basch (1976a, 1977, 1983) when he argues that our knowledge of information processing allows us to model the particular hermeneutic activity that purportedly lies at the basis of clinical psychoanalytic practice. More generally, this is the view of psychoanalytic knowledge advanced by such diverse clinical theorists as Gedo (1979), Modell (1981), and Brenner (1983), all of whom assert that psychoanalysis is a fusion of science and humanism which properly encompasses *both* the experiential and the non-experiential realms.

Roy Schafer, as I see it, rejects this traditional picture of psychoanalytic knowledge. It is not only that (following in the footsteps of Gadamer) he rejects the objectivism of empirical-analytic science, but also that he rejects the objectivism of traditional hermeneutics. For Schafer—the historical psychoanalyst—there are thus no "inside" depths to be hermeneutically plumbed, and no "outside" relations to be analytically abstracted. Hence, there can be no privileged (objective) point of view, whether positioned from the inside or whether positioned from the outside; thus, there is no problem of (a) reconciling or harmoniously joining two discrepant points of view, and (b) neither is there any necessity to resign oneself to a bifurcated system of psychoanalytic understanding. There is, in truth, only one, unitary, and sufficient system of psychoanalytic understanding,

and it is neither traditionally hermeneutic nor traditionally metapsychological, nor an amalgam or mix of each. It is, in Gadamer's sense, a unitary
system of *situated* and *contextual* understanding.

In the interpretation I now offer, "action language" (Schafer 1976) is
just an early and imperfect anticipation of such a system, while the papers
collected in *The Analytic Attitude* (Schafer 1983) articulate a more mature
and fully realized approximation of the situated and contextual conditions
of psychoanalytic understanding. In other words, whereas Schafer's earlier
study was colored and controlled by its polemic against traditional metapsychology (for which action language was unwisely offered as a replacement), his later work is relatively free of such rhetorical pressure, and is
focused, instead, on the dialogical context of psychoanalytic practice and
on the historical situatedness of psychoanalytic discourse. It is thus in *The
Analytic Attitude* that Schafer emerges, finally, as a philosophical hermeneuticist; and it is the radically historical (and narrativist) psychoanalysis
that appears therein that must eventually occupy our attention in the
pages to follow.

My first task, however, is to undertake a critical review of Schafer's
action language proposal. I do so with two objectives in mind: (a) to
expose the idea of theory that is implicit in that proposal, and (b) to
identify the limits and ambiguities of "theory," so construed—since the
argument will be advanced as this chapter proceeds that these are largely
overcome and resolved in Schafer's narratively oriented exposition in *The
Analytic Attitude*. I begin in this section with a consideration of the first
objective, and move on in the next with a consideration of the second.

Recall that Schafer proposes action language as a replacement for traditional metapsychology. He is able to do so because he regards the latter
as a self-contained linguistic system (a "language game" of forces, energies, structure, and apparatus), whose contents not only communicate
what is intended by the theory, but also *constitute* the object of the
theoretical account. In other words, traditional metapsychology (and,
arguably, empirical-analytic science as such) is not essentially referential,
referring to an extralinguistic and real (if hypothetical) world of structures
and processes, but is rather analytical and self-constitutive, generating its
own linguistic universe of internally interrelated meanings. And so Schafer
observes, with respect to traditional metapsychology, that:

In line with this strategy, reasons become forces, emphases become energies, activity becomes function, thoughts become representations, affects become discharges or signals, deeds become resultants, and particular ways of struggling with the inevitable diversity of intentions, feelings and situations become structures, mechanisms and adaptations. (1976 103)

Metapsychology is thus dispensable, not only because its propositions may no longer be congruent with observation, and not only because they may embody a logically confused conflation of theory, model, and speculation, but chiefly because they belong to (and constitute) a non-referential language game that is inappropriate to the recognition and comprehension of human conduct. More exactly, it is Schafer's point that the language games of traditional psychoanalytic metapsychology (and empirical-analytic science in general) are incapable of speaking of or to the discourse of human conduct. Since "theory" is not referential, but only constitutive, metapsychology and natural science are disqualified because they cannot *constitute* (describe and redescribe) a world of human conduct (Schafer 1978 60). This means, for example, that the explanations, models, and metaphors of metapsychology are actually beside the point, since what these describe, conceptualize, and explain is never the identifiable action as such,[17] but only (at best) some hypothetical process presumed to underlie or circumscribe it. The two-part premise, then, of Schafer's revisionary program is that: (a) the language games of traditional metapsychology (and, arguably, of empirical-analytic science in general) are non-referential, self-constituting linguistic systems, which (like all such systems) can only "explain" through rule-governed redescription; and further, that (b) these language games (the discourses of science) are a priori incapable of representing "the person as agent and maker of meaning" (Anscombe 1981 225), with which psychoanalysis, in Schafer's view, has always been centrally concerned in practice.

Given this premise, Schafer is in the position to claim that action language can perform "the same type of explanatory job" as traditional metapsychology: namely, "it establishes an orderly universe of propositions concerning the definition, description and interrelationships of psychological phenomena or 'psychic reality,' now viewed as actions in various modes" (1976 211). Within the rules of such a linguistic system, what are decisive are never the "external" causes or processes which underlie or "produce" human action, but how these are reflected and represented (consciously and unconsciously) in the *reasons* that individualize a person's subjective experience or psychic reality. In sum, all explanation is through reasons, and psychoanalytic explanation is therefore advanced as a subtype of "rational explanation." Yet it is evident that such explanation (like metapsychological explanation) is necessarily descriptive or redescriptive in nature. Hence:

> in giving reasons for particular actions . . . one restates these actions in a way that makes them more comprehensible. A reason is . . . another vantage point from which to view and define an action or its context. . . . it may involve a shift to another level of abstraction for the designation of actions . . . (which) serves interests other than those which dictated the initial version of the action in question. This kind of explanation continues to set forth significant features of the analysand's psychic reality. *In this view, the traditional distinction between description and explanation is discarded.* (Schafer 1976 210–11, emphasis in original)

My first conclusion, then, is that Schafer's action language proposal yields a "descriptive theory" of psychoanalysis, which means—in effect—that psychoanalytic understanding ("explanation") is always *redescriptive* and must be so in terms consistent with a view of human conduct as rule-governed (or rule-following) performance. In Schafer's view, action theory should thus reject the classical Freudian argument that the "true cause" of action is some unconscious motive striving for expression, *if* that motive is construed as a logically independent "mental event" which is a component of some hypothetical or inner "process." Within action theory, there are no external causes or inner processes; the task of psychoanalytic understanding is simply to make sense (through rational explanation and redescription) of the individual's misunderstanding or disclaimer of the psychoanalytically relevant features of his conduct and activity. For in Schafer's view, nothing is gained by seeking to "explain" action in terms of events and processes, since the scientific language game within which such explanation must be pursued necessarily abstracts from the "goings-on" of human conduct and activity, and *decontextualizes* them in such a way that they can no longer be identified as such, namely, as exhibitions of human intelligence, as subscriptions to practices, and as meaningful performances which have reasons. To paraphrase one commentator (Oakeshott 1975 15): a wink is not a blink, and the language game of science does not allow the wink to appear as a recognizable expression of human conduct.[18]

Summing up the discussion thus far: action language implies a descriptive (or redescriptive) theory of psychoanalytic understanding; what is being redescribed, recontextualized, and thematically reduced are the conflicts that the analysand has unconsciously defined, and the compromises he or she has unconsciously arranged. The rules of action language explicate the "logic" of such redescription, and this logic pertains to the mapping of internal conceptual relations, not to delineation of causal connections. So, for example, the rules of action language would now require that the psychoanalytic theme of the resolution of conflict be construed in terms of a redefinition or redescription of paradoxical (conflictual) situations such that they are (a) no longer paradoxical, (b) no longer the only possibilities envisaged, (c) no longer the principal issues, and (d) no longer the actions to persist in (Schafer 1978 100). Viewed in this way, psychoanalytic theory *is* the description and redescription of psychoanalytically relevant actions and modes of action (e.g., actions viewed in terms of infantile erotic and aggressive conflicts, meanings, and the variations of these that the analysand has continued to fashion); as such, psychoanalytic theory is neither explanatory in the usual sense, nor empirical in any obvious sense. Schafer virtually concedes the latter point when he observes that action language is "not a set of empirical psychoanalytic propositions," but rather "a strategy for stating these propositions clearly and parsimoniously" (1978 185), just as it is (perhaps more perspicuously) an approach through which the implicit and practical strategies of clinical interpretation may be classified and explicated. In other words, the "theory" of action language belongs to a *second order* of discourse: it is that which makes psychoanalytic understanding possible by constituting a linguistic world of psychoanalytically relevant actions and modes of action; hence, action theory, operating at this second order of discourse, pertains to setting the rules for interpreting those linguistically mediated events and experiences of a human life that are of special psychoanalytic interest, and that are defined and organized through the psychoanalytic method.[19] It is in this "non-empirical" and "non-explanatory" sense that action language stands as Schafer's initial and imperfect anticipation of a comprehensive historical theory of the conditions of psychoanalytic understanding.

Action, Agency, and Language: The Preliminary Critique

We complete this introductory overview by identifying certain ambiguities and limitations of Schafer's action language proposal. Just as the
previous discussion has not pretended to be comprehensive in scope, the
critique which now follows has only a selective and schematic intention:
its purpose is simply to lay the groundwork for an extended treatment of
Schafer's mature position in *The Analytic Attitude*. I take up the critique
under the following three headings: (a) the conceptualization of action;
(b) the primitivity of personal agency; and (c) the problem of linguistic
prescriptivism.

(a) *The Conceptualization of Action*. Schafer puts forth the concrete distinction between action and happening—the latter referring to "those
past and present events in the coming about of which the person has
played no part" (1976 361). I perform an *action* when I take a stroll, and
I suffer a *happening* when a cinder block falls on my head. Happenings
(environmental and bodily) are assimilated to actions, and hence become
accessible to psychoanalytic understanding, only when they are given
meaning by the person as agent. Thus Schafer's view that "psychoanalytic
interpretations say why people do what they do; not what makes people
do what they do, even when such significant happenings as trauma are
taken into account" (1978 195). Accordingly, causes are external and
extrinsic to action, and are only assimilated to it when they are reflected
or represented as *reasons* by the person as agent. Psychoanalytic understanding therefore traffics only in reasons (actions), not in causes (non-
actions), even when such events (happenings, causal processes, and other
non-actions) provide the occasion of significant actions and are influenced
by them. But this position clearly poses a problem for psychoanalytic
understanding, when it is being construed (as it is in this chapter) as a
mode of historical understanding. For even a "perfect" description and
redescription of all individual actions qua actions would not constitute a
well-explained history. The problem is not just that such a history would
omit the "causal impact" of all factors not "mentioned" in human reasons
(or would misjudge the force and direction of those so mentioned); the
problem is further that the *retrospective stance* of the historian cannot help
but attribute meaning to actions of which the historical actor would (or

could) not have been aware. For it is the historian, and not only the actor, who organizes actions into an overall action (episodes into stories), and who is thus able to know the significance of even the unintended consequences of an agent's actions. *Historical meaning* is thus the outcome of narrative structure imposed upon actions (and events) from a position subsequent to them; it inheres not in the intentions or reasons of "persons as agents," but in the retrospective consciousness of historically situated interpreters (Danto 1985). The conclusion follows that the rules of action language—focused as they are in securing primacy of place to "the person as agent"—fail to insure a space (within the same linguistic system) for the historically situated interpreter, who, as much as the historical actor, is himself a bearer of meaning. In short, action language, through its rigid and definitional exclusion of "cause" from personal action, also excludes (specifically) historical meaning from its universe of discourse. This is a deficiency which is mostly remedied, I believe, in the historical or narrativist psychoanalysis advanced in *The Analytic Attitude*.

There is, in addition, a certain bias which distorts Schafer's conceptualization of human action. We recall that any event may have (a) an action aspect and (b) a non-action aspect.[20] The former includes such interrelated concepts as reason, situation, meaning, and intention, while the latter encompasses the processes, structures, and capacities which hypothetically produce some behavior which itself "overlaps" with an identifiable action. In such an account, both the action and non-action aspects of an event are concretely inseparable, though analytically distinguishable. *Ex hypothesi*, each aspect is the outcome of analytic abstraction. But Schafer's system is ill at ease with such a position, and seems to imply the view that the world constituted through the rules and specifications of action language is somehow more "out there," more phenomenologically sound, than the analytically abstracted universe of non-action. Indeed, one commentator (Spence, in Reppen 1985) has even cited this bias as evidence for a kind of behaviorism. If so, it is surely a linguistic (and not a psychological) form of behaviorism;[21] and it is a behaviorism which has unfairly privileged "action," discounting the truth that it is as much the product of analytic abstraction as are the "remote" inner events and hypothetical entities of empirical-analytic science.

(b) *The Primitivity of Personal Agency.* The bias just noted is surely connected to Schafer's presumption concerning the primitivity of the concept

of personal agency (Anscombe 1981; Meissner 1979). For Schafer—
following the conventions of British analytical philosophy[22]—treats "the
person" as an indefinable, core construct, which contains in it all the
familiar attributes of "action," e.g., intentions, reasons, purposes. There
can be, by definition, no agencies other than the person "such as drives,
the ego, introjects and the emotions," and the person is thus left alone
and privileged in this linguistically constituted field, "as sole agent, uniquely
responsible for his actions, and without legitimate recourse to disclaiming
his own actions since there would be no other entity or powers (such as
being overcome with anger) to which he could attribute responsibility"
(Anscombe 1981 226).

It has been argued, perspicuously by Anscombe, that such a presumption is: (a) *conceptually* confused because the concept of the person, thus
construed, is so inclusive that its sphere of application can't be circumscribed; and (b) *empirically* inadequate since "the person regarded as a
general explanatory theory . . . cannot cope with commonplace clinical
observations" (240). The point I now add is just that Schafer's conceptualization also sacrifices (or distorts) the developmental dimensions of
psychoanalysis, in that there is no way to address the human being's
transition from organism (e.g., infancy) to personhood, or its retrogres-
sion from personhood to organism. Action language is a *rational* and
normative theory which presupposes the potential possession of "fully
developed" capacities,[23] and whose real point (as Schafer states) is to offer
a non-mechanistic account of the way in which analysts and analysands
do traditionally interact and the way in which analysands do customarily
change for the better as a result of being in analysis (1983 191). In other
words, Schafer's premise is surely that something "true" and "transformative" occurs in psychoanalytic practice, and that psychoanalytic theory
must somehow account for how this is possible. The rules of action
language are thus predicated on an ideal (and idealized) representation;
and the theoretical interpretation of the analytic situation, informed by
these rules, proceeds in terms of a certain normative model and in terms
of a certain regulative ideal. As a consequence, action language is not
easily able to acknowledge deviations from the norm, such as those which
follow from empathic failure and distorted communication in the analytic
field (Basch 1988). More generally, it is so biased toward the ideal of the
person as agent and maker of meaning (i.e., the primitivity of the concept
of personal agency) that it fails to recognize the psychoanalytically rele-

vant *biological past,* and its clinical appearance or repetition through the "archaic transferences" of the analytic situation (Gedo 1984). In summation, the rules and specifications of Schafer's action language—by presupposing the primitivity of the concept of personal agency—remove the *organism* from the sphere of psychoanalytic understanding, and thereby distort the recognition (and interpretation) of the biological past, whether in the genetic context of development or whether in the narrational context of the transference. It remains a vexing dilemma—as yet unresolved—whether Schafer's later version of historical psychoanalysis is as successful in recovering the "past in nature" as it is the "past in narrative."

(c) *The Problem of Linguistic Prescriptivism.* We complete the preliminary critique by questioning the coherence and viability of Schafer's overarching strategy of linguistic prescriptivism. The rules of action language prescribe an autonomous linguistic system (a) through which psychological and psychoanalytic phenomena are translated into a conceptual universe of internally related meanings, which are then (b) interpretable according to the rules so stipulated.

In this view, action language neither represents nor refers to a reality external to the self-constituted linguistic system. It now becomes clear (contra Spence) why Schafer cannot properly be labeled a behaviorist. For even though he appears to recast psychoanalytic theory in terms of what can be *looked at* and *pointed to* (Spence, in Reppen 1985 69), such ostensible psychological data ("actions") can never be interpreted as dependent variables which are the functions of environmental events, or alternatively, of neurophysiological events, or of theoretical networks involving hypothetical or abstract structures and processes. The point, for Schafer, is that "actions" are neither (a) genuinely observable, nor (b) insertable into functional (causal) relations, nor (c) representative of an extralinguistic reality.

- Actions are not observable (introspectively or empirically) because they are *meanings* which are constituted by, and only become accessible through, interpretation (i.e., description and redescription).
- Actions are not insertable into external or functional relations because, as meanings (and not just events), they become intelligi-

ble only through the network of *internal* (conceptual) relations
which specifies their context and hence their content.
- Lastly, actions lack extrinsic reference; that is, they do not represent or refer to an extralinguistic reality, because Schafer is evidently committed to a strict construction of Proposition 2 (see
Chapter 1), which—we recall—denies that knowledge is ultimately reducible to a relationship between knower and known,
and maintains that it is rather a self-constituting activity, carried
on inside the circle of a particular, authoritative speech community. In summary, Schafer prescribes or stipulates a particular
epistemic circle in which the idea of meaning and truth as "negotiable" sense necessarily displaces the idea of meaning and truth as
reference—since there is now, by definition, no foundational reality (outside the circle) to be mirrored or referred to.

In the account just sketched, theoretical understanding in psychoanalysis is purely linguistic and non-referential,[24] and its scope is rigidly
circumscribed by the "language rules" stipulated, and by the interpretative
practices prescribed. Such an account is questionable, not only because it
eschews science's supposed commitment to "look beyond the appearances
and to envision a real hypothetical structure" (Meissner 1979 100), but
also because it prematurely restricts the range of hermeneutic (and historical) understanding. The philosopher Bernard Williams captures this intuition when he suggests that

> our understanding of reality already includes the conception of it as existing
> independently of us and our understanding. (Berlin 1981 xii)

Williams' point is that our *natural* use of language already incorporates
the idea of referentiality (of intrinsic reference), and that referentiality is
thus an *intra*linguistic (or metalinguistic) condition of hermeneutic understanding. True, hermeneutics will construe this condition differently
from empirical-analytic science, but it is bound by it nonetheless. However, by departing from the natural use of language, and by attempting to
"reform" it through a rigid, definitional strategy of stipulation and prescription, Schafer loses access to this intuition (of intralinguistic referentiality), and hence loses access to the prelinguistic and extralinguistic
dimensions of interpretable experience. Schafer, in short, has endorsed a
literalist or strict construction of Proposition 2, forgetting that that proposition, itself, must become an object of hermeneutic reflection. Again to

paraphrase Habermas, hermeneutic consciousness is incomplete as long as it does not include a reflection upon the limits of hermeneutic understanding.

The implications or consequences of Schafer's strategy should now be evident. Since the theory and domain of psychoanalytic understanding have been restricted to a non-referential and linguistically stipulated universe of meaningful actions and communications, it becomes impossible (a) to account for how such actions and communications are systematically distorted by extralinguistic causal influences,[25] a concern which would seem to be of great relevance for *clinical psychoanalysis,* and (b) to interpret such actions and communications as parts of more general (non-linguistic) biological, psychological, and social processes, a concern which would seem to be of great relevance for what has traditionally been called *metapsychology.*

At the more concrete level of clinical discourse, Schafer is also obliged —by virtue of his non-referential linguisticism—to accept a patient's account as constituting the experience, so that it is this account (or narrative) that requires explanation (or interpretation), and not the extralinguistic experience of which the account is ostensibly a report. As Meissner (1979) puts it:

> If the patient reports a certain passivity or suffering in his emotional experience, the action language approach makes a presumption of activity and responsibility and wants to know the reasons why the patient would give such a passive and victimized account. The natural science approach, however, would accept the patient's account of his experience as a fact, and direct its effort to explaining or understanding the conditions and/or causes of that experience. (100)

But the real point in the above is that Schafer's action language approach cannot tolerate the presumption of extralinguistic referentiality (nor does it seem to recognize referentiality as an intralinguistic condition of hermeneutic understanding). To do so would be to depart from a linguistically prescribed universe of internally related meanings and reasons ("accounts"), from which there is no exit.

I thus conclude that *linguistic prescriptivism* unduly inhibits psychoanalytic understanding, even when such understanding is conceived of as a form of hermeneutic (or historical) discourse. It also generates the following paradox: while psychoanalytic interpretation (pursued within the frame of action language) is certainly capable of arriving at new "truths" (meanings) which seem to imply the existence of a reality outside the horizons of language and semiotic construction,[26] the parameters of Schafer's program appear to forbid further interpretation of this possibility. It is arguable, at this point, whether Schafer's historical psychoanalysis (to be introduced shortly) actually resolves this paradox. The problem we are thus left with is this: to what extent, or in what manner, does psychoanalytic understanding presuppose an extralinguistic "reality"? This is also a problem which has preoccupied contemporary philosophers of history (see Chapter 3 of this book). Thus, there are those like Dray, Gallie, and Mink who continue to believe that narrative or historical discourse (however different from scientific or paradigmatic discourse) is indeed capable of representing the "real past," while there are others, like Hayden White (1981, 1984), who have proposed that historical narrative is only *intrinsically* referential, and might be best understood as a construction of a story about reality, rather than as a (putative) direct representation of it. In other words, the problem of extralinguistic referentiality will indeed resurface in Schafer's historical psychoanalysis, but this time in a more articulated interpretative context—one in which "referentiality" belongs to an enduring debate over history's cognitive function: i.e., whether or not that function presupposes the "objectivity" of a real past which narrative discourse somehow reconstructs or represents.

To conclude, our review of Schafer's action language proposal has led us to the brink of historical psychoanalysis. We will discover shortly that "action" is recontextualized within the frame of narrative, and that the omniscient and atemporal perspective of linguistic stipulation is replaced by the historical situatedness of psychoanalytic understanding. But the question introduced above will continue to vex us. In other words, do all our tales lead to events, or do they lead just to other tales, "to man as a structure of fictions he tells about himself" (Brooks 1984 277)?

History and Hermeneutics: The Narrative Substructure of the Psychoanalytic Past

There is a subtle shift of emphasis in the later writings of Roy Schafer (1982, 1983, 1984). It is not at all that action language disappears in the papers collected in *The Analytic Attitude,* but rather that it is recontextualized as narrative discourse, and relocated within a program of historically situated psychoanalytic understanding. Action (or "activity") remains the ultimate category and everything within psychoanalytically relevant experience can be redescribed or interpreted in terms of it. But any activity is now seen to have a narrative form or character, tentative and inchoate in the beginning, but more definite and articulate as it is practiced more widely. Thus, to know any specific activity is to know it *historically,* i.e., (a) to comprehend its character and content in all its historical (narratively constructed) complexity, and yet (b) to know it reflectively from within a historically situated horizon. This is the first and preliminary sense in which Schafer now advances a form of historical psychoanalysis.

At the same time, there is a certain thread that continues to run through Schafer's work over the past two decades. For that work surely reflects the conviction (shared by most psychoanalysts) that something *true* and *transformative* can indeed occur in the analytic situation. It is possible, of course, that psychoanalysts are universally mistaken in this conviction. But if not, the question remains: how are we to make sense of it? What does it mean to claim that something true and transformative is achieved through psychoanalytic practice? The answer sought cannot be an empirical one, for our present concern is not with contingent fact, but rather, with those conditions of psychoanalytic understanding that would allow us properly to articulate and explicate the working premise that psychoanalysis is, in principle, truthful and transformative. Such a concern, I take it, is also Schafer's. Hence, in this reading, his historical psychoanalysis is also a *philosophical* and *hermeneutic* psychoanalysis, in the specific non-objectivist sense given to these terms by Gadamer. Schafer's project is thus presented below as both (a) a psychoanalytic application of "philosophical hermeneutics," and (b) an exemplary expression of historical and hermeneutic psychoanalysis, an important purpose of which is to establish a region of discourse within which the claim that "psychoanalysis is truthful and transformative" may be properly interpreted and justified.[27]

The focus of this section falls on certain salient features of Schafer's project. These are conveniently summarized through a brief review of the three core issues of the critical philosophy of history (see Chapter 3), namely, (1) retrospection and empathy, (2) narrative as inquiry, and (3) historical truth. My task is now to discern how these core issues figure in Schafer's historical psychoanalysis.

1. *Retrospection and Empathy*. Schafer, we recall, is not a traditional hermeneuticist. The empathic activity of the analyst does not mean that he or she is reliving or reproducing the experience of the analysand. There is no presumption of unmediated access to (or identification with) the patient; for the patient's experience is not "objectively" available, and cannot be grasped or inspected as such—whether through an act of cognitive intuition or through an act of affective attunement (Stern 1985 145). In Schafer's view, the analyst can only be empathizing with the analysand *as he or she exists in some constructed model*; for the analyst, then, "the analysand is not somehow objectively knowable outside this model. . . . As an analyst, one empathizes with one's idea of analysand" (Schafer 1983 35). Moreover, given the variety of theoretical orientations in psychoanalysis, as well as the reality of individual differences in style and temperament, "there are numerous, perhaps countless, mental models of any one analysand that may be constructed, *all* more or less justified by 'data' and by reports of beneficial effects on empathizing and the analytic process" (1983 40).

Yet the model thus constructed is not an arbitrary one and is not unconstrained by formal considerations. It is a model, for example, which presupposes that in imagining (or narrating) their own self-presentations, analysands are always responding to the current structure of their analytic situations, "and to their analysts' modes of thinking and responding" (42). Hence, the model that is constructed is (or should be) a model of the patient's self *only* insofar as it is in analysis with a patient's analyst.[28] It is therefore, a dialogical and ideographic model (one which presupposes the presence-to-the-patient of a *particular* therapist), and it is in this sense that Schafer calls it a model of the patient's "second self." But this second self (in terms of which the person of the patient appears to the analyst) is mirrored by the *analyst's* second self, through which he or she approaches the analytic encounter.

An important feature of this equally "fictive" (or artificial) second self is the so-called "affirmative orientation" of the analyst, described by Schafer as follows:

> In empathizing, the analyst assumes, at least implicitly, that whatever the analysand is doing or experiencing, it is what is essential that he or she do under the extremely adverse circumstances that prevail unconsciously or in "psychical reality." (1983 45–46)

Not only must the analyst's second self *grant* that whatever the patient is doing is "reasonable" (i.e., what anyone would do under such dangerous psychic circumstances), but further, that the patient's actions and experiences comprise a "meaningful totality" (a "text"), defined most exactly through their mutual implications. It is in this "fictive," unsentimental (and non-psychological) sense that the analyst empathically affirms the analysand by assuming, "coherence and potential intelligibility in everything the analysand brings up or refrains from bringing up" (47). The empathic action of the analyst is thus most evident *not* when he or she is successfully "decoding" target utterances of the patient or uncovering the "real" experience of the patient, but when he or she is "listening horizontally," and opening him- or herself up to the text, making contact with it, and recognizing "distinctions between what has never been said before, what is being repeated, and what is repeated but slightly changed" (Spence, in Reppen 1985 230). In this connection, one cannot help but recall Gadamer's notion of the *anticipation of completeness:* that is, the presumption in hermeneutics that the object of understanding forms a potential, intelligible unity, a self-coherent whole, and that one can therefore use the regulative ideal of unity to assess the adequacy of one's interpretations of its various parts. The conclusion follows, then, that Schafer's conception of empathic activity likewise involves the presumption (or narrative fiction) of the patient's intelligible unity. It is as if the patient's psychical reality (itself accessible only through explicit or implicit narrative accounts) constitutes a potentially intelligible, and indefinitely interpretable, *text.*

For Schafer, empathic activity is thus conceivable only within the dialogical context of a "fictive" analytic relationship, whose twin poles are the narrative devices of the analyst's and analysand's "second selves." But if empathy is conceivable only in this mode, how, then, is it to be identified and recognized? Now the scientist, in wrestling with such a question, seeks to specify the process that hypothetically underlies empathic activity, and in this manner, identify (or predict) instances of such a process as these are likely to occur under certain conditions, prospectively in time. In marked contrast, for the historical psychoanalyst Schafer, "there is a major retrospective aspect to the identification of empathizing" (1983 55). What counts as an example of empathizing will often only be learned after the fact, by looking backward, when the analysand, having changed, "will be using a new perspective on the history of the analytic relationship, and the original empathizing may have helped make the change of perspective possible . . ." (55). In other words, from the narrative position (or retrospective stance) of the analyst's second self, there may well be more to an action than could have entered into its creation at the moment of its execution. Prior "goings-on" (e.g., the original empathizing) now become significant, but only by virtue of being linked to important events which follow: most notably, the revised edition of the patient's self-narrative, with respect to which the analyst's original conduct can justifiably be *redescribed* as empathic. The analyst, we recall, is never encountering the patient's subjective experience in its aboriginal form; he or she is always viewing it as constructed and reconstructed (as told and retold), and is therefore accessing it only through implicit or explicit narrative accounts. But the patient's narrative is ineluctably *retrospective,* and the analyst's retelling of that narrative is no less so. Thus, what now counts as empathy is known only by virtue of looking backward. And the analyst, having the advantage of hindsight (as well as "theory"), will tell a different "empathic story" now or in the future than the one he and the analysand might have told in the past.

The fact that empathizing is retrospectively identified suggests that in this way (as in others), Schafer is proposing a historical model of psychoanalytic understanding. Surely his point is this: that the logic of such understanding must hinge upon an essential tension or interplay between empathic awareness here and now (and there and then) and its subsequent retrospective formulation. There is, more exactly, a back and forth movement (or circular loop) between empathy and retrospection, so that it becomes possible, for example, to assert that

> the more freely and completely one knows relevant versions of the past, the richer one's empathic comprehension of what is taking place in the psychoanalytic session, and the keener one's interpretations of transference and resisting. (Schafer 1983 208)

Such circular understanding in psychoanalysis can also be visualized as a kind of spiral of narrative knowing, in which empathic action is always being retrospectively narrativized, and in which such narrations, in turn, engender new and richer (hermeneutic) understandings of empathic practice. This, in short, is the kind of knowledge (as argued in Chapter 3) which is historically structured, because it exhibits and reflects the "dialogue" between empathy and retrospection.

2. *Narrative as Inquiry.* Historical psychoanalysis is limited to making meaning out of our experience of the past. But accordingly to Schafer, such experience is always viewed as constructed and reconstructed, and the analyst only encounters it through explicit or implicit narrative accounts (1983 186). From the analyst's point of view, there is thus no "independent" biographical material that counts; all "facts," be they facts of the analysand's past or facts of the here and now, exist only in *narrated* versions of them (1983 195). This is why it is reasonable to assert, for example, that Freud's theory of the development of the female is a theory based on an interpretation of the analysand's history (or of the evidence of narration), not on the nature of being female.[29]

It follows that the patient appears to the psychoanalytic clinician and theorist as a set of actual or potential narrative actions—so that even disclaimed actions (e.g., "the impulse overwhelms me") and acts of imagining and fantasizing are now construed as "narratives or tellings that constitute experience" (243), rather than as reports of some objectively existent introspectible experience, fact, or process. There is veritably no exit from the circle of narrative. The historical analyst does not traffic in objectively existent experience and process, and is himself confined to retelling (reinterpreting) the tellings and retellings of the patient. At the same time, Schafer argues, narrative is also *productive:* it constitutes or brings into being "new experience":

> The life history keeps being rewritten, not just because there are fewer gaps, disguises, misunderstandings and limitations, but also because there are more perspectives or strategies of definition and organization. In this way, *new actions constantly come into being.* (Schafer 1983 87, my emphasis)

This, then, is the paradoxical achievement of narrative as inquiry: it not only retells or redescribes the past; it also constitutes or brings something new into being. The question now becomes: how, exactly, is this achieved; how does this paradox figure in the construction of what Schafer calls the "psychoanalytical narrative"?

The psychoanalytic narrative is regarded "as a co-authored text produced and progressively revised by two members of the same narrative and interpretative community" (Schafer 1984 404). It is actually an endpoint of a dialogical-hermeneutic process, whose beginning consists in the narrative actions (tellings and retellings) of the analysand. The analysand is typically understood as embodying a narrative strategy through which various story lines are used "to develop ever new opportunities for repeating and perpetuating unconsciously maintained infantile psychosexual dilemmas and dangers" (Schafer 1983 271). In other words, the analyst (notwithstanding his empathic or "affirmative" orientation) does not and cannot take the patient's story at face value; he or she must rather see in that story its usefulness for representing the necessity for renunciation, inhibition, punishment, and compromise (Schafer 1983 258). The patient, in short, is recognized as being in unconscious danger, which is why the therapeutic (or *practical*) task for the therapist "is to help the analysand consciously to recognize danger situations and to understand how in his or her life history these situations evolved and persisted and the means that were adopted to cope with them" (96).[30]

The psychoanalyst begins by listening to the patient's story, realizing that each tale or narration told thus points beyond itself to something the storyteller did not intend to say.[31] Eventually, the analyst retells something told by the analysand, and reflects on the historical significance of the analysand's response to that narrative transformation. "In the narration of this moment of dialogue," writes Schafer, "lies the structure of the analytic past, present and future" (239). This is how the "psychoanalytic life history" comes into being. It is no normative, chronological ("developmental") life history; it is rather a story that "begins in the middle," in the transferential present of the analytic situation. The psychoanalytic life history proceeds to be repeatedly retold and reinterpreted, and in an important sense there is no single or conclusive life history to be told. The narrative account changes as themes and questions change, and in Schafer's view, it will require "several basic themes at least to help retell a life story adequately along analytic lines" (Schafer 1984 404). Yet, while themes and story lines may vary widely (generating different histories of the "past"), there is always a certain constancy in the *plot*. For any well-formed psychoanalytic life history is emplotted: (a) through themes or story lines stated in terms of conflictual, sexual, and aggressive wishing and imagining; (b) in the form of narrative actions susceptible to reinterpretation in the context of the transference (and resisting); or (c) as interpretations whose content typically stresses the archaic, bodily meanings of narrative actions (Schafer 1978). It is also in such a sense that the psychoanalytic life history necessarily *constitutes* psychic reality. For psychic reality is actually the product of narrative structures (e.g., themes, plots, narrative stances); thus, the psychoanalytic life history is not "about" psychic reality, as if it actually represented an objective or extralinguistic reality, but is, in fact, a construction of it.[32]

The psychoanalytic life history is not, however, the end point of the interpretative process. The ultimate "object" of the historical narrative is not the patient's "life," nor even his or her psychic reality. It is rather the analytic encounter itself. In Schafer's words:

> Developing the psychoanalytic biography retains great importance, but what is more clearly recognized now is that the importance of the biography depends on the extent to which it enhances the understanding of the analysis itself. (1983 208)

This means that psychoanalysis, as a theoretical (and historical) enterprise, is actually viewed as the reflexive study of itself. The significance of the psychoanalytic life history is therefore dependent upon its recontextualization within the history of the analytic encounter. What is called the "psychoanalytic narrative" is, in fact, this superordinate narration of the history of the analytic encounter; as such, it has as its "objects" not only the psychic reality of the analysand but also that of the analyst, since *both* are implicated (as historically situated "texts") in changing and alternative versions of the past.

The "psychoanalytic narrative" is thus the *terminus ad quem* of a dialogical-hermeneutic process in which psychical realities are creatively redescribed and narratively configured, and in which the analysand joins in the "retelling" as the analysis progresses. As such, the psychoanalytic narrative is also an expression of *situated* and *contextual* understanding (Gadamer 1975). It is situated because there is no neutral (unsituated) vantage from which to assess the "real" meaning of past and present experience;[33] and it is contextual by virtue of the "dialogical structure" of its own practice. Schafer's historical psychoanalysis in this way appears to instantiate Gadamer's "conditions" of hermeneutic understanding.

3. *Historical Truth*. The question of historical truth pertains to the validity and referentiality of narrative discourse. To what extent, for example, does the psychoanalytic narrative (or an aspect of it) represent some extralinguistic reality, such as the *unconscious past*? Schafer's answer to this question is characteristically Gadamerian, in that it affirms the thesis that the unconscious subtext of the psychoanalytic narrative is both found and made. We recall that, for Gadamer, effective understanding involves a

"fusion of horizons" in which the historically conditioned concerns of the interpreter are integrated with the object of understanding in such a way that this integration determines the content of the object. This means: (1) that the object of understanding (e.g., past experience) cannot be recovered in its pristine purity, since to attempt to do so would only be to deprive it of the meaning it must have from the historian's current and prejudiced perspective; (2) that the historical distance (from the object) that is implicit in the situatedness of understanding is not an obstacle to valid knowledge, but an ontological condition of it, since it decisively determines the very nature of that which we try to understand. In short, for both Gadamer and Schafer, the object of understanding (e.g., the "unconscious") is at once dialogically encountered (or "found") and narratively constructed (or "made"), and this is as it should be in light of the situated and contextual conditions of understanding in general.

The view that the "unconscious past" is both found and made is nicely illustrated by Schafer's treatment of transference-repetitions:

> But once they get to be viewed as historically grounded actions and subjectively defined situations, as they do upon being interpreted and worked through, they appear as having always been . . . inventions of the analysand's making and so, as his or her responsibility. In being seen as versions of one's past life, they may be changed in significant and beneficial ways. Less and less are they presented as purely inevitable happenings, as a fixed fate, or as the well-established way of the world. (1983 131)

It is worth observing that in these remarks, Schafer not only depicts the past as both found and made, but also as conceptually implicated in the present. Recall that we have access to the unconscious past only through implicit or explicit narrative accounts—and that such accounts (narrative reconstructions of the infantile past and the transferential present) are logically interdependent. This is why Schafer is again in accord with Gadamer when he concludes that analytic work (i.e., hermeneutic understanding) "is temporally circular rather that unidirectionally retrospective, and the so-called past and present may not be regarded as independent variables that are testable one against the other" (196). A final observation is also in order. In representing the unconscious past as both found and made, Schafer succeeds in eliciting a key feature of the analysand's movement from a "practical" to a "historical" relationship to his or her past—this being, as I have argued elsewhere (see Chapter 3), essential to the acquisition of historical self-understanding, and hence, to the therapeutic action of psychoanalysis.

The fact remains that the problem of historical truth is not quite settled or resolved by viewing the psychoanalytic narrative as both found and made. The issue of "referentiality" needs now to be confronted directly. We do so by first recognizing that any historical narrative is composed of at least two kinds of referents: (1) a first order of referents which are the events, characters, and actions that make up the story; and (2) a second order of referents—namely, the *plot,* which configures episodes, events, and actions into some sort of whole (or unity). Clearly, first-order referents may contain information which possesses extrinsic reference, or represents some extralinguistic reality. But as I have already argued in Chapter 3, historical truth does not primarily pertain to the determination of such extrinsically referential facts of the first order. It must pertain, instead, to the validity of the plot, that is, to the second order of referents which contains information generated by the specific type of coherence used to order narrative sentences into an intelligible and unified discourse (Polkinghorne 1988). Now surely, the second-order plot will somehow "fit" the (first-order) facts, and no historical narrative can justifiably deny, ignore, or falsify relevant facts. But it is equally true that a variety of organizing schemes (plots) can fit the same facts (e.g., see Spence 1982, on narrative truth; and Eagle 1984b). Hence, we are still left with the question of whether *plots* are extrinsically referential, or if not, how to assess their cognitive status,[34] and how to choose among equally reasonable and believable candidates.

As noted earlier, critical philosophers of history are divided over whether narrative can ever represent the extralinguistic reality of the past. It is not at all clear that the logic of emplotment can generate a true representation of the coherence of reality (or that human actions are actually configured in the form of plots). This is why there is a certain skepticism toward the claims of those like Marx and Engels (Tucker 1961 126–29), who argued that the specific logic of dialectical emplotment actually corresponds to the real coherence of history and nature. But though we rightly remain doubtful that plots can be *extrinsically* referential, we may still speculate that they are *intrinsically* so. As introduced above, the notion of intrinsic reference (or intralinguistic referentiality) rests on the intuition that "our understanding of reality already includes the conception of it as existing independently of us and our understanding." Such an intuition closely resembles Brentano's and Husserl's idea of *intentionality,* according to which such mental acts as judgments, beliefs, desires, and valuations are always *about* or *of* this or that. In other words, on the occasion of any mental act, whether there be an objectively existent referent or not, there is always an "intentionally inexistent" object; so that, for example, when I desire the apple in front of me, the apple is the object of my desire in one sense of "object" . . . but there is also another object, the intentionally inexistent apple, which is the common and peculiar element in all desire for apples (Husserl 1964). It is in such a sense, then, that *intrinsic reference* implies, for the narrative author and agent, a linguistically mediated experience of some intelligible unity, the truth or validity of which is of a different order from the coherence generated by such non-narrative discourses as empirical-analytic science. In this view, there is thus a distinctive meaning (or intentional object) created or constituted through narrative emplotment, of an intrinsically referential type, which cannot be translated into scientific discourse without distortion or loss.[35]

As we return to Schafer's psychoanalytic narrative, and specifically, to the *logic* of its emplotment, we find that the "psychoanalytic past" can now be characterized as an intrinsically referential (or intentional) object of the second order. As such, as a historical object of understanding, this "past" is also viewed as an outcome of a "fusion of horizons" (Gadamer 1975), in which our historically conditioned concerns are integrated with the object of understanding in such a way that this *integration* determines the content (or meaning) of the object for us.

It follows from such an account that alternative narratives of the psychoanalytic past are not necessarily competing candidates for a correct depiction of how things were. For the "psychoanalytic past" (the product of such narratives) is neither an objectively accessible "given," nor simply an arbitrary or imaginative construction. The underlying idea (in Schafer's presentation) is rather as follows: although past events cannot be changed, one can alter the form of the plot that is used to configure them into a whole and connect them to the present.[36] In this way, even the accidents and happenings of the past can be turned into actions (i.e., events for which one is now willing to accept responsibility).

What Schafer is actually proposing is a certain logical innovation which I shall here label "the causal efficacy of emplotment," and its essential thrust is this: (a) that past events are not meaningful in themselves, but are given significance as "living representations" by the configuration (or plot) of the narrative; and (b) that since the past is seen as meaningful (and efficacious) only *because of* the current (transferential) narrative, what is now brought into question is the logical assumption that prior events cause succeeding events, or that "facts" have precedence over the meanings attached to them (Culler 1981). As Schafer puts it, the conventional distinction between past and present no longer holds, insofar as narrative emplotment in the here and now is always operating to reinterpret meaningless past events in order to give them a "force" they did not originally have. The past, in this radically historicist interpretation, is "caused by" the present, and is experienced as an intelligible unity of meaning, intrinsically referential, and generated in the here and now through the logic of psychoanalytic emplotment. This past (the unconscious past) may be viewed as found: (1) because it must accommodate or "fit" the facts of the first order; (2) because it is dependent upon raw materials (meaningless or extralinguistic past events) which are "narratively reprocessed" into present meanings; and (3) because its claim to truth is ultimately based on evidence.[37] Yet this past—the psychoanalytic past—is also viewed as made, because it is an artifact of the logic of narrative emplotment, and because its claim to *truthfulness* is ultimately based on acceptance or conviction (Freud 1937b; Spence 1982). Indeed, since the "psychoanalytic past" has such a complex character, or logic, Schafer can propose the following:

> Because the reconstruction of the psychoanalytic past necessarily takes place in the here and now clinical dialogue, it remains an interpretable and reinterpretable feature of the here and now. This means that the past is always taken as that which is currently being told in one or another conflictual analytic context. (1983 194)

Since the past is always taken as that which is currently being told and retold, it follows finally that

> analytic interpretation . . . far from unearthing and resurrecting old and archaic experiences as such . . . develops new, vivid, verbalizable and verbalized versions of those experiences. (Schafer 1983 189)

Conclusion. This section has had two interrelated objectives. The first and more general one has been to discern in Schafer's mature views evidence of a historically conditioned conception (or model) of psychoanalytic knowledge. The second and more specific objective has been to introduce, in broad outline, Schafer's version of the "psychoanalytic past," recognized here as both *found* and *made,* and hence, as a distinctive and exemplary expression of historical understanding.

1. With respect to the first objective, I contend that Schafer succeeds in developing a historically conditioned *model* of psychoanalytic knowledge, explicable according to the following formula:

(a) the analyst is engaged in historically structured and historically situated listening
(b) in a dialogical, transactive, and transferential context
(c) and in this way, generates narrative productions.

Two points are immediately worth stressing. First, the "co-authored" narrative productions (c) feed back as input (via a circular loop) to both analyst and analysand (historically situated interpreters), and help to organize the "horizon" (or effective history) of historically structured listening (a). Second, the entire process, viewed as either an interminable or terminable unity (Freud 1937a), may itself become the recursive object of historical and hermeneutic interpretation—the outcome of which is called the psychoanalytic narrative—the reflexive history of the analytic encounter whose beginning lies always in the transferential "middle" (or present). Of this overarching narrative (and its subversion of any chronological or "developmental" structure) Schafer has the following to say:

> The present is not the autobiographical present. . . . Once the analysis is under way, the autobiographical present is found to be no clear point in time at all. One does not even know how to conceive that present; more and more it seems to be both a repetitive, crisis-perpetuating misremembering of the past and a way of living defensively with respect to a future which is . . . imagined fearfully and irrationally on the model of the past. (1983 238)

2. Turning to the second objective, I have argued that the psychoanalytic past comes into view as a narratively constructed "experience of the past," as the *intentional object* of the analysand's ever-changing and continuously revised psychoanalytic life history. But this life history (in terms of which the psychoanalytic past first appears) never stands as a direct representation of how the past really was, and is itself only a subordinate narrative moment within the more inclusive context of the psychoanalytic

narrative. Therefore, the psychoanalytic past, at its most historically coherent, is actually an artifact of the psychoanalytic narrative, or more exactly, of the logic of its emplotment.

To summarize and recapitulate, the psychoanalytic past counts as (a) a historical construction of the psychoanalytic past, (b) an expression of hermeneutic understanding, and (c) a constitutive element of a normative psychoanalytic theory.

- Schafer's construction of the psychoanalytic past is *historical* because: (1) it exhibits and reflects the dialogue between empathy and retrospection; (2) it discovers as well as constitutes new kinds of meaningful experience or knowledge, and therefore validates itself as a form of inquiry; and (3) its understandings of the past are assessed not only as historically true (or false) in terms of what the evidence obliges us to believe, but also as *truthful* (or not) in terms of their power to command conviction and assent, and in terms of their pragmatic value for performance to come and as instruments for change.
- Schafer's version of the psychoanalytic past is an expression of *hermeneutic* understanding because: (1) as an object of such understanding, it is the outcome of a "fusion of horizons"; (2) as an intersubjectively mediated object of understanding, it fulfills the Gadamerian requirement that understanding is possible only by virtue of being conditioned by both its effective history and its dialogical structure; and (3) thus stands over and against the *objectivism* inherent in both traditional hermeneutics and empirical-analytic science.
- Finally, Schafer's interpretation of the psychoanalytic past is a *normative* one because it belongs to a theoretical project, an important purpose of which is to justify how psychoanalysis can be understood as a "truthful" and "transformative" practice.

The Narrative Past and the Objective Past: A Comparative Perspective

By viewing Schafer's project as a specialized expression of philosophical hermeneutics, I have been able to elicit its historical, hermeneutic, and

normative features. It is in terms of these same features that the prototypical idea of the psychoanalytic past comes into view. For purposes of ease
of exposition, this particular (though exemplary) version of the psychoanalytic past is now designated the "narrative past." It is only one of
several distinguishable variants of the historically constructed psychoanalytic past. And it is therefore to the *comparative* analysis of such historical
constructions that I now turn my attention.[38]

The contrast which is most decisive is that between the narrative past (as
introduced above), and what must now be termed the "objective past."
The latter is no mere conceptual fiction or figure of speech. For unlike the
narrative past which is intersubjectively mediated and intrinsically referential, the objective past is a past in which events and experience are
presumed to possess an inherent structure and force, independent of the
imaginative or narrative activity of mind. This past is extrinsically (or even
extralinguistically) referential, and what it refers to are the so-called "living representations" of past conditions: these representations being either
present effects and/or current expressions of past conditions. The objective past (so viewed) is no narrative device, but is given as a stable and
preexistent object of knowledge, the nature of which is not at all determined by the historical distance between it and the historically situated
historian.

The objective past may be authenticated in two modes. (a) In the mode
of the *actual* past, the past is articulated as closely as is possible through
the concepts and categories of the historical actors, authors, and texts.
The actual past is therefore the past in terms of the knowledge, beliefs,
and self-understandings of historically situated agents. We recall that this
is the past that is elicited when traditional (or objectivist) hermeneutics
"empathically" reconstructs the original message, meanings, or intentions
carried in cultural life-expressions. (b) At the same time, objectivity is also
realized in a second mode, the mode of the *real* past. The real past is the
past articulated as closely as possible through the concepts and categories
of the scientific historian, and is therefore the past in terms of the knowledge, methods, and techniques of scientific abstraction. In its most extreme form (when retrospection has not only displaced empathy, but has
itself been divested of any temporal perspective), this mode is no longer a
historical construction at all, but is tantamount to a scientific construction
(of the psychoanalytic past), in that it rejects all contextual and configura-

tional understanding in favor of atemporal analysis and analytic abstraction (see Chapter 3, "Science and History: Diverging Commitments"; and Chapter 5).

Since my concern in this chapter is with the *historical* construction of the psychoanalytic past, it must be conceded that the objective past is most relevant in either its actual mode or in its mixed mode. But upon closer inspection, it appears that the purely actual mode of the objective past is as unacceptable as the purely real mode. For psychoanalytic understanding can never rest content with reconstructions solely in terms of the agent's (or patient's) concepts and categories. If it were thus restricted to the reconstructions of the patient's actual past, it would lose access to the patient's "inner world" or "psychic reality" (insofar as these concepts imply a "depth" which is beyond the purview of the *conscious* concepts and categories of historically situated agents). We must therefore conclude that the objective past is necessarily authenticated in a *mixed* mode. In other words, the historically constructed objective past is always expressed as a *composite* past, as some compound or mix of the actual and real pasts (see also Chapter 2, "The Mixed Construct of Psychoanalytic Development").

Most clinical theorists are at least in part historical psychoanalysts; but unlike Schafer, they operate within an objectivist (Proposition 1) tradition and cannot give credence to the reality of the narrative past. It follows that notwithstanding their apparent differences, such theorists are all firmly committed to some version of the objective past, and in this way echo Freud's fundamental observation in "The Dynamics of Transference" (1912c) that the childhood capacity to love forms a cliche or "stereotype" which perpetually repeats and reproduces itself as life goes on. Thus clinical theorists as opposed as Kernberg (1975) and Kohut (1971) may differ in the weight they give to the actual versus the real past (with Kohut's "experience-near" discourse, for example, weighted more heavily toward the actual mode); but both are at one in their commitment to the *objectivity* of the psychoanalytic past, and must grant that the "living representations" (of which I spoke earlier in this discussion) are, indeed, the extrinsic or even extralinguistic referents of an objective past. Moreover, both analysts are in further accord that such representations are mental representations signifying more or less unconscious beliefs, expectations, and intentions, as well as more or less unconscious images of self and others; and that as living representations, these are to be construed as either present effects (or current expressions) of some past condition or *prototype,* i.e., some real or imagined event or situation which is (a) prefigurative, (b) prior in time, and (c) causally related to the present representation (or behavior). The past prototype, following Freud, is assumed to survive in (or be carried by) the present representation. And in this depiction, which seems fundamental to any traditional view of psychoanalysis as a "truthful" theory and "transformative" practice, no current difficulties can by themselves neurotically impair one's mental health, except as they are vivified by *memories* (of the past?) which persist inappropriately in the present.

In summary, representations are "alive" and efficacious (and thus, potentially dangerous) because they carry within them the power or imprint of a past "prototype." I will now briefly review two clinical formulations from the recent literature, since they seem to me to count as paradigmatic examples of the relevance of the objective past for historical and scientific psychoanalysis.

1. First, the concept of unconscious pathogenic beliefs is central to the "updated and sophisticated ego psychology" of Weiss, Sampson, and their colleagues (Weiss and Sampson 1986; see also Eagle 1984a 18, 95–106). This research program (which incorporates both scientific and historical components) will be examined at some length in Chapter 5; for now, it is sufficient to observe that it is a program based on a cognitive psychoanalytic theory which assumes "that a patient's psychopathology stems largely from unconscious beliefs developed during childhood" (Curtis et al. 1988 257). Pathogenic beliefs are so called because they are frightening and constricting; they are, in short, "irrational," and along with the associated fears, guilt, and anxieties, they "hinder or prevent a person from pursuing goals," notwithstanding the individual's "strong unconscious wish to change these beliefs, overcome the inhibiting feelings which stem from them, and thereby gain greater control of his or her inner and outer worlds" (Curtis et al. 1988 257–58).

An example of such a belief is the patient's conviction that he or she is capable of seriously harming others (e.g., Mother) if he or she does not seriously tend to them.[39] Such a belief is assumed to be a *living* representation, because it carries within it the power and imprint of a past prototype. Moreover, such a belief is *pathogenic* only because some current situation is infected by memories (of the past prototype) which persist "inappropriately" in the present. Weiss, Sampson, and their colleagues further assume that the patient is characteristically motivated to test the therapist (within the transference) to disconfirm the aforementioned pathogenic belief, and that this assumption must underlie and enlighten any rational plan of therapy. Summing up, then: the Weiss-Sampson research program includes (as we shall see further in Chapter 5) certain crucial empirical-analytic components; for now, however, it is enough to infer that unconscious pathogenic beliefs are also recognized as "living representations" of a historically constructed objective past, and that this past—an objective psychoanalytic past—is authenticated as a composite past, as some variable mix or compound of the real and actual pasts.

2. The second example cited is the concept of splitting, which in my view, is as central and pivotal to object relations theory and borderline psychopathology as pathogenic beliefs are to ego psychology and neurotic conflict. Following Kernberg (1975), Volkan (1976), Horowitz (1977), and Grotstein (1981), "splitting" is taken to refer to an underlying and hypothetical *process* by which mental representations of the self and others are segregated, such that part rather than whole images are formed. Thus, "objects" come to be seen as either good or bad, rather than as having both good and bad attributes.

Now the hypothetical process of splitting properly belongs to an empirical-analytic or scientific system of psychoanalytic understanding. But the segregated affect states and object representations (which are said to result from the process) may also be construed as constituents of a historically constructed objective past. As such, the patient's split self-concept, good/bad image of others, and unstable expectations concerning interpersonal relations, must again be assumed to be "living" representations, because they carry within themselves the power and imprint of past prototypes.

In the present case, however, it is *not* that memories persist inappropriately in the present, but rather, that the person (or patient)

> has no access to modulating memories of previous positive feelings which might temper the reaction to frustration. The sense of perspective, which requires the integration of mixed experiences across time, is impaired, leading to an unrealistic and at times dramatic overreaction to the experience of the moment. (Marmar and Horowitz 1986 23)

In other words, what gives power in the here and now to the past prototype is the *absence* (and not the repressed presence) of certain narratively reconstructed memories (i.e., memories associated with self-regulation and with affective self-modulation).[40] It would seem, then, that these split self-images and object images are indeed the "living representations" of an objective (and extralinguistic) psychoanalytic past, but they are only such by virtue of the *presence of an absence*. The patient's sense of narrative or historical perspective (through which he or she might integrate mixed experiences over time) is somehow impaired. We are thus tempted (from this *historical* point of view) to postulate a deficit in or loss of "narrative competence," just as we may be tempted (from an empirical-analytic point of view) to postulate a developmental arrest (or regression) in "cognitive functioning." But whichever the preferred mode of explanation (history or science), it seems sufficient to observe, for the discussion at hand, that the process of splitting presupposes the existence of an objective psychoanalytic past—and that this past (at least insofar as it is historically constructed) is authenticated as a composite past—and points to a prelinguistic or extralinguistic (or even biological) "prototype," which survives in (or is carried by) the living representations of the present.

Causality and Narrativity: The Dialectics of Historical Construction

So far, discussion has focused on the substantive features of the psychoanalytic past, or on the constituent components of the objective past, but not on how these are historically connected or coherently organized into some narrative construction. Let me therefore turn, in the following pages, to the specific problem posed by the *historical construction* of an objective past.

Recall, first, that Roy Schafer constructs a hermeneutical (or Gadamerian) history of the analytic encounter. It is an *acausal* history, because the concept of action which lies at its base compels us to regard each (narrative) action "as inherently spontaneous, as starting from itself . . ." (Schafer 1978 48). This acausal history Schafer calls the "psychoanalytic narrative," and its product (or intentional object) is designated the "narrative past." The narrative past (an artifact of the logic of psychoanalytic emplotment) is conceptually implicated in, or is an interpretable aspect of, the narrative (and transferential) present and its principle of coherence is the regulative ideal of interpretive unity and meaningful continuity. As we turn to the objective past, the situation is very different. For it is evident that the objective past, which is contingently and existentially distinct from the empirical present, belongs to a history whose principle of coherence is at least, in part, causality; we are therefore forced to ponder the relation between an acausal and hermeneutical narrative on the one hand (Schafer's), and a causal history on the other (Edelson 1986). The competing claims of *narrativity* and *causality* are thrown into relief, and we now wish to learn if a historical construction of the psychoanalytic past can possibly do justice to both.

Edelson (1985, 1986) is one of a relatively small number of psychoanalytic theorists who has explicitly argued for the validity and reliability of a historical construction of what I have here termed the objective past. In his view, for example, Freud used his narrative case studies not only to establish facts (or to illustrate clinical phenomena), but also to tell a causal story. Thus Edelson writes:

> A single case is often used to spell out causal mechanisms: this is a particularly important feature of Freud's case studies. What is called a psychoanalytic narrative by some is in part at least an effort to explicate causal mechanisms, to show how one kind of state of affairs or events can lead to, produce, or generate another, or how relations among constituent entities can cause or be realized by the properties of a certain kind of structure. (1986 592)

It follows, then, that in Edelson's account psychoanalytically relevant psychological entities (e.g., inhibitions, compulsions, representational anomalies, etc.) must be viewed as concrete and occurrent in the patient's mind;[41] only by being viewed in this way can they or their component properties ever count as real causes, and hence, as open to manipulation and control in such contexts as those of therapeutic treatment and empirical-analytic (experimental) investigation. At the same time, however, it remains a legitimate task for causal history (independent of treatment and experiment) to construct an *argument* for the real existence of such psychological causes by showing

> that a cause has the power to produce its effects by virtue of its structure or properties, and also just how—by virtue of what processes or mechanisms—its causal influence is propagated from one space-time locale to another. (1986 97)

Now Edelson takes great pains to defend the utility of such an "N = 1" narrative argument. Our present concern, though, is not with his controversial position regarding the probative value of a "historical" case study (see also Grunbaum 1984; and Spence 1982), but rather, with the nature and role of causality as such in the historical construction of the psycho-analytic past.

Our understanding of the nature of psychoanalytic causality is ad-vanced by Edelson's carefully drawn distinction between (a) etiological explanation on the one hand, and (b) constitutive explanation on the other (see Salmon 1984 269–70 for a general account). In the former case (the etiological), causes are external to (but impinge upon) the system whose properties are to be explained. Edelson offers the classic example of "the effect of one moving . . . body upon the motion of another with which it collides" (1986 100). In the latter case, the case of constitutive or functional explanation, causes are internal to (or constitu-ents of) the system whose properties are to be explained; the example now offered is of pressure inside a container being caused by (or being the expression of) the impact of moving molecules on the side of the vessel.

Of particular relevance to my argument in this chapter are Edelson's constitutive (or internal and functional) explanations, for the following two reasons:

1. First, these are the kinds of explanations for which transference phenomena offer relevant evidence. As Edelson puts it:

> Such explanations involve inferences about causally efficacious psychologi-cal entities existing or occurring in the here and now (including . . . memo-ries or fantasies of the past in which early important objects play a part in the state of affairs represented). (1986 110)

But Edelson immediately goes on to add that "explaining the origin of such causally efficacious . . . entities is logically independent of the consti-tutive explanation." In other words, the explanation of the origin or survival of what I earlier called the past prototype lies beyond the scope of the *constitutive* causal narrative, since the latter pertains only to contexts where "cause lies in the presence of an unconscious conflict or dilemma in the here and now" (1986 111). Edelson's point is that etiological or genetic explanations are at a different level than constitutive or functional explanations. This implies, contra Grunbaum's claim (1984), that the psychoanalyst need not use here and now transference phenomena as question-begging evidence for *etiological* causal explanations. On the con-trary, it now appears that the primary value of the historically constructed clinical case study is that it can offer evidence for the scientific credibility of *constitutive* explanations (explanations involving events occurring in, or proximate to, the psychoanalytic situation).

Several implications follow from such a thesis. First, it is evident that other forms of inquiry, such as non-historical empirical-analytic investigations, are needed to develop credible *etiological* explanations, inasmuch as only these are the kinds of explanations that can cope with remote, extraclinical events (prototypes), and the problem of the propagation of their causal influence over time. Second, it appears that any constitutive causal history which purports to represent the psychoanalytic past can, at best, postulate the original prototype as a necessary assumption (or as a speculative hypothesis), but cannot properly resolve the problem of its origin within the historical account itself. Thus, the causal history of the objective psychoanalytic past can never really settle matters of origin;[42] so, in this important sense, the objective past (as a historical construction) can only exist as a conceptual ideal, never as a fully realized or actualized state of affairs in a causally connected historical narrative. A third implication of Edelson's thesis is that the ultimate task of organizing etiological and constitutive explanations within one coherent system may well belong to psychoanalytic metapsychology. For it is metapsychology, and not clinical theory, which seems best equipped to generate the *developmental* models needed to explain intentionality and constitutive causality (in the here and now) in terms of "biological finalities" (and/or developmental and prototypical origins).[43]

2. The second reason for our present interest in constitutive causal explanations concerns its logical relation to Schafer's endeavor to develop an acausal, historical, and hermeneutical psychoanalysis. Recall that constitutive explanations refer to functional systems in which entities are internally (though causally) interrelated, and in which any one entity is "known" by virtue of its participation in the systemic whole. Now it can be reasonably asserted that these are precisely those systems which Schafer characteristically recomposes as networks of internally interrelated *meanings,* which are then interpretable (and redescribable) in terms of a continuous series of mutually implicative narrative actions. Any one narrative action or episode is thus "known" by virtue of its relation to (and role within) the story as a whole (Mandler 1984).[44]

Let us now turn to a specific instance in which Freud is said to offer a constitutive explanation of a patient's phobic symptoms. It should be readily apparent that this is exactly the kind of explanation which Schafer reformulates as a historical-hermeneutic interpretation of narrative action. In the instance cited, the phobic symptoms "express" (or are a function of) an unconscious conflict, but more precisely are *caused*

> by the patient's retrospective interpretation of a memory or fantasy of seeing, at a very early age, his mother and father having intercourse, in light of later sexual researches (and his preoccupation with castration); his simultaneous realization that gratification of his wishes for passive pleasure from his father seemed then to entail his being castrated; the fear of his father aroused by this realization; and displacement of the fear of animals. (Edelson 1986 102)

According to Edelson's account, conflict "causes" anxiety or fear, whose displacement results in the "effect" of phobic symptoms and this whole process is actually embodied in a functional system of more or less contemporary multicausal relationships. But Schafer (as we have already seen) would wish to reject any causal characterization of psychoanalytically relevant behavior; he would not see, in this connection, any point in bringing in notions of causality. For in his view, "acting anxiously" is an essential aspect of what we mean by conflict, "both when we interpret it clinically and when we speak of it theoretically" (1983 93). Hence, it becomes tautological to invoke causality (even constitutive or functional causality), since "the cause and that which it is supposed to explain are not logically independent and often they are identical" (Schafer 1983 93). Because *meanings* (actions, narrations) are in this way logically or conceptually imbedded in (or interrelated with) one another, they lack the necessary independence and contingency that would allow them to participate as true and concrete causal entities in functional relationships. Moreover (the argument continues), because such meanings, actions, and narrations are necessarily redescribable (by both agent and interpreter), and are therefore open to many different identifications, how can the causal historian (e.g., Edelson) ever be sure that he has hit upon the "real identity" motivating the agent's behavior?

Schafer's critique has thus brought us back to the original theme of this section: namely, the competing claims of "narrativity" and "causality," and whether or not a historical construction of the psychoanalytic past can possibly do justice to both. But this theme, we have just observed, really throws into relief the issue of the relation between objective facts or events on the one hand, and subjective (or intersubjectively mediated) meanings and narrations on the other. For example, is there ever sufficient regularity in the assignment of meanings, or in the identification of actions, to permit a place for causality in the historical construction of the psychoanalytic past?

My position is that there is, and for two reasons: (1) first and self-evidently, the interpretative communities to which persons belong largely determine the meanings of events for them (Fish 1980), and in this way are the most obvious source of regularities in the assignment of meanings; without such consensual validity and interpretative stability, communication within and among groups and subgroups would not really be possible; (2) second, and more specifically, the range of viable "identities" (for any human action or set of human actions) is surely constrained by "reality," that is for example—(a) by contextual cues surrounding an action, by the difficulty of an action (or task), and by the agent's experience with an action (Vallacher and Wegner 1987); as well as (b) by the organizational structures hypothesized to be inherent in the development of emotional and cognitive experience (Piaget 1971; Greenspan 1979; Lane and Schwartz 1987).

In other words, in the argument I am now advancing, the validity of the Schafer-Gadamer thesis is still affirmed: namely, the view that human action is indeed open to different identifications, translations, and narrative reconstructions, and that these are achieved through a "fusion of horizons," and thus depend not only on the agent's phenomenal organization of action, but also on the historically situated interpreter's "prejudices" and prejudgments. At the same time, however, I also propose that such narrative meanings and understandings do not merely comprise a system of internally related and linguistically mediated concepts, but may also be seen as constrained, conditioned, and stabilized by such reality factors as those just cited (e.g., organizational structures and contextual cues, as well as biological needs and reinforcement contingencies). Thus I am arguing on the one hand: (a) that actions and narrations possess an interpretative variability (and density) which many empirical-analytic psychologists are too prone to overlook and discount; and on the other hand, (b) that these same actions and narrations (meanings) reflect a stability and regularity which hermeneuticists are often unwilling or unable to recognize. In short, narrative actions, contra Schafer, qualify at least in part as *contingent* or *empirical* performances, and as such, may belong to "causal histories"; in this key respect, at least, Edelson's "objectivist" point of view is vindicated. But such actions and narrations also bear witness to the precedence of meaning over fact and therefore qualify as intelligible (or interpretable) events, open to the kind of historical-hermeneutic inquiry which Schafer has attempted to pursue in the context of American psychoanalysis.

Conclusion. My own position can now be summed up in the following way. Schafer's project remains the prototypical expression of historical understanding in American psychoanalysis, and it stands as such by virtue of its grounding in the philosophical hermeneutics of Gadamer. If Schafer's discourse is thus at the very epicenter of historical psychoanalysis, its outer regions are occupied by Edelson's causal narrative, which proceeds in the objectivist tradition common to both traditional hermeneutics and empirical-analytic science. Were we to posit a "continuum of historicality," its positive pole would thus be occupied by Schafer's discourse, and its negative pole by Edelson's. In between are a variety of psychoanalytic discourses, more or less historical (in terms of the argument developed in Part I of this book) and more or less hermeneutic (in terms of the Gadamerian tradition explored in this chapter). Beyond Edelson's causal narrative, which defines its outer limits, the "continuum of historicality" shades imperceptibly into empirical-analytic science, where discourse is characterized by its commitments to objectivity, to quantitative communication, and to analytic abstraction (see Chapters 3 and 5). It is recognized, of course, that any concrete example of psychoanalytic discourse is almost surely a *mixed* discourse, at once both more or less historical and more or less scientific, and more or less coherent in its expression as a composite or mixed discourse.

Focusing directly on historical psychoanalysis, the prototypical expression of which is Schafer's discourse, I now suggest the following conclusions:

1. meanings always have logical precedence over the facts to which they are attached;
2. causal analysis, though legitimate, can only play an adjunctive or ancillary role in the historical construction of a psychoanalytic past; and
3. the objective past remains a subordinate or subsidiary concep-

tion, since the psychoanalytic past, at its most historically coherent, is ultimately constituted as a narrative past.

These conclusions (though in my judgment hermeneutically acceptable) could not be fully endorsed by Schafer. He could not, for example, permit causal entities or causal connections to enter into the psychoanalytic narrative, since to do so would be to depart from any continuous sequence of historical interpretation and reinterpretation. Likewise, he could not allow the objective past to figure in the psychoanalytic past, since to do so would be to posit an abstraction (the "past prototype") which the evidence does not oblige us to believe. There is, in short, an unbridgeable gulf between the objective past as presented above, and the narrative past, which is—for Schafer—a past that is created as it is being spoken under the modifying influence of the analyst to whom it is ostensibly addressed (see also Leavy 1980 49).

In opposition, then, to Schafer's radically hermeneutic recommendations, I am suggesting that the "narrated actions" of both patient and analyst, agent and historian, are not only meaningful, interpretable, and historically situated performances, but also contingent and empirical ones; therefore, historical psychoanalysis is most validly characterized as involving a *dialectical tension* or interplay (but not a "Great Divide") between fact and meaning, causality and continuity, the objective past and the narrative past. Interestingly, and perhaps paradoxically, Schafer's entire project reflects and exhibits this dialectical tension, in the form of a sustained argument against objectivism in American psychoanalysis. Yet, were we to take Schafer's theoretical conclusions literally and *unhermeneutically*,[45] this tension would be lost and with it, the "historicality" of his psychoanalysis. And so the following conclusion may now be submitted: when this tension is no longer evident, as in purely literary expression and as in purely empirical-analytic discourse, historical understanding (in psychoanalysis as elsewhere) has been voided, disclaimed, or proscribed.

The Scope of Historical Psychoanalysis

We recall that for Schafer, psychoanalytic understanding is hermeneutically specified by its dialogical, transactive, and transferential conditions. In other words, the "truth" of such understanding is contingent on the clinical circumstances of its constitution—and in this sense must always be distinguished from the "truth" of psychoanalysis as an *extraclinical* empirical-analytic science (see Chapter 5). Even Edelson's non-hermeneutic "constitutive causal history" is logically bound to the clinical context, insofar as evidence for its explanations is derived from the *transferential* phenomena of the here and now. It is therefore the case that historical psychoanalysis, whether conceived as hermeneutical history (Schafer), or as constitutive causal history (Edelson), is necessarily dependent upon the evidence and/or conditions of analytic practice in the clinical setting.

It is hardly surprising, then, that historical psychoanalysis, so viewed, generates its own distinctive hermeneutic explications of clinical concepts (e.g., empathy, countertransference, resistance, and so on), and is capable in this way of advancing toward a coherent interpretation (or internal analysis) of therapeutic practice as a meaningful and self-moved activity, whose character is explicable in terms of principles inherent in it.[46] Yet historical psychoanalysis is not just relevant as a hermeneutical interpretation of the analytic encounter; its scope of application is far wider, and its range of relevance is by no means confined to the conceptual analysis or explication of therapeutic discourse. It therefore becomes my purpose in this section to convey the natural scope of historical psychoanalysis, particularly in its prototypical expression as narrative and hermeneutic inquiry. The potential scope of historical psychoanalysis is conveniently illustrated by focusing on two basic concepts of clinical psychology and psychiatry, and on the central features involved in their hermeneutic formulation. These are the concepts of (1) psychopathology, and (2) development.

1. *Psychopathology.* Although the word pathology has a passive sense, referring to that which one suffers, it seems wrong (or one-sided) to believe that a neurosis, for example, is simply passively experienced. Schafer, as a historical psychoanalyst (and as a logician of discourse), puts forth the alternative view when he writes:

> A neurosis is created and arranged and protected. It is . . . the construction of danger situations and the construction of emotional actions to take in these situations. Consequently, the diagnosis of neurosis is the diagnosis of the actions we are used to calling symptoms, neurotic character traits, impulses, defenses, affects, and functions. (1983 111–12)

In this constructivist position, it is not just the contents of psychopathology, but also its forms, which are viewed as meaningful constructions and as narrative achievements (or actions). What is thus called into question is a certain traditional psychoanalytic conception of psychopathology, which sees it solely as a function of regressive *processes,* in which "states of mind more primitive chronologically and developmentally gain ascendancy and . . . resemble, in structure and function, those postulated to be operative during infancy and early childhood" (McGlashan 1983 911).

To presume, as Schafer does, that neurotic or even psychotic conditions are intelligible as meaningful constructions and as narrative achievements, is not of course to see such conditions as purely volitional or as purely uncaused; nor is it to deny that genetic, neurobiological, and physiological factors play a role in the etiology and maintenance of such conditions. It is just to affirm that human meanings (which can and must be understood) frequently appear to arise from systems that themselves cannot be understood;[47] thus, our real concern (at least as historical psychoanalysts) is not, paradoxically, with eliciting the "natural history" (Nemiah 1961) of clinical syndromes (e.g., their incidence, onset, etiology, course, etc.), but with comprehending the historical construction (and reconstruction) of psychopathological biographies.

From within these parameters, it now becomes possible to introduce, in broad outline, some salient features of a historical-hermeneutic approach to psychoanalytic psychopathology. Such an approach is directed toward actual and fantasized past contents and past plights, but only insofar as these are more or less open to being constituted and reconstituted in new narrative accounts. In other words, the degree to which a patient's self-narrative is in the "subjunctive" mode (Bruner 1986), or is open to being "rewritten," becomes a relevant indicator of psychopathology; so that what is now diagnostically decisive is not the specific content of an individual's traumatic or conflictful past,[48] but rather *the capacity here and now* (in a dialogical context) to generate new and more empathic narrative perspectives on one's ineliminable past. Hence, the import of Erikson's well-known definition of ego integrity as "the acceptance of one's one and only life cycle as something that had to be, and that by necessity, permitted of no substitutions" (1963 263–69). For it is surely the case that historical psychoanalysis is particularly concerned with the recognition and explication of precisely those narrative practices, strategies, and competencies that seem to inhibit or promote the empathic acceptance (or historical awareness) of one's own ineliminable past (see also Chinen 1984; Schafer 1984; Wallulis 1990).

Viewed in this way, historical psychoanalysis is also disclosed as a *normative* endeavor. I mean by this that in its approach to psychopathology, it is always directed toward the identification and diagnosis of disordered or deformed narratives; this implies not only the possibility of a well-formed or canonical narrative (e.g., "ego integrity"), but also an ideal of "narrative rationality" in terms of which variations in narrative competence may be recognized and elucidated. Although it is beyond the scope of this book to spell out the norms and standards of narrative rationality, I suggest that these are implicated, most fundamentally, in what Schafer terms the psychological capacity for *reflective self-representation* (1968): here taken as the individual's reliable awareness that he or she is the thinker (or narrator) of the (narrated) thought. When such background awareness is not present, or is otherwise attenuated or degraded, there is no firm basis for distinguishing between a thought (or narration) and the concrete experience or reality to which it refers, resulting in a drop in the level of "reality testing," or in a loss of the sense of "narrative reality."

In the present context, then, psychopathology is viewed as an impairment or disturbance in reflective self-representation (or narrative self-awareness), just as it may be more generally conceptualized as an expression of the degradation of those capacities[49] that support narrative rationality. Examples of such capacities are: (a) the capacity for voluntary control; (b) the capacity to distinguish self and other; and (c) the capacity to distinguish past, present, and future. It is possible, of course, to explain the degradation of these capacities in terms of underlying psychological *processes,* but such an account (of causally lawful processes) belongs not to historical psychoanalysis, but to an empirical-analytic science of psychology and psychoanalysis (see Chapter 5). It is also possible, indeed likely, that the degradation of those capacities that support narrative rationality has its basis in constitutional or biological factors (e.g., factors related to non-optimal tension regulation). If such is the case, however, the psychopathology in question is only ambiguously psychoanalytic[50]—since it pertains to preverbal or presymbolic biological dispositions, which may or may not be "assimilated within networks of subjective wishes of later origin . . ." (Gedo 1984 165).

The historical psychoanalyst, however, need not traffic in such inner processes or biological suppositions. It is really not incumbent upon him or her to *explain* the degradation of the capacities that support narrative rationality. It is enough that he or she postulate the possibility, and allow that *interpretable evidence* of such degradation may be coded into the spatial and temporal scheme of a narrative, as, for example, whenever there is no clearcut distinction between the here-and-now of the narration and the there-and-then of the narrated; whenever, for instance, we do not know whether we are on one level or the other. The use of "we" in this context reminds us that narratives are always meant for some imagined reader (or hearer), and that historical psychoanalysis is therefore required to return to the transference scene, or at least to the dialogical clinical setting, in order to discover and elicit "degraded capacities" and other pathologically relevant aspects of narrative discourse and practice. For, as remarked early on in this section, the "historical truth" of psychoanalytic understanding is intrinsically contingent on the clinical circumstances of its constitution. And this must mean that psychoanalytic psychopathology, as a specialized expression of historical discourse, can only be recognized and conceptualized in its dialogical, transactive and transferential conditions. Thus the hermeneutic task becomes one of apprehending and interpreting such phenomena as the "disjuncture" between narrative form and narrative content (Olinick and Tracy 1987) — since it is features such as these in the patient's storytelling (to an imagined interlocutor, in the presence of the therapist) that reveal or offer evidence for the workings of the transference, and hence of the manner in which "psychopathology" is constructed and deconstructed *in situ*.[51]

2. *Development.* The psychoanalytic construct of development has already been introduced in Chapter 2 of this book. It was then argued that this construct was a mixed construct, and that the "past" thus constituted was a composite past. Thus, on the one hand, there is (a) the empirical-analytic developmental knowledge which comes from looking forward in time, and which seeks to explain whether and how earlier components are incorporated into a newer and more integrated organization; and on the other hand, there is (b) the historical or retrospective knowledge of development which comes from looking back, and which imagines the past in terms of present traces, and which is realized as a narrative of identity in difference or continuity in change. The former has as its object the "genetic" (or objective) past, which is a past that is ultimately reduc-

ible to underlying processes, patterns, and structures. The latter has as its object the "narrative" past, which is an intersubjectively mediated past existing in narrative time, and which is never reducible to extralinguistic, unintelligent or unlearned processes (be they biological or psychological in nature). Traditional psychoanalytic discourse is thus envisaged as a mixed discourse which aims to conserve a complex image of the past-in-the-present. Neither the historical nor the scientific past is by itself a sufficient representation of the psychoanalytic past. It follows, then, that the idea of development must be *doubly conceptualized*[52] (both historically and scientifically) in any inclusive or comprehensive treatment of psychoanalytic discourse (e.g., Stern 1985; and Chapter 2, "The Mixed Construct of Psychoanalytic Development" and "The Double-Edged Critique").

From Schafer's hermeneutic perspective, however, the mixed model (as sketched above) is radically misconceived. What it characteristically generates—the *normative analytic life history*—"is no more than a second order retelling of clinical analyses," and one which "confusingly deletes reference to the history of the analytic dialogue" (1983 238). Such normative life histories, which vary in detail from analytic school to analytic school (but which all purport to delineate the stages and phases of the life span, beginning with biological and prehistorical "origins"), are not only unscientific, but unhistorical as well. They are unhistorical because they have been abstracted from the dialogical, transactive, and transferential context of historical (psychoanalytic) understanding and in this way fail to acknowledge that the life history is only intelligible as an aspect of the superordinate psychoanalytic narrative which is co-authored by patient and therapist under the conditions of the transference. Schafer's point, in short, is that the normative or developmental life history is nothing more (and also nothing less) than a *mythic* interpretation (a decontextualized plot), and that this is so because the hermeneutic history of the analytic encounter has been abridged (or abstracted) in such a way that it is now viewed as embodying a timeless, paradigmatic pattern.

In place of this second-order analytic life history (a pseudo-normative myth of development), Schafer urges renewed attention to the history of the analytic dialogue. Such a hermeneutical history will disclose the narrative logic (or temporal structure) of psychoanalytic development, but in Spence's words, "will not survive translation into something more general" (1982 296)—since such a history is recognized as contextually conditioned (Gadamer 1975) or as intrinsically contingent on the clinical circumstances of its constitution. It follows that such a first-order hermeneutical history never begins with extraclinical biological or autobiographical beginnings ("origins"), but rather "begins in the middle, which is the present: the beginning is the beginning of the analysis" (Schafer 1983 238). As a hermeneutic-historical construct, "development" thus starts from the narrative present with a narrative account of the analyst's retelling of something told by the analysand, and the analysand's response to that narrative transformation. "In the narration of this moment of dialogue lies the structure of the analytic past, present and future" (Schafer 1983 238). This is simply to say that historical psychoanalysis, to the extent that it is itself narratively articulated, retrospectively exhibits the temporal (or narrative) structure of psychoanalytic development. Historical psychoanalysis therefore represents, but does not empirically demonstrate, the psychoanalytic relations of the "self now" to the "self before." In such a theoretical context, the personal past (the "self before") is uniquely one's own and nontransferable to others; the second-order normative life history will thus have only the purely heuristic function of helping to control (or emplot) the many tellings and retellings of the analysand's nontransferable life history. It follows, then, that the normative (or decontextualized) life history is not at all theoretically privileged, and is only relevant as an interpretative technique or narrative device, one of the many ways in which the historical analyst uses (or invents) a "general past" (i.e., a transferable past) to help constitute the individualized present (the "self now").[53]

Schafer's developmental hermeneutics can now be generalized as follows: the *domain* of psychoanalytic development does not consist in the events, behaviors, and processes of an individual's biological or experiential past, but rather in the narrations in terms of which these events, behaviors, and processes are meaningfully represented and reconstructed. In Schafer's account, what develops is not just the human life as such (i.e., its intrinsic maturational potentials, or its cognitive and affective capacities), but also, the manner in which, and the perspective from which, the *story* of a life is told and retold (Cohler 1981; Freeman 1984; Chinen 1984). Human beings are not simply constructions based on past events or processes; they are also (as self-aware agents and makers of meaning) the interpretable expressions of narrative structures and their transformations. The psychoanalytic developmentalist will therefore want to recognize and understand such narrative structures and their transformations, and one of the ways in which to do so is historically.[54]

As a historian, the psychoanalytic developmentalist assumes a retrospective stance; he or she "stands on the far side of the end, in human terms, on the far side of death" (Brooks 1984 95), and from this vantage seeks to "describe" what kind of story an individual is in, or how an individual (more or less narratively self-aware) has narratively revised the past in order to arrive at his or her present narrative position. But in trying to understand narrative development (how narrative change from beginning to end has taken place), the historical psychoanalyst brackets conventional notions of "beginnings" and "endings," since the ordinary temporal assumptions of chronology and autobiography no longer hold under the transactive, transferential, and dialogical conditions of the analytic (and hermeneutic) situation. Within the boundaries of such a paradigm, the task cannot be to unveil some uniform or expectable trajectory across the life span (e.g., Erikson 1963); that task is in any case a futile one as Gergen (1977) and Gergen and Gergen (1986), among others, have argued. The task is rather to conceptualize identity in difference (continuity in change) across the *analytic* life span, across the analytic past, present, and future—and in the course of doing so, to represent the psychoanalytic relations of the "self now" to the "self before." When successful, such a "history" will not only reconstruct the narrative substructure (or "story") of an individual's psychical past, but will also yield a narrative of identity: a psychoanalytically relevant apprehension of, and reflection upon, the unity and continuity of selfhood, the "truth" of which is intrinsically contingent on the clinical circumstances of its constitution.

Conclusion. My purpose in this section has been to illustrate the potential scope of historical psychoanalysis, and to argue that it offers not just a hermeneutical interpretation of the therapeutic encounter (a "theory of therapy"), but also a unique perspective on the "development" and "disorders" of psychic reality. I must concede, however, that certain important issues have still gone largely unexamined, namely: (a) the relevance of historically constructed psychoanalytic concepts for empirical inquiry and investigation; and (b) the relevance of historical psychoanalytic understanding for the art and practice of psychotherapy. Consideration of these issues will be postponed till Chapter 5: that chapter is focused not only on the problem of the scientific construction of the psychoanalytic past, but also on such decisive matters as the relationship of scientific psychoanalysis to historical psychoanalysis, and the relationship of both to "practical knowledge."

It is worth noting, as I conclude, that Chapter 5 of this book elaborates a "scientific argument" in support of a major claim advanced in this section. I have repeatedly asserted that historical psychoanalysis (as a form of narrative discourse) is *uniquely* suited to represent the psychoanalytic relations of the "self now" to the "self before." In putting forth this claim (that "narrativity" is the language structure having temporality as its ultimate referent), I have deliberately abstained from any further discussion or defense of it. Instead, I have implicitly endorsed Paul Ricoeur's proposal that

> between the activity of narrating a story and the temporal character of human experience, there exists a correlation that is not merely accidental but that presents a transcultural form of necessity. (1983 52)

What my presentation has presupposed, in short, is that the historically constructed psychoanalytic narrative, *and it alone,* (a) can symbolically represent the experience of temporality, and (b) thus advance toward a specifically psychoanalytic apprehension of, and reflection upon, the unity and continuity of selfhood. This presupposition becomes scientifically credible when Michael Basch (1976a) and Pinchas Noy (1979) recommend a new model of primary and secondary process—an important implication of which is that narrative discourse (and not scientific discourse) is, by virtue of its own underlying cognitive processes, uniquely able to represent or symbolize the human experience of time.

The Limits of Historical Psychoanalysis

The limits of historical psychoanalysis have been amply documented throughout this chapter, and by implication, throughout the first part of this book. It should now be clear, for example, that historical psychoanalysis: (a) characteristically involves the explication of intentionalistic structures of meaning (narratives), rather than the abstraction of causal and lawful processes; (b) characteristically depends for its validity on the clinical circumstances from which its data arise, rather than on the extra-clinical evidence and conditions of biological development and biograph-ical history; and (c) characteristically represents its "object-domain" as a linguistically constituted world, rather than as an extralinguistic reality (and so illustrates a certain circularity in understanding in that it uses language to interpret language). To summarize and recapitulate, historical psychoanalysis is thus limited in the following three respects: by its lack of direct access to *process*; by its apparent inability to exploit *extraclinical* evidence; and by its lack of unambiguous reference to *extralinguistic* realities. It follows, then, that the specifically historical construction of the psychoanalytic past is likewise limited in each of these ways.

The scope and boundaries of historical psychoanalysis are, in general, defined and circumscribed by the limits of hermeneutic understanding itself. Yet these limits, it would appear, are trespassed and violated by the problematic thesis of hermeneutic universality (Habermas 1980). Let me now inspect this thesis more closely. It begins by validly postulating that interpretative (linguistic) practices comprise a significant part of what goes on in the social and psychological world; and further, that our access to this world is necessarily via our (interpretative) understanding of these interpretative practices. At this juncture in the argument, however, a certain fallacy is commonly committed: for it is falsely inferred that these interpretative practices are *all* that exists, or all that can be *known* to exist. The thesis of hermeneutic universality (in this fallacious form) appears, therefore, to reject the possibility of valid knowledge of a human world "beyond interpretation" (e.g., Gedo 1979). It fails to allow that intelligi-ble and interpretable linguistic communication is (conceivably) "part of" more general social, psychological, and biological processes; that these processes, though prelinguistic or extralinguistic in nature (and though non-meaningful and non-intentional by definition), may still constrain, underlie, or give rise to those very interpretative practices which, alone, can be understood.

The fallacy of hermeneutic universality consists, therefore, in (a) the universalization of historical or hermeneutical reason,[55] (b) the hyposta-tizing of signifying practices, and (c) the "reduction" of meaningless systems (processes) to meaningful ones. What seems to be required, then, to counteract this error (and to restore the historicity of interpretation), is further hermeneutic reflection on the limits of hermeneutic understanding. Such reflection, for example, ought at least to admit the possibility that the predictable and repetitive behavior (or lack of it) of natural, causal, and non-intentional systems and processes is inherently involved in the way we conceive, diagnose, and interpret our situations and purposes, and in the way we choose means to alter them and/or bring them to fruition (Vallacher and Wegner 1987; Apel 1977; Ricoeur 1974).

Such reflection, in short, will acknowledge that there *is* a human world beyond historical and hermeneutical interpretation, and that the legitimacy of historical interpretation (and hence, of historical psychoanalysis) paradoxically depends on the steadfast acknowledgment of this fact. Otherwise, historical psychoanalysis is in danger of sacrificing its specifically psychoanalytic identity, and is in danger of dissolving into a wholly linguistic and solipsistic enterprise. What will be lost is the *psychoanalytic* implication of the existence of a reality outside of the horizons of the semiotic system of psychic reality; what will be lost is the recognition (or presumption) "that inner psychic reality is created on the rock of anatomical and external realities and on the truth of infantile desires" (McDougall 1985 285).

In this, the traditional or normative view, the proper locus of psychoanalytic discourse is never far from the "borderline" between history and nature, meaning and force, mind and body. Hence the enduring relevance of Freud's pivotal proposal in *The Interpretation of Dreams* (1900) that instinct (libido) bridges the frontier between body and mind; and the import of his later suggestion in *Beyond the Pleasure Principle* (1920) that the compulsion to repeat seems not to be explicable in terms of subjectively accessible strivings (or intentionalistic structures of meaning), but is rather to be accounted for in terms of the phylogenetic history (or evolutionary biology) of instinctual life. More recently, Gedo (1979, 1981, 1984) has sought to update this understanding of the extralinguistic (or prelinguistic) significance of psychoanalytic discourse by arguing that

> early biological experiences continue to exert a determining influence on subsequent behavior without mental representation. The concept of repetition compulsion explains that early biological experiences which, from our usual psychological perspective, are passively endured, affect later behavior through automatic repetition in the active mode. In my view, the fact that this occurs is what Freud was bringing to our attention through his contin-

ued insistence that the unconscious is ultimately unknowable. (1981 314–15)

Gedo is proposing, in effect, that psychoanalytic understanding (whether theoretical or practical in aim) cannot be viewed as wholly interpretative, historical, or hermeneutical—since to do so precludes recognition that

> the most essential of our therapeutic activities pertain to *preverbal* and even *presymbolic* issues, including *optimal tension regulation* and the establishment of a stable hierarchy of *biological* aims and *patterns,* especially in the *affective* realm. (1984 165, my emphasis; see also Chapter 1 of this book, p. 22.)

I therefore conclude that historical psychoanalysis exceeds its proper scope to the extent that it commits itself to the thesis of hermeneutic universality. Moreover, when rightly reflecting on its assumptions, historical psychoanalysis comprehends its own limits and points to its complement, scientific or empirical-analytic psychoanalysis—since it is the latter alone which has access to causal or lawful process, to extraclinical evidence and conditions, and above all, to the extralinguistic (or prelinguistic) realities of affective experience and the peremptoriness of desire.[56] And from within such parameters, the psychoanalytic past is no longer knowable as an altered and alterable past, the meaning and significance of which are conditioned by the historical situatedness and dialogical structure of understanding. On the contrary, scientific psychoanalysis restores or resurrects the *objectivity* of the psychoanalytic past, disengages it from reflective, narrative, or historical self-awareness, and in this manner, recognizes it as having "a condition independent of mind" (Lewis 1956). We will shortly discover in the next chapter how this past is constituted or established in terms of two distinguishable but interrelated strategies: (a) on the one hand, through the specification of those underlying processes which help to explain how the human being is (or emerges as) an agent and maker of meaning; and (b) on the other hand, through the representation of "that organization underlying human life which cannot be rendered in terms of the person as agent and maker of meaning" (Anscombe 1981 225).

Concluding Reflections

Everything is real so long as we do not take it for more than it is. As we now negotiate the transition to science, and to the scientific construction of the psychoanalytic past, it is wise to recall the merits of historical psychoanalysis, as expounded thus far in this book. For its value is not to be dismissed. We are reminded, first, that history does indeed engender new and usable knowledge; and unlike memory, it does so intentionally and reflectively. We are reminded, as well, that patients, even psychotic patients, deserve to be *historically understood,* and are not necessarily mistaken when they feel that therapists who seek to "correct" their thoughts are stealing their own pasts from them. We are reminded, finally, that the "past"—though known to be altered and alterable—is nevertheless imperishable. It is the necessary postulate (or intentional object) of our self-awareness as historically situated agents and makers of narrative meaning. In sum, historical psychoanalysis affirms the theoretical and practical truth that in psychoanalytic discourse (as in other discourses), history destroys those who are unable to speak rationally about it. Historical psychoanalysis specifically empowers us to speak rationally about our psychical pasts and personal histories. Within the boundaries of its world (and so long as we do not take that world for more than it is), historical psychoanalysis enables us to know and not merely to repeat. And it can only do so because it acknowledges the historical situatedness and dialogical structure of its own understandings.

NOTES

1. In characterizing historical psychoanalysis as a typically American achievement, and in regarding Schafer's project as its exemplary expression, I do not dismiss the contributions of such European analysts and theorists as Lacan (1977), Ricoeur (1970, 1974), Chasseguet-Smirgel (1984), and Melanie Klein (1975). My point is just that certain local and national assumptions help to shape the theory and practice of psychoanalysis. In Edith Kurzweil's words: "Every country creates the psychoanalysis it needs, although it does so unconsciously" (1989 1). I thus assume that American psychoanalysis—whether cast in the idiom of science, history, or practice—will bear the imprint of such native assumptions as presentism, pragmatism, contempt for the authority of the past, and commitment

to the idea of progress. Such assumptions, along with the intellectual controversies and cultural fashions associated with them, determine the character of Schafer's exemplary American venture in historical psychoanalysis. For another perspective on the "Americanization" of psychoanalysis, see Rieff's *Triumph of the Therapeutic: Uses of Faith after Freud* (1968).

2. I do not claim that Schafer has been consciously influenced by Gadamer. On the contrary, it would appear that Schafer's acknowledged debts are to the British philosophers of mind and action, including most notably, Ryle, Austin, Wittgenstein, and Hampshire. My objective in this chapter, however, is not to reconstruct Schafer's original intentions or to describe an actual line of intellectual influence. It is rather to display the true scope and limits of historical psychoanalysis. This objective is most likely to be met if Schafer's "logical debt" to Gadamer is recognized and appreciated, and if historical psychoanalysis, in general, is understood as a specialized application of philosophical hermeneutics.

3. This image of the influence of the analyst is most persuasive in the context of therapeutic work with the neurotic (or conflicted) patient. Such a patient possesses sufficient ego structure to tolerate a "small shift in narrative perspective," and to risk "rewriting" his or her self-narrative. For the predominantly neurotic individual, then, the personal past is "safely" alterable, and he or she need not experience the analyst's influence as an assault on his or her identity or as a theft of it. Consider, in contrast, the predicament of a thought-disordered schizophrenic patient whose delusions are "shields" required for psychic survival. Delusions offer schizophrenic individuals something similar to the sense of identity that normal or neurotic people get from their memories or self-narratives—a knowledge of their place in the world and how they came to be what they are. It is hardly surprising, then, that schizophrenic patients, prone to psychotic anxiety (McDougall 1979), may experience the therapist's influence as an intrusive violation and are often unable to tolerate a "small shift in narrative perspective." Such patients conclude that therapists who seek to "correct" their thoughts are actually stealing their pasts from them (Baur 1991). For such severely disturbed and terror-struck patients, the co-construction of a psychoanalytic narrative is thus an unlikely (though not an impossible) therapeutic option. See also Notes 49 and 56.

4. As noted in the text, the nature and scope of countertransference have been widely debated, and definitional controversy has surrounded the use of the term. Winnicott (1947), for example, in his well-known paper "Hate in the Countertransference," argued for the notion of an "objective" countertransference in which the analyst's response is induced or evoked by "objective data" emanating from the patient. In such a view, countertransference is a *total* reaction to the patient's (and analyst's) "reality situation": it follows that the analyst's responses to the patient (which may or may not be communicated to him) need not be seen as stemming only from his own neurotic needs, and need not be viewed as expressing an unconscious reaction to the patient's transference. In short, although Winnicott did warn about the negative influences of some countertransferences on the analyst's professional conduct, he was among the first psychoana-

lysts to contradict Freud by considering countertransferential reactions as potentially valuable sources of information about the patient's pathology and progress in clinical treatment.

It is worth noting that the *empirical* literature on countertransference also relies on what might be called a "totalist" definition—resulting in the measurement of all accessible reactions of the therapist to the patient. For a useful review of this literature, see McClure and Hodge (1987), who make a notable attempt to quantify the extent and direction of countertransference. Their research appears to establish a significant relationship between strong affect (positive or negative) on the part of the therapist, and the manner in which the patient's expressed personality is perceptually or cognitively distorted. Therapists, in short, should be cognizant of the operation of countertransference, especially when they have *strong* feelings about their patients.

5. The argument developed in the preceding pages implies that therapeutic strategy (guided by the hermeneutic "reading" of countertransference data) may be transactional and not interpretative in emphasis. Interpersonal learning (even if unaccompanied by conscious insight) can therefore stand as the necessary and sufficient condition for therapeutic progress.

6. For an explicitly hermeneutic-phenomenological conceptualization of the analytic encounter, see Atwood and Stolorow (1984).

7. My point is that Schafer's numerous critics have missed the mark because they have failed to discern the *relevant* philosophical (Gadamerian) rationale of his hermeneutic and historical project. I contend that Schafer's revisionary psychoanalysis appears most coherent when it is understood as a specialized application of philosophical hermeneutics. It deserves, therefore, to be criticized as such. When it is not, the critique is essentially misconceived, even if it raises useful points.

8. In recent decades, however, the archaeological view of memory has fallen into disrepute, and with it, the archaeological interpretation of the psychoanalytic process. Thus Spence (1982) has argued that the archaeological metaphor should be discarded because memories are irrevocably changed by the process of recollecting and narrating them:

> More than we realized, the past is continuously being reconstructed in the analytic process, influenced by (a) the repressed contents of consciousness; (b) subsequent happenings that are similar in form and content; (c) the words and phrases used by the analyst in eliciting and commenting on the early memories as they emerge; and (d) the language choices made by the patient as he tries to put his experiences into words. The past, always in flux, is always being created anew. (93)

9. See Blight's argument (1981) that both empirical-analytic science and traditional hermeneutics share a set of common tenets (a positivist metatheory), and that they are distinguished only by their different attitudes toward, and evaluations of, the non-empirical domain of the "Great Divide." In terms of the thesis advanced in this book, each is an objectivist (or Proposition 1) form of human knowledge—and in this respect, each is distinguishable from the non-

objectivist theory of historical and hermeneutical understanding propounded by Gadamer. Gadamer, like Blight, aims to move beyond the "Great Divide" established by nineteenth-century positivist metatheory. However, unlike Blight (who offers Popper's evolutionary epistemology as a new, unifying paradigm), Gadamer recognizes the need to return to philosophy, and to undertake an inquiry into the *conditions* of understanding and into the underlying dimensions of interpretation. Such an inquiry is perfectly general, and is not to be confused (a) with a new methodological program for the human sciences, or (b) with a psychological investigation of the conditions (or causes) of human thought.

10. Gadamer is advancing an *ontological* claim: namely, that the object of understanding is never given as preformed, preexistent, or prestructured—but is, instead, an outcome of a "fusion of horizons." This object is not the traditional positivist object of knowledge, which is stable and immutable and which exists "out there" waiting to be known by the knower, but is more aptly described as an "intersubjectively mediated object of understanding," encountered and made within the condition of dialogue.

11. Gadamer stresses the situatedness of *all* understanding. The condition of effective history is relevant not only for historical interpretation, but for the natural and social sciences as well. This claim becomes more credible when we realize that forms of scientific knowledge themselves constitute traditions, and that all understanding (or observation) of an object-domain involves a "prejudgment" in terms of a particular interpretative paradigm or set of prejudices. There is, in short, no "observation" or confirmation that is not conditioned by (historically situated) tradition. There is no "objective" point of view, and the prejudices of an investigator (or scientific tradition) are actually preconditions of the possibility of understanding. Similar arguments concerning the dependence of observation on theory, and the conventional character of the confirmation and rejection of theories, have been advanced by Quine, Kuhn, and Feyerabend—leading contemporary philosophers of science.

12. To assert that there is no neutral or unsituated vantage point is to affirm the futility of any attempt to attain an "objective" point of view, since the attempt to do so inevitably falls victim to the historical embeddedness of natural language. If we assume (with Gadamer) that objectivity and neutrality are inconceivable within the boundaries of natural language (or historically situated discourse), then recourse may still be sought in the construction of a neutral, descriptive metalanguage, in terms of which all naturally occurring historical discourses could be redescribed and "objectively" inspected. This, in essence, is the proposal advanced by Rubenstein (in Reppen 1985 105), when he recommends devising a neutral language model of mental functioning, "faithful to the worlds of both persons and organisms."

13. The hermeneutic circle delineates an experience of understanding in which there is a movement from a first prejudgment of the meaning of the whole, in which the parts are understood, to a change in the sense of the meaning of the whole because of subsequent encounters with the detail and individuality of the various parts. This dialectical movement back and forth between whole and parts

(which Dilthey first described as the hermeneutic circle) is actually a *spiral*—in which each movement from part to whole (to part ...) increases the depth of understanding. It is important to appreciate that the hermeneutic circle, in the form given to it by Gadamer, is no mere methodological device, but is rather an ontological and structural element of understanding itself. It is therefore insufficient to dismiss the hermeneutic circle as a vicious circle (just because one's understanding of individual parts may appear to confirm one's assumption as to the meaning of the whole, and vice versa). The more important issue is *how* one is led to revise one's understanding of a whole, if one begins to understand individual parts in light of an *assumption* as to the meaning of the whole.

14. The "regulative ideal of unity" is a principle for the interpretation of lives, insofar as lives are recognized as narratively articulated and as narratively represented. Unity or self-coherence remains just an *ideal*, approached but never reached, so long as the narrative can be revised or retold.

15. The text or text-analogue is not, in Gadamer's view, a fixed or immutable object of knowledge whose original message or intention can then be reconstructed. Texts are altered according to the various historical horizons within which they are received. Any particular text is therefore a kind of skeleton, a set of schemata waiting to be "concretized" in various ways by various interpreters at various times. It follows that a text is capable of "communicating" to an interpreter, and is capable of meaningful self-transformation in dialogical contexts. However, it is also evident that the text or text-analogue (when not a living human interlocutor) cannot respond to an interpreter's communications. This is said to distinguish the hermeneutical and historical context of *interpretation* from the clinical and practical context of *intervention,*

> where it is response of the subject of one's interpretations to these interpretations that defines issues of accountability and effectiveness ... [and which] makes it immediately apparent that, in contrast to historical inquiry, in the clinical context interpretations are above all interventions. (Eagle 1984a 169)

16. This is the traditional (or normative) format for the integration of Freudian metapsychology and clinical or case theory. Whether or not this integrative format is conceptually coherent, theoretically cogent, or therapeutically useful, remain lively topics of argument and controversy in contemporary American psychoanalysis.

17. See Vallacher and Wegner (1987) for an important inquiry into the problems associated with the identification of action. Though empirical-analytic psychologists, both researchers concede that any segment of behavior can be consciously identified in many different ways, and that the identification of action appears to be open-ended, limited only by our constructive and labeling capacities. At the same time, their research approach aims to delineate the factors that restrict the range of viable identities. Vallacher and Wegner thus offer one solution to the problem of the relationship of behavior (and underlying process) to interpretable action and meaningful conduct.

18. Oakeshott's argument has as its premise the thesis that the movement of

an eyelid is a categorially ambiguous identity, in that it may count as a wink or a blink. The former is an expression of human intelligence which is interpretable in terms of *reasons,* while the latter is a component of a process which is understood in terms of *law* or *cause.* Oakeshott assumes that the language game of science is only applicable to the analysis of a "blink," and that science commits a category mistake when it seeks to comprehend a "wink" in terms of its own concept of a lawful or causal process.

19. This implies that Schafer's theoretical discourse presupposes consensual validity with regard to the key concepts of "psychoanalytic interest" and "psycho-analytic method." Such concepts are presumed to be sufficiently well established and unambiguous that they may be translated into the terms of action language. Schafer's second-order discourse cannot, by itself, define what is of psychoanalytic interest, nor can it legislate the content of psychoanalytic method. Moreover, since the concepts of "psychoanalytic interest" and "psychoanalytic method" de-rive, in large measure, from Freud's metapsychological and clinical theories, it is evident that Schafer's discourse is (paradoxically) parasitic on the "discredited" normative tradition of psychoanalysis.

20. According to Schafer (1983 84), the class of non-actions "includes reflex movements, normal maturational change, bodily secretions and stimuli, and other anatomical, motoric, and physiological processes."

21. Linguistic behaviorism is a position sometimes associated with the philos-opher Gilbert Ryle, and is enunciated in his book, *Concept of Mind* (1949).

22. I refer, in particular, to such philosophers as Ryle, Austin, Wittgenstein, and Strawson—all of whom agree that *persons,* and not minds or bodies, are the ultimate subjects of human actions. This point is made most explicitly by P. F. Strawson in *Individuals* (1959).

23. The claim is that action language theory offers an interpretation of analytic discourse which presupposes an *idealized* patient, who is potentially in possession of fully developed linguistic, symbolic, and narrative capacities. See in this chapter, "The Scope of Historical Psychoanalysis" for further discussion of the normative and rational character of historical psychoanalysis in general, where it is argued that an ideal (or norm) of "narrative rationality" informs the hermeneutic inter-pretation of psychoanalytic psychopathology.

24. My contention is that such theoretical understanding lacks *extrinsic* refer-ence to extralinguistic realities. The possibility, however, that such discourse may possess *intrinsic* reference is not excluded. See also Note 35.

25. The problem is that pathological distortions in an individual's self-under-standing and ability to communicate with others may remain unclear and opaque at the level of ordinary communication (where one is hermeneutically clarifying assumptions and implications). As long as one is at this level, the distortion in a patient's expression of meaning may remain inaccessible and invisible. Hence the view of Habermas (1971) and Apel (1977) that hermeneutics fails to see the extent to which individuals react to causal factors rather than act for themselves, and the consequent distortion involved in the intentions, reasons, and purposes they express. Schafer (following Gadamer) is thus considered guilty of hypostatiz-

ing language, and of presuming that linguistically articulated consciousness determines the material practice of life. Against this *idealist* point of view, Habermas and Apel argue that the objective framework of social and psychological action is not exhausted by intersubjectively intended (and symbolically transmitted) meanings.

26. The psychoanalytic implication of an extralinguistic reality requires a philosophical (and not just an empirical) elucidation. Consider Barratt's (1984) account below:

> The movement of psychoanalysis is neither circular nor solipsistic. It arrives at something new at each moment of its odyssey. And thus it seems to imply the existence of a reality 'outside' of the horizons of the semiotic system of psychic reality. In a certain sense, this is correct, for psychoanalysis does indeed demonstrate that psychic reality is not exhausted by semiotic construction. . . . By pointing to the nonidentity of signification, psychoanalysis vindicates the authentic concreteness of desire and materiality that is not held captive in any hypostatized signifying practices. (265)

27. Historical psychoanalysis is thus exposed as a normative as well as hermeneutic enterprise, since *valid* empirical analyses of the "psychoanalytic situation" presuppose prior explication of the "premise" of psychoanalytic discourse: namely, the principle that something true and transformative occurs in psychoanalytic practice. The explication of this normative principle establishes the *domain* of psychoanalytic theory, hence the boundaries within which valid empirical psychoanalytic investigations can be conducted.

28. Joel Kovel in *The Age of Desire* (1981) has commented on the analyst's lack of knowledge of the analysand's extra-analytical life. In a meditation on his work with Curtis, an investment banker, he comes to recognize that "like Freud, I do not know this analysand either. Or rather, I know only what he tells me and what I infer from it" (38). The analyst is doubly turned away from the patient's public life, because, first, that life must be cut off from the private, intimate life "where we can be with people in a trusting way," and second, because even that intimate life is cut off by yet another degree from the life of subjectivity, from the inner world of psychical reality.

29. This is just to say that historical psychoanalysis is limited to making meaning out of our *experience of* the past; it is limited to the mental. It is therefore unacceptable to try to verify the mental by acquiring evidence from outside of it —as Freud at first sought to do in attempting to establish the reality of the seduction scene.

30. The comprehension, recognition, and testing of "danger situations" are also central to the empirical psychoanalytic theory of Weiss and Sampson (1986), discussed in Chapter 5 of this book.

31. Wyatt (in Sarbin 1986) offers an account of "psychoanalytic listening," in which it is recognized that the analyst is not only on the lookout for the unconscious intent of the story, but also understands it as testifying to an unending process of coping and experiencing. See also Spence (1982).

32. If the plot actually represented or referred to an extralinguistic reality, it would follow that that reality could be investigated empirically. The task of empirical-analytic science would then be to describe the extralinguistic reality of psychic reality. But as we have seen, the plot of the psychoanalytic narrative does not represent (or refer to) psychic reality, but is rather a construction of it.

33. The analyst's lack of neutrality (his or her historical situatedness) is subject to the following observation by Spence (in Reppen 1985): "At the same time, as the analyst appears less neutral than we once assumed, it becomes increasingly urgent that we develop a neutral metatheory—a theory that can handle all possible narratives and provide a framework for all clinical observations. Thus the focus shifts from the neutral analyst (an impossibility) to a neutral theory . . ." (80–81).

34. See Spence (1982) for an attempt to assess the cognitive status of narrative truth. His argument is that such truth is always contingent, never absolute. "By that we mean that its truth is a function of other things besides the statement itself; in the case of an interpretation, it depends on such factors as the state of the transference, its relevance to other parts of the conversation, its timing, its phrasing, and other aspects of its persuasive appeal" (271–72). Moreover, the analyst, himself, is truthful, not because he is committed to the factual truth of his narrative interpretation, but because he believes in the therapeutic utility of his formulation. He believes it will facilitate the process of therapy.

35. For empirical substantiation of the distinction between narrative discourse and scientific (or paradigmatic) discourse, see Mandler (1984). The argument is offered that while science structures information according to a categorical or taxonomic format, narrative structures information according to a schematic format. According to the latter, events or entities are known through their participation in a collection (as part of a scene viewed). Schematic knowledge is therefore organized in terms of a part-whole configuration.

In the present context, I am also arguing that the "objectivity" of narrative discourse (as distinguished from scientific discourse) is to be understood in terms of *intentionality*. This is the doctrine that consciousness is always consciousness of, that it always intends (directs itself toward) an object which it distinguishes from itself. There is no necessity, in this view, to presuppose an extralinguistic reality. Objectivity is accordingly viewed as *intrinsically* referential. An important implication is that self-awareness is always mediated: one cannot be aware of oneself without at the same time being aware of something other than oneself; alternatively, whenever one is aware of oneself, one is aware of oneself as standing in relation to something else. Awareness (or understanding) thus implies the "objective correlation" of the *self* and *object* of awareness. According to my argument, then, it follows that the historical construction of the psychoanalytic past actually entails the creation or constitution of the "past" as an intentional object of narrative (or self-) awareness.

36. The capacity to alter the plot is also involved in what Bruner (1986) calls "subjunctivity." See in Chapter 1 of this book, "Prolegomenon."

37. The evidence in this context refers to the "data" of transference and countertransference.

38. See also Chapter 2 for an account of the traditionalist and revisionary points of view, in terms of which the *comparative* analysis of the psychoanalytic past is first introduced.

39. See Schafer (1984), where a similar pathogenic belief is *narratively* elaborated.

40. The "absence" of certain memories (associated with affective self-regulation, etc.) implies their inaccessibility as subjectively intended or encoded meanings. In Gedo's view (1979), this is explained by the hypothesis that there are certain early, preverbal, biological experiences which continue to affect later behavior but which are beyond interpretation. His hypothesis, in turn, has been questioned by more traditional analysts such as McDougall (1985), who postulate a process of primal repression (or psychic repudiation) which "ejects" early experiences or meanings from psychic reality. Such experiences or meanings may still be "heard" as enactments in the analytic situation, and "read" as indications of pain not yet felt by the patient as personal suffering. In McDougall's words: "This form of psychic rejection needs to be distinguished from denial and disavowal, which are defenses against neurotic anxiety; the rejection described here is marshaled to deal with preneurotic anxiety: narcissistic fears for bodily and ego integrity, terrifying sadistic fantasies linked to archaic sexual impulses, and self-object confusions of the earliest mother-child relationship" (1985 185). What is still unclear, according to this formulation, is how such psychic fears and fantasies are encoded or registered in the inner world of the preverbal infant. See also Stern (1985).

41. Note that Edelson's causal entities are postulated as concrete and occurrent and are *not* an outcome of analytic abstraction. This means (in terms of my argument) that Edelson's discourse deviates from empirical-analytic science, and qualifies, least in part, as a historical discourse.

42. The conceptualization of "origins" remains a vexing issue for psychoanalytic theory. It has been remarked, for example by Schimek (1975a), that Freud's speculative hypothesis of inherited memories was a way of grounding the contents of universal fantasies in actual events, but now events in the "history of the race," if no longer in the history of a specific individual. Freud's move was necessary if he wished to avoid reducing the unconscious wish to a biological drive. By making the unconscious wish a memory trace of the phylogenetic history of the race, its intentionality is assured, and the autonomy of psychic reality is vindicated. Psychoanalysis is therefore recognized as an interpretative or hermeneutic psychology, as well as an empirical-analytic and biological science.

43. Psychoanalytic metapsychology is examined in Chapter 5 of this book, where it is argued that it offers a developmental (or biological) framework for psychoanalytic discourse.

44. See Mandler (1984) and Note 35. Mandler undertakes an empirical inquiry which allows her to distinguish four cognitive structures (of which narrative

is one). Each of the four structures encodes and stores information according to different formats; the variations in time required to learn and recall information organized by these (hypothesized) formats would appear to be the result of distinct strategies of organization.

45. My point, of course, is that Schafer's proposals always require interpretation; they become, themselves, the objects of historically situated and dialogically structured hermeneutic understanding. Were they to be accepted as fixed protocols, to be dogmatically "applied in practice," they would lose their character as authentic expressions of historical understanding.

46. See also Chapter 1, "The Price of the 'Unity of Inquiry,' " where it is argued that the internal analysis or explication of psychoanalytic practice is not reducible to a "theory of intervention," since the latter is necessarily an *external* account of psychoanalytic therapy. For further discussion of the underlying philosophical point, see Oakeshott (1962 113).

47. For a more thorough examination, see Schwartz and Wiggins (1986). It may seem needlessly paradoxical to assert that non-intentionalistic and organic systems cannot be understood, since these are precisely those systems which are abstracted and analyzed by empirical-analytic science—knowledge of which enables us to predict and control extralinguistic reality and nature. But because such systems are governed by causal laws (and not by rules), and because these laws do not have to be learned in order to be operative, the systems themselves are neither meaningful nor intelligible; more precisely, they are only interpretable in terms of the ahistorical rules of empirical methodology and statistical inference. Upon some consideration, my argument will seem plausible enough in the fields of molecular biology and psychophysics; confusion arises in such borderline disciplines as social psychology, sociology, and psychoanalysis, where investigators fail to distinguish what can be explained (in terms of causal laws) from what can be understood (in terms of interpretable rules), and hence distort the character of, and interrelationship between, meaningless and meaningful systems. It follows from this thesis that schizophrenic persons, for example, are not only organic systems which require explanation, but also intentionalistic entities which merit understanding.

48. It should be noted, of course, that trauma and conflict from the past may influence subjunctivity in the here and now. The capacity (in the analytical present) to alter narrative perspectives, and to "rewrite" one's plot, is itself empirically conditioned by past experiences and events, and the propagation of their influence over actual time.

49. The degradation of such capacities is associated with the severe psychiatric disorders of schizophrenia and psychotic depression. From a psychoanalytic point of view, degradation may reflect developmental arrests (Stolorow and Lachman 1980) and/or primal repression (e.g., McDougall 1985; and see also Note 40), and may involve such psychic phenomena as narcissistic fears for bodily and ego integrity and self-object confusions of the earliest mother-child relationship. In other words, what seems to be involved in the degradation of these capacities is what McDougall terms "psychotic anxiety," the pervasive and primitive fear over

one's right to exist and to possess a separate existence without the dread that one will be attacked and damaged by others. Such fear is usually associated with an exceptional vulnerability to self-fragmentation and boundary loss, and helps to explain why severely disturbed patients (*or* their analysts) are often unable to tolerate that "small shift in narrative perspective" which is inherent in the therapeutic action of psychoanalytic treatment. See also Note 3.

50. What should count as psychoanalytically explicable psychopathology? According to Edelson (1986 107), "when there is 'something wrong' at the psychological level, and there is no condition, event, or process fitting the description 'something is wrong' at the neurophysiological level or in the social situation that is sufficient to produce the 'something wrong' at the psychological level, we have a psychological phenomenon that is an appropriate subject for psychological explanation."

51. An enduring question for psychoanalytical theory is whether such narrative phenomena offer evidence for the existence and workings of *archaic* transferences (Gedo 1979, 1984)—transferences which reflect the continuing influence of repetitive biological dispositions on current behavior and experience. Are these dispositions somehow "registered" in the inner world of the infant's subjective reality? If so, are they then assimilated into the network of subjective wishes, strivings, and meanings that comprise the narrational dimension of psychic reality? Because such questions concern the manner in which non-intentional states give rise to (or are absorbed by) intentionalistic structures, they may not be readily susceptible to an empirical-scientific solution. For an interesting discussion of the "advent of the intentional," see Erickson's philosophical study, *Language and Being: An Analytic Phenomenology* (1970).

52. The idea of "double conceptualization" (as history and as science) is reconsidered in Chapter 5 through a discussion of Noy's model of the development of primary and secondary process. Noy (1979) argues that primary process categorizes and represents the world as *experience,* while secondary process categorizes and represents the world as *knowledge.* Any item of information is categorized twice (doubly processed). It is hypothesized that the maintenance of the unity and continuity of the self depends upon this double representation of the self as experience and as concept. I shall argue, in the chapter to follow, that Noy's hypothesis lends support to an important contention of this study: that historical, as well as scientific discourse, is essential to any coherent and comprehensive exposition of psychoanalytic understanding.

53. In Schafer's words (1983 238):

> It soon becomes evident that, interpretatively, one is working in a temporal circle. One works backward from what one is told about the autobiographical present in order to define, refine, correct, organize, and complete an analytically coherent and useful account of the past, and one works forward from various tellings of the past to constitute the present and that anticipated future which are most important to explain. Under the provisional and dubious assumption that past, present, and future are separable, each segment of time is used to set up a series of questions about the others and to answer questions addressed to it by the others.

Note that in this account, there is no exit from the circular logic of historical psychoanalytic understanding; the role of the "general past" (the normative life history) is thus, at most, an ancillary one.

54. Narrative structures and their transformations may also be understood and explained non-historically. See, for example, Sarbin (1986), Bruner (1986), Freeman (1984), Mandler (1984), and Cohler (1981)—all of whom advance more or less empirical models for the ahistorical investigation of narrative functioning and narrative development.

55. The "universalization of historical or hermeneutical reason" appears to mirror the positivistic universalization of technical reason (see Chapter 1 of this book, p. 8). It is not certain, however, that Gadamer (1975, 1976) has actually committed this error since his theory of understanding allows for the autonomy of the natural and social sciences, and only requires that these sciences recognize that their interpretative elements cannot be expunged. In psychoanalysis, for example, we are well aware that empirical explanations typically involve assumptions about the relation between early childhood experiences and neurotic symptoms. But these assumptions have at some point to be applied to individual cases; that is, they have to make *sense* of an individual's history for him or for her, and therefore have to be *interpreted* in light of the individual's life (or in light of the narrative representation of that life). Clearly, such interpretative elements can never be expunged from psychoanalytic discourse, nor can their presence be easily reconciled with any view of psychoanalysis as an exclusively objective and explanatory science. This, then, is Gadamer's real point: it is not that historical or hermeneutic reason is *universally* appropriate, or that interpretation is the only method of knowing; it is rather that science, itself (i.e., scientific psychoanalysis) is unable to overcome the conditions of prejudice and situatedness.

56. I have assumed all along that historical psychoanalysis, in its radically hermeneutic form, is at most *intrinsically* referential and lacks reference to extralinguistic or prelinguistic realities. This has been deemed a profound limitation of hermeneutics per se, as well as an implicit argument for the *extrinsically* referential discourse of science. But must such an assumption be endorsed without qualification? I have only granted it because (following Schafer), it has been presumed that "meaning" is what is possessed by words, phrases, discourses, narratives, and other linguistic entities. It follows that if historical psychoanalysis is limited to making meaning out of our experience of the past, then its domain must be confined to "meaningful" linguistic entities and must exclude "meaning-less" extralinguistic or prelinguistic entities.

But is it actually unreasonable to maintain that experiences, actions, situations, and objects—in their extralinguistic dimensions—have or possess meanings, and no less so than words, phrases, and narrative discourses? In short, if meaning were accessible in its extralinguistic dimensions, then historical psychoanalysis might, in principle, elicit it. The assumption to be granted is that experience, itself, *prior* to its linguistic appropriation, serves as a linguistically mute criterion for its own description and interpretation. Meaning must be *antecedent* to language; and the theoretical problem now concerns language's relation to prelinguistic meaning, just as the practical or clinical problem centers on how language (or therapeutic discourse) can appropriate the unexpressed.

If such speculations are persuasive, then it appears that the boundaries of historical-hermeneutical psychoanalysis have been enlarged, and that Gedo's forceful critique must be qualified. It now follows that Gedo's archaic or preverbal transferences are not necessarily beyond interpretation (or linguistic appropriation)—though it remains a separable issue of clinical or practical judgment whether or not such interpretations (of prelinguistic affective-biological dispositions) should be offered or transmitted in the actual conduct of psychotherapy.

5

The Scientific Construction of the Psychoanalytic Past

Analogies of this kind are only intended to assist us in our attempt to make the complications of mental functioning intelligible. . . . We are justified, in my view, in giving free rein to our speculations so long as we retain the coolness of our judgement and do not mistake the scaffolding for the building.

—Sigmund Freud

It is no cause for wonder, then, that within psychology it never becomes clear . . . what it is to which ideas are attributed and referred. . . . Here everything remains in question; and yet the scientific findings are correct.

—Martin Heidegger

Introduction: Psychoanalysis and the Tyranny of the Past

In the Freudian tradition, the past is primary. What is decisive, theoretically and therapeutically, is the manner in which the past influences our lives through obtruding itself into the present. Psychoanalysis, then, has always been concerned with how and why the past contaminates the present, with how and why the influence of the past can become excessive. Once Freud dismissed the seduction hypothesis[1] in 1897, it became clear to him that the agency of such excessive influence was most likely fantasy (and not mere memory as he had earlier supposed). The past exerts a tyranny over the present through fantasy. But the past that explains how and why this is so is not the past of real events, or of experienced trauma, or of recollection and remembrance. It is rather the "past of phases" (e.g., phases of psychosexual or instinctual development). It is this *analytically*

178

abstracted past—the so-called developmental past—which is presumed to be explanatory, accounting not only for the structure and content of pathogenic fantasy (why it is as it is, why it means what it means), but also for its force, intensity, and dominance in the present.

Let me begin by reviewing the traditional Freudian account.[2] It proceeds more or less as follows: dominant fantasies are as they are because they contain desires that belong to past phases (of psychosexual development); and it is because the desires that such fantasies contain *do* belong to past phases that the fantasies are dominant. These desires do not simply arise or originate in past phases; it is rather that the "pastness" of such phases remains stamped all over them. These, then, are *archaic* desires. They belong to an earlier (infantile) period or phase, and as such, are unintelligible in the here and now. The person who has them can no longer tell what kind of pleasure he or she could hope from these desires were they actually to be satisfied. It follows, then, that fantasies as well are unintelligible—not only for the archaic desires (and conflicts) that they contain or imply, but also for the way in which they conceal or disguise these desires and conflicts. Because fantasies are in this way unintelligible to the person who has them, they are likely to be felt as obligatory (or as excessively forceful), since they can't be easily tested and disconfirmed in the circumstances of everyday life. Hence, for example, the self-estranged plight and neurotic predicament of the "Rat Man" (Freud 1909a), whose possibilities are both defined and diminished by the tyrannical force of "obsessional" or intrusive ideas. For what the "Rat Man" really wants of his father are things he can no longer understand because he lacks "concrete understanding" of his own *archaic* desires.

Such concrete understanding has traditionally been construed as affective as well as cognitive in kind (Freud 1915a; Loewald 1960), as at once experiential and conceptual. In this book, such understanding is also regarded as a form of historical understanding—transmitted, modeled, and acquired through the therapeutic practices of clinical psychoanalysis, and explicated and rationalized through a theory of therapeutic action. The theory of therapeutic action therefore comprises one aspect of the theoretical discourse of psychoanalysis. But that discourse encompasses not only a theory (or model) of therapeutic action, but also distinguishable theories (or models) of psychoanalytic development and pathology —the chief aims of which are to establish how the "past" enters: (a) into the explanation of personality and psychic reality; and more particularly

(b) into the explanation of fantasy, of its emergence, dominance, and dynamics in the present.[3]

Recall that "history" and "science" are viewed as the principal avenues toward theoretical knowledge in psychoanalysis. Each constitutes a theoretical discourse; each articulates a distinctive construction of the psychoanalytic past, and each construction (in its own fashion and in its own sphere of application) is theoretically legitimate. Thus, it has already been argued that *historical psychoanalysis* offers one valid approach to recognizing and explicating the meaningful contents of psychic reality (including, for example, wishes, fantasies, and related acts of imagining). Such acts are interpreted as internally interrelated meanings, or as mutually implicative narrative actions (Schafer 1983); and their objective correlate or intentional object is designated the "narrative past," i.e., the historically constructed psychoanalytic past. This past, though, is a hermeneutic construct, an artifact of the logic of narrative emplotment. It is only meaningfully connected (not necessarily causally related) to the fantasies and imaginings of psychic reality and subjective experience. As such, this "inexistent past" (an interpretable feature of the here and now) can help to specify the meaningful content and form of fantasy, and may therefore constitute an argument for its intelligibility; but it cannot, qua narrative past, account for the conditions of fantasy's occurrence or emergence, or for its underlying affective and cognitive processes, or for the magnitude of its force or intensity in real time and real space.

For such a theoretical account or argument, we now turn to *scientific psychoanalysis*. It alone recognizes wishes, fears, fantasies, and their conflicts as developmentally generated, insofar as it alone abstracts an explanatory and objective past. We will find that it is this "past"—the scientifically constructed psychoanalytic past—which purports to describe (a) not only those underlying processes which help to explain how the human being emerges as an agent and maker of meaning, but also (b) those extralinguistic, prelinguistic, and biological realities which cannot be rendered in terms of "the person as agent and maker of meaning" (Anscombe 1981).

The Structure and Scheme of Scientific Psychoanalysis

The central and crucial task for scientific psychoanalysis, as introduced above, is to construct an "explanatory past" (a model of development), and to argue for its bearing upon the structures, contents, and processes of psychic reality. This project is the point of psychoanalysis as a scientific mode of theoretical discourse, and accordingly, sets the theme for the present chapter. At the same time, the discussion which follows is inescapably a dialectical one—since its focus falls on the tension or interplay between *two* modes of psychoanalytic understanding: science and history. Both, together, comprise the theoretical discourse of psychoanalysis; the concepts, categories, and constructions of scientific psychoanalysis only come into view in argument with those of historical psychoanalysis. Furthermore, as already noted, science is a specifically *theoretical* discourse.[4] Its relevance for psychoanalysis as a therapeutic practice (or as a form of treatment) cannot be thoughtlessly presumed. What, really, is the relationship between "psychoanalytic theory" and "psychoanalytic practice"? Are clinical practices, for example, logically entailed within theory? And if not, are there other formal or informal relationships which hold between theory and technique, between empirical consequences and practical knowledge? This chapter, then, has a twofold objective: (a) it aims not only to specify certain concepts, categories, and structures of scientific psychoanalytic argument, but (b) seeks also to set such an inquiry in comparative and dialectical perspective.

In Part I of the book, empirical-analytic science was identified and distinguished in terms of its commitments to objectivity and to quantitative and analytical abstraction. Psychoanalytic inquiries are more or less scientific precisely to the degree that these commitments are upheld; in my view, such commitments are most relevantly upheld (or instantiated) at the level of conceptualization, rather than at the levels of theory formation and theory testing.[5] It is fortunate that this should be the case, since full-fledged theories remain largely unrealized in scientific psychoanalysis. A scientific theory, we recall, is generally regarded as a statement of variables, relationships among variables, and predicted consequences of the interaction of the variables. The relationships and predictions are formulated deductively, but the resultant hypotheses are stated in operational terms, so that they may be validated or falsified through the use of accepted empirical or statistical methods. The hallmark of scientific theory is therefore a set of rigorously formulated deductive hypotheses presented in a form that makes them amenable to inductive testing (in academic psychology, see, for example, Hull 1935). It is evident, however, that empirical inquiry in psychoanalysis (and in the "softer" fields of psychology as well) scarcely meets this hypothetico-deductive standard. Only the rare research program, such as that of Weiss and Sampson (1986)—to be reviewed later in this chapter—appears to approximate the requirements of *theoretical* (as well as empirical) adequacy.

So, in a certain sense, it would now seem misleading to speak of the "clinical theory" or "metapsychological theory" of psychoanalysis. "Theory" (at least from the scientific point of view) is being used honorifically; what we are really describing, when we use that term, are sets of more or less integrated concepts and classificatory schemes. Such schemes may further conceptual innovation: e.g., Freud's extension of the concept of "psychical" (Freud 1917c), but they need not be associated with the construction or promulgation of new theories. In short, such schemes (as orientations or approaches to analysis) focus chiefly on definition, classification, and categorization; it is even possible (though not necessary) that the resultant concepts and taxonomies can be used to generate empirically testable hypotheses. But these analytical approaches are still less than full-fledged theories, if only because the worth of the suggested models, categories, and hypotheses remains in question until empirical analysis has been done. Scientific psychoanalysis is characteristically at the point of not yet establishing the "worth" of its numerous approaches or orientations; and many in the field would thus argue that this unfinished business is (or should be) its chief occupation in the years to come. My perspective, however, is different. As a non-empirical theoretician, my concern is not at all to validate or establish the worth of some particular approach or model within the purview of scientific psychoanalysis; it is rather to estimate the "relative worth" of scientific psychoanalysis as such. And this more general objective (a non-empirical one) can only be met through comparative reflection upon the assumptions and presuppositions which control *conceptualization* in "science," "history," and "practice."[6]

Given the considerations advanced above, it now becomes possible to reconsider certain current views regarding the structure of psychoanalytic thought. Surely, the most familiar of these proposes that it is hierarchically layered, with experience-distant "metapsychology" at the most abstract, general, and transdisciplinary level, and with experience-near "clinical theory" at the most concrete, ideographic, and clinically relevant level. It may be further argued that the former (with its focus on the classical concepts of instinctual discharge, psychic energy, and psychic structure) contains and explicates the assumptions upon which the latter is based (Freud 1917b); or that the latter (with its focus on the concepts of transference, neurosis, and interpretation) is actually derivable from the former. From such a vantage, recent controversy (Holt 1976, 1989) in the American psychoanalytical community has centered on (a) the nature, use, and abuse of Freudian metapsychology, (b) candidates for its replacement (ranging from Schafer's "action language" to Rubenstein's "neutral language" to Basch's reformulation in terms of cybernetics, neurobiology, and systems theory), and (c) proposals for its elimination altogether.

In the course of this controversy, the onus has clearly fallen on abstract metapsychology. It is metapsychology (in both its Freudian and revisionist expressions) which is called upon to justify itself. In contrast, the role of clinical theory is generally seen as self-evident, though its epistemic character (more or less empirical-analytic, more or less hermeneutic) may still be left open for debate (e.g., Basch 1986). Upon closer inspection, however, the nature, role, and function of clinical theory, and indeed, its legitimacy as a distinct level (or layer) of psychoanalytic thought, turn out to be problematic and uncertain. On intuitive grounds, for example, it would seem that what is *called* clinical theory is substantively heterogeneous. It has to do with understanding and managing psychopathology (Gedo and Goldberg 1973), with understanding such processes as interpretation, resistance, and transference (Schlesinger 1981), with understanding what the analyst is actually doing (or ought to be doing) in psychoanalytic practice (Schafer 1983), and with understanding and explaining the forces and processes that further the presumed goals of psychoanalytic treatment (Weiss and Sampson 1986).

Clinical theory, then, is many things. It is a presumptive theory of pathology (and development); it is a theory of therapy and therapeutic action; it is a theory of technique and/or a phenomenology of practice. It is "concrete" and "experience-near" and yet, as Klein (1976) observes, it is still a general psychological theory whose terminology—though no less theoretical than metapsychology—is somehow closer to experience. The fact of the matter is that we cannot adequately specify what is meant by "clinical theory" and that there is scant reason to suspect that it even exists as a distinct, hierarchic level of psychoanalytic thought. Moreover, as already noted, neither metapsychological nor clinical theory is actually *theoretical* in the rigorous (hypothetico-deductive) sense suggested above. Perhaps the most that can be said is that scientific clinical theory is, at present, more promissory proposal than established fact: what is usually being proposed is that it be the generic label applied to hypothesis-driven empirical (and descriptive) inquiry—one of whose aims would be to evaluate the worth of (metapsychological?) models and approaches. This, perhaps, is what Rubenstein (1977) had in mind when he put forth the following proposal:

> Clinical psychoanalytic theory has two functions: (1) to explain our observations; and (2) to contribute to the confirmation of those explanations. (247)

Whether or not "clinical theory," so characterized, can prove *clinically useful,* or be relevant to what transpires in clinical practice, or advance therapeutic effectiveness, remains legitimately in doubt. For it is hardly unreasonable to suppose, as does Keat (1981), that

> therapeutic success, explanatory theories, and theories of techniques, may display a high degree of logical independence from one another. (16)

My position, then, is that the structure of scientific psychoanalysis is not adequately represented by the conventional distinction between metapsychological and clinical theory. I suggest, in its stead, an alternative conception, one which brackets the question of whether or not psychoanalytic theory, as such, is hierarchically layered.

The conception I now offer is more or less descriptive: it emerges from the commonalities of American psychoanalytic argument, and reflects the implicit or explicit strategies of such diverse theorists as Gedo (1979, 1981, 1984, 1986), Kohut (1971, 1977), Kernberg (1975), Basch (1976a, 1977, 1981, 1983, 1986, 1988), and Stern (1985), among others. Winnicott (1965) is an important precursor, but Freud, himself, I believe, conformed to the conception under consideration. Its essence is that there is always a certain parallel between the issues, processes, and interactions of child development, and the issues, processes, and interactions in the psychoanalytic therapy of adults. According to this *analogical rationale,* infant-child pathology is translatable into adult pathology, and the "interpersonal world of the infant" (Stern 1985) is translatable into the adult therapeutic environment. The consequences of this analogical premise are perhaps most prominently (and literally) displayed in Kohut's (1971, 1977) approach, in that it directly correlates the environmental needs of the child (during the narcissistic development era) with the "analogous" therapeutic needs of the adult (who exhibits disturbances of the self).

My proposal is therefore as follows: the conceptual scheme of scientific psychoanalysis is logically organized by this problematic "parallel" between the vicissitudes of child development and those of adult pathology and psychotherapeutic interaction. As I have already observed, the "parallel" (or analogy) is problematic (e.g., Shapiro 1989), and scientific psychoanalysis is thus obligated to sustain and justify it through *argument*.

The structure of such argument typically incorporates three distinguishable (but interrelated) theories or models: a theory of development (an "explanatory past"); a theory of pathology; and a theory of therapeutic action. It follows that, in light of this prototypical scheme, scientific psychoanalysis is characteristically concerned with the "rules of translation" that govern the correspondence between (a) the affective and cognitive processes of infancy and childhood, and (b) those underlying psychopathology in adults as well as attachment and understanding in psychotherapeutic interaction. This helps explain, in part, why Basch (1988) is able to state that psychoanalytic psychotherapy is "applied developmental psychology":

> The therapist uses his or her knowledge of normal development to reach some conclusions about the reasons for a patient's malfunctioning and how one may enter the developmental spiral either to foster or to reinstate a more productive . . . developmental process. (29)

It is important, though, to recognize that such a view of the structure or scheme of psychoanalytic argument does not presuppose (or reinstate) the conventional distinction between metapsychological theory and clinical theory. *Each* of the three interrelated models (development, pathology, therapeutic action) may operate at many levels of abstraction and generality (and may even embrace the metapsychological concern for biological origins and physical substrates), and no single model is validly separable as "clinical theory." Not even the model of therapeutic action (the so-called theory of therapy) constitutes a clinical theory—if by the latter is meant a theory from which clinical techniques and practices (as well as "practical knowledge") are actually deduced or derived.[7] In Fairbairn's (1958 385) words, how analysis works "is not adequately understood." And I make no assumption in this book that such (practical?) understanding is necessarily guaranteed by *theoretical* discourse in general, or by the scientific mode of theoretical discourse in particular.

My strategy in this chapter should now be evident, for it follows from the conception just introduced. I have two aims: the first (and primary one) is to reconstruct the argument underlying the prototypical scheme of scientific psychoanalysis, while the second is to explicate the relationship of that scheme to "history" and "practice."

The Idea of Development: Orthogenesis, Epigenesis, and Repetition

Commenting on his analytic work with a suicidal patient, Gedo (1984) concludes that what really counted was the savagery of the struggle. Gedo believes, of course, that he has discerned clinical evidence for a *biological propensity to repeat*. Specifically, very early psychological events are alleged to leave their mark on patterns of affectivity; and the human organism is said to be so constituted that it seeks the repetition of the *patterns* of such experience (where these involve not only qualitative aspects,[8] but also such quantitative aspects as intensity, duration, and rates of change).

Gedo portrays his position as a conceptual innovation. The focus of psychoanalytic attention shifts from the unconsciously motivated or psychodynamic repetition of a wholly intentional system (a "person"), to the biopsychological or prepsychodynamic repetition of a partly non-intentional system (an "organism"). Thus the transference reenactment of infantile experience remains central, but what now seems theoretically and clinically salient is its affectively charged character and not, for example, just the psychodynamic inference or narrative interpretation of imagined fusion with an omniscient mother (Gedo 1984). In other words, the symbolically encoded content of affective memory becomes secondary to (and distinguishable from) the enactively encoded experience of early preverbal affect (here viewed as the precipitant of a primal repetition). In the course of this chapter, Gedo's revisionist proposal will be examined further, but what seems most pertinent for this discussion is the psychoanalytic *orthodoxy* of its commitment to "repetition." That commitment has already been highlighted in Chapter 2, where it was asserted that traditional Freudian theory requires that "the major mode of development is the repetitive mode, and the dominant characteristic of its concept of development is inertia" (Zukier 1985 12). There is, at the very least (Zukier would argue), a certain tension between the psychoanalytic idea of repetition and the scientific construct of development (whose focus is clearly on prospectively directed change and the hierarchical reorganization of earlier structures).

Moreover, even analysts who disregard such metapsychological considerations as repetition-compulsion cannot avoid recognizing the repetitious character of psychotherapy itself. The same territory must be won again and again, and the clinician is therefore said to come up against "resistance"—that is, the *conservatism* of the personality in face of any external attempt to change it. As Shapiro (1989) has expressed it:

> Resistance in this sense has no motive. It refers to a reactive tendency of the personality, not to an intentional action on the part of the person. (209)

So conceptualized, the personality itself is a system, and its resistance to therapeutically induced change (development?) "is merely a special case of its self-regulating and self-stabilizing capacity" (Shapiro 1989 200). Resistance, then, is not just a psychodynamically motivated pattern of oppositional intention (Greenson 1967), but also a *systemic process*[9]—and in fulfilling its "self-regulating and self-stabilizing" functions, the personality (construed as a system) thus reflects a biological as well as psychological propensity to repeat.

Repetition is therefore basic to psychic life. All psychic functioning, whether or not unconsciously motivated, is in some way repetition. It is in this sense that repetition is also a subtext of scientific psychoanalytic discourse. For repetition is, at one and the same time, (a) "resistance" to development (or change), yet (b) implicated in its psychoanalytic conceptualization. How can this be? Is it really possible to conceive of "psychoanalytic development," or is the very formulation a *reductio ad absurdum* as Zukier has already insinuated? It thus becomes necessary, at this juncture, to identify and explicate the assumptions and presuppositions of "development" in order to see if these can be reconciled with the centrality of repetition in psychoanalytic science. This discussion will lay the groundwork for the sections to follow, in which the "model of development" (i.e., the conceptual scheme of Basch, Noy, Gedo, etc.) is explicitly introduced.

The scientific idea of development consists in the analytic abstraction of an explanatory past, and it originates as an attempt to solve the problem of continuity in change.[10] According to the *orthogenetic* principle which underlies its formulation (Werner 1948), "development" is conceived (a) as a series of quantitative and qualitative reorganizations, (b) among and within behavioral, biological, and other systems, (c) which take place by means of differentiation and hierarchical integration. And it is precisely because of hierarchical integration that continuity (in functioning) can be maintained despite rapid biological, behavioral (and other) changes, especially during the earlier years of human development. It is further assumed that variables at many levels of analysis (e.g., genetic, neurobiological, psychological variables, etc.), in dynamic transaction with one another, determine the character of these adaptive integrations and reorganizations. *Normal* development, in short, is presumed to occur through the reorganization and integration of earlier competencies into new and later behavioral and biological structures. *Pathological* development, however, is marked by defective or diminished differentiation over time, or by the lack of integration of competencies relevant to achieving adaptation at a particular developmental level (Kaplan 1966). Because early structures are often incorporated into later structures, any early deviation in functioning may ultimately lead to (or contribute toward) the emergence of larger future disturbances, including enhanced susceptibility to regression (reversion to less differentiated structures and modes of functioning).

The orthogenetic principle is often supplemented by the principle of *epigenesis* (Piaget 1971). According to this latter principle (borrowed from the discipline of embryology), organismic growth, or biological development in general, is characterized by a *prescribed program* of phases or stages, each being necessary to the following one in a constant order. At the same time, each stage or phase (with its associated functional capacities)—though followed by another—is nevertheless presumed to persist or reverberate throughout the life span of the organism; so each phase, once established, is seen as capable of exerting a certain influence upon the organism for the remainder of its life span. It follows that the developmental past (as a level of organization and mode of functioning) is not only the precondition of the present, but is also incorporated into it; developmental (or maturational) change may thus be said to "repeat" or recapitulate the past, albeit at a further stage of organization, differentiation, and hierarchical integration. It was in fact this very principle that Freud first exploited in *Three Essays on the Theory of Sexuality* (1905a), in which the development of libido is retrospectively portrayed as an epigenetic series (see also Gedo and Goldberg 1973; Erikson 1959).

The idea of development, as I have presented it, is a *scientific* conceptualization; it involves the analytic abstraction of an explanatory past, and in this way is categorially distinct from the historical construction of the psychoanalytic past, which consists in the narrative abstraction of a meaningful past. The idea of development is thus a scientific construction, in that it analytically abstracts the past in terms of the principles of orthogenesis and epigenesis. But these principles (which formally define the scientific scheme of development) are biological in origin and application. Their plausibility as developmental postulates depends upon their reference to those "transhistorical" processes (and/or extralinguistic realities) that underlie the interpretable world of meaningful appearances. Hence the rationale for Freud's original focus on libidinal and instinctual vicissitudes, since what in this instance is being "developed" or (transformed) is presumably the symbolic representation of a *biologically prescribed program*. Moreover, Freud seems to be similarly justified in privileging the developmental processes of infancy and early childhood, since these early periods are (on empirical grounds) more "biologically loaded" than those, for example, of young adulthood and middle age. Thus psychoanalytical theorists like Erikson (1963), who seek to extend an orthogenetic and epigenetic approach throughout the life span (and across historical cultures), are probably misguided, since their accounts (though intuitively plausible and clinically appealing) lack genuine biological leverage and often constitute disguised evaluations of how normal people should evolve (see also Gergen 1977; Gergen and Gergen 1986).[11] As a science, then, and as a discourse defined by its biological presuppositions, psychoanalysis is thus entitled to maintain that the vicissitudes of later development are (in an important and non-trivial sense) based upon the definitive experiences of infancy and childhood (A. Freud 1965; Mahler 1968). Even the normal adult still carries a certain psychic (or psychobiological) burden "deposited" by the past. But such claims are only warranted on account of the biological principles of orthogenesis and epigenesis, in terms of which an explanatory past is analytically abstracted, and an idea of development is scientifically constructed.

If psychoanalytic development is grounded in the biological past, or experiences of infancy and childhood, then this must also mean that it is focused on the identification and negotiation of early stage-salient issues, and that these issues typically revolve around the origins and vicissitudes of interaction, reciprocity, and attunement (Stern 1985). Thus, the earliest (biopsychological) issues of development concern *homeostatic regulation* (Greenspan 1979), when the infant must establish basic cycles and rhythms of sleep and wakefulness and of feeding and elimination. Stabilization of these bodily processes allows the infant to interact more extensively with the outside world, and to begin to achieve a reliable signaling system. Yet it is also evident that the *caregiver* plays a crucial role in facilitating the development of homeostasis, in that he or she must be able to provide a physical and emotional environment (a protective, predictable, and engaging environment) in which the infant can balance inner states and external stimuli. In other words, human development in its earliest phases presupposes the infant's need for an external source of psychological regulation; homeostasis therefore designates a *relational* as well as *biological* prototype of development. It is a prototype based on the biological notion of the infant's emerging self-regulatory capacities that can be directed *both* outwardly in a request for the environment to help and inwardly toward self-soothing or to such stimulatory behaviors as sucking.

Mastery of homeostatic regulation, and the development of reliable patterns of signaling (as illustrated by the emergence of the social smile), contribute to an increased capacity for sustained attention to (and interaction with) the environment so that behaviors which were previously endogenously stimulated and reflexive in nature are replaced by contingent responses to exogenous stimulation. This stage (4–6 months) is characterized by increased intensity and differentiation of affect. The crucial task for infant and caregiver, through a kind of coordinate attunement, is to negotiate the management of "tension" or affective arousal.

Later stages usually cited include: (a) the development of a secure *attachment relation* (Bowlby 1980), marked by increased attention to the pleasures and pains of interpersonal interaction and recognition; (b) the development of a so-called autonomous self (18–24 months); and finally (c) the development of symbolic representation (24–36 months) whereby children—through language, play, imagination, and fantasy—become more able to label (and share) emotions, intentions, and cognitions, and to exhibit their growing social awareness (Beeghly and Cicchetti 1987). This is also the stage at which fantasy distortion (hence psychic reality in its usual sense) becomes conceivable. As Stern (1985 255) has argued: prior to this stage, prior to the advent of symbolic thinking and linguistic and narrative competence, the cognitive capacity for defensive (psychodynamic) distortions of reality is not normally available (see also in Chapter 2 of this book, "Saving the Mixed Model?").

My brief survey of the phases of early ("preoedipal") development is not meant to be psychologically or psychoanalytically comprehensive; yet it does direct attention to the vast data base accumulated through systematic infant observation, and even more importantly, illustrates the idea of an epigenetic series that is orthogenetically organized.[12] According to this prototype of development, the infant-child is "biologically programmed" to negotiate intersubjective (or intended) meaning—and to do so by mastering such sequential tasks as homeostatic regulation, the management of affective arousal, the acquisition of a secure attachment relationship, and the attainment of symbolic (and self-) representation. There is, in short, a genetic and physiological blueprint underlying the expectable development of affective experience and cognitive structures during the early years (and it is *this* developmental process which facilitates the evolution and expression of psychoanalytically relevant object relations). Moreover, each stage or phase of infantile development is relationally structured, and each is conceived as a qualitative and quantitative reorganization of its precursor in time. Later stages are necessarily more differentiated than earlier ones, although the needs, issues, strategies, and tasks of infantile development are presumed to persist into adulthood, even if they are no longer so salient as they once were.

It is such a model that defines the current meaning of "psychoanalytic development"; and it is such a model (or ideology?) which appears to shape argument, theory, and research in the American tradition of scientific psychoanalysis. Thus Gedo and Goldberg (1973) and Gedo (1979, 1981, 1984) have advocated a comprehensive framework (a hierarchy of modes of functioning) which postulates five developmental eras within an epigenetic scheme, along with five "corresponding" therapeutic modalities. As one would expect, the earlier developmental eras are tied to such *psychobiological* concerns as (a) prevention of traumatic overstimulation and (b) self-regulation of internal sensation and affective arousal. To illustrate: Gedo's first developmental era (the "reflex arc" era, or the aforementioned stage of homeostasis) is correlated with the environmental or caregiving function of "pacification." However, (a) since epigenesis requires the persistence (or availability) of early modes of functioning in later and more differentiated developmental phases, (b) and since Gedo posits, further, a biological propensity to repeat (in order to help account for the current salience of infantile issues like tension regulation), it follows that adult pathologies and archaic transferences are allowed to reflect and express the presymbolic and/or presubjective dysfunctions of infancy. In such circumstances (Gedo would affirm), it is incumbent on the analyst "to patch over this deficit by assisting the patient via measures aimed at 'pacification'" (1984 132). More generally, however, the patient's predominant developmental organization *at any moment* dictates the nature and intent of the therapeutic intervention—although it is usually to be expected that any particular patient will be functioning on *several* developmental levels, and will therefore (over the course of treatment) be the object of several "corresponding" modalities of therapeutic intervention (ranging from "supportive" pacification and unification, through optimal disillusionment, and interpretation and witnessing).[13]

To sum up the discussion thus far: the epigenetic and orthogenetic idea of development is both illustrated by and articulated in John Gedo's conceptual scheme for clinical psychoanalysis. Within the boundaries of such a scheme, it is presumed that patients (whether neurotic, borderline, or psychotic) not only repeat the meaningful and interpretable events and interactions that once made them uncomfortable (a reflection of the psychodynamics of psychic reality), but also reenact the *affectively charged experience* of discomfort itself (a reflection, perhaps, of the biological propensity to repeat).[14] According to Gedo's argument, psychoanalytic science is therefore required to recognize and explain two analytically distinct (but often concretely inseparable) expressions of "repetition" in development; and the clinical management of such repetitions (now known as transference-repetitions) may well necessitate (as we have already observed) not only such therapeutic measures as interpretation, but also those that are "beyond interpretation" (Gedo 1979).[15]

I can now proceed to summarize this discussion through the following two sets of observations.

1. The psychoanalytic presumption of "repetition" turns out to be not at all inconsistent with the scientific construct of development, since it is evident that orthogenesis and epigenesis each implies repetition (and conservation) as well as change and hierarchical reorganization. According to the principle of orthogenesis, prior or past levels of organization are incorporated in (or are *repeated* in) later and more differentiated organizations; and according to the principle of epigenesis, earlier modes of functioning (and the issues, needs, and structures associated with them) persist in (or are *repeated* in) subsequent and later levels of development, though they are not normally so salient as they once were at their original phase-appropriate level. Hence, the idea of repetition is implicated in the scientific formulation of development, even if its role and function are now magnified by such specifically psychoanalytic postulates as (a) the biological propensity to repeat and (b) the psychodynamic propensity to regress.[16] I thus propose that the normative notion of development is *psychoanalytically* modified, in that it now reflects the "regressive pull" of (a) external trauma and stress, (b) intrapsychic anxiety and conflict, and (c) innate biological (or constitutional) pressures and processes (Freud 1937a). "Psychoanalytic development" thus generates a field of opposing vectors or forces: in its normal as well as pathological course, it always signifies a tension or "conflict" between an analytical vector of regressive disorganization and an analytical vector of hierarchical reorganization (Arlow and Brenner 1964). In this way, as in others, "conflict" (whatever its narrative content), and conflict-resolution (whatever its dynamic nature), remain central to the definition of psychoanalysis as a theoretical and scientific discourse.

2. If "psychoanalytic development" is formally conceptualized in terms of orthogenesis, epigenesis, and repetition-regression, then it is substantively characterized in terms of the *affective experiences* and *cognitive structures* of infancy and childhood. The adult is "regressively pulled" to repeat such infantile prototypes (and their derivatives as well), but this does not necessarily bespeak the direct effect of early experience on adult behavior, but rather implies the mediating role of an intervening developmental process (Shapiro 1989 170).

According to my argument, what is repeated are: (a) the qualities and quantities of affective experience; and (b) the cognitive representations and symbolic transformations of such experience. The first class of repetitions pertains to affective dispositions whose origins and conditions are (in large measure) biological; the second class of repetitions pertains, more generally, to the affectively charged relational representations (and/or memories) of childhood experience, and more particularly, to those that elaborate and symbolize the meaning of interpersonal attachment. I assume, of course, that both classes are initially registered in the "inner world" of the infant, at first as the preverbal, enactive, and sensorimotor schemata of subjective experience (Piaget and Inhelder 1969; Stern 1985), and later, as the more or less unconscious *self-schemata* (desires, fears, fantasies, etc.) of psychic reality (Horowitz 1988). So registered, they enter into the developmental process and contribute to the further development (and/or distortion) of the adult personality. As Freud (1937a 238) states: "The adult's ego . . . continues to defend itself against dangers which no longer exist." It is in this general, albeit elliptical, sense, that the adult personality reflects the imprint of the infantile past; and it is in such a sense that this personality—*as an adult organization*—is regressively prone to reenact (repeat) the contents, patterns, and structures of the infantile past.

Michael Basch (1988), we recall, has described psychotherapy as "applied developmental psychology." Given the prevalence and influence of this view, it is not surprising that the infantile prototype (as sketched in this section) is often transferred, *in toto,* to the clinical context—as if therapeutic change were merely the engineered resumption of a developmental process that had been frozen or arrested in childhood. However, as Eagle (1984a 136), among others, has observed: "No process, physiological or psychological, unfolds in an adult as it would have when we were 1, 2 or 3 years of age." This important objection notwithstanding, the infantile prototype of development is still relevant (in my view) to the theory and practice of therapy, especially insofar as it yields a model for the interaction of affective experiences and cognitive structures. The influence of such a model, to be introduced in the next section, is clearly evident in clinicians' increasing acceptance of an interconnection between (affective) attachment and (cognitive) understanding at all stages of therapy within any given case. In other words, the infantile prototype of development reminds the therapist that affective enactments facilitate reflective awareness and cognitive competence, just as cognitive mastery can facilitate efficient tension regulation and the emergence of empathic responsiveness. If we grant that these affective-cognitive interactions of infancy and childhood are somehow "paralleled" in adult psychotherapy, then it follows that the oft-drawn distinction between the analyst's *interpretative,* insight-facilitating function and his *empathic,* relationship function may well be misconceived—especially to the degree that it implies that there are two distinct modes of therapy for two distinct classes of patients: i.e., classical "insight-oriented" therapy for neurotics, and non-analytic "supportive" therapy for those suffering from preoedipal or narcissistic pathologies.[17] It would rather seem that support and interpretation, attachment and understanding, and affect (experience) and insight (concept) are inextricably joined in any concrete therapeutic engagement, and that, as Eagle (1984a) puts it:

> The establishment of conditions of safety can itself be seen as an implicit interpretation to the effect that the patient is not in the original traumatic situation and that the therapist is different, in important respects, from the traumatic figures of the past. (105)

In this section, I have sought to describe the structure of the scientific construct of development, and to place that construct in psychoanalytic context. In the discussion below, I introduce the developmental formulations of Michael Basch and Pinchas Noy. These convey (as one would expect) a more precise depiction of the psychoanalytic prototype of infantile development and specifically offer (a) a credible *model* for the developmental interaction of affective experiences and cognitive structures; as well as (b) an *argument* for the relevance of such a model to the practices of therapy and to the processes of therapeutic action.

From Psychoanalytic Metapsychology to Developmental Psychoanalysis

In this section and in the two which follow, I reconstruct a prototypical model of psychoanalytic development. This model is based largely on proposals advanced by Michael Basch (1976a, 1976b, 1983, 1988) and Pinchas Noy (1969, 1979). Though distinctive in certain respects, it also illustrates a typical and exemplary approach to scientific conceptualization in American psychoanalysis. As such, it provides the foundation for the tripartite structure of scientific psychoanalytic argument: from its underlying scheme of affective-cognitive development follow the psychoanalytic paradigms of the nature and conditions of psychopathology on the one hand, and the nature and conditions of therapeutic action on the other.

I begin with the thesis that the scheme of affective-cognitive development (as described below) stands as a "scientific" surrogate for traditional psychoanalytic metapsychology.[18] According to the latter, what gets the organism moving is a biological drive transformed into "instinctual" psychological energy called *id* (Freud 1933). This id-drive toward life-pleasure or death-aggression creates a tension pushing for discharge, and thus signifies that the most basic (or underlying) tendency of the organism is immediate discharge of excitation. It is the impossibility of doing so, however (due to the resistance of physical and social reality), that precipitates the development of ego functions and object relations and places the child's inner self into adaptive contact with the external world (Eagle 1984a 6–19). "Development," then, is an unnatural but inevitable detour from nature, which is caused or propelled, in the first place, by unremitting pressure for instinctual discharge. It follows that, in terms of this traditional metapsychological scheme, the quality and quantity of affective awareness and affective events are just the conscious (or behavioral) expressions and derivatives of the instinctual drives of sexuality and aggression. Thus, though the *locus* of pleasure-unpleasure may change over the course of development (oral, anal, genital), and though the primary objects of emotion may also change, the meaning of the drives themselves (and of derivative affects as well) do not. In other words, according to the traditional theory: (a) the baby's attachment to the mother is as "erotic" and sexual as is his or her later attachment to a lover; and (b) while anxiety in infancy may be experienced and expressed differently from anxiety in adulthood, its theoretical function is constant throughout the life span. It must be concluded, then, that even if traditional Freudian theory gives primacy of place to affects and emotions (as instinctual derivatives), and even if it regards cognitive states as epiphenomena of changes in the emotional domain, it cannot quite generate a valid or persuasive theory of affective-emotional development; and this it cannot do owing to its fundamental commitment to the *changelessness* of instinct.

Along with many other contemporary American theorists, Basch and Noy reject (or at least reformulate) such metapsychological propositions as those cited above and no longer assume, for example: (a) that psychobiological (or intrapsychic) development is "driven" by the pressure for instinctual discharge; or (b) that the relative intensity (or affective force) of thought, fantasy, and desire is a function of the ebb and flow of "psychic energy." In place of this traditional and discredited instinct-driven theory, it is now posited that behavior and development are biologically programmed for the acquisition and expression of (some degree of) competence, mastery, and relatedness; and moreover, that the intensity or force of thought and desire is due *not* to some "cathexis" of psychic energy, but rather to the patterns and processes of temperament[19] and affective communication, as these are disclosed biologically and developmentally in interaction with cognitive structures.

In the model proposed by Basch and Noy, an "explanatory past" (a genuinely developmental past) is therefore offered as a scientific alternative to the traditional (and pseudo-developmental) metapsychology. This revisionist formulation presumes, in the first place, that there are entities, experiences, or events that can be referentially labeled as "affects," formally excised and abstracted, and then treated as objects (or paths) in abstract space by an independent observer; and in the second place, that affect (as arousal) is variably regulated and experienced, and is eventually assimilated to schemata that become more differentiated and integrated over time, so that emotional awareness, itself, is seen as a type of cognitive processing (a) which has its own organizational structure and (b) which has its own developmental history. Finally, unlike more familiar American alternatives to traditional metapsychology—which address chiefly the *psychosocial* vicissitudes of ego-formation, object relations, and self-development—the Basch-Noy model retains Freud's original, dual focus on *both* the biological substrate and the relational sources (real and fantasized) of motivation and development, leading to a recognition:

- that human behavior is affectively motivated;
- that affect originates as a form of biologically programmed communication, initially independent of language and lexical (or subjective) representation;
- that affect, so construed, possesses its own organizational structure, and has its own line of orthogenetic development;
- which interacts with analytically distinguishable cognitive structures and processes;

- that are, themselves, developmental systems which are epigenetically constituted and orthogenetically organized.

Let us then assume—in introducing the Basch-Noy model—that affect and cognition comprise two distinct, yet interactive systems (Hesse
and Cicchetti 1982), and that an important task for scientific psychoanalysis is to reframe traditional issues and inquiries in light of such an
assumption. From such a premise, Basch (1976a, 1976b, 1983) begins,
first, by constructing a model in which emotional awareness and empathic
communication are seen as originating in orthogenetically more primitive
affective states. Such elementary state-processes (conditions of affective
arousal) are construed as biologically fixed reaction patterns (subcortically
controlled)—"somatic responses to the quantity or intensity of stimulation of the nervous system, and not to the content, quality or symbolic
significance of the stimulus" (Basch 1983 107). With this as his point of
departure, Basch proceeds to generate "affect" as a developmental process,
elaborating, for example: its linkage to encoded (sensorimotor) memory
traces; the transformation into signals of the infant's original affective
responses; and the early (but psychoanalytically decisive) vicissitudes of
parent-child affective communication (see also Stern 1985).

But in advancing such a model in which transitions from one level to
the next are defined by transformations in the schemata for processing
incoming information, Basch tacitly concedes a certain *discontinuity* in
affective development. For the development of affect is held to progress
in discrete stages (affect—feeling—emotion—empathy); and the integration of these stages or levels within one *continuous* process (as an
internally coherent explanatory past) is not at all an outcome of inference
from the empirical evidence, but is actually a logical implication or corollary of the principles of orthogenesis and epigenesis.

Consider, for example, the details of Basch's argument: affect in infancy is not properly labeled a psychological event, in that it is still devoid
of those organizational structures that facilitate self-awareness, symbolization, reflection, and reasoning. Only later, perhaps between 14 and 24
months (after much "transformation" in the schemata for processing
incoming affective information)[20] is the infant fully capable of a psychological intentional experience of affect ("feeling"), since it is only then
that the child's organized sense of self clearly emerges. Likewise, "emotions"—which involve implicit cognitive appraisals—represent still more

complex and developmentally advanced forms of affective experience and communication. Finally, at the summit of this developmental line, stands "empathy," here understood as the awareness of another person's emotional experience which is based on the *knowledge* one has of one's own inner world.[21] Basch regards "empathy," so viewed, as the most sophisticated transformation of affective communication, since it figures as an advanced cognitive skill which depends on decentering—the capacity "to take an objective view toward one's self through both *reflection*[22] and what Vygotsky called 'inner speech' " (1983 119).

In short, Basch introduces a persuasive model of emotionality and its development—in which the simplest affective-biological states are always epigenetically preserved in the later and more advanced forms of empathy, and in which "precursors" to empathy are uncovered in the infant's earliest affective states, and indeed, in the biological substrate of its neural activity and in the underlying circuitry of its brain. Development, in such a scheme, presupposes *continuity in change* (affective-biological arousal leads, inexorably, to empathic understanding); but this presupposition, we realize, is warranted only by commitment to the principles of orthogenesis and epigenesis.

Interesting implications follow from Basch's scheme. These include the propositions: (a) that the affective experience of any individual is normally characterized by a variable "distribution" of affect (as arousal), and more or less modulated, more or less conscious feeling, emotion, and empathy—each, of course, organized at a different level in the continuum of development; (b) that psychopathology is always a function of some "non-optimum distribution" of affect, feeling, emotion, and empathy; (c) that psychopathology, in general, is a function of *disorganization* in each level or stage of affective development, resulting in maladaptive affective states that are characteristically either undermodulated or overmodulated (see also Horowitz 1988 15–18); (d) that empathic communication, which requires the advanced cognitive capacity for self-distancing reflection (without incurring an irreversible loss of affect, feeling, or emotion), is actually a refined form of intelligence and understanding[23]—and so, for example, the analyst's empathic responsiveness

> implies that an accurate appraisal has been made of the context in which the affect is mobilized, the overall level of maturation . . . and the actual level of maturity being exhibited under the circumstances. (Basch 1983 123)

There is at least one further corollary to Basch's argument. It now becomes possible, in principle, not only to assess empirically the *analyst's* empathic responsiveness (see above), but also to diagnose and influence the empathic behavior and performance of the patient. This is just to say that it is reasonable to conceive of retrospective historical reconstructions (the self-narratives of Schafer and Spence) as evincing more or less empathic understanding; in this way, the narrational capacity to assume an empathic, hence reflective stance toward oneself, or to display an empathic understanding of one's own ineliminable past, becomes a scientifically coherent goal (or norm) for development and therapy.[24] Conversely, deviation from an empathic understanding of one's past, or inability to sustain a genuinely empathic stance toward oneself, becomes a diagnostic indicator of "deficits," and/or reality-distorting conflicts and regressions in one's affective-cognitive development.

As I close this phase of the discussion, I add a final cautionary note: in Basch's model, the affective past is analytically abstracted as an explanatory past; precisely on this score, precisely because it serves as a *scientific* conceptualization, Basch's model does not so much account for "qualitative" change (affect . . . empathy), as, in truth, it nullifies it. For though the principles of orthogenesis and epigenesis enable us to translate the problem of qualitative transformation into a scientific ("biological") discourse, they by no means manage to resolve that problem. Such a translation (in which affective development is conceptualized in terms of increasing differentiation, articulation, and hierarchical reintegration) does not succeed in explaining fundamental *qualitative* transitions. Hence, it is never made clear how the organism advances (a) from elementary affective-biological states (affects as "objectless objects" or non-intentional processes), (b) to emotional-empathic communications which cannot really be described or understood apart from the total (meaningful) situation in which they are experienced. How, in short, does the organism move from a condition in which some essential function or capability is lacking (e.g., language, intentionality, etc.) to one in which that competence is exhibited? Such a question appears to signal the perplexity encountered by *all* scientific attempts to explain (or model) *any* developmental change that involves "qualitative changes in status" (Feffer 1982; Danziger 1985); indeed, it is a problem or perplexity that Basch, too, cannot really resolve or assuage—notwithstanding his scientific intention to derive "personhood" from organism, or narrative meaning (empathic understanding) from an inherently meaning-less state.[25]

The Psychogenesis of the Symbolic Concept of Self

As I am presenting it, the Basch-Noy model offers a psychoanalytic rendering of the proposition that affect and cognition comprise two distinct, yet interactive developmental lines. In the previous section, "af-fect" was introduced as a developmentally intelligible scientific idea—as an analytically abstracted aspect of an "explanatory past." My task is now to specify how affect, so construed, is cognitively processed, how it is symbolized and represented, and how it interacts with cognitive struc-tures which are themselves developmentally organized and psychoanalyti-cally significant. We will discover, in the end, that "psychoanalytic signifi-cance" resides in a radical reformulation of Freud's original model of primary and secondary process.[26]

The starting point is once again Basch: namely, his proposal that a central function of the human brain is to turn experience (information) into symbols. The brain's primary or distinctive activity consists of "ab-stractive transformation" (Basch 1976a), and it is this abstractive transfor-mation which constitutes symbolization.[27] Following the philosopher Langer (1967), Basch proceeds to distinguish two forms of symboliza-tion, discursive and presentational. The discursive form, consisting of words and mathematical symbols, is abstract and linear; information is transmitted by a step-by-step arrangement of words or symbols. In sharp contrast, symbolism is described as *presentational,* precisely because infor-mation is transmitted more or less instantaneously as in a dream image, religious ritual, or work of art. Like Freud's primary process, presenta-tional symbolism cannot express negation, lacks true-false values, and states no propositions.

Basch believes that presentational symbolism is the true thematic of Freudian psychoanalysis. Freud is said to have discovered the hidden language and logic of presentational symbolism (of primary process), and by so doing, demonstrated that it could be *translated* into a verbal discur-sive mode, and hence become susceptible to scientific investigation. This discovery, states Basch (1976a 419), "is comparable to the discovery of the calculus, which made the systematic study of the organic-molecular level possible."

According to Basch, the presentational mode of symbolization is peculiarly suited to express and represent the meaning of experience, or more exactly, the meaning of affective experience. For the meaning of any particular message is taken to lie in its effect on the disposition of the organism; and such dispositions and attitudes are usually classified as *affective* insofar as they

> relate to the symbolic concept of self rather than to the purely adaptational demands made by the physical surround of the organism. (1976a 418)

We can now discern the relevance of Basch's earlier treatment of empathy, in which he traced the development of affective experience from its "meaningless" origins in the biology of temperament and in the conditions of somatic arousal, through its expression, articulation, and modulation in primitive cognitive structures, and finally, to its supposed actualization in the capacity for reflection or empathic understanding. It appears that presentational symbolism participates in (or interacts with) this same developmental line. Affective meaning is developmentally disclosed *as* presentational symbolism, by virtue of the cognitive processes which underlie (or give rise to) its expression. In short, the symbolic encoding of developing (but often opaque and unintelligible) affective experience is normally in the presentational mode rather than in the discursive mode. Moreover, this is as it should be in that such affective experiences (affect —feeling—emotion—empathy) are characteristically self-related: that is, they pertain to the meaning of the symbolic concept of the self.

It follows that a distinctive feature of psychoanalytic *intervention* is its tendency to translate the presentational symbolization of affective meaning into its discursive counterpart.[28] Much of the work of psychotherapy therefore consists of *formulating* experience for the first time,[29] of verbalizing hitherto unverbalizable experiences—whether such experiences refer to early patterns of affectivity (e.g., Gedo 1981), or to later, cognitively more complex, affectively charged and defensive symbolic representations (e.g., fantasies and similar psychodynamic schemata). So in terms of both the present discussion and the model examined in the previous section, it is evident that psychoanalytic therapy is directed toward "verbalizing the unverbalizable," either (a) by translating presentational symbolism into a discursive mode, or (b) by verbalizing the "feeling potential" of affect, the "emotional potential" of feeling, and the "empathic potential" of emotion. Once again the psychoanalytic past is disclosed as both "found" and "made"; I mean by this that relatively non-discursive *(unverbalizable)* affective experiences and affective meanings are viewed as derivatives of an objective developmental past, repeated and reenacted (or "found") in the context of transference, while *verbalized* formulations or interpretations of such experiences and meanings are apparently constructed (or "made") in the dialogical and narrative context of the psychoanalytic encounter.[30]

One of the basic functions of presentational symbolism is to help maintain (or constitute) the unity and continuity of the symbolic concept of self. *Only* presentational symbolism is capable of expressing and representing the continuity of self-experience, involving as it does the concept of lived time. As Basch states:

> Inevitably, the reflexive activity of the brain becomes in turn a subject for reflection, and the resulting symbolic concept of self becomes objectified as a permanent "self." . . . [But] it is the relation of the self *now* to the self *before* that cannot be discursively symbolized and presentational symbolism seems to me . . . to be the outgrowth of the brain's symbolizing in this area . . . (1976a 417)

The following claims are thus advanced: (a) first, that the experience of temporal continuity is central to the coherence of the symbolic concept of self, to the preservation of personal identity, and *mutatis mutandis,* to the expectation of a sense of psychic security; and (b) second, that the apprehension of the unity and continuity of selfhood is impossible within an exclusively discursive mode of symbolization. Scientific or paradigmatic discourse[31] is accordingly disqualified from expressing or representing the experience of temporality, and is unable, in particular, to represent the psychoanalytic relations of the "self now" and the "self before." Now in Chapter 4 ("The Scope of Historical Psychoanalysis"), I have already asserted that *historical* psychoanalysis (as a specialized expression of narrative discourse) is singularly suited to represent these relations, and that (following Ricoeur), "narrativity" is the language structure having temporality as its ultimate referent. Basch, however, could not exactly endorse my position since historical psychoanalysis (narrative) is clearly a discursive mode of symbolization. We will soon discover, though, that Pinchas Noy (1979) proposes a yet more radical revision of primary process (presentational symbolism)—which further elaborates its developmental properties, and which also models its ongoing interaction with parallel secondary process. Most importantly, Noy allows primary process to employ "economic sign representation," hence enabling us to redefine narrative discourse as a particular mode of primary process ideation, notwithstanding its representation through signs in both speech and text. Given Noy's reconceptualization of primary process (or presentational symbolism), it now becomes possible to account for (a) the rationality of the narrative (historical) representation of the experience of temporality, and likewise, (b) the rationality of the narrative (historical) apprehension of, and reflection upon, the unity and continuity of personal identity. It is, by the way, this last claim which helps to legitimate historical or hermeneutical psychoanalysis as a *theoretical* discourse. For what is being "theorized"[32] is the experience of temporality as it is psychoanalytically relevant to the unity and continuity of the symbolic concept of self.

There is, to conclude, a third claim that Basch advances—one which leads directly to our treatment below of Noy's reconceptualization of primary and secondary process. According to Basch, Freud was in error in theorizing that primary process (presentational symbolization) was more primitive than secondary process, that it was "a hierarchical precursor of the later discursive symbolism" (1976a 417). On the contrary, Basch endorses the *evolutionary* hypothesis that presentational symbolism represents "the brain's attempt to cope with the newest of evolutionary developments," namely meaning. Primary process (contra Freud) is no longer understood as a primitive discharge mode, but is rather regarded as a cognitively sophisticated developmental achievement. Its principal function, we recall, is to process affective information—information relevant to needs, attitudes, and dispositions which are self-related—and to *represent* such information in terms of the meaning of the symbolic concept of self. We end, then, with this observation: that it is perhaps a constitutive paradox of Basch's project that it aims to encompass—within the presuppositional horizon of *one* developmental paradigm—(a) not only the most primitive affective states (presubjective and biological conditions of arousal and temperament which are inherently meaningless) but also (b) the most "advanced" and "developed" expressions of emotional, empathic, and aesthetic communication (historical and cultural conditions which pertain to the meaning of the symbolic concept of self).

The Duality of Cognition in Psychoanalytic Development

If the classical instinct-drive theory is rejected, then affect is no longer reducible to an aspect of instinctual discharge and instinctual tension. Affect becomes, instead, a derivative of *development*. What is experienced as feeling, emotion, or empathy is actually the consequence of the cognitive processing of affective arousal; the cognitive process itself undergoes a sequence of structural transformations during development which determine the structure (and phenomenology) of subsequent emotional awareness and experience. And according to Basch's formulation, such awareness and experience are normally symbolized through the presentational mode, itself a sophisticated developmental achievement and an outcome of the operations of primary process.

It is Pinchas Noy's (1969, 1979) special contribution to have fashioned a comprehensive revision of Freudian primary process. In doing so, he not only has enlarged our understanding of how affective information might be processed and organized, but also has expanded our view of psychoanalytic psychopathology, and of the rationale for therapeutic intervention. Like Basch, Noy rejects the traditional view that primary process must be construed as a "primitive discharge mode." He argues, instead, that two distinct, yet interrelated, *developmental lines* can be abstracted from concrete cognitive functioning: the first, self-centered or primary process thinking; the second, reality-oriented or secondary process thinking. Each line is epigenetically and orthogenetically organized, and each continues to evolve and mature in tandem with the other: the development of both being determined largely by the same intrinsic maturational factors.

Noy proceeds to outline the hypothetical developmental course of each of these modes, focusing on such crucial cognitive functions as categorization, the representation of reality and self, and causal reasoning. For the purposes of the present discussion, it is important that Noy recognizes the original biologically rooted, self-regulatory function of primary process (its epigenetic origins in the biology of temperament and affective arousal), as well as its gradual specialization (or orthogenesis) to deal efficiently with the "expanding self." One might say, in summary, that Noy's primary process categorizes and represents the objects, events, and phenomena of the world as *experience* (always involving such "self-ele-

ments" as need, wish, or affective-emotional state); whereas emerging
secondary process organizes reality as *knowledge:*

> An inner representation of some hypothetical outer reality which is com-
> posed of things, beings and events that act, change, appear and disappear
> without any relation to the self. (1979 180)

Primary and secondary process therefore constitute two developmental
lines of cognitive functioning: the former generating a symbolic of *experience* (of which, presentational symbolism is one important type); and the
latter generating a symbolic of *knowledge* (as illustrated by discursive
symbolism in general, and scientific discourse in particular). Noy further
assumes: (a) that any item of information is capable of being categorized
twice (or doubly processed), first as subjective experience and then as a
piece of objective knowledge; (b) that neurophysiological structures and
processes exist to transform data processed by one of the modes into the
other; and (c) that (contra Basch), primary process may employ "economic sign representation" whenever required by a particular task of "self-
assimilation."

Proceeding from such assumptions, Noy (1979 189) is able to argue
that the maintenance of the unity and continuity of the self can only be
assured by the *double* representation of the self as an experience (primary
process, presentational symbolism) and as a concept (secondary process,
discursive symbolism). In other words, affective information can be doubly processed, and the symbolic concept of self (the locus of affective
meaning) is most efficiently established, expressed, and represented when
data processed by one of the modes are transformed to the other. An
important implication of this hypothesis is that psychoanalytic psychopathology is always a function of some imbalance (or non-optimum fit)
between experiential and conceptual representations, between primary
and secondary process operations. It is possible, for example, that one
cognitive line (e.g., primary process) is relatively underdeveloped, and
that such mental tasks as the mastery of a trauma or the assimilation of an
emotional experience may therefore be unsuccessfully performed. More
generally, any imbalance between the two developmental lines is likely to
result in feelings of derealization and depersonalization. As Noy states:

> Feelings of depersonalization and derealization generally appear together,
> because any imbalance between the experiential and conceptual modes of
> representation usually affects both the creation of the self-image and the

inner representation of reality. We see these two symptoms in such a broad spectrum of psychopathological states—from cases of severe schizophrenia, through borderline or narcissistic personality disorders, to transient neurotic disturbances—that the symptoms in themselves have no prognostic value, until the exact disturbance that prevents the normal fit is located. (1979 190–91)

The idea of "double representation" (or dual information-processing) not only serves to clarify the nature of psychopathology (as above), but also helps to specify the psychoanalytic-developmental *processes* which underlie narrative discourse. Let us assume that these cognitive processes are characterized by a particularly salient form of "double representation," such that data processed by one of the modes (e.g., primary process) are *exceptionally susceptible* to transformation into the other mode. According to this proposal, narrative discourse (or historical understanding) is hypothesized to be a particular mode of *discursive* primary process thinking, which is exceptionally susceptible to (parallel) secondary processing. One advantage of this proposal is that it succeeds in distinguishing narrative discourse from (a) on the one hand, scientific argument and technical reason (conceptual secondary process) and (b) on the other hand, art, music, dreamlife, and ritual (non-discursive presentational symbolism). Narrative discourse is therefore *mediatory:* it mediates between the (a) conceptual reality requirements of scientific discourse and the (b) obligatory demands of presentational symbolism—and it always articulates or expresses some *balance* of experiential and conceptual modes of representation. Indeed, the specific appeal and utility of narrative (in psychoanalysis, for example) may inhere in its character as an "in-the-service-of-the-self" imaginary reality which is, at the same time, exceptionally susceptible to parallel processing and critical emendation by (conceptual) secondary process.

It is of further interest that Noy's developmental scheme implies that narrative is susceptible not only to parallel secondary processing but also to critical transformation by so-called *autonomous thought* or reflection. Autonomous thought (or the reflective capacity of one section of the human cognitive processes) is, like Basch's empathic understanding, the climax of a developmental line (in this case, of secondary process). Noy speculates that the emergence of autonomous thought depends on the ability of thought to think about itself (1979 201). Consequently, autonomous thought—which is able to control and direct its own operations,[33] disengaged both from the compelling needs of the self *and* from the pressing demands of reality—becomes

> the first biological information-processing system that could liberate itself from dependency on fixed preset programs (instincts). . . . This development created an entirely novel condition—a biological system which was no longer dependent upon the programs provided by nature, but which could *program itself by itself.* (1979 203)

In this sense, the biologically rooted symbolizing activity of the brain now becomes an *end in itself,* and in Basch's words:

> the reflective activity of the brain becomes in turn a subject for reflection, and the resulting symbolic concept of self becomes objectified as a permanent "self." (1976a 417)

I have already asserted that a crucial feature of narrative discourse is its susceptibility to critical transformation by autonomous or reflective thought. We can now see what this might mean. Reflective thought is itself irreducible to scientific discourse on the one hand, or to narrative discourse on the other. It may be, in Bruner's (1986) terms, a third "natural kind." At any rate, it is the distinguishing feature of autonomous thought that it is capable of *reflecting* upon the differentiation between reality and fantasy, between "knowledge" and "experience," without succumbing to the imperious demands of either.[34] Noy elaborates this view by proposing that autonomous thought—whether it appears as philosophical intuition, psychoanalytic insight, or creative imagination—signifies a special integration of (and a sound balance between) primary and secondary modes of communication—such that the boundaries of autonomy temporarily expand to include part of the "territory" hitherto reserved for "obligatory" self-centered and reality-controlled thinking (Noy 1979 215).

Given such a perspective on the development of cognition and on the emergence of autonomous thought, it is now possible to put forth the following characterization of the *psychoanalytic narrative* (previously explicated from a historical point of view in Chapter 4 of this book): the analytic narrative, co-constructed by patient and therapist in the context of the transference, may be described (ideally) as the ongoing endeavor to reduce obligatory trends, while expanding the boundaries of autonomy. In bringing both presentational and discursive symbolism under the aegis of *reflection,* the "analytic process" is thereby accelerated toward at least one of its presumed goals,[35] which Basch has already described as the "symbolic transformation of the conceptualization of self." From this self-consciously scientific or developmental perspective, psychoanalytic practice can now be construed as implicating special *hermeneutic* procedures for the reflective transformation of narrative discourse, for the "symbolic transformation of the conceptualization of self."

Conclusion and Recapitulation. There is a tripartite structure to scientific argument in psychoanalysis. The structure of such argument incorporates three interrelated models—the model of development, the model of psychopathology, and the model of therapeutic action. The model of development is here viewed as foundational, as the *locus classicus* of psychoanalytic science. And as reconstructed above, the Basch-Noy version illustrates *one* particular though exemplary approach to scientific conceptualization in American psychoanalysis.[36] Among the model's notable features are the following:

1. the conceptualization of affective experience as a derivative of development, rather than of instinctual discharge or instinctual tension;
2. the conceptualization of affect and cognition as comprising two distinct, yet interractive, developmental lines;
3. the conceptualization of cognitive functioning as two sets of parallel processes (primary and secondary process), each operating according to its own organizational rules, but *both* determined by similar maturational factors, and both responsible for determining the quality, intensity, and organizational structure of emotional experience;
4. the conceptualization of "reflection" as the orthogenetic culmination of the processes of cognitive development, and as the orthogenetic culmination of the processes of affective development (i.e., the emergence of empathic understanding).

It has not been possible, given the limits of my inquiry, to specify the model in fine detail; so, for example, the question of the development of conflictual states of mind has gone largely unattended, and the problem of the emergence of affective-cognitive *defenses* has been mostly ignored (but for useful discussions of these topics, see Horowitz 1988; Basch 1988; Shapiro 1989). Moreover, as an exercise in conceptualization, the

Basch-Noy model is not necessarily focused on the formulation of testable hypotheses, or on the matter of their empirical exploration. Such issues must remain open to future study.[37] Nevertheless, this model is still advanced as a presumptively *scientific* construction of the psychoanalytic past, and for these reasons:

1. it conforms to the objectivist thesis of Proposition 1 (see Chapter 1, "Two Propositions");
2. it upholds and articulates the three essential commitments of empirical-analytic science (see Chapter 3, "Science and History: Diverging Commitments");
3. it presupposes the truth and applicability of the biological principles of orthogenesis and epigenesis;
4. it encompasses meaningless, physicalist processes (e.g., those underlying basic affective-biological states) and meaningful psychical experiences (e.g., those constitutive of neurotic styles) within the formal structure of a single, internally coherent developmental scheme.

The developmental past, as modeled by Basch and Noy, is an analytically abstracted past. As such, it constitutes a scientific construction of the psychoanalytic past, and is categorially distinct from the past as narratively abstracted, as historically constructed in Chapter 4 of this book. It is important to bear in mind, however, that while the scientific past cannot displace (or replace) the historical past, it can nevertheless purport to explain it. For as suggested above, the psychoanalytic past (as scientifically constructed) specifies precisely those cognitive-affective processes and structures which hypothetically underlie "narrativity" in human discourse. Since narrativity is an essential element of historical understanding in general and of historical psychoanalysis in particular, it appears that scientific psychoanalysis thus explains the nature and utility of historical psychoanalysis. In short, the Basch-Noy model not only provides a developmental and cognitive account of the underlying nature of narrative (and of the psychoanalytic narrative), but also constitutes an argument for its clinical utility and theoretical legitimacy. (a) Historical psychoanalysis is *clinically useful* since only the narrative it generates has temporality as its ultimate referent. Only the psychoanalytic narrative can apprehend and symbolize the unity and continuity of self-experience (and so represent the relationship of the "self now" to the "self before") which is presumably so important to positive therapeutic outcomes. (b) At the same time, historical psychoanalysis is *theoretically legitimated* since only it (and not scientific psychoanalysis) is capable of reflecting upon the unity and continuity of self-experience; only historical psychoanalysis succeeds in generating a *discursive formulation* (or "hermeneutical theory") of the psychoanalytically significant relations of the self now to the self before.

In summary, I have argued that scientific psychoanalysis accounts, in principle, for the nature, necessity, and utility of historical psychoanalysis. It follows that the scientifically constructed psychoanalytic past ("development") underlies and legitimates the historically constructed psychoanalytic past ("narrative"). The latter evidently presupposes the former; and while the "narrative past" (an intersubjectively mediated past) can never be replaced by the scientific past (an objective and explanatory past), it nevertheless requires the latter to serve as its regulative principle.[38]

Development, Pathology, and Therapeutic Action

According to my argument, the model of development is privileged—it supplies the foundation for the larger edifice of scientific psychoanalysis. That edifice or structure, however, also includes the interrelated and derivative conceptualizations (models) of psychopathology and therapeutic action. There is, in short, a tripartite structure to scientific psychoanalytic argument. My purpose in this section is to exhibit that structure "in the round," and to do so by examining the developmental dimensions of psychoanalytic psychopathology on the one hand, and those of psychoanalytic therapy on the other.[39]

1. *Psychopathology.* Given the primacy of "development" in the logic of scientific psychoanalysis, psychopathology must, in general, be viewed as a disorder or disturbance in the developmental processes. For example, if normal development reflects the orthogenetic principle of increasing differentiation and hierarchical reintegration, then psychopathology will be expressed in the reverse processes of disintegration and de-differentiation. Such an approach can be found in Arieti's (1967) *The Intrapsychic Self*, where schizophrenia is conceptualized as a process of disintegration and de-differentiation. Arieti argues (like Basch, Noy, and Gedo) that in normal development, primitive forms of affect and cognition are hierar-

chically integrated into increasingly more advanced forms. The earlier affective forms ("protoemotions") decrease in developmental importance as they become transformed into higher, more modulated, and more differentiated types of emotion. As one would expect, this process is facilitated by a certain, expectable evolution in interpersonal relations (particularly with regard to those involving mother or primary caregiver). However, given biological vulnerability on the one hand, and the cumulative stress of distorted affective communication on the other hand, these primitive schemata ("protoemotions") can again become available to the psyche. In such circumstances, the schizophrenic typically resorts to an *earlier* mode (or level) of affective and cognitive development in order to cope with (or reduce) overwhelming anxiety. But this solution turns out to be pathological or maladaptive, because the patient originally functioned at a higher level—and it is presumably not possible for him or her to adjust *adaptively* to an earlier level of functioning.

Given such typical formulations as Arieti's, it seems reasonable to propose that psychoanalytic psychopathology, in its widest sense, be *conceptualized* in terms of disorders or disturbances in development. But "development" (as Gedo, Basch, and Noy would each concur) incorporates within the formalism of a single model (a) presubjective and preverbal biological-affective processes, as well as (b) the symbolic or imaginative transformations of meaningful, relational representations (where such representations include wishes, fantasies, and their conflicts). Hence, the sources or etiologies of psychopathology are *both* biological (e.g., genetic or constitutional vulnerability) and relational (e.g., environmental, interpersonal, or intrapsychic perceived stress). But whatever the source, and whatever their relative weights in any given case, pathological conditions can always be conceptualized in terms of disorders of (or disturbances in) the biopsychical developmental process.

Psychoanalytic psychopathology, as a clinical art and research discipline, is interested in identifying various patterns of (early) distorted affective communication between infant and caretaker, including, for example, such patterns as affective withdrawal, lack of pleasure, inconsistency, unpredictability, shallowness, and ambivalence (Gaensbauer and Sands 1979).[40] It is indeed an assumption of scientific psychoanalysis that the vicissitudes (and consequences) of early affective communication provide an enduring preverbal sense of what the infant *may expect* of the world (Basch 1988 98). Although this preverbal "set" will doubtlessly be influenced and modified by future maturation (Shapiro 1989), it is preserved (epigenetically) and is easily "reactivated" under conditions of environmental (or intrapsychic) stress and/or biological vulnerability.[41] Moreover, according to the model of development (which assumes that earlier structures are incorporated into later structures), any early deviation in functioning may ultimately lead to the emergence of larger future disturbances. Thus, early distortions in affective communication will tend to have a cumulative negative impact on the future—so that the adult becomes more than normally susceptible to *regression* (reversion to less differentiated cognitive and affective structures and modes of functioning).[42] Under such unfavorable circumstances, the disturbed individual may now be prone to resort to the "primitive" defenses of delusional projection, psychotic denial, and splitting, as opposed to the more "mature" defenses of intellectualization, isolation, repression, and reaction-formation (A. Freud 1936; and see Vaillant 1986, for an empirical approach to the developmental classification of defenses).

It is worth recalling, however, that it is not development in the abstract which determines the nature and severity of psychopathology, but rather the specific development of underlying affective and cognitive structures (as sketched in the three previous sections). Thus, on the one hand, Weiss and Sampson (1986 79) may be in part correct in presuming that "most or perhaps all, psychopathology is rooted in pathogenic beliefs,"[43] and that such unconscious beliefs often arise as the result of trauma, chance, and accident. On the other hand, it is surely also the case that (a) the intensity with which such beliefs are held, (b) the degree to which they persist over time, (c) the ease (or rigidity) with which they are applied to situations, and (d) perhaps even the very meaning and content of such beliefs, depend on the specific vicissitudes of affective and cognitive development (as these are played out in each and every level of functioning). We have already observed—in the earlier discussion of the Basch-Noy model—that there are, in fact, several distinct possibilities for the pathological development of affect and cognition. To recapitulate, these include:

(a) disorders in the affective line of development (e.g., non-optimum "distributions" of affect, feeling, emotion, and empathy —or deficits in the acquisition of the organizational structures which are prerequisites for one or more of the aforementioned *levels* of affective development);

(b) imbalances or disequilibria between the *rate* of affective development on the one hand, and that of cognitive development on the other (such that affective-cognitive interactions are accordingly less efficient and less adaptive);

(c) imbalances or misfits between primary and secondary process (reflecting developmental arrests in one or the other cognitive mode, and resulting, in an excessive or maladaptive role for one or the other mode of cognitive functioning).[44]

According to this taxonomy, the nature and intensity of psychoanalytic psychopathology are always functions of (some degree of) developmental disorganization of affective and cognitive structures. And the etiological sources of such disorganization, we recall, are *biological* (constitutional) as well as *relational* (environmental and interpersonal). When such developmental disorganization is experienced phenomenologically, the person-organism finds itself open to threats of deformation or annihilation (anxiety). In order to protect itself, the person-organism tends to close itself off to stimuli, or otherwise to "reduce its experience" (Horowitz 1988 21). These attempts at defense, closure, or self-protection result in a certain diminution of experienced (or actual) autonomy. The patient (e.g., the neurotic, the borderline, the psychotic) finds himself *repeating* a preordained pattern, reenacting repressed, unconscious, or otherwise unintelligible experiences, often in a compulsive or obligatory manner. The patient's "passive repetition" no longer contributes to further development, and is indeed an obstacle to it. Not until the patient in some sense becomes conscious[45] of his current experience as a "repetition" of past modes will it be possible for him or her to assume an active role and so transform or elevate the experience to a new developmental plane. In this "proactive mode," the old is mastered, if not eliminated or abolished,[46] and the orthogenetic trend of development is reasserted. Such, perhaps, is the substance of Freud's famous utterance, "Where id was, there ego shall become." For what is here intended is not only the traditional formula of *psychoanalytic therapy* (see below), but also the aim of ego or self-development in general (Loevinger 1976).

2. *Therapy and Therapeutic Action.* The model of psychoanalytic therapy seems to depend upon the plausibility of the "analogical rationale"— namely, the view introduced earlier in this chapter that the issues, pro-

cesses, and interactions of child development are in some sense analogous to the issues, processes, and interactions of adult psychoanalytic psychotherapy.

The analogical rationale therefore designates a certain parallel between the "interpersonal matrix" of early development (Werner and Kaplan 1963; Bruner 1983) and the dyadic context of the analytic encounter. Surely, though, this cannot mean (a) that the adult patient is merely reproducing (or reverting to) the affective disturbances of infancy, or (b) that the adult patient is merely repeating or reenacting "nuclear conflicts" (cognitive-affective distortions and fantasies) from childhood, or (c) that the analyst is just performing the corrective role of the good parent or competent caregiver. In sum, the analogy in question cannot constitute a *literal* correspondence: for example, the analyst does not become the mother in some total sense; rather, it is just that the analyst is now entitled to interpret some piece of affective communication (or miscommunication) between him or her and the patient *as if* it had once been between the patient and her mother. The presumption of a "mother transference" simply reaffirms the belief that the therapeutic situation can be viewed *as if* it were a setting which somehow facilitates the "reactivation" of primitive, perhaps once adaptive, but now self-defeating patterns of behavior. But this belief, in turn, depends upon the validity of the developmental (and psychoanalytic) principle that early affective-cognitive patterns are relatively immutable, or are at least epigenetically preserved. Only if this principle is upheld can it then be argued that such basic patterns

> play themselves out, when treatment is successful, in the transference to the therapist. Or to put it another way, the affects transferred to, or re-activated with, the therapist are expressions both of the patient's problematic . . . past attempts at affective communication *and of the effects of these on the patient's character.* (Basch 1988 79–80, my emphasis)

In thus emphasizing Basch's concluding phrase, I also underline the merely analogical (or metaphorical) character of "reactivation." For as Shapiro (1989 173) has argued (at least in the context of neurotic estrangement), "childhood conflict is not preserved intact, but it may distort development in ways that are not easily reversed." In other words, the adult personality (as the contemporary expression or outcome of development) "is more densely organized than psychoanalysis, even in its elaboration of the ego, has so far conceived it to be. It is far less a mere transmitter or simple template of its own early history than was thought" (Shapiro 1989 177).

If the analogical rationale is now metaphorically construed (and no longer implies literal correspondence or literal reactivation), how, then, is it applicable to the theory of therapy or to the conceptualization of therapeutic action? Basch (1988) points to one possible solution when he argues for a fundamental distinction between (a) the *level* and form of the transference on the one hand, and (b) the *content* (or narrative significance) of the transference on the other.

Basch assumes, first, that the analyst's empathic understanding, along with his scientific knowledge of development, enable him to recognize the patient's *maturational level* of affective communication (e.g., is the patient unable to tolerate any affective pressure; is the patient responding affectively, but unable to put his or her experience into words?). The analyst, then, is not only entitled to categorize the patient's current behavior in terms of a developmental paradigm, but also to see in it evidence of some distortion or failure in early affective-cognitive development. Thus, the analyst's *empathic understanding* (which implies his or her ability to exploit the evidence of countertransference) [47]

> permits him or her to introduce into the therapeutic relationship interventions that address the patient's difficulties in a manner that is phase-appropriate—that is, interventions that take into account the cognitive and affective level of development that the patient is displaying in relationship to the therapist at any given time. (Basch 1988 130)

Because such empathic-developmental knowledge apparently guides the choice of intervention (see, for example, Gedo and Goldberg 1973; Gedo 1979), it is important that the therapist is thus able to infer *when* in development a patient was adversely affected. The reasonable belief that primitive affective-biological patterns can be transferentially "reactivated" simply lends further weight to the required inference. But while there may be sufficient biological and developmental reasons to support the clinical relevance of the "reactivation" hypothesis, at least insofar as *archaic* transferences are concerned (and insofar as the maturational *level* of the transference is concerned), the situation is surely less clear-cut with regard to the *content* of the transference. By content, we mean those typical thematic issues or plots (e.g., psychosexual issues, autonomy and power issues, attachment issues, etc.), in terms of which the analyst establishes the transferential significance of the patient's message (or narrative). In this connection, the following questions arise: (a) is such significance *validly* established by correlating the patient's messages to the supposed facts of his or her past, or to disturbances inferred from his or her developmental past; (b) is the endeavor (in this way) to establish genetic significance psychoanalytically obligatory—or at all necessary to assure positive outcome in psychoanalytic therapy?

Recall that these are among the chief problems with which Roy Schafer (1976, 1983) is concerned, and for which his historical (and hermeneutical) psychoanalysis is advanced as the solution. For according to the historical approach, there is no longer any point to searching for the supposed source or origin of the patient's potentially meaningful communications. What is really required is only to ascertain the *narrative* point of origin (Stern 1985; and Chapter 2 of this study, "Saving the Mixed Model?"). The clinical objective, of course, is not at all to reconstruct the past "as it actually was," but rather to co-construct a "narrative past" as an instrument for change.

In sum, the thesis I am urging is this: the model of development indeed lends credence to the view that early affective-cognitive patterns of behavior are "reactivated" in the transference, and that such patterns can be inferred through the analyst's scientifically informed and empirically grounded empathic understanding. Hence, the conviction that the level (and form) of the transference can be plausibly construed as a reenactment, repetition, or reactivation of a developmental (or scientifically constructed) psychoanalytic past, and that "phase-appropriate" interventions can be designed and implemented.[48] This, then, is the first part of the thesis I am now proposing.

Its second part asserts (in contrast) that the meaningful or narrative *content* of the transference is not best viewed as a reenactment, repetition, or reactivation of some moment or phase of a real or actual past. It is true that wishes, fantasies, and their conflicts are developmentally generated, and are thus (in some sense) "stamped" by the pastness of early developmental phases. But to regard such meaningful contents as "archaic" is not necessarily to endorse the view that some "real past" can be validly inferred or interpretatively recovered from the evidence of the patient's current behavior and discourse in the analytic situation; nor is it to endorse the view that such efforts at interpretative recovery are therapeutically beneficial (Spence 1982; Schimek 1975a; Schafer 1982, 1983). Thus, in the thesis I am now upholding, all expressions of the *content* of the transference (even those that explicitly refer "to the past") are properly interpretable as indirect allusions to the "here and now," since the past (now the "narrative past") is only known and relevant through *current* interpretations of it. More generally, all analytic "reconstructions" of childhood history (starting indeed with Freud's own cases) are actually hermeneutic constructions of the "remembered present"; and one can no longer adhere, for example, to the traditional notion of "preserved nuclear infantile conflict," not just because of the constant remolding of fantasy and memory over the life course, but also because such a notion circumvents the existence (and density) of adult personality, as well as the influence of the intervening developmental process (Shapiro 1989 170).[49]

Given the distinction between the *level* and *content* of the transference, and given the implications that flow from it, it now appears that therapeutic interventions fall into two distinct classes. I do not mean "support v. interpretation," since that distinction (or antinomy) is vitiated by such arguments as Eagle's (1984a) in which the establishment of conditions of safety ("support") is itself viewed as an implicitly transferential interpretation. Accordingly, the relevant distinction is not now between supportive and interpretative interventions, but between *developmental* and *narrative* interventions.

The former can be legitimately construed as "phase appropriate" interventions, which means that they are always correlated with the *maturational level* of the transference. Such interventions depend for their validity (and hypothetical efficacy) (a) on the truth-value of the model of development, (b) on the analyst's capacity for empathic understanding, and (c) on the verisimilitude of the "analogical rationale"—all of which, together, help the therapist to identify, justify, and implement an indefinite variety of *developmental interventions,* including, for example, Gedo's (1979) modalities of pacification, unification, and optimal disillusionment, as well as Kohut's (1971) modality of transmuting internalization.[50] Such interventions are supportive-interpretative (in the sense cited by Eagle above), and are aimed at enabling the patient to progress from the obligatory (or passive) repetition of early preverbal, affective-biological patterns to some form of reflective self-regulation, whereby unrecognized biological needs are now brought within the purview of awareness. It is assumed that, by virtue of such interventions, the patient is better positioned to "resume development"—to elevate a previously obligatory, unintelligible (or preverbal) experience to a new developmental plane; it is in this sense that the old pathogen is said to be mastered and assimilated, if not exactly eliminated and abolished.

Narrative interventions (Spence 1982) are likewise both supportive and interpretative. But as interpretations, at least, they do not promulgate developmental renderings of the content of the transference; nor, of course, do they consist in the historical reconstruction of a veridical past. Narrative interventions, then, are *not* genetic interpretations; it follows that the "pasts" they construct are neither objective nor extrinsically referential.[51] In short, narrative interventions generate (or cause) "narrative pasts." Such hermeneutical pasts—far from simply replenishing the gaps of memory—really yield believable and livable accounts of where the patient has come from, where he or she wants to go, and how he or she is working (unconsciously) to get there.[52] "Narrative pasts," in other words, are artifacts of the logic of narrative emplotment; it is in this specific sense that narrative interventions are said to constitute hermeneutic procedures for the transformation of narrative discourse, and for the constitution of "inexistent" narrative pasts. It follows, then, that such interventions are concerned not just with interpreting the objective psychodynamic (conflictual) content of the transference, but also with bringing into being such content as a linguistically constituted and newly verbalizable domain of intentionality. The patient is thereby assisted (perhaps for the first time) in *formulating* and *apprehending* the unity and continuity of his or her self-experience,[53] in that the psychoanalytic narrative (the achievement of the psychoanalytic dialogue) is seen as singularly suited to represent the temporal relations of the self *now* to the self *before* (see also Leavy 1980). To sum up: narrative interventions are viewed as hermeneutic procedures which further not only the reflective transformation of the patient's narrative discourse (as explored in Chapter 4 of this book), but also the symbolic transformation of the patient's experience of intentionality, of his conceptualization of self. As Basch (1976a 418–19) states: "The patient actually becomes a different person as a result of the symbolic transformation of his conceptualization of 'self.' "

In concluding this discussion, we need to keep in mind that developmental and narrative interventions, though analytically distinct, are concretely inseparable in each and every therapeutic engagement. *Any* particular intervention has both its developmental and its narrative aspects;[54]

and there are no patients or pathologies (at least in a psychoanalytic treatment context) for whom or for which just one or the other class of intervention is either desirable or possible (see also Gedo 1979 6).[55]

Scientific Psychoanalysis: Evaluation and Critique

In the course of this chapter, I have sought to reconstruct the characteristic conceptual scheme of scientific psychoanalysis. My purpose is now to submit that scheme to an evaluation and critique.

Let me begin by recalling a fundamental assumption of my project. The idea of scientific psychoanalysis (as I understand it) is not at all equivalent to an empirical research program, since such a program would necessarily involve not only the construction of theories or models to account for bodies of empirical data, but also the submission of these theoretical claims to empirical test. But it is evident that researchers such as Gedo, Basch, and Noy do not undertake a systematic empirical exploration of their conceptual formulations; it follows, therefore, that the empirical worth of their contributions is not yet established. Recall that this is the *normal* state of affairs in scientific psychoanalysis and only the rare venture, such as the Mount Zion Psychotherapy Research Program (Weiss and Sampson 1986; Curtis et al. 1988; Silberschatz et al. 1989), actually generates an empirically testable theory of the psychoanalytic process and submits it to empirical test in the clinical situation.[56] In the pages which now follow, we will have ample reason to return to the Mount Zion program since, in key respects, it complements, clarifies, and corrects the *prototypical scheme* of scientific psychoanalysis (as introduced in this chapter). But we must begin, first, by acknowledging that this scheme itself cannot be submitted to empirical test. Its contribution or content, after all, is essentially *conceptual;* there is no question of falsifying or verifying it. We must therefore be content with just a conceptual critique. Such a critique, moreover, cannot pretend to be comprehensive or conclusive, though it may further our appreciation of scientific psychoanalysis as a theoretical discourse, and as a discourse which is complementary to (though distinguishable from) those of "history" and "practice" (Oakeshott 1962). I proceed to take up the critique under the following three headings: (a) the continuity of biological and psychological life; (b) the psychogenesis of repetition; and (c) the meaning and conceptualization of clinical relevance.

(a)*Biological and Psychological Life.* In psychoanalysis, "continuity" refers to the *continuity of the psychical.* Prior to Freud, the psychical was conventionally equated with the conscious, and the psychology of consciousness never went beyond broken or discontinuous sequences that were obviously dependent upon something else, e.g., neurophysiological structures and processes (Solms and Saling 1986). It was Freud's great contribution to have reestablished psychical continuity by extending the concept of the psychical to encompass the unconscious (Freud 1915c, 1933). Henceforth, it was to be the *psychological* or *intentional* unconscious (not neurophysiology) which was seen to explain or underlie the structure and content of consciousness. With its domain now specified in terms of principle of psychical continuity, and with its method now defined in terms of the sufficiency of mentalist explanation, psychoanalysis was thus able to constitute itself as an autonomous psychological science. This tradition (the autonomist tradition) is ably upheld by the ongoing Mount Zion Research Program (Weiss and Sampson 1986), which proceeds independently of any biological (or non-psychological) considerations, and which explores the hypothesis that patients come into therapy with an *unconscious plan* or strategy for disconfirming unconscious pathogenic beliefs. Note that such a hypothesis is purely psychological: it eschews all reference to energic, instinctual, and other biological factors, and relies, instead, on the wholly mentalist concept of "unconscious decision" (or plan) in order to model continuity and change in human behavior.

It is evident that the prototypical scheme of scientific psychoanalysis (as sketched in this chapter) is not just committed to the continuity of the psychical, but is also committed to the more comprehensive continuity of psychological and biological life in general. Hence Gedo (1984), for example, has underscored the psychoanalytic significance of such presubjective issues as *optimal tension regulation,* and has also postulated the assimilation of *biological-affective* dispositions into networks of subjective wishes of later origin. Similarly Basch (1976b, 1983) has stressed the developmental generation of emotional experience, so that empathic understanding is seen as continuous with (and as emerging from) primitive biological states of arousal and reactivity. Such trends recall Freud's seminal proposal that instinct is the concept which stands on the borderline between the mental and the somatic, and which looks backward to its biological substrate, as well as forward to its "psychical representative" (Freud 1915a 123). What is never quite clarified, however, is the relationship between the biological substrate of the instinctual drive and its so-called psychical representative. One never learns, for example, how to model the transition from a (theoretically) quantifiable libido (a) to the meaningful life-historical behaviors in which fixation and regression manifest themselves, (b) and to the fantasies, recollections, and narrations which the analyst actually encounters in the clinical situation. This ambiguity remains, even when energic considerations are ignored and the instinct-drive theory is discarded; it simply resurfaces as the perennial problem of the relationship between *mental* (or psychical) events and *physical* (or brain) events, especially as this relationship (interaction?) figures in the diachronic context of development. So, for example, the relevant questions now become: how does one model the assimilation of biological (physicalist) dispositions into subjective (mentalist) wishes of later origin; and what are the implications of such *biopsychical continuities* for the processes of development, pathology, and therapeutic action?

In my own view, this problem (the problem of mind and body, also known as the problem of biopsychical continuity) is "settled," if not solved, in the developmental paradigm of scientific psychoanalysis. Within the boundaries of that paradigm, the principle of orthogenesis (hierarchical integration) guarantees that continuity in functioning is maintained despite rapid biological and behavioral changes, and despite such presumptive "qualitative" transitions (e.g., physical—mental) as those marked by first language acquisition, self-other differentiation, and the advent of subjective wishing and desiring. Within such a paradigm, the organism's functioning is seamlessly and ontologically continuous, *not* because this is what the evidence obliges us to believe, but because this is what is required by the principle of orthogenesis. All scientific (or empirical) observation must accordingly be conducted within this *presuppositional frame*. It is for this reason (a logical or non-empirical reason) that "discontinuities" between the biological and the psychological are ultimately inadmissible.

My initial conclusion, then, is that scientific psychoanalysis cannot tolerate the possibility of an ontological split between the psychological and the biological. There is no exit from "biopsychical continuity."[57] But is the inference now warranted that the mental can actually be traced back to the physical? We have already noticed that Basch, Noy, and Gedo appear to hold to such a thesis (a reductionist or biologist thesis), and that Gedo even asserts the following:

> In postulating the assimilation of a set of biological dispositions into the hierarchy of an individual's personal aims, I believe I have provided one solution to the problem of bridging the gap between the separate levels of organization we term "physiological" and "psychological," that is, Descartes' *res extensa* and *res cogitans*. (1984 165)

My own position, however, is more circumspect. I concede, of course, that physical conditions and biological substrates are obviously necessary for conscious and unconscious processes to exist. But I also assume that such processes are *irreducible* to physical entities and biological phenomena (e.g., "chemical depression," strictly speaking, is a *non sequitur*).[58] Or to paraphrase Parisi (1987 237): psychoanalytic science, properly understood, appears to rest upon an *emergentist* position, one which admits of the material aspects (and origins) of mind and psychical reality, while at the same time making illogical the reduction of mental life to these material aspects (or origins). In this view, there is indeed biopsychical continuity (in functioning), but the biological level of life is in no way ontologically privileged, nor of course is the primary level of explanation biological. As Parisi (1987 242) aptly states: "for Freud, there was no primary level."

It follows that scientific psychoanalysis may admit an *explanatory* split, if not an ontological one. It is conceded, for example, that biology cannot sufficiently explain such psychologically emergent properties as the apparent meaningfulness of a dream, or the unconscious plan to disconfirm a pathogenic belief. There is thus scientific scope for psychological or "mentalist" explanation.[59] Yet this position is perfectly consistent with the view that neurological structures and processes underlie such behaviors as fantasizing, interpreting, and decision-making, as well as those of affective life in general. In other words, the desires, fears, and fantasies of psychic reality are indeed developmentally generated, and must therefore bear the imprint of a *biological*-presubjective, as well as *psychological*-intentional past.

To recapitulate, the thesis of the continuity of biological and psychological life follows, logically, from the *developmental* (or orthogenetic) conception of scientific psychoanalysis. That thesis requires that we recognize the psychoanalytic past as ontologically indivisible: from the standpoint of science, at least, the biological and psychological properties of the psychoanalytic past are simply analytically abstracted aspects of a single and unitary continuum of functioning; as such, they are each equally open to psychoanalytic scrutiny and conceptualization, and neither is ontologically or epistemically privileged. Because scientific psychoanalysis is in this way cognizant of biopsychical and developmental continuities (e.g., Gedo's "archaic transferences"), and because scientific psychoanalysis (unlike its historical counterpart) is thus directed to *both* the biological and psychological aspects of concrete behavior (as evident, for example, in its conceptualization of affective-emotional states), it cannot truly be construed as a pure or autonomous psychology. Scientific psychoanalysis cannot be *just* a psychology. It must be more than psychological. It appears then, that the prototypical scheme of scientific psychoanalysis follows in the metapsychological footsteps of Freud himself, whose project too was to bridge the unbridgeable: to bridge the "gap" between the physiological and the psychological, and to account for the "emergence" of the latter from the former.

(b) *Repetition*. In one of his earliest comments on the psychogenesis of repetition (the "compulsive manner towards repetition"), Freud (1905a) describes the apparent tendency among neurotics for repressed sexual instincts to strive for expression. "It is necessary to assume," he writes "that these early impressions of sexual life are characterized by an increased pertinacity or susceptibility to fixation in persons who are later to become neurotics or perverts." Almost a decade later, in 1914, we notice the first appearance of the phrase "compulsion to repeat" (the locus of which is now the psychotherapeutic encounter in the clinical setting):

> As long as the patient is in the treatment he cannot escape the compulsion to repeat. . . . We soon perceive that the transference is itself only a piece of repetition, and that the repetition is a transference of the forgotten past not only on to the doctor but also on to all other aspects of the current situation. We must be prepared to find, therefore, that the patient yields to the compulsion to repeat which now replaces the impulsion to remember. (Freud 1914 150–51)

Building upon such observations and conjectures, Freud soon came to fashion a new theory of instincts based upon the premise that "an instinct is an urge inherent in organic life to restore an earlier state of things" (1920 36). Yet even if this speculative doctrine is dismissed in its entirety (even if the repetition compulsion is no longer understood as "an expression of the inertia inherent inorganic life"), one cannot but be convinced that "repetition" counts as the archetypal psychoanalytical phenomenon, and that the "repetition of the past in the present" remains the *terminus a quo* for psychoanalysis, both practical and theoretical. In the guise of the former (as a clinical treatment modality), psychoanalysis aims to interrupt or alter the "vicious circle of repetition" (Thoma and Kachele 1975 108–11; Basch 1988 108–9); in the guise of the latter (as a scientific or historical discourse), psychoanalysis aims to comprehend it as a psychological, psychobiological, or narrative phenomenon—e.g., what is it that is being repeated, why and how (by virtue of what means, mechanisms, activities, or processes)?

We recall, moreover, that historical psychoanalysis is as committed as its scientific counterpart to a *theoretical* formulation of "repetition"; indeed, in its exemplary hermeneutical version (Gadamer 1975, 1976; Schafer 1978, 1983), it yields its own distinctive construction of the "past" and its own understanding of "repetition," such that its specific theoretical task is simply to interpret the meaning of a narratively emplotted repetition of a narrative past in a transferential present. It is never presumed, of course, that an objectively existent piece of the past is reenacted in the present, nor is it supposed that repetition is a species of real recurrence or true reappearance. It is rather that the past is conceived as actually being created as it is narrated; its "repetition in the present" is therefore viewed (from the hermeneutical and historical vantage) (a) as a function of the structure of narrative discourse (the ultimate referent of which is "temporality"), and (b) as a function of the phenomenology of the intersubjective analytic encounter (Leavy 1980; Spence 1982; Schafer 1983; Atwood and Stolorow 1984; Danto 1985; Ricoeur 1985; Sarbin 1986).

Returning to the scheme of scientific psychoanalysis and to its rendering of the "repetition of the past in the present," we immediately recall that the "past" is *developmentally* (and not narratively) constituted. In the earlier discussion ("The Idea of Development: Orthogenesis, Epigenesis, and Repetition"), this signified, simply, that the scientific (or developmental) past is orthogenetically and epigenetically organized. But what may be overlooked in such a formulation is something more basic: namely, the principle that whatever is being repeated must necessarily be construed as some function of an analytically abstracted explanatory past (as some function of the "phases of development"). Since science is only interested in the particular insofar as it is an instance of the general, this principle further requires that whatever is repeated be viewed as an instance of some abstracted class, and never just as a concrete or phenomenological particular. It follows, then, that a crucial task for scientific psychoanalysis is to identify, distinguish, and classify these abstract classes (e.g., biological, biopsychical, and psychological, etc.)—since it is only these (or the "members" these classes contain) which are actually represented in any *scientific* account of the psychogenesis of repetition. It is therefore an inherent limitation of scientific psychoanalysis that it cannot recognize or model the repetition of phenomenological particulars (e.g., meaningful mental contents), except insofar as these can be "translated" into members (or instances) of abstracted classes.

The limitation I have just cited is a limitation of science as such; it is not a defect in the particular conceptual scheme I elaborate in this chapter, and should thus be sharply distinguished from the critique to follow. For in my view, the real defect of scientific psychoanalysis is its evident inability to specify what it means for an *adult* to repeat early and infantile patterns, contents, and organizations of behavior. And notwithstanding its developmental substructure, this defect implies (paradoxically) that the prototypical scheme of scientific psychoanalysis remains insufficiently developmental; what it still fails to supply are the "rules of translation" by which one takes into account: (a) the effect of the intervening developmental process on what is repeated, how, and why; and (b) the effect of the *adult* personality organization on the "obligatoriness" of reenactments and on the "compulsive manner towards repetition" (Shapiro 1989). In other words, were such "rules of translation" available and explicit, it might then begin to be possible to assess the influence of the intervening developmental process on the underlying nature of psychoanalytic repetition—i.e., under what developmental conditions is the process of repetition more or less intentional; and under what conditions is this process simply equivalent to a "biological propensity to repeat" (Gedo 1981, 1984)?

In their comprehensive review of the problems of metascience and methodology in clinical psychoanalytic research, Thoma and Kachele (1975) have argued that no psychoanalytic theory deserves to be taken seriously if it does not present testable hypotheses for the psychogenesis of repetition.[60] I have maintained, perhaps more strictly, that no scheme of scientific psychoanalysis is internally coherent or adequate in scope unless it incorporates those "rules of translation" which specify what it means for an *adult* to repeat the infantile past in the present. Although it is evident that such rules are still unavailable, and that their adequate formulation is dependent upon unforeseeable conceptual innovations, it is noteworthy that at least one psychoanalytic research program has "jumped the gun" and taken up the challenge of Thoma and Kachele. I refer, of course, to the Mount Zion Research Program which has not only generated and tested specific hypotheses for the psychogenesis of repetition, but also defended a particular conception of the intentionality of repetition. According to Weiss and Sampson (1986), repetition (transference-repetition) is inherent in the patient's *strategy* or *plan* to test or disconfirm an unconscious pathogenic belief. In this view, the patient "in making a powerful pull or demand on the transference, may unconsciously be carrying out a trial action to test an unconscious infantile belief" (1986 269). What seems clear, in this formulation, is that the psychological process of repetition, though obligatory (or "compulsive"), is also thoroughly intentional. The patient is presumed to be able to exert considerable *control* over his or her unconscious mental life and to make and carry out *plans* (in interacting with the analyst) in order to change pathogenic beliefs. The patient, then, may be "compelled to repeat," but the compulsion itself originates in the patient's intention,[61] in his or her desire to ward off the recurrent danger that stems from the pathogenic belief.

In summary, the Mount Zion model stipulates that the patient's transference demand (or repetition) is not only maximally intentional, but is also rational and realistic (given the presence, of course, of pathogenic beliefs); it follows that this transference-repetition is not at all "an expression of unconscious wishes seeking gratification without regard to reality" (Weiss and Sampson 1986 268). The latter position (Freud's) has aptly been termed the automatic functioning hypothesis, since it implies a kind of automatic or "subintentional" interplay of psychic forces (e.g., impulses and defenses); whereas the Mount Zion model (derived from another trend in Freudian theory) is termed the higher mental functioning hypothesis, since it argues for an unconscious mental process which is as fully intentional and as fully competent as the more familiar conscious mental process. The Mount Zion Research Program thus figures as an interesting anomaly in psychoanalytic discourse: it is advanced as a *purely intentional* theory (and in this respect resembles Schafer's approach) and yet it is thoroughly *empirical-analytic* in its formulation and structure.[62] Moreover, the central claim of this theory (a scientific and non-hermeneutical theory) is said to pertain to "an unconscious wish for mastery"; and the repetition of the past in the present is actually seen as nothing other than an expression of that wish, now lent substance and weight by the human agent's supposed affinity for unconscious planning and unconscious decision-making.

As strict empiricists, Weiss, Sampson, and their colleagues believe it essential that theoretical claims be submitted to empirical test. Hence their particular approach to the unwieldy corpus of Freudian theory, which (as we have just seen) involves the abstraction of *two* logically consistent theories which can actually be tested against one another. The intentional theory (based on the higher mental functioning hypothesis) prevails empirically, but the more basic point is that the traditional "omnibus theory" (a loosely organized mixture of *both* models) doesn't really lend itself to being tested at all. For that reason alone, it deserves to be superseded in psychoanalytic inquiry and research. Moreover, the scheme of scientific psychoanalysis (as I have presented it in this chapter) would almost certainly be regarded as just another version of the "omnibus theory," albeit one much refitted and much revised.[63]

My own position, however, is that the Mount Zion model is best viewed as exemplifying only *one* cognitive level in the prototypical scheme of scientific psychoanalysis. In addition to that level (the psychological level of the purely intentional), there are surely other psychological levels which correspond to such "quasi-intentional" phenomena as the behavior of self and personality *systems* (e.g., Basch 1988 108). It would seem to me, for example, that such behaviors and phenomena (e.g., the Zeigarnick effect, etc.) designate the reactive tendencies and tensions of systems and organizations, not the wholly intentional actions (conscious or unconscious) of persons (Shapiro 1989 200). But beyond even these considerations, it must surely be questioned whether psychoanalytic data reveal *only* the manner in which human biology is psychologically mediated or symbolically represented. For it has been an important contention of mine that scientific psychoanalysis, properly understood, is *meta*psychological, and therefore apprehends not only psychologically emergent properties (whether intentional or quasi-intentional), but also such prepsychological, psychobiological, and subintentional properties as those that pertain to the maintenance of an optimal level of stimulation. As Gedo (1981 313) has forcefully argued, many analytic patients are struggling with presubjective and prepsychodynamic issues, and "never have any conception, conscious or unconscious, of the nature of their deficit."

It follows that for such theorists as Gedo, Basch, and Noy, it is crucial that clinical psychoanalysis (as a theoretical discourse) not only represent the human being as an "intentional agent and maker of meaning," but also describe the underlying processes (including those that are subintentional or prepsychological) which help to explain how the human being *develops into* an intentional agent. The conclusion which must follow is that the Mount Zion model figures as just *one aspect* of a far more comprehensive venture of scientific conceptualization in American psychoanalysis. In terms of the present discussion, this means, simply, that Weiss, Sampson et al. have succeeded in analytically abstracting one class of psychoanalytically significant repetitions, namely that class which is here viewed as "maximally intentional." We have seen, however, that the more comprehensive approach to the "psychogenesis of repetition" requires that we recognize a "continuum of intentionality" and that we also acknowledge the psychoanalytical relevance of repetitions which are biological, biopsychical, and quasi-intentional in character.

(c) *Clinical Relevance*. I complete my evaluation of scientific psychoanalysis with a critique of the idea of clinical relevance, the meaning of which remains arguable and equivocal, if only because the relation of theory and practice is seldom clear. Consider, for example, the following thesis: if we grant (as I think we must) that efficient practice precedes the theory of it, then it is evident that psychoanalytic theory, in general, is of only questionable value for the skilled practitioner. In Waelder's (1962 620) words: ". . . some of the best analysts I have known knew next to nothing about it."[64] The reverse, by the way, seems also to be true, namely, that a complete mastery of psychoanalytic theory may exist alongside a complete inability to practice the activity (psychotherapy) to which it supposedly refers.

Moreover, it appears to be a matter of historical record that psychoanalytic practice did not originate deductively from a theory of analytic therapy (or from a theory of pathology or development); on the contrary, it is usually supposed that clinical practices and techniques have emerged "empirically," that is, through a professional tradition of trial and error. As Freud (1912b) himself expressed it:

> The technical rules which I am putting forward have been arrived at from
> my own experience in the course of many years, after unfortunate results
> had led me to abandon other methods. (111)

In other words, there is "a continuous sequence of trials and errors, as we
check our technical procedures by their immediate consequences and by
their therapeutic results" (Hartmann 1951 33). It follows that if psychoanalytic practice ever actually advances in its efficiency and effectiveness,
it need not do so through the "application" of theory. It need not do so
because the intelligent pursuit of an activity (the practice of analytic
therapy) does not consist, apparently, in the application of theories and
principles. And even if it did, the *knowledge of how to apply them* is not
given in knowledge of them. My first thesis, then, is that there is a certain
discontinuity between psychoanalytic theory and psychoanalytic practice,
so that it is even reasonable to suppose that it is primarily in the practice
of an activity that we acquire the knowledge needed to practice it.

   Such a thesis, however, is both paradoxical and counterintuitive in that
it immediately discounts *any* theory's claim of clinical relevance. We are
understandably reluctant to endorse it, recognizing that it is still widely
believed that theory and practice are closely related, and that theory (or
science) somehow succeeds in conveying the *impression* of clinical relevance. I suggest, however, that theory only succeeds in doing so insofar
as it functions: (1) to codify, organize, and abridge psychoanalytic practice (e.g., Havens 1986); (2) to explicate the rules and principles which
seem to inhere in it (Schafer 1976, 1983); and (3) to help to account for
the efficiency (or inefficiencies) of therapeutic practice (e.g., Gedo 1979;
Weiss and Sampson 1986; Basch 1988). In performing these typical
functions, psychoanalytic theory thus manages to convey the impression
of clinical relevance by generating the "background assumptions" and/or
hypotheses which are held to facilitate clinical listening and therapeutic
intervention in the psychoanalytic situation (Spence 1982 284). Yet,
having said all this and having thus conceded the appearance of clinical
relevance, the following propositions are still affirmed: (1) that practice
proves often to be efficient; (2) that efficient practice precedes the theory
of it; and (3) that it is in the practice of an activity that we actually acquire
the knowledge of how to practice it. The second thesis I propose is
therefore this: that psychoanalytic theory, in general (whether historically
or scientifically constructed), actually consists in a kind of *retrospective
rationalization* of what is already understood to be a successful and trans-

formative practical activity.[65] In other words, psychoanalytic theory "tacitly knows" psychoanalytic therapy in advance. It is equally true, however, that such theory is always "behind" psychoanalytic practice, trying to catch up with it; and it is in this peculiar sense that its "clinical relevance" is inevitably belated and therefore equivocal.

Given these two theses, how are we now to construe the clinical significance of the theoretical scheme of scientific psychoanalysis? Recall that this scheme incorporates closely interrelated models of development, pathology, and therapeutic action, and appears to involve a logical relationship among its components, such that the "clinically relevant" theory of therapeutic action is regarded as a logical corollary of the theory of development. Within this prototypical scheme, the principles of psychoanalytic practice are actually seen as "based on" rational deductions from certain conceptions of psychic functioning and human development. Hence, for example, Gedo's (1979 16) argument that if *development* follows an epigenetic scheme, so must *therapy,* in that all earlier (or past) vicissitudes must be dealt with if the unfavorable outcome of any phase-specific developmental crisis is to be reversed. But upon closer inspection, it isn't at all obvious that Gedo's argument is either deductively sound or empirically valid: (1) for orthogenetic and epigenetic schemes of development are, in fact, compatible with a variety of different (even mutually contradictory) therapeutic approaches;[66] (2) moreover, there seems to be no logical deductive tie between the premise of an *epigenetic developmental scheme* (one variant of the scientific psychoanalytic past) and the techniques and practices proposed to deal, therapeutically, with the hypothesized residues of developmental vicissitudes found here and now in adult patients.

Gedo's error is the emblematic error of theoretical and scientific psychoanalysis. It is replicated, as well, in Basch's (1988 29) assertion that psychotherapy is nothing but "applied developmental psychology." It is an error (1) because it falsely presupposes a logical relation between theory and practice, (2) and because it wrongly assumes that theory can (or should) dictate practice. I call this error the *rationalist fallacy* (Oakeshott 1962), in that it implies that practical activity is nescient simply because it is partially blind to what it does. Since practical activity is seen as nescient or unintelligent, it follows that it must be "rationalized" or made right by theory. This is accomplished either by prescribing the "application" of theory to practice, or by positing the "derivation" of practice from theory. In both instances, the nescience of practice is purportedly overcome, because practical activity has now been assimilated to theory and because practical knowledge (which actually exists only in use) has now been translated or converted into an abstract idiom of rules, principles, and techniques. The rationalist fallacy thus defines the meaning of clinical relevance within the prototypical scheme of scientific psychoanalysis; its principal effect, we have just seen, is to uphold the doubtful thesis of logical continuity between theory and practice. Moreover, it is evident that from the vantage of this scheme, it is now *inconceivable* that the inefficiency and ineffectiveness of analytic therapy may be compatible with the truth of psychoanalytic theory, or that the efficiency of such therapy may be unrelated to psychoanalytic theory or provide scant support for its scientific truth.

Let me now summarize my own position on "clinical relevance." The scheme of scientific psychoanalysis indeed articulates certain truths, but these "truths" (the truths of development, pathology, and therapeutic action) express a desire or craving for intellectual order and conceptual structure. In this respect, they are distinguishable from (or discontinuous with) the narrative truths of psychoanalytic practice which articulate the needs of affective relations, and which defer to the special exigencies of efficiency and effectiveness in practical activity. Viewed in this way (from outside the ambit of the rationalist fallacy), it does not seem that psychoanalytic theory, as customarily understood, speaks *directly* to psychoanalytic practice; it cannot, for example, explain or account for its own application (or use) in the concrete clinical situation. The conclusion which must follow is that the knowledge (or truth) it generates is of only doubtful clinical relevance—if by clinically relevant knowledge we mean: (a) principles and truths which are actually derived from practical activity (rather than the reverse); (b) knowledge which is therefore of practical use in the conduct of therapy; or (c) knowledge that can validly supersede (or replace) the practical knowledge implicit in the efficiency of therapeutic practice.

According to the thesis I am now asserting, clinical relevance (as distinct from the impression of it) cannot really be substantiated in scientific psychoanalysis. The various proposals and claims of Basch, Noy, and Gedo et al. may well be correct, but they are not, on that account, clinically relevant. Even from a strictly scientific perspective, it would now seem that clinical relevance can only be furthered through the development of a more or less *autonomous* theory of therapy. And since "rationalism" in psychoanalysis is rejected (and the rationalist fallacy is recognized for what it is), such a theory may owe little to the prototypical scheme of scientific psychoanalysis, or to its "closely interrelated" models of development, psychopathology, and therapeutic action. In other words, such an autonomous theory of therapy need not be indebted to the "psychoanalytic past," or to any specific conceptualization of it; nor, in fact, need such a theory even be recognizably psychoanalytical, since it will rest largely on "reliable empirical data identifying the interactions and interventions that are effective for particular goals, and the processes accounting for whatever effectiveness is achieved" (Eagle 1984a 163). It is thus quite possible that an autonomous theory (disengaged from the traditional logic of scientific psychoanalytic argument, and unencumbered by the "psychoanalytic past") will now find it expedient to translate the psychoanalytic phenomena of clinical interaction into their non-psychoanalytic equivalents, especially if it is also claimed that *all* therapies share a common core of therapeutic processes (Stiles et al. 1986). For, from the vantage of the autonomous theory of therapy, the key point is that it is no longer what is psychoanalytically distinctive that counts, but what is therapeutically effective. Again to cite Eagle: "Whatever the accompanying theory of personality and conception of human nature, one's psychotherapeutic approach must stand or fall on its pragmatic accomplishments" (1984a 163).

I end with three paradoxes. (a) First, for a scientific theory to be clinically relevant, it must now be construed as an autonomous theory of therapy. I have already noted, however, that such a theory need not presuppose the "psychoanalytic past," nor even the scientific (or developmental) construction of such a past. In short, there may well be a "Great Divide" between a scientific theory of development and an autonomous theory of therapy (or intervention), and the clinical relevance of the latter may actually depend upon the exclusion or interdiction of the (scientific) idea of the psychoanalytic past. (b) Second, it is evident that a clinically relevant (or autonomous) theory of psychoanalytical therapy may yet turn out to be a non-psychoanalytical theory of the therapeutic process (see Stiles et al. 1986), rather than a distinctively psychoanalytic theory of a psychoanalytic (therapeutic) process (e.g., Weiss and Sampson 1986). (c) Third, it seems reasonable to conclude that such an autonomous theory (whatever its psychoanalytic content) must still uphold the commitments of empirical-analytic science—which requires it to *abstract* from practice some concept of "therapeutic process" (Greenberg and Pinsoff 1986), and to analyze that concept in the usual way. But the empirical findings and theoretical claims thereby produced, though quite possibly "correct,"[67] do not necessarily constitute a *practical* (or clinically relevant) account of therapy, or a veridical representation of the practical knowledge that characterizes it. Such claims and findings may indeed yield a more correct explanation of the conditions of "effective intervention" (and of the processes that underlie it), but these variables cannot be presumed to be equivalent to those which define the "efficiency" and "effectiveness" of psychoanalytic therapy as conceived, experienced, and enacted in the idiom of practical knowledge (see in Chapter 1 of this study, "Prolegomenon"). This third and last paradox therefore reminds us that there is not only a certain discontinuity between theory and practice *within* scientific discourse, but that there is also a certain (more profound) discontinuity between "science" and "practice" as such, or between the distinguishable discourses of scientific and practical psychoanalysis.

Science, History, and Practice: Pluralism in Psychoanalysis

My purpose in this chapter has been to reconstruct the argument underlying the conceptual scheme of scientific psychoanalysis, and to subject that scheme (a prototypical scheme) to an evaluation and a critique. What I have sought to do, in sum, is to advance a specific interpretation of the nature and role of scientific discourse in the psychoanalytic enterprise. But it seems to me that the work of interpretation, in its very essence, is comparative and contextual. I mean by this that any object of understanding is most effectively grasped (a) when reflected upon comparatively, (b) when characterized in terms of what it is not, (c) and when viewed as an aspect of some totality or whole of which it is (hypothetically) a part. Given this interpretative approach, it is scarcely surprising that psychoanalysis should come into view as a plurality of distinct discourses, each of which stands in some specific relation of similarity and difference to the other, as well as to the "whole" of which it is a constituent part.

I have already observed, for example (in the previous discussion of clinical relevance), that "science" and "history" are not only distinguishable psychoanalytic discourses, but are also differently related to psychoanalytic practice. Thus, for historical psychoanalysis, particularly in the form given to it by Schafer (1983) and Gadamer (1975), there is really no question of "applying" theory to practice: instead of imposing upon practice an external theory which is alien to it, historical theory aims to identify, explicate, and reflect upon the rules which inhere in psychoanalytic practice, or which are tacitly imbedded in it. It is assumed that such rules are actually derived from practice, do not exist in advance of it, and cannot provide the impetus or cause of the activity. So viewed, historical psychoanalysis is not "applicatively" related to psychoanalytic practice since its clinical relevance does not consist in the application of some universal (or theory) to a concrete case. It is rather that the universal is always seen as implicit in the concrete case, and it is therefore only in an explicit (or reflective) grasp of the concrete situation that we acquire an actual understanding of the universal (Gadamer 1975 305). It is that actual understanding or insight which constitutes the *theoretical dimension* of historical psychoanalysis.

It follows from my argument that historical psychoanalysis is less likely than its scientific counterpart to distort the "internal structure" of psychoanalytic practice; because of this, its theorizing is more likely to be "clinically relevant" in the specific sense of making explicit the sort of knowledge which may be of practical use in the conduct of therapy (see, for example, Leavy 1980). Historical psychoanalysis, then, neither explains[68] nor prescribes practice; it yields instead a narrative interpretation of the "tacit knowledge" of clinical discourse and therapeutic activity. It is in such a sense that historical psychoanalysis offers an *explication* (but not an explanation) of the goings-on of psychoanalytic practice.

In sharp contrast, scientific psychoanalysis remains convinced that what we learn about the "natural course of therapy" (about its underlying processes) will indeed be of practical and prescriptive use for the therapist. It is important to recall, however, that in the act of "observing" therapy, scientific discourse is also obliged to derive psychoanalytic practice from principles, rules, and theories which are external to it. This means, in effect, that psychoanalytic practice is reconceptualized as a "therapeutic process," and that the latter constitutes an analytic abstraction of the former. Science thus requires not only the imposition of an alien knowledge upon the practical knowledge of analytic therapy, but also its *replace-*

ment by an analytically abstractive discourse of theories, methodologies, and techniques (see, for example, Danziger 1985; also, "The Methodological Circle" in Chapter 1 of this book). Science, in sum, mandates the maximal distortion of the internal structure of psychoanalytic practice; in this respect, the knowledge it generates can only be of doubtful clinical relevance. Yet, it is also evident that science, alone, can bring into being an *autonomous theory* of therapy—the principal virtues of which are that it accounts for the efficiencies and inefficiencies of analytic therapy and contributes, as well, to the development of more effective clinical techniques; in these respects, to be sure, science (in elucidating processes of change and in yielding technologies of intervention) is indeed relevant or applicable to the strategies and tactics of psychotherapy.[69] It is in such a sense that scientific psychoanalysis offers an *explanation* (but not an explication) of the goings-on of psychoanalytic practice.

Psychoanalysis, I have said, comes into view as a plurality of discourses. Psychoanalysis speaks in more than one voice; this is the "root metaphor" of my project, and it serves as the basis for a taxonomy or framework for the varieties of psychoanalytic understanding (see Figure 2). This taxonomy is represented in terms of three interlocking circles. It is thus apparent that scientific psychoanalysis, historical psychoanalysis, and practical psychoanalysis *each overlaps the other,* although the area of overlap of history and practice (HP) is significantly greater than that of science and practice (SP). This is as it should be because historical psychoanalysis, though a theoretical discourse, nevertheless seeks to articulate (as faithfully as is possible in light of its own assumptions) the rationality of practical knowledge and the coherence of psychoanalytic practice.

But Figure 2 also reminds us that practical psychoanalysis is itself a distinct and autonomous discourse. For in my view, psychoanalytic practice does not merely designate an object of explanation ("science") or explication ("history"), and does not simply signify a domain (or data base) for theoretical operations. In short, practice is not just another form of theory and the essential features of psychoanalytic practice may not be satisfactorily conveyed through the theoretical discourses of history and science. The latter, in particular, would seem to imply "the reduction of *praxis* to *techne*" (McCarthy 1978 22), and the illegitimate extension of purposive-rational action and technical reason to all spheres of life and activity (Habermas 1971).

S = Scientific Psychoanalysis
H = Historical Psychoanalysis
P = Practical Psychoanalysis

<u>Overlaps</u>

SP =
HP = ////
SH = |||||

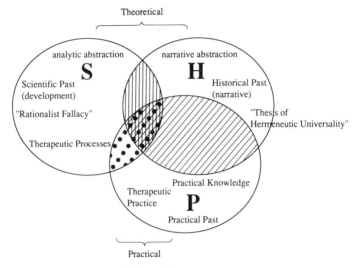

Figure 2
The Three Discourses of Psychoanalysis

I suggest, therefore, that the principle of pluralism requires that we acknowledge the *necessity* of practical psychoanalysis[70] and recognize its autonomy and legitimacy as a distinct discourse. There is thus an unmet need for an "extratheoretical" formulation of psychoanalytic practice, and of the practical knowledge which characterizes it (see in Chapter 1, "The Price of the 'Unity of Inquiry' " and in Chapter 6, "Pluralism and Practical Psychoanalysis," for further discussion). Such a formulation, however exactly understood, is categorically distinct from theoretical formulations of psychotherapy and therapeutic practice; it follows that its "presenting problem" is not so much the tyranny of the past (recall the introductory section of this chapter), as it is the *practical knowledge* of how to live in the present. Practical psychoanalysis is therefore "presentistic": it recognizes that analytic therapy prescribes no solutions, explanations, or insights except to live in the present; and it is learning how to do so (in a specialized interpersonal context) which defines its agenda as a distinct discourse.

Several psychoanalytic authors have already sought to approach psychoanalysis in this way (e.g., Etchegoyen 1991; Sullivan 1970; Leavy 1980; Levenson 1983; Havens 1986); and workers in adjacent fields have similarly sought to underscore the particularity of practical knowledge (e.g., Polanyi 1958; Garfinkel 1967; Geertz 1983; Sternberg and Wagner 1986), as well as subtle issues that arise from the exigencies of practical action and rhetorical discourse (e.g., Bruner 1986; Blumenberg 1987; Argyris et al. 1985; see also "The Practical Past" in Chapter 3 of this book). But in American academic psychoanalysis at least, the recognition of the autonomy of practice has been blocked and obscured, partly out of a groundless fear of succumbing to "antiscientific irrationalism," but mostly because of an unalterable conviction that the truth and veridicality of psychoanalytic theory must be mirrored and verified in therapy—a conviction which is incidentally mired in an enduring confusion between the explanatory and the therapeutic contexts of experience and understanding (for additional elaboration, see Eagle 1984a 172–81).

It is beyond the scope of my project to specify in detail the *program* of practical psychoanalysis (but for concluding observations, see in Chapter 6, "Pluralism and Practical Psychoanalysis"). It is enough to say that it begins, after all, by acknowledging the difference between practice and the understanding of practice, and takes on its specific shape by allowing that the latter need not (and cannot) be purely historical or scientific in character. But it is necessary to suppose, further, that such a program will also include the close observation and "thick description" (Spence 1982; Geertz 1983) of clinical interaction, and will be free to make use of the theoretical discourses of science and history (as well as such others as phenomenology) in order to accomplish its specific aims and purposes *in accord with its own particular assumptions*. It is important to underline this point since it is obvious that psychoanalytic practice cannot explicate itself and must therefore depend (for its own self-understanding) upon the various theoretical discourses. And yet, though in this way dependent, practical psychoanalysis is nevertheless distinct and autonomous. What distinguishes practical psychoanalysis, and what validates it as an autonomous discourse, is the manner in which it uses the various languages of explanation and explication in order to accomplish its specific aims and purposes in accord with its own assumptions. Chief among these assumptions is the proposition that practical psychoanalysis emerges through participation in therapeutic activity. It is the activity itself which defines the appropriate questions as well as the manner in which they are answered. Practical psychoanalysis is a distinct discourse because (unlike historical and scientific psychoanalysis) it emerges *only* through participation in the concrete activities of therapy. It is this participation (and not "theory" of any type) which is the cognitive source of the therapist's power to solve any particular *practical problem,* and indeed, it is the therapist's "knowledgeable" participation in the concrete (interactive) activity which presents the problem itself.[71]

But why is such a program needed? If practical psychoanalysis simply formulates what good analysts already do anyway (whatever their theoretical predilections or rationalizations), and if such practice is typically articulated as tacit or practical knowledge which exists only in use and resists conceptual formulation, why even propose (or recommend) such a program?

It is true that practical psychoanalysis is not directly dependent upon the theoretical contents of science and history (i.e., the developmental and narrative constructions of the psychoanalytic past), and that it stands on its own as an autonomous discourse and practice. It would indeed survive the demise of scientific or historical psychoanalysis and persist (however impoverished) as a cultural tradition of therapeutic practice, as a tradition of "persuasion and healing" (Frank 1973). But it is precisely *because* scientific and historical psychoanalysis are likely to survive (and even flourish) that a reflective program of practical psychoanalysis is warranted. For such a program seems necessary if therapeutic practice—always an affair of particulars, not generalities—is to retain its identity (as a form of conduct) and withstand the steady encroachments of science and history.[72] Psychoanalytic practice, in my view, should be neither remodeled as the "psychoanalytic narrative" of historical discourse, nor reduced to the "therapeutic processes" of scientific discourse. The reflective recognition of practical psychoanalysis as a distinct discourse is thus required if psychoanalytic practice (praxis) is to preserve its individuality and avert assimilation to psychic engineering (techne) and hermeneutic interpretation (exegesis).

NOTES

1. It has never been adequately explained why Freud discarded the seduction hypothesis (in which all neurotic patients are presumed to have suffered experiences of incest or seduction), and why he then adopted the alternative theory that repressed sexual memories are not of actual experiences but of fantasies. It is now evident, however, that the "reality" of the seduction was never quite so factually grounded as is sometimes supposed. As Schimek (1987) notes, Freud's *evidence* of the original pathogenic sexual seduction did not include unambiguous recovery of memories of it, but relied instead on what Freud construed as a "reproduction" of the events in the therapeutic situation. Thus, even in his earlier theoretical formulation, "real" or extraclinical facts recede in importance, while the symbolic or "psychical reality" (as reproduced in the context of patient-therapist interaction) emerges into the foreground.

2. The explanatory account outlined in this paragraph closely follows that offered by Wollheim (1984) in Chapters 5 and 8 of *The Thread of Life*.

3. See Horowitz's *Introduction to Psychodynamics* (1988) for an updated account of the psychodynamics and cognitive processes of fantasy.

4. It is important to recognize that science (as a theoretical discourse) is more than merely empirical. Of course, empiricism requires that theoretical claims be amenable to empirical test. But first there must be a theory to test, and the *construction* of such a theory (or model) is a non-empirical activity.

5. I assume that conceptualization, theory formation, and theory testing are discrete activities, though each is an essential feature of the scientific enterprise, taken as a whole. Frequently, though, the logical autonomy of scientific conceptualization goes unnoticed, for it is true that "one may . . . construct new concepts without promulgating a new theory about them" (Kukla 1989 789).

6. See in Chapter 3, "History, Science, and Practice," for a review of the divergent assumptions of historical, scientific, and practical conceptualization.

7. See in Chapter 1, "The Price of the 'Unity of Inquiry,'" for a brief treatment of practical knowledge and its relationship to science and technique.

8. In the present context, the *qualitative* aspects of affect do not designate meaningful mental contents (e.g., fantasies) but certain constitutive experiences. Wilson (1986), for example, suggests that the quality of anaclitic depressive affect is manifested in experiences of helplessness, depletion, desperate object-seeking, and emptiness.

9. The same phenomenon can be abstracted as a *systemic process* or as an *intentional action*. The former is a prototypically scientific mode of (analytic) abstraction; the latter is alternately scientific or historical. In other words, "intentionality" can be narratively or analytically abstracted. Compare, for example, the projects of Schafer (1983) and Weiss and Sampson (1986).

10. According to Feffer (1982), however, all scientific developmental explanations founder upon the paradox of discontinuity. It appears that the Cartesian doctrine (upon which modern science is supposedly based) constructs an "un-

bridgeable gulf" between developmental stages that require continuity. Cartesianism thus seeks to connect events it has rendered unconnectable. Developmental science does not overcome this paradox, but aims to circumvent it through its commitment to the principle of orthogenesis.

11. This is not to deny that biological (or "instinctual") factors are relevant to *adult* development. Such periods of life as menopause and old age undoubtedly involve the expression of a "biologically prescribed program" which is susceptible to symbolic or psychical representation. It is fair to assert, though, that *adult* development seems most relevant for clinical practice when its focus is on vulnerability to developmental dysynchrony. That is, people who enter psychotherapy because of "developmental issues" appear to do so when they are experiencing life transitions and are feeling "offtime." The patient is distressed by the sense that a significant aspect of what he or she wished for at this point of life is not coming to pass, and may never come to pass. It is evident that the therapeutic treatment of such distress ("developmental dysynchrony") is at least as dependent on the *narrative* substructure of historical psychoanalysis, as it is on the *developmental* schemata of scientific psychoanalysis (Cohler 1981).

12. The foregoing account is not psychoanalytically comprehensive in that it neglects the conceptualization of "multiple lines of development" (A. Freud 1965), including those that pertain to the evolution of ego structures, object relations, and "self." See also Gedo and Goldberg (1973 73–100).

13. It is important to stress that Gedo dissents from the view that "interpretation" (the verbal resolution of unconscious intrapsychic conflict) is the only legitimate psychoanalytic treatment modality. Recall that each of the other modalities (pacification, unification, optimal disillusion) is seen as *psychoanalytically* significant, and each is construed in relation to the other as a necessary feature of the unified psychoanalytic treatment situation (Gedo and Goldberg 1973 159–65).

14. It is assumed, in psychotherapy, that patients often repeat events or interactions which once made them uncomfortable. But it is no easy task to distinguish between the repetition of a meaningful situation and the repetition of the affectively charged experience itself. Is the patient's discomfort secondary to (or a function of) a meaningful and interpretable experience, or is it rather a preverbal and presymbolic manifestation of a "biological propensity to repeat"? Consider the case of a patient who seems to be reliving what the parent did to him by doing it to the therapist (often by abusing the therapist). Is such a transference (based on identification with an abusing parent) really amenable to verbalized interpretation, or is it actually a kind of "archaic repetition" which requires instead the support of pacification or unification? There is no easy answer to this question, but it seems clear, in practice, that the therapist (contra Gedo) will probably grant *intentionality* to the patient: he or she will assume that the patient "really hopes" that the therapist won't be devastated by this sequence of interaction (which would be the patient's usual reaction). In other words, the practical task of the therapist is to *tolerate* such repetitions (whatever their underlying nature); it is assumed, as a consequence, that the patient will "learn" that one can be subjected to this kind of pressure and abuse and not be devastated. My point in this example

is that it is the therapist's reflective "toleration" which is presumably mutative, and that this is more relevant clinically than the specific choice of intervention (e.g., unification or interpretation). For a brief discussion of the aforementioned type of transference based on identification with an abusing parent, see Karon (1984).

15. However, the traditional distinction between interpretative and supportive interventions is probably overdrawn or misconceived, and it is doubtful whether Gedo actually subscribes to it. See Eagle (1984a 105) and Note 17 below.

16. See Arlow and Brenner (1964) for a traditional psychoanalytic account of regression, fixation, and related concepts.

17. The dichotomy often drawn between supportive and insight-oriented therapies is increasingly viewed as unhelpful (Schlesinger 1969); as Gedo, Eagle, and others have argued, elements of both "support" and "insight" are required in most treatments, with patients at multiple levels of functioning and with moment-to-moment needs for both affective containment and interpretative insight (insofar as these can actually be distinguished from each other).

18. There is an enormous critical literature on metapsychology, but much of it revolves around competing concepts of the intellectual identity of psychoanalysis. For a definitional formulation which is removed from this "core controversy," consider the following statement offered by Laplanche and Pontalis in *The Language of Psychoanalysis* (1973), in which metapsychology is described as

> a term invented by Freud to refer to the psychology of which he was the founder, when viewed in its most theoretical dimension. Metapsychology constructs an ensemble of conceptual models. . . . Examples are the fiction of a psychical apparatus divided up into agencies, the theory of the instincts, the hypothetical process of repression, and so on. Metapsychology embraces three approaches, known as the dynamic, the topographical and the economic point of view. (248)

19. "Temperament" is described by Horowitz (1988 25) as originating in "biologically determined variations in how a person is able to regulate and consciously experience various types of emotional arousal."

20. "Incoming information" refers to (a) sensory data from the external world, and (b) emotional arousal from the internal world. Since these are different domains of knowledge, they may not be organized at the same level in a given individual (Lane and Schwartz 1987).

21. If empathic responsiveness is based on the knowledge one has of one's own inner world, it follows that the analyst's empathic understanding depends in part on his moment-to-moment awareness of the meaning of his own *countertransference* experience. In other words, empathic responsiveness is the outcome of an *interactive* process in which the therapist receives and processes projective identifications from the patient.

22. The idea of "reflection" is first examined in Chapter 1 of this book ("The Plurality of Ends"), where it is conceptualized as "the formation of ideas of ideas"

(Hampshire 1977), and is regarded as a method of inquiry. Reflection, so viewed, is obviously a philosophical (or epistemological) concept, not a psychological one.

23. Basch is thus in agreement with Schafer that the analyst's empathy is not, in essence, a feeling of harmony or closeness with the patient; nor is it some kind of welcomed identificatory experience on the part of the therapist. For both Schafer and Basch, empathy is a complex expression of understanding. For Schafer, "understanding" is a hermeneutic concept: e.g., the analyst empathically affirms the analysand by assuming coherence and potential intelligibility in everything the analysand brings up or refrains from bringing up, whereas for Basch, empathic understanding is developmentally modeled as a form (or level) of information processing (Basch 1988 78–79 146–53).

24. By asserting that "empathic competence" is a scientifically coherent clinical concept, I mean that it can be derived from a plausible model of psychoanalytic development. Whether or not this concept can be *empirically* formulated in a useful way still remains an unresolved issue.

25. Note that I have just reiterated the "perplexing" point that "science"— grounded in the *objectivist* assumptions of analytic abstraction—may well be incapable of describing and accounting for "fundamental qualitative transitions." In the words of Laplanche (1976 18): "Deriving an object from an objectless state seems so unpromising a theoretical task to certain analysts that they do not hesitate to affirm—in a reaction which is laudable in its intentions but which only leads to a different error—that *sexuality per se* has an object from the beginning." It is evident that Basch, too, has not managed to explain how we are to picture the *qualitative transition* from a monad shut in upon itself (an objectless object) to a progressive (developmental) discovery of the object. See also in this chapter "Scientific Psychoanalysis: Evaluation and Critique."

26. Freud (1911) originally referred to multiple forms of thinking when he divided the formative organizing principles into primary and secondary process. Primary process rules for forming thought were regarded as the earliest means through which desires channel themselves into actions; according to these rules, highest priority is always given to the immediate and direct gratification of wishes. Thinking (e.g., dreaming) in this form may seem irrational, incorrect and/or creative, since the products of such thinking typically include symbols, fluid displacements of attributes of one object to another, as well as magical assumptions about meaning (Horowitz 1988). Freud further argued that the rules of secondary process *develop from* the original matrix provided by primary process. Secondary process thinking increasingly corresponds to the "real world," and is thus viewed as rational, logical, and consistent. Specifically, secondary process facilitates *delays* in impulses toward immediate gratification, since its organizational rules (about time) make it possible to expect the future and plan for it.

27. The brain's symbolizing or imaginative activity is not to be confused with linguistic competence or naming. As Basch (1976a) observes, thought processes are neurological events that occur independently of naming *per se* (which is why it is possible for us to think without words). At the same time, naming promotes the transformational activity of the brain by generating new hierarchical orders of

classification and abstraction. It is only in this secondary sense that naming (or linguistic behavior in general) is a form of symbolizing activity.

28. But the opposite is also true: it is often appropriate for psychoanalytic intervention to translate the discursive symbolization of affective meaning into its presentational counterpart. For example, alexithymic patients not only have difficulty expressing feelings in words, but also have a paucity of fantasy life and are usually able to describe their emotional experience only in mechanistic terms. The therapist may thus need to specify the nature of the patient's emotional arousal when it cannot yet be meaningfully put into words; the ultimate point of such an intervention will be to formulate the *presentational* symbolization of affective meaning, or to proceed *inward* from expressive (verbal) behavior to preverbal inner meaning. See also Chapter 2, Note 15.

29. As Stern (1985) has argued, much of the work of psychotherapy actually consists of formulating experience for the first time, as opposed to altering defensive processes that conceal fully formed mental contents residing in the unconscious. Such an argument implies an enhanced role for developmental theory, in that areas of experience which are relatively *underdeveloped* must initially be identified in order that they be "constructed" (or formulated) for the first time.

30. See Erickson (1970) on important conceptual and phenomenological issues that pertain to the relationship of the verbal and preverbal domains of experience.

31. Bruner (1986) has distinguished "two irreducible modes of cognitive functioning . . . each meriting the status of a 'natural kind.' " The first mode—the logico-scientific or *paradigmatic* mode—aims at context-free and universal explications, establishing truth through formal verification procedures and empirical proof. In contrast, the second or *narrative* mode entails particularistic, context-sensitive explications; instead of focusing on the question of "how to know the truth," it centers on the wider question of "the meaning of experience." It is evident that Bruner's classification of cognitive "natural kinds" overlaps with the taxonomies of Basch and Noy. See also Chapter 2, Note 11.

32. This argues against the view that hermeneutics, while perhaps of clinical relevance, lacks any function (or role) in theoretical psychoanalysis (e.g., Eagle 1984a). My claim is that historical-hermeneutical psychoanalysis "theorizes" the temporal relations of the self now and the self before. The fact that such discourse is non-scientific does not detract from its theoretical function.

33. What seems relevant in this context is that "recursion" is the hypothetical process whereby the mind (or a computer program) loops back on the output of a prior computation and treats it as a given that can be the input for the next operation. Without invoking such a notion, it seems impossible to conceive of "autonomous thought," since it is only recursion which can account for how the mind turns around on itself to create the kind of summary of its capacities that might constitute a "sense of self" (Bruner 1986).

34. It is important to recognize that autonomous thought is *specifically* characterized by its freedom from the necessity to respond automatically to any feedback information (Noy 1979 203–4). In other words, autonomous thought

"*may* use itself for self-monitoring, but it does not *have* to do so," and is actually free to manipulate feedback information according to its own purposes. Noy regards autonomous (or reflective) thought as the orthogenetic culmination of the development of secondary process. He accordingly views science, philosophy, and art as exemplary achievements of autonomous thought.

35. It may rightly be wondered whether psychoanalytic therapy is properly viewed as having goals. As Shapiro (1989) has argued, such therapy is essentially open-ended, and proceeds according to the *patient's* interests and concerns and not according to the therapist's premeditated design. It is possible, of course, that the "goal" in question (the symbolic transformation of the conceptualization of self) does not imply a plan, theory, or protocol, but is rather an expected outcome (or consequence) of successful or efficient psychoanalytic praxis.

36. There are, of course, other trends in scientific conceptualization in psycho-analysis. Some, for example, focus on the process of therapy, and exclude from consideration the extraclinical domains of development, pathology, and psycho-dynamics. But the Basch-Noy model is exceptional not only in its striving to encompass *both* clinical and extraclinical domains, but also in its attempt to explicate the historical (or narrative) past in terms of the underlying processes of an objective, scientific, or developmental past.

37. However, see Weiss and Sampson (1986) for a systematic attempt at psychoanalytic theory formation and theory testing. The empirical psychoanalysis of the Mount Zion Research Program is also explored later in this chapter under "Scientific Psychoanalysis: Evaluation and Critique."

38. I am arguing that even though the patient's past is irrecoverable, some notion of its "objectivity" is required for both clinician and theorist alike. The idea of an objective, explanatory, and scientific past (a "developmental past") is thus viewed as indispensable. It is not that the scientific past determines the specific features of the historical (or narrative) past; it is rather that the former insures that the latter is "anchored" in the extralinguistic conditions of biological nature and orthogenetic development. And so, while the hermeneuticists are correct in suggesting that one's sense of self has some of the characteristics of a generator of possible narratives, they err in failing to ground this insight in the "wordless" vicissitudes of affective-cognitive development. They forget that the idea of an objective or scientific past is required as a regulative principle for any reasonable interpretation of the nature and use of the historically constructed psychoanalytic past. Without such a regulative principle, historical-hermeneutical psychoanalysis is in danger of asserting the "totalization of the semiotic system" (Barratt 1984 266).

39. Compare this section to the corresponding one in Chapter 4, "The Scope of Historical Psychoanalysis."

40. See Note 8 which comments on anaclitic depressive affect, a presumed consequence of distorted affective communication between infant and caregiver. I would suggest that what psychoanalysts commonly regard as "preoedipal pathol-ogy" is largely the outcome of such early patterns of distorted affective commu-nication.

41. This preverbal set is also reactivated in the psychoanalytical situation, perhaps as an "archaic" transference-repetition, where it may become the object of interpretation, as well as of supportive measures that are "beyond interpretation" (Gedo 1979, 1984).

42. But regression does not imply a simple return to infantile modes of functioning, since such reversions are always mediated by the *adult* personality organization (Shapiro 1989). It is likewise fallacious to argue that, *as adults,* we are just "frozen" or fixated at arrested points in childhood. It follows that psychotherapy is not specifically concerned with permitting "arrested configurations to unfold as they would have in the normal course of development" (Eagle 1984a 136); nor is it concerned with the *direct repair* of such developmental impairments as those implied by regression and fixation.

43. The concept of pathogenic beliefs is introduced in Chapter 4 of this book, under "The Narrative Past and the Objective Past: A Comparative Perspective." See also (in this chapter) "Scientific Psychoanalysis: Evaluation and Critique."

44. Imbalances between primary and secondary process may result, for example, in the defensive state of isolation. Isolation, according to Noy (1979 211) "is a part of the general defense mechanism that autonomous thought enacts in order to defend itself against the danger of being flooded by the obligatory self-centered processes." It succeeds in doing so only by pretending that it does not recognize the language of the self-centered processes at all. As a consequence of this unconscious maneuver, the productive interaction of primary and secondary processes is impeded, and the development of each suffers by virtue of its isolation from the other.

45. "Becoming conscious" need not require that the patient is in possession of *conceptual knowledge* of his or her narrative and developmental pasts; what is suggested is actually a form of *experiential awareness* which is the outcome of interaction in the clinical situation. For example, the patient may now be able to apprehend that he or she is no longer in the original traumatic situation "and that the therapist is different, in important respects, from the traumatic figures of the past" (Eagle 1984a 105).

46. Compare this formulation (in which the old is presumably mastered, if not exactly eliminated or abolished) to the *movement* from the practical to the historical past as explicated in Chapter 3 of this book ("Clinical Psychoanalysis and the Model of History").

47. As stated by Basch (1988 148): "To decenter one's affective experience is to be able to step back from what one is feeling and think about it dispassionately." Decentering permits the therapist to think about what the patient is feeling, and not just about what he or she is feeling about the patient. By decentering his affective reaction to the patient, the therapist is able to recognize his own countertransference for what it is, and thus hear the full import of the patient's affective communication. Such *empathic understanding,* when joined to a theory of development, can also aid the therapist in deciding whether, and if so, how, he or she will respond to the "need" being signaled by the patient's affective communication.

48. Such interventions may be simultaneously construed as (a) supportive, (b) educative, and (c) interpretative. They are *supportive* in that they seek to simulate a "phase-appropriate" developmental environment (as well as a safe, predictable, and engaging environment); they are *educative* in that they aim to bring unrecognized biological needs into the purview of the patient's experiential awareness; finally, they are *interpretative* (or quasi-interpretative), in that they help the patient to apprehend that he or she is not in the original traumatic situation.

49. See also Freud's own paper "Constructions in Analysis" (1937b) in which there seems to be a significant reversal of his usual emphasis on how much depends (therapeutically) on making the unconscious conscious.

50. It is important to remember that, for any given patient, the therapist needs to use more than just one of these clinical modalities (interventions). In Gedo's words:

> We believe each of these modalities to be absolutely necessary to every psychoanalytic effort, even if in varying proportions, depending on how often the analysand functions in which mode. In other words, the use of the various modalities should be a routine feature of psychoanalytic treatment technique; it is *not* a departure from classical procedures, as Eissler (1953) seemed to suggest when he called any intervention on the part of the analyst other than verbal interpretation "a parameter." (1979 6)

51. For discussion of this topic, see Chapter 4 of this book, especially "History and Hermeneutics: The Narrative Substructure of the Psychoanalytic Past."

52. To reiterate, the "narrative past" does not constitute a real or actual past, but a believable or livable one. Its purpose, as an "inexistent past," is to serve as an instrument of change—and one of the ways in which it may do so is by furthering the patient's experiential awareness of his pathogenic beliefs. As Weiss and Sampson (1986) argue: the disconfirmation of such beliefs is the practical object of psychoanalytic therapy, and narrative interpretations (though not necessarily historically veridical) may still help the patient by guiding him in his unconscious striving to overcome his pathogenic beliefs. It is thus paradoxically the case that though pathogenic beliefs are presumptively veridical (and count as *bona fide* representations of an objective past), the clinical narratives within which they must be imbedded are not so; nevertheless, the patient's processing of such narratives (and of the "pasts" they generate) appears to be an essential feature of the patient's competence (and capacity) to overcome his pathogenic beliefs, and to liberate himself from the tyranny of the past.

53. Assuming that narrative interventions help to formulate the unity and continuity of the patient's self-experience, it is still an empirical question whether or not they are effective in therapy. It is also of theoretical interest *why* such interventions should be effective or beneficial, and why they should be so in any given case.

54. Although any specific intervention has both developmental and narrative

aspects, their translation into operational and measurable dimensions is an empirical task quite distinct from my present purpose and beyond the scope of this study.

55. I mean by this that there are no "purely" preoedipal or oedipal patients (for whom just one *or* the other class of intervention is appropriate). More generally, as Eagle (1984a 137–43) has observed: "There is no need for a dichotomy . . . between a psychology of developmental arrests and one of dynamics or structural conflict"; and it certainly seems oversimplified to argue, as does Kohut (1977), that oedipal issues do not surface until (or if) preoedipal concerns with self-cohesiveness have been resolved. It seems more reasonable to suppose that "issues of conflict, self-organization and ego functions . . . are all inextricably linked" (Eagle 1984a 143).

56. In observing that the Mount Zion Research Program submits its theoretical claims to empirical test *in the clinical situation,* I am not just asserting that this research program seeks "clinical sanction" for its formulations. *All* schools of psychoanalysis claim clinical sanction for their "theories"—a phenomenon which Grunbaum (1984) has noted in his sustained argument against the use of "contaminated" clinical data as support for psychoanalytic theorizing. My point is rather that the Mount Zion Research Program has sought to meet Grunbaum's objections (as summarized in his epistemological liabilities argument), and thus stands as a pioneer attempt to test competing psychoanalytic hypotheses in a therapeutic context. If the evidential value of the Mount Zion Research Project is too hastily discounted, we are left asserting the dubious proposition that psychoanalytic hypotheses and theories can only be assessed in *extraclinical contexts.* Such a proposition is dubious because, in the words of Thoma and Kachele (1975), "no testing of psychoanalytic theory is possible without considering that the method is imbedded in human interaction."

57. Compare this to the assertion in Chapter 4 (p. 127) that there is no exit from the linguistic *circle of narrative.*

58. There is growing trend in psychiatry to reduce the *concept* of depression to a definition which equates it with a series of biochemical phenomena correlated with "experience." Hence the emergence of terms like "chemical depression," an example of how the experience of depression, or of "darkness visible" (a linguistically mediated context of interpretation) yields to a presumed biological substrate. There is, in truth, no natural necessity for such a shift to occur. It is simply a rhetorical or ideological convention, the latest reconstruction of emotional reality. The term "chemical depression" thus reflects shifting social interests, not the "real" nature of depressive phenomena.

59. Recall, however, that mentalist explanation is not tantamount to hermeneutic interpretation. The former may be causalistic, objectivistic, and in general fulfill the usual requirements of scientific discourse. See, for example, Edelson (1984, 1986).

60. Thoma and Kachele (1975) appear to employ the concept of repetition compulsion in its clinical or non-metapsychological sense. They state, for example, that:

Sooner or later, however, those relatively stable situations with which psychoanalytic theory concerns itself . . . will again exist, because they constitute the core of . . . different disorders. We mean the repetition compulsion. That the repetition compulsion is a superordinate essential characteristic of psychic disorders is unquestionable. No theory deserves to be taken seriously that does not present testable hypotheses for the psychogenesis of the repetition compulsion. (109)

61. In other words, the *sense of compulsion* need not presuppose the force of non-intentional biological-affective dispositions (such as those involved in manic behavior); nor need it be equated solely with the reactive tendencies of psychological (or personality) systems.

62. This is just another way of indicating that historical and scientific psychoanalysis are each capable of representing human intentionality. The former does so in terms of the requirements of *narrative abstraction,* while the latter does so in terms of the requirements of *analytic abstraction.* This means that for psychoanalytic science, "intentionality" is discerned in analytically abstracted aspects of behavior and functioning; the task of theory is to synthesize (or rejoin) these aspects into an empirically testable representation of a human process. Such intentional representations (even though "mentalist") are always construed as "emerging from" the subintentional and biological aspects of behavior and functioning. Science, in short, not only aims to rejoin events which its premises have previously disconnected, but also seeks to reestablish the unity (and continuity) of body and mind, of the subintentional and intentional aspects of human experience. In this respect, science diverges from history or hermeneutics, in that the latter is predicated on a certain *discontinuity* between the intentional and the subintentional. The divergence between science and history is underscored by Modell (1981), who (speaking as a scientific psychoanalyst) puts it in the following way:

> Words cannot be separated from affects and affects have unquestionably evolutionary, that is, biological significance . . . for at bottom the psychoanalyst is unlike the historian in that he observes the psychological representations of biological phenomena. (397)

63. The prototypical scheme of scientific psychoanalysis is a revisionary scheme. In other words, the positions expounded by Basch, Noy, and Gedo not only marginalize traditional metapsychological formulations, but also involve a rejection or reconceptualization of Freud's instinct-drive theory. At the same time, it cannot be denied that the prototypical scheme retains elements of both the automatic functioning hypothesis and the higher mental functioning hypothesis; in this respect, it is still classifiable as a "mixed model," or as what Weiss and Sampson term an "omnibus theory."

64. Waelder is referring, specifically, to psychoanalytic *metapsychology;* but his point holds, I believe, for psychoanalytical theorizing in general.

65. In Chapter 4, I refer to the universal conviction among analysts that "something true and transformative occurs in psychoanalytic practice." It seems to me that theoretical psychoanalysis articulates this conviction, and seeks to

justify it in terms of the prevailing conceptualizations of development, pathology, and therapeutic action. In other words, the theoretical question is always: how do we reconcile our informal or "tacit knowledge" of the success and truth of psychoanalysis (as a practice) with our formalized knowledge of development, pathology, and therapeutic action? Psychoanalytic theory thus operates *as if* it possessed "tacit knowledge" of psychoanalytic therapy (in advance of such theoretical formulations which purport to explain or account for its efficiency and effectiveness). One must therefore conclude that psychoanalytic theory is providing retroactive logical rationalizations (or deductive rationales) for "theories" and "practices" that have actually evolved more or less informally.

66. See Kohut (1971, 1977), who also puts forward an epigenetic scheme for development, while apparently recommending a therapeutic approach which is at odds with Gedo's. My concern, however, is not to adjudicate between these competing approaches, but to suggest that there can be no simple deductive relationship between the premise of an epigenetic developmental scheme and the inference of specific therapeutic strategies for the treatment of adult pathologies. There can be no simple relationship of this sort because of fundamental psychological differences between the child and the adult—differences which complicate (if not invalidate) any direct correspondence between the "issues" of child development and those which pertain to the psychotherapy (and psychopathology) of adults (e.g., Shapiro 1989; Eagle 1984a).

67. Recall the following passage from Heidegger's *What Is Called Thinking?* which introduces this chapter: "Here everything remains in question, and yet, the scientific findings are correct." To maintain in this way that science is merely "correct," but not true, is to imply that science is able to make statements about the nature of reality without its really knowing what reality is as such. Heidegger (1967) addresses the relationship of scientific knowledge to a more fundamental knowledge in the following passage from *What Is a Thing?*:

> *With our question, we want neither to replace the sciences nor to reform them.* On the other hand, we want to participate in the preparation of a decision; the decision: Is science the measure of knowledge, or is there a knowledge in which the ground and limit of science and thus its genuine effectiveness are determined? However, with our question we stand outside the sciences, and the knowledge for which our question strives is neither better nor worse but totally different. (10)

68. Remember that Schafer (1978, 1983) is not seeking to develop an explanatory or empirical theory. As he states: "Action language is not a set of empirical psychoanalytic propositions; it is a strategy for stating these propositions clearly and parsimoniously" (1978 185).

69. But bear in mind my earlier argument that such an empirical-analytic (autonomous) theory of therapy does not really constitute a *practical* account of therapy, or a veridical representation of the practical knowledge that characterizes it.

70. Practical psychoanalysis refers, in general, to "knowing how" to partici-

pate in the therapeutic activities of psychoanalytic practice. The term "practical," however, is ambiguous, since it pertains not only to (a) the practical knowledge implicit in human conduct (e.g., moral conduct, political conduct, parental conduct, entrepreneurial conduct, etc.), but also to (b) knowing how to participate in a practice as such. This second usage is not exclusive to conduct, but also pertains to scientific and historical inquiry, both of which are engagements in *theoretical* understanding, released in large measure from the considerations of conduct. In other words, there is a significant component of practical knowledge in the (theoretical) activities of science and history (see, for example, the works of Thomas Kuhn, Imre Lakatos, and François Jacob in science, and those of Marc Bloch and J. H. Hexter in history and historiography); it is evident, then, that the practical conditions of these activities do indeed define the "appropriateness" of questions, as well as the manner in which they ought to be answered. In sum, practical knowledge cannot be expunged from the theoretical discourses of science and history (Gadamer 1975, 1976, 1981).

My present focus, however, is not on the practical knowledge which is present in theoretical discourse, but on the practical knowledge which is present in the therapeutic conduct of psychoanalytic practice. Because therapeutic conduct is a subcase of practical conduct in general, it involves such "skills" as the skill in desire and aversion, as well as the skill to bind another self to one's desires (Oakeshott 1962 208–9). Such practical skills are always modulated by the requirements of the psychoanalytic situation. For example, the skill in desire and aversion now requires that the therapist (notwithstanding his or her unpleasant feelings toward the patient) overcome the wish to retaliate and resist the urge to seek relief; similarly, the skill to bind another self to one's desires is obviously involved in strengthening the therapeutic alliance (always an important aim), but the effective therapist soon learns that this may be most efficiently accomplished when the patient is allowed to have the experience of becoming intensely angry at the therapist without the usual disastrous consequences. Such skills (which comprise the practical knowledge of psychoanalysis) are neither deduced from a theory of countertransference, nor properly viewed as "applications" of such a theory. It is rather that this practical knowledge (which may indeed enable the therapist to exploit the transference and countertransference) is engendered through participation in the interactive therapeutic activity. It is the activity itself (and not a theory of it) which generates the knowledge base of practice.

71. The authentic problems of practical psychoanalysis (those problems which actually must be managed or resolved for the activity to retain its specific identity) are not initially recognized, conceptualized, or occasioned through psychoanalytic theory; they rather present themselves as a result of the therapist's "knowledgeable" (but non-theoretical) engagement in the concrete (interactive) activity. For further discussion of the nature and use of practical psychoanalysis, see in Chapter 6 of this book, "Pluralism and Practical Psychoanalysis."

72. The assimilation of psychoanalytic practice to science is characterized as follows by Leavy (1980):

> One might understand the situation as a very sophisticated variety of medical consultation, in which the patient brings his narrative to the physician as the object of a scientific scrutiny, which is to result in the application or remedial words to it. . . . What such a view leaves out is the dialogue. It moves in the direction dear to the modern scientist, toward the computerized management of illness, in which the therapeutic action is taken by an instrument free of human passions and therefore of blind spot, as well as incapable of participating response. (62)

Unlike Leavy, perhaps, I do not wish to imply that practical psychoanalysis is the "true language" of psychoanalysis, or that practical discourse is more concrete or more experience-near. On the contrary, I believe that practical discourse is in no way epistemically privileged. It is just one more abstraction from experience, and there is as much danger that historical and scientific psychoanalysis should be assimilated to it as the reverse.

My real point is that the three discourses of psychoanalysis are not properly viewed as composing a hierarchy, or as engaged in an argumentative struggle for logical supremacy. *They may differ without disagreeing.* The appropriate image or metaphor of their relationship is not that of an argument or a debate, but that of a *conversation.* As Oakeshott (1962) has written in "The Voice of Poetry in the Conversation of Mankind":

> It is with conversation as with gambling, its significance lies neither in winning nor in losing but in wagering. Properly speaking, it is impossible in the absence of a diversity of voices: in it different universes of discourse meet, acknowledge each other and enjoy an oblique relationship which neither requires nor forecasts their being assimilated to one another. (198–99)

6

Pluralism in Psychoanalysis: A Recapitulation

Nothing will ever be attempted if all possible objections must be first overcome.

—Samuel Johnson

All who study our Talmud know there are no final proofs in the arguments of its interpretations. . . . In this discipline there are no clear demonstrations, as there are in geometry.

—Nahmanides

Analysands are divided selves. They are divided between there and then and here and now. They are people who are largely locked up in the past, with only so much energy available for the present and future. It is hardly surprising, then, that psychoanalysis should be concerned with how and why the past influences our lives through obtruding itself into the present. The exact nature of that influence has been much debated, and questions have been raised regarding the extent to which the past is explanatory (and its recovery mutative)—or whether, indeed, there is *any* genuine connection between what happens in analysis and what happened in the past.

In this book, I have endeavored to respond to such concerns by offering an account of the conceptualization of the past in American psychoanalysis. I have sought, throughout, to explore *how* the idea of the past figures in the various worlds of psychoanalytic discourse, and by doing so, to comprehend the conceptual complexity of the past, particularly the complexity that is engendered by the scientific, historical, and

253

practical constructions of the past. As my inquiry has taken shape, it has become apparent that the "past" is no simple or self-evident idea, and that psychoanalytic understanding is more perspicuous when it acknowledges and exploits the multiple versions of the past at its disposal.

In this book, then, I have obviously cast a very wide net. It may therefore be useful, as I now conclude, to take stock of what has (or hasn't) been achieved, and to attempt a concise statement of my aim or intention. I thus offer below:

- a summary of this book's argument and theme;
- reflections on the nature and use of practical psychoanalysis;
- a review of the more telling objections to my argument and approach; and
- comments regarding directions for further inquiry.

The Argument Summarized

This book offers an argument for pluralism in psychoanalysis. According to the philosopher and psychologist William James, pluralism is the orientation which affirms that "there is no possible point of view from which the world can appear an absolutely single fact" (James [1910] 1975 6). But, as James also reminds us, pluralism by no means precludes a practical monism. Philosophy, itself, can be defined as the quest for the world's unity, and pluralism's real concern with unity is whether it can be so instituted as to assure that alternative viewpoints receive a fair hearing. In other words, "experience is a process, [so] no point of view can ever be *the* last one" (James [1910] 1975 55); thus the problem of pluralism is just to guarantee that any intellectual unity established on pragmatic or provisional grounds does not slide into an unwarranted or misconceived totality.

Given such an understanding, pluralism appears capable of recognizing and accommodating the legitimate claims of practical unities. It is therefore most exact to state that the argument of this book (just because it is a pluralist one) necessarily reflects and embodies a certain tension between pluralism and monism in American psychoanalysis. Thus, in this study, I have expounded and defended a pluralist conception of the unity or coherence of psychoanalytic discourse in which the exclusivist and totalist claims of both scientific (unitarian) and hermeneutic (dichotomist) psychoanalysis are clearly repudiated.

Upon close inspection, it is evident that the former (or unitarian) model insists on the unity and uniformity of explanation across all domains and subject matters, and culminates in the requirement that psychoanalytic knowledge be homogeneous in nature and form. The goal or purport of such a model is seemingly unobjectionable: it is to transform psychoanalysis from a speculative armchair discourse to a reliable empirical science (a) in which it would now be possible to test the validity of psychoanalytic theories in order to use them more advantageously in understanding the nature of psychoanalytic phenomena, (b) and in which it would also be possible to demonstrate how relations among the many components of therapeutic, developmental, and mental processes must be considered in making a prediction about any single component. The danger in this stance, however, is totalism—the view that all psychoanalytic understanding is reducible to scientific (or paradigmatic) discourse, and that all other discourses are simply defective or weak variants of that superordinate or foundational discourse.

The second (or dichotomist) model asserts, in contrast, that the methods and epistemologies appropriate to the investigation of physical and biological processes may not be suitable for exploration of the "human realm." The human realm must be approached with "an openness to its special characteristics and a willingness to let questions inform which methods are appropriate" (Polkinghorne 1983 289). Such a model, however, cannot help but sanction the dualistic thesis that nature and culture are severed by a "Great Divide" (Blight 1981), and that each (ontically distinct) realm implies and requires its own peculiar mode of knowing. So it appears, on the one hand, that the goal or purport of the dichotomist model is (also) unobjectionable: it is to respect the "special characteristics" of the human realm in order to gain access to it and to know it more truly. Yet, on the other hand, the risk in employing such a model is clearly to sever that realm from biology and nature, and the danger is thus to exclude any prospect for a unified or coherent system of psychoanalytic understanding. It follows, then, that hermeneutic (or dichotomist) psychoanalysis is as susceptible to totalism as is its scientific counterpart. It, too, risks premature closure through a policy of metaphysical exclusion (dualism), and through an artificial (a priori) arrestment of experience.

. . .

The pluralist argument, as set forth in this book, asserts that what is required is not the unification of psychoanalysis into a homogeneous discourse (unitarianism), but rather the recognition of where, when, and how each *mode* of discourse is applicable and appropriate. In other words, the pluralist argument allows for a plurality of discourses (or modes of discourse)—but contra hermeneutics, does not presume an inherent "split" between the natural and the human realms. History, science, and practice are thus recognized as distinguishable modes of discourse; yet, each mode is equally able to abstract any domain or subject matter—whether or not, for example, that domain or subject matter belongs to the so-called human or natural realms. In brief, totalism (in whatever form) is rejected because no point of view (e.g., unitarianism or dichotomism) "can ever be *the* last one." It follows that no single mode of psychoanalytic understanding is so epistemically privileged as to offer *the* mirror of nature, psychical reality, or the psychoanalytic past; and no particular discourse (history, science, practice, etc.) is unconditionally entitled to supersede or replace the other. In this, the pluralist understanding, the objective is not to develop a superordinate, scientific, or "neutral" language for psychoanalysis, but is rather to discern (as noted above) where, when, and how each discourse or language game is applicable. Pluralism in psychoanalysis therefore asserts that understanding may be (more or less) scientific, historical, or practical in character, and that each form of understanding demarcates a specific modality of discourse. There are no a priori constraints upon the referents of such discourse, and any single mode may legitimately refer to any domain or subject matter. Thus a scientific abstraction of "mind" (or psychical reality) is as valid as (but no more so than) a historical abstraction of "mind" (or psychical reality). Each mode of abstraction (from the process of experience) is equally legitimate, though each will surely differ from the other in its relevance or usefulness for the realization of specific aims and purposes in particular contexts.

Because there is a plurality of discourses (or modes of discourse), there is a plurality of "pasts." Psychoanalytic understanding generates and exploits multiple versions (or constructions) of the past—and in this book, these have been designated the scientific (or developmental) past, the historical (or narrative) past, and the practical (or pretheoretical) past. Each "past" is constructed, not given, and each "past" is necessary (and irreplaceable) in any comprehensive account of the unity and coherence of psychoanalytic understanding. Furthermore, each "past," though categorially distinct, is also related to the others in certain specifiable and interesting ways, and each past contributes to the "depth" we wish to associate with psychoanalytic understanding in general. Herbert Schlesinger (1969 204) has justly observed that "a psychotherapy in which the patient is not helped to express something of the depth of himself would be quite unthinkable." But how is psychoanalytic thought properly to picture this depth? In this book, its recognition and its explication have necessarily been complicated by the pluralist principle that psychoanalytic understanding is heterogeneous, and that the "depth" of the psychoanalytic past must thus be perceived from at least three parallel points of view, as simultaneously a scientific construction, a historical construction, and a practical construction. It may even be hypothesized that the analyst's (or theorist's) reflective understanding of the plurality (and coherence) of psychoanalytic pasts will somehow help the patient "to express something of the depth of himself." (Whether, in fact, this is really the case, whether or not such help is actually forthcoming in psychotherapy, and whether or not it furthers personality change, are of course empirical questions—albeit ones which must first be articulated in terms of the principle of the plurality of discourses.)

The pluralist proposal is thus offered as a reasonable alternative to the unitarian (scientific) and dichotomist (hermeneutic) positions which appear to dominate contemporary controversy in American psychoanalysis. Long-standing (and possibly sterile) debates may now be seen in a new light, and perhaps be reformulated or circumvented if not actually resolved or settled. Accordingly, in the preceding chapters, I have sought to illustrate the utility of the pluralist thesis by reexamining and reframing such traditional controversies as (a) narrative truth versus historical truth in psychoanalytic interpretation, (b) the clinical theory-metapsychology debate, (c) the argument between hermeneutics and science, and (d) the problem of the relation of psychoanalytic theory to therapeutic practice. Concerning the last, for example, I have questioned the automatic assumption that theory (whether scientific or historical) is clinically relevant. I have done this *not* because I perversely wish to dismiss the value of psychoanalytic theory (or argue for some kind of mystical doctrine of knowledge by direct acquaintance), but because I seek to underline the non-utilitarian aim of psychoanalysis in general. For it seems to me that the pluralist thesis reminds us that the actual objective of psychoanalysis (recognized now as a practical unity, or as a whole comprised of scientific, historical, and practical aspects) is neither "truth" nor "effectiveness." Its objective is rather *thought itself* (Heidegger 1968). I mean by this that the psychoanalytic enterprise, at its most coherent and reflective, offers the possibility of "thought-ful" self-understanding rather than therapeutic amelioration (Oremland 1991).[1] Philip Rieff (1968) makes a similar point in *The Triumph of the Therapeutic* when he juxtaposes Freud's rigorously rationalistic and non-utilitarian psychoanalytic orientation with the remissive therapeutic requirements of Carl Jung, Wilhelm Reich, and D. H. Lawrence.

Thus, to insist upon thought (or thinking) as the actual objective of psychoanalytic understanding is no idle, frivolous, or irrelevant eccentricity. It is simply to acknowledge that

- each mode of psychoanalytic discourse (history, science, practice) is absorbed by its own internal struggles and is unreflectively defined by its own logical limitations;
- psychoanalytic understanding, at its most coherent, transcends such struggles and limitations through reflection upon the assumptions of each mode of discourse, without committing itself to the aims or requirements of any single mode of discourse.

It is in such a sense, then, that the psychoanalytic orientation is indissolubly connected to the "interminable" requirement of thinking and is characterized by a singular appreciation of the powers and limitations of rational or reflective understanding. Indeed, it is only insofar as we abstract from the paramount objective of thought itself, and hence arrest the process of experience and curtail the possibilities of thought, that we arrive at the subordinate or derivative objectives of truth and efficacy in psychoanalysis. In short, psychoanalytic understanding, in my view, suffers no loss of dignity or relevance when its non-practical (non-utilitarian) aim is admitted; nor is that aim at all incompatible with the theorist's laudable pursuit of truth and correctness and the clinician's professional duty to be useful, helpful, and accountable to the patient.

Pluralism and Practical Psychoanalysis

It is a paradox of the pluralist argument that it not only evokes the "non-utilitarian" aim of the psychoanalytic orientation (see above), but also helps to validate its practical character as well.

Recall, for example, the claim in Chapter 5 of this book ("Science, History, and Practice: Pluralism in Psychoanalysis") that the problems and methods of scientific and historical psychoanalysis are derived from their respective traditions of inquiry, while those of practical psychoanalysis are derived from the conduct of practice itself. In other words:

- practice is a legitimate source of knowledge;
- the knowledge base of practice is generated by practice itself, not by research efforts divorced from the context of practice;
- practice is no longer the mere application of scientific or theoretical findings, but the locale for knowledge development through practical reasoning and practice-based inquiry and action.

It follows from my thesis that psychoanalysis (as a practical discourse) appears as a form of knowledge-in-practice, constituted wholly in the settings of practice, and acquired and transmitted exclusively through the processes of guided participation or apprenticeship (Rogoff 1990). Indeed, the practical or practicing knowledge of the novice analyst is established not only through his or her "real" apprenticeship with an expert analyst, but also through his or her quasi-apprenticeship with certain "memorable" patients (Dryden 1987). "Apprenticeship," in this wider sense, thus involves the sharing and partial sharing of intentional worlds, as well as the appropriation of techniques and methods. The analyst-as-apprentice therefore depends on knowledge elicited from the experience of direct interaction, even as he or she masters the art of establishing and fostering intersubjectivity in the dialogical and transferential circumstances of practice (circumstances which, by nature, are unstable, uncertain, and often non-benign). The analyst is concretely engaged in a tradition of conduct—and the problems or methods which are relevant to such conduct are those that arise through participation in the practical activity itself. It follows, then, that practical psychoanalysis (as a discourse or mode of discourse) is self-sufficient and owes nothing essential to the research-generated knowledge of science or to the hermeneutically driven knowledge of history.

Let me now illustrate what I mean by this last (and admittedly difficult) point. Consider the situation of an analyst or psychotherapist working with a child who is coping with the traumatic effects of the violent and sudden death of his mother. On the one hand, the research-generated knowledge of science will probably direct the analyst to focus on the developmental or maturational level of the child-as-research-object, in the expectation that therapeutically useful and theoretically justified interventions will follow logically from such an assessment. On the other hand, the hermeneutical discourse of history may well direct the analyst to attend to the split between past and present in the experience of the child-as-narrator, in the hope that such an interpretative exploration will eventually help the child to construct a livable and coherent self-narrative. In sharp distinction, practical discourse—as a form of engaged cognition— owes nothing to these theoretical traditions of inquiry and understanding. From within the specific parameters of practical psychoanalysis, the grieving, disturbed, or traumatized child is:

- neither an object of research or assessment,
- nor the presumptive narrator of a not-yet-well-formed life history.

The child is rather seen and heard as an agent in distress, who requires immediate and urgent attention in the here and now. The analyst, in turn, is primed to listen and to act, precisely because he or she will have already acquired (through apprenticeship) such *principles of action* as:

- a child can't wait;[2]
- a child's memory of loss makes no mistakes (Wiesel 1990).

In actuality, the child is always leading the analyst, moment-to-moment, session-by-session, and the analyst (though "theoretically informed") lacks a premeditated design or plan (Shapiro 1989). Perhaps for this very reason, the analyst is free and must be free to "turn on a dime" and act decisively in the intersubjective present. In doing so, he or she is enacting (as well as interpreting) such principles of action as those above—which themselves derive from participation in the practical activity and can be neither validated nor falsified by scientific or historical discourse. Such principles of action, we recall, are not "applied" (i.e., they are not equivalent to theoretical or scientific research findings), but are enacted or expressed through the sharing or partial sharing of the intentional worlds of the adult analyst and child analysand.

More generally, the practical or practicing knowledge of psychoanalysis supplies principles of action which, among other things, enable the analyst:

- to figure out what to do, at this particular moment, about his feelings (pleasant or unpleasant) toward the patient;
- to figure out, moment by moment, what role to play (and how to play it) in order to avoid destructive reenactments of the patient's vicious circle in human relationships;
- to figure out, here and now, how to be truthful and respectful to this particular patient, even while being required by the situation to enact a professional role.

Such principles of action comprise the timing, tact, and know-how[3] of clinical practice. As core elements of the analyst's practical knowledge, they are not only derived from the experience of practice, but also help to reshape and inform the analyst's interactions with his or her patients. Yet, as elements of practical knowledge, such principles also resist explicit translation into the theoretical discourses of science and history—or if so formulated, do not contain in them the actual knowledge required for their own use in the shifting contexts of practice.

It should be evident by now that the pluralist argument succeeds in establishing practical psychoanalysis as an autonomous mode of discourse. Practice is *not* just another form of theory, and the knowledge base it generates is quite distinct from that generated through scientific research or historical interpretation. Yet it must also be conceded that if the pluralist argument of this book legitimates practical psychoanalysis, it is by no means able to delineate its specific features as a practice-based inquiry or as a reflective mode of discourse. I admit, then, that practice does not speak for itself, and that its comprehension will require a program of conceptualization and reflection which lies far beyond the scope of this study. What is certain, however, is that such a program or project will need to demonstrate a more subtle understanding of the cognitive processes of practical reasoning, and must eventually succeed in formulating the variety of "methods of generating practicing knowledge and the criteria used to judge its value and acceptability" (Hoshmand and Polkinghorne 1992). Once this is achieved, once we are able to comprehend, on its own terms, the specific form of knowledge derived from the experience of psychoanalytic practice, we may then be in a favorable position to reframe the science-practice (or theory-practice) relationship in psychoanalysis, psychotherapy, and professional psychology in general. This, by far, is the most important consequence of this book's argument and points to the most urgent direction for further inquiry (see also the section of this chapter entitled "Directions for Further Inquiry"). In this book, I take a first step in that direction; and I have done so by pursuing the implications of the pluralist thesis, by recognizing practice as a legitimate source of knowledge.

Objections Reconsidered

Let me again respond to the most familiar and persistent objection to a project of this type. This is a non-empirical inquiry. It is a fact that psychology has always been the most aggressively empiricist of all academic (or even scientific) disciplines.[4] From its vantage, it is often difficult to assess, evaluate, or see the point of any inquiry which does not revolve around the collection and interpretation of data. Numerous critics have challenged this empiricist objection, and recently, Kukla (1989) has actually supplied a catalog of non-empirical activities which are indispensable to the advancement of psychological (or psychoanalytic) knowledge. These include: the construction of theories (and the derivation of empirical consequences); the investigation of the logical coherence of theories or models; the discovery and elucidation of logically necessary truths (along with distinguishing them from the contingent claims of a theory); the identification and explication of propositions too basic to be submitted to empirical test (e.g., contingent a priori presuppositions); and finally, the specification of what Kukla terms "pragmatic a priori beliefs" (1989 793). Each of the above non-empirical activities, to a greater or lesser degree, belongs to my project—and this fact, alone, should lead us to dismiss the empiricist objection once and for all. And yet, it clearly retains a certain force. Why?

The problem is not (as is sometimes claimed) that there are no solid criteria with which to evaluate the worth of non-empirical contributions in psychology and psychoanalysis. If this were indeed the case, then much work in philosophy, criticism, the social sciences, and even biology and physics would actually fall outside the purview of rational criticism. The problem is rather, I think, that it is difficult to *measure* the contribution of non-empirical research to the "progress" of a discipline which is militantly empiricist, and which is unified methodologically, even as it is fragmented theoretically (Danziger 1985). Empirical research in psychology (however trivial) is automatically processed by the prevailing methodological paradigm. It is therefore easy to conclude (however fallaciously) that such research "adds" to psychological and psychoanalytic knowledge, if only because its methods and results belong to well-demarcated problem areas. In sharp contrast, non-empirical inquiries tend to question or avoid established methods, and are likely to revise or recast the familiar map of a discipline. It follows that the contributions of such non-empirical inquiries may even be experienced as cognitively dissonant, as impossible to accommodate within the traditional model for the measurement of disciplinary progress. So it is therefore the case that in academic psychology, at least, non-empirical (or theoretical) psychology is always problematic. The temptation is to dismiss that endeavor as an exercise in "armchair psychology," as an unfortunate regression to psychology's speculative origins in the philosophies of Aristotle, Hobbes, Hume, and J. S. Mill (among others). Such fears to the contrary notwithstanding, it must nonetheless be concluded that the empiricist objection to my project, though most familiar and most tenacious, is also least substantial and least warranted.

Having just considered the most general of objections, it should now be possible to proceed to a more concise review of those which seem directly relevant to the specific form and content of the argument of this book.

Because my approach is *synoptic* (as well as non-empirical), the objection will be made that it strives for breadth of treatment, but at an unacceptable cost in depth of treatment. Numerous topics of psychoanalytic interest (e.g., transference and countertransference, empathy and psychopathology, the analysand's attitude to the past, truth and efficacy in interpretation, etc.) are encountered and even discussed at some length. But the obligation to achieve a synoptic perspective (and thus to retain the thread of the underlying argument) has often tended to cut short such discussions—leaving, at times, an impression of superficiality and/or incompleteness. It is true that I have sought to neutralize this objection through the use of explanatory notes which follow each of the five principal chapters; and the attentive reader will observe that these notes frequently extend or qualify discussions which are introduced in the main text. Nevertheless, I cannot deny that this is an imperfect solution to an insoluble problem. Clearly, I have chosen to approach my subject in such a way that it might lead to a more perspicuous *overview*. And for such a choice (as with any choice) there are consequences and costs.

A more substantial objection is founded on coherence. Criticisms directed toward coherence and internal consistency are especially significant for non-empirical inquiries, since logical (rather than methodological) considerations are now most salient. Given the pluralist argument expounded in this book, it is reasonable, then, to question whether history, science, and practice constitute an internally consistent and logically coherent depiction of the "unity" of psychoanalytic understanding. In other words, are these discourses (or modes of discourse) sufficiently justified as distinguishable, yet interrelated, discourses (or modes of discourse)? Have I adequately shown, for example, how the theoretical discourses of science and history are validly coordinated in psychoanalytic inquiry, or how the different forms of information each discourse generates can be most effectively exploited in psychoanalytic research? Even more to the point, have I succeeded in elucidating "practice" as an autonomous discourse which merits further inquiry and exploration—or has my (too brief) treatment foundered in the paradox of "what explicates practice" (if not the *theoretical* discourses of science and history)? In all these respects (and especially the last), the coherence of my overall argument may be legitimately questioned, and any defects in the above will likely be reflected in the analyses of the nature and role of each version of the psychoanalytic past, and of the ways in which each is related to the other in any comprehensive (or unified) system of psychoanalytic understanding.

At the very outset of this book, I asserted that it must be judged, in the end, by its relative fruitfulness, by its ability to open up new avenues of inquiry, practice, and self-understanding. It is fitting, then, that the final objection centers on the conundrum of "utility." Does the pluralist thesis, as expounded throughout this book, actually make a difference somewhere in the world of human experience? Does it really matter?

Let me concede first that if the utility of my project is measured by its value in guiding (or prescribing) the specifics of psychoanalytic practice, then it must frankly be regarded as relatively useless. According to my own arguments, psychoanalytic theory is not prescriptive; no more so is this book's attempt to advance an account of the coherence of psychoanalytic understanding. The most that I can claim is that the reflective study of psychoanalytic thinking (or the recognition of a plurality of psychoanalytic discourses) is somehow necessary for an authentic understanding of psychoanalytic practice. Such an understanding, at the least, may then help the practitioner to avoid the hollowness of mere technique and application. But such an understanding cannot constitute a cookbook (or protocol) for the conduct of psychotherapy, nor can it supply a substitute for the practical knowledge of psychoanalysis.

The genuine utility of my project must really reside in its ability to clarify (and perhaps resolve) certain intellectual dilemmas, and hence open up new avenues of inquiry. I believe, for example, that this book succeeds in explaining why historical discourse (in contrast to scientific discourse) does not describe a "real past," but rather constructs a "narrative past"— now recognized as an intentional object of historical consciousness. I suggest, further, that this is an important contribution which not only clarifies the complex nature of psychoanalytic understanding (and the meaning of psychoanalysis as a "life historical" discipline), but also illuminates the therapeutic action of psychoanalysis (see, in particular, Chapter 4). I will even generalize this claim by asserting that my effort in this book to distinguish and legitimate a historical mode of psychoanalytic understanding can be of real use to the consumer of psychoanalytic literature. He or she will now be better positioned to make sense of the arguments, case studies, and theoretical claims of important psychoanalytic authors. For according to my thesis, the writings of such authors are often ambiguous and opaque, not the least because they unwittingly conflate historical and scientific arguments (and almost always fail to apprehend the nature and role of practical knowledge in psychoanalysis). In short, an important contribution of my project may consist in its promoting a more intelligent and critical reading of the literature of the field.

Although I am convinced that this book is most useful in exposing the way in which we think (or ought to think) in specialized psychoanalytic contexts, I would also urge that it opens up new avenues of self-understanding in general. I believe it was Proust who quipped that everything has already been said, but since no one pays attention, it has to be repeated every morning. Likewise, much that has been said in this book may seem obvious (or already said). But it has been necessary for me to repeat and reframe the obvious, perhaps in a new context, perhaps with a new nuance—if only to breathe new life into such tired psychoanalytic truisms as: "Analysis leaves its scars; it cannot cure the past, but only lay it to rest in a forgivable way" (see "The Equivocality of the 'Past'" in Chapter 2 of this book). For some readers, then, my project may be of more than academic interest. One of its uses (I hope) is that it may actually help us to speak more rationally about our personal pasts—not just in the contexts of psychoanalytic theory and practice, but also in those of everyday life, and not only through the languages of science, but also through those of history and practice.

Directions for Further Inquiry

This study has been offered as an exercise in thinking. My purpose, though, has not been to prescribe what to think or which truths to hold, but to enlarge the boundaries of permissible inquiry. To that end, numerous research problems have been cited and documented throughout the preceding five chapters, and their relationships to (and dependence upon) the arguments of this book have been described in some detail. What now follows is by no means a comprehensive catalog (or inventory) of such problems, but rather a selection designed to illustrate just a few of the more promising directions for further inquiry.[5]

1. *Empathic Narrative.* According to one of my principal arguments (see, in particular, Chapter 4), the empathic narrative is the verbal or linguistic medium through which the past is laid to rest "in a forgivable way," and through which the past is mastered and assimilated, if not exactly abolished and eliminated. But what, precisely, are the formal characteristics of such a narrative, and how do psychological or psychodynamic processes figure in its construction and in its therapeutic effect? Under what circumstances, for example, is empathic narration avoided, resisted, or disavowed? How does the analyst's attitude toward the analysand's past (and toward his or her own) affect the construction of the empathic narrative? What, specifically, are its empirical antecedents and consequents, and through which research designs (and methods) may these be most reliably and validly explicated? What underlies the capacity to generate new and

more empathic perspectives on one's own ineliminable past (and why is it that people differ in their possession of this capacity)? How might such narratives be fostered in psychotherapy?

2. *Narrative Development.* According to a basic tenet of historical psycho-analysis, people derive their identities from the stories they tell about themselves. Human beings are not simply the developmental outcomes of past events and processes, but are also (as self-aware agents and makers of narrative meaning) the expressions of narrative structures and their trans-formations. What develops, then, is not just the organism as such (e.g., its intrinsic maturational potentials, its cognitive and affective capacities), but also the manner in which, and the perspective from which, the story of a life is told and retold. And yet, very little is actually known, empiri-cally, about the processes of "retelling," or about *narrative development* throughout the life span and its relevance for psychoanalytic theory and therapy. How and why do our stories change (or fail to change), both within the clinical context and outside of it? What role has self-deception in storytelling, and how does it figure in our explanations of narrative change? Does it matter if our knowledge of such change comes from looking backward in time or looking forward in time? And in what ways, if any, is the history of our storytelling related to the biological and psychological processes through which—according to scientific psycho-analysis—we become aware of our own existences?

3. *Presentism in Psychoanalysis.* Although an important aim of my book has been to lay bare the multiple versions of the past that figure in American psychoanalytic discourse, it has become increasingly probable —as this inquiry has progressed—that there may well be no robust relationship between "what happens in analysis" and "what once hap-pened in the past" (see, in particular, Chapter 5). In the vocabulary of this book, the scientifically constructed psychoanalytic past ("develop-ment") may be neither logically entailed within, nor empirically relevant for, a psychoanalytic theory of therapeutic change. In other words, there may well be a *disjunction* (within psychoanalytic discourse) between the theory of development and the theory of change. Further inquiry, both conceptual and empirical, is needed to explore the implications of such a disjunction. Does it now follow, for example, that the analyst's attitude toward the past is inconsequential for practice, or that the historically

constructed psychoanalytic past ("narrative") is *also* to be expunged from
the psychoanalytic theory of therapeutic change? If so, won't such a
presentistic theory (now an "autonomous" theory of therapy) be altogether deprived of its psychoanalytic character and identity? In short, has
psychoanalysis any future as a theory of intervention (or as a theory of
treatment or theory of change), or does its future—at least as a theoretical
discourse—actually lie elsewhere?

4. *Comparative Psychoanalysis.* The pluralist principle, as elaborated
throughout this book, is a kind of hermeneutic device (or heuristic) which
can help to further the much-needed enterprise of comparative psychoanalysis (Schafer 1983 282). For if the interpretative analysis of the
various schools of psychoanalytic thought is pursued from a narrowly
unitarian (or dichotomist) viewpoint, the results of such an inquiry are
not only likely to be biased by initial assumptions, but even worse, are
likely to confirm these assumptions. Such an approach can purport to
"correct" the logical defects of certain psychoanalytic schools, but most
assuredly, cannot do justice to the authentic aims and objectives of these
schools. In contrast, the pluralist position (though also not a neutral or
unsituated point of view) has the advantage of bracketing or suspending
the "biases" specific to unitarian and dichotomist psychoanalysis. Hence
its comparative inquiries are more likely to appreciate *all* the discourses of
psychoanalytic understanding, rather than presuming that any single discourse (or mode of discourse) is epistemically privileged, or unconditionally entitled to replace or supersede the others.

To illustrate: when the pluralist critic evaluates the varied contributions
of Freud, Sullivan, M. Klein, Winnicott, Erikson, Kohut, etc., he or she
will identify and distinguish scientific, historical, and practical modes of
discourse as these are woven through the assumptions, concepts, and
methods of each "school." The pluralist critic will also appreciate—in the
work of each analyst or school of analysis—the relative weight and import
of these modes of discourse (and of the corresponding versions of the
psychoanalytic past), and will seek to elicit the implications of such variations and differences: e.g., the relevance of such differences (a) for exploit-
ing different forms of information about psychic life and the psychoanalytic past, (b) for adjudicating what counts as evidence for key propositions,
and (c) for specifying how these propositions are (or are not) connected

to the analytic methods which are supposedly practiced within each school. In these ways as in others, the pluralist approach can help to enrich the study of comparative analysis. Because that approach, itself, constitutes a conceptual innovation, it may lead to more perceptive and unanticipated interpretations of the commonalities (and differences) in the various schools of psychoanalysis. Such findings will not only serve to illustrate (or "test") the pluralist hypothesis, but also to increase confidence in its validity.

Final Comment

History and science comprise the theoretical discourse of psychoanalysis. My purpose has been to understand what is right in each—perhaps in the hope that through a kind of simultaneous contemplation, I might move toward a more perspicuous *overview* of why we are torn between them as competing modes of psychoanalytic understanding. It follows, then, that the intelligibility (or plausibility) of my project has depended on the "negative capability" of its potential audiences: their capability, as the poet Keats first described it, to contain *competing truths* (e.g., of science, of history), and above all, to resist the call to certainty and closure.

In my final comment, then, let me therefore restate these truths so that it becomes apparent why I cannot choose between them. Historical psychoanalysis (especially in its radically hermeneutic form) is founded on the proposition that *language creates the world we inhabit;* paraphrasing Gadamer (1975), language is not just one of man's possessions in the world, but on it depends the fact that man has a world at all. From the vantage of history, this proposition is deemed too basic to be submitted to empirical test, and yet its truth is presupposed in any coherent account of the hermeneutic conditions of human understanding.

In sharp contrast, however, the truth of science is founded on the falsity of the linguistic proposition. Far from being regarded as untestable but true, the proposition in question is now deemed testable and false. Language does not create the world we inhabit, for it is regarded as an empirical truth that our concepts are, in origin, non-linguistic "and can be achieved as a result of interactions with the world and other members of our species in the absence of speech" (Edelman 1989 267). From the vantage of science, then, concepts precede language, and unlike language, are neither conventional nor arbitrary, nor linked to any specific speech community. There is thought and there is language, but strictly speaking, there is no "language of thought." Concepts are *about the world,* and though language vastly enhances conceptual categorization, it does not (contra hermeneutics) create or constitute the world we inhabit.

I hope it will be agreed that the dispute between science and history cannot be resolved through an appeal to science. Such a "resolution" would violate the pluralist thesis that "no point of view can ever be *the* last one" (James [1910] 1975 55). It is wiser, then, not to choose between the competing truths of science and history. Psychoanalysis has always understood this, and this, I believe, is its distinguishing virtue. In Ricoeur's (1974) words, psychoanalysis remains a "mixed discourse." My distinct contribution in this book has been to repeat Ricoeur's insight, albeit in a new context and with a new nuance. To acknowledge the plurality of psychoanalytic pasts is to concede the truth of pluralism in psychoanalysis: the truth that universes of discourse (science, history, and practice) may differ without disagreeing.

NOTES

1. My thesis is eminently debatable, as Sperling (in Panel, 1954) implied when he observed that psychoanalysis may provide an unparalleled psychological education, but the goal of therapy is a better-functioning ego. Recall, though, that psychoanalysis is not only a form of treatment or therapy, but also a cognitive and existential stance. This stance is indissolubly connected to the requirement of *thinking,* and thus affords the possibility of interminable insight to analyst and analysand alike: The question "What is called thinking?" can never be answered, however, by proposing a psychological or psychoanalytic definition of the concept of thinking. Heidegger (1968) and others have reminded us of the fruitlessness of such reflection. It follows that the goal or aim of psychoanalytic understanding lies outside the purview of psychoanalytic understanding. The answer to the question "What is called thinking?" can never be just a psychoanalytic answer.

2. This comment is attributed to Albert J. Solnit, M.D., Sterling Professor Emeritus of Pediatrics and Psychiatry at Yale University, and Commissioner of Mental Health for the State of Connecticut.

3. I owe this particular formulation of practical knowledge to an individual who chooses to remain anonymous.

4. It is a curiosity of intellectual history that though other disciplines such as physics and molecular biology have been more successful as science, academic

psychology has surely been most dogmatic in its adherence to empiricist and positivist norms of investigation and justification.

5. Recall, however, that the most obvious direction for further inquiry has already been introduced under the heading "Pluralism and Practical Psychoanalysis."

References

Anscombe, R. 1981. Referring to the unconscious: A philosophical critique of Schafer's action language. *International Journal of Psychoanalysis* 62: 225–41.

Apel, K. O. 1977. Types of social science in light of human interests of knowledge. *Social Research* 44: 425–70.

Arendt, H. 1968. *Between past and future.* New York: Viking Press.

Argelander, H. 1976. *The initial interview in psychotherapy.* New York: Human Sciences Press.

Argyris, C., Putnam, R., and Smith, D. M. 1985. *Action science.* San Francisco: Jossey-Bass.

Arieti, S. 1967. *The intrapsychic self: Feeling, cognition, and creativity in health and mental illness.* New York: Basic Books.

Arlow, J., and Brenner, C. 1964. *Psychoanalytic concepts and the structural theory.* New York: International Universities Press.

Atwood, G. E., and Stolorow, R. D. 1984. *Structures of subjectivity: Explorations in psychoanalytic phenomenology.* Hillsdale, N.J.: Analytic Press.

Barratt, B. B. 1984. *Psychic reality and psychoanalytic knowing.* Hillsdale, N.J.: Analytic Press.

Bartlett, F. C. 1932. *Remembering: A study in experimental and social psychology.* Cambridge: Cambridge University Press.

Basch, M. 1973. Psychoanalysis and theory formation. *Journal of Psychoanalysis* 1: 39–52.

———. 1976a. Psychoanalysis and communication science. *The Annual of Psychoanalysis,* Vol. 4, 385–421. New York: International Universities Press.

———. 1976b. The concept of affect: A re-examination. *J. Amer. Psychoanal. Assn.* 24: 759–77.

———. 1977. Developmental psychology and explanatory theory in psychoanalysis. *The Annual of Psychoanalysis,* Vol. 5, 229–63. New York: International Universities Press.

———. 1981. Psychoanalytic interpretation and cognitive transformation. *International Journal of Psychoanalysis* 62: 151–75.

273

Basch, M. 1983. Empathic understanding: A review of the concept and some theoretical considerations. *J. Amer. Psychoanal. Assn.* 31: 101–26.

―――. 1986. Clinical theory and metapsychology: Incompatible or complementary? *Psychoanalytic Review* 73: 261–73.

―――. 1988. *Understanding psychotherapy.* New York: Basic Books.

Baur, S. 1991. *The dinosaur man: Tales of madness and enchantment.* New York: Edward Burlingame Books/Harper Collins Publishers.

Beck, A. T. 1976. *Cognitive theory and the emotional disorders.* New York: International Universities Press.

Beeghly, M., and Cicchetti, D. 1987. An organizational approach to symbolic development in children with Down's Syndrome. *New Directions for Child Development* 36: 5–29.

Benjamin, W. 1968. *Illuminations,* trans. and ed. H. Zohn and H. Arendt. New York: Harcourt, Brace & World.

Berlin, I. 1981. *Concepts and categories: Philosophical essays.* New York: Penguin Books.

Betti, E. 1962. Hermeneutics as the general methodology of the Geisteswissenschaften. In *Contemporary hermeneutics: Hermeneutics as method, philosophy and critique,* ed. J. Bleicher. London: Routledge & Kegan Paul, 1980.

Binswanger, L. 1945. Insanity as life-historical phenomenon and as mental disease: The case of Ilse. In *Existence: A new dimension in psychiatry and psychology,* ed. R. May, E. Angel, and H. Ellenberger. New York: Basic Books, 1958.

Bleicher, J., ed. 1980. *Contemporary hermeneutics: Hermeneutics as method, philosophy, and critique.* London: Routledge & Kegan Paul.

Blight, J. 1981. Must psychoanalysis retreat to hermeneutics? Psychoanalytic theory in light of Popper's evolutionary epistemology. *Psychoanalysis and Contemporary Thought* 4: 147–206.

Blumenberg, H. 1987. An anthropological approach to the contemporary significance of rhetoric. In *After philosophy: End of transformation?* ed. R. Baynes, J. Bohman, and T. McCarthy. Cambridge: MIT Press.

Bowlby, J. 1980. *Attachment and loss: Loss, sadness, and depression.* New York: Basic Books.

Brenner, C. 1974. On the nature and development of affects: A unified theory. *Psychoanalytic Quarterly* 43: 532–56.

―――. 1983. *The mind in conflict.* New York: International Universities Press.

Brooks, P. 1984. *Reading for the plot.* Oxford: Clarendon Press.

Bruner, J. 1983. *Child's talk: Learning to use language.* New York: W. W. Norton.

―――. 1986. *Actual minds, possible worlds.* Cambridge: Harvard University Press.

―――. 1990. *Acts of meaning.* Cambridge: Harvard University Press.

Burrell, M. 1987. Cognitive psychology, epistemology and psychotherapy: A motor-evolutionary perspective. *Psychotherapy* 24: 225–32.

Chasseguet-Smirgel, J. 1984. *Creativity and perversion.* New York: W. W. Norton.

Chinen, A. B. 1984. Modal logic: A new paradigm of development and late-life potential. *Human Development* 27: 42–56.

Cicchetti, D., et al. 1988. Stage-salient issues in infancy and toddlerhood: Implications for a transactional model of intervention. In *Developmental psycho-pathology and its treatment,* ed. E. Nannis and P. Cowan. San Francisco: Jossey-Bass.

Cicourel, A. V. 1982. Language and belief in a medical setting. In *Contemporary perceptions of language: Interdisciplinary dimensions,* ed. H. Brynes. Washington, D.C.: Georgetown University Press.

Cohen, M. 1952. Countertransference and anxiety. *Psychiatry* 15: 231–43.

Cohler, B. J. 1981. Personal narrative and life course. In *Life-span development and behavior,* Vol. 4, ed. P. B. Baltes and O. G. Brim. New York: Academic Press.

Collingwood, R. G. 1946. *The idea of history.* New York: Oxford University Press.

Crites, S. 1986. Storytime: Recollecting the past and projecting the future. In *Narrative psychology: The storied nature of human conduct,* ed. T. Sarbin. New York: Praeger.

Culler, J. 1981. *The pursuit of signs: Semiotics, literature, deconstruction.* Ithaca: Cornell University Press.

Curtis, J. T., Silberschatz, G., Sampson, H., Weiss, J. Jr., and Rosenberg, S. E. 1988. Developing reliable psychodynamic case formulations: An illustration of the plan diagnosis method. *Psychotherapy* 25: 256–65.

Dallmayr, F. 1981. *Twilight of subjectivity: Contributions to a post-individualist theory of politics.* Amherst: University of Massachusetts.

Danto, A. C. 1965. *Analytical philosophy of history.* Cambridge: Cambridge University Press.

———. 1985. *Narration and knowledge.* New York: Columbia University Press.

Danziger, K. 1985. The methodological imperative in psychology. *Phil. Soc. Sci.* 15: 1–13.

Deutsch, F. 1957. A footnote to Freud's "Fragment of an analysis of a case of hysteria." *Psychoanalytic Quarterly* 26: 159–67.

Dilthey, W. 1906. The contribution of the historical world in the human sciences. In *W. Dilthey: Selected writings,* ed. H. P. Rickman. Cambridge: Cambridge University Press, 1976.

Dray, W. 1957. *Laws and explanation in history.* Oxford: Oxford University Press.

———. 1964. *Philosophy of history.* Englewood Cliffs, N.J.: Prentice-Hall.

———. 1985. Narrative versus analysis in history. *Phil. Soc. Sci.* 15: 125–45.

Dryden, W., ed. 1987. *Key cases in psychotherapy.* New York: New York University Press.

Dunn, J. 1978. Practicing history and social science on realist assumptions. In *Action and interpretation,* ed. C. Hookway and P. Pettit. New York: Cambridge University Press.

Eagle, M. 1984a. *Recent developments in psychoanalysis.* New York: McGraw-Hill.

———. 1984b. Psychoanalysis and narrative truth: A reply to Spence. *Psychoanalysis and Contemporary Thought* 7: 629–40.

Edelman, G. M. 1989. *The remembered present: A biological theory of consciousness.* New York: Basic Books.

Edelson, M. 1975. *Language and interpretation in psychoanalysis.* Chicago: University of Chicago Press.

Edelson, M. 1984. *Hypothesis and evidence in psychoanalysis*. Chicago: University of Chicago Press.

———. 1985. The hermeneutic turn and the single case study in psychoanalysis. *Psychoanalysis and Contemporary Thought* 8: 567–614.

———. 1986. Causal explanation in science and analysis. In *The Psychoanalytic Study of the Child*, Vol. 41, ed. P. Neubauer and A. Solnit. New Haven: Yale University Press.

Epstein, L., and Feiner, A. H., eds. 1979. *Countertransference*. New York: Jason Aronson.

Erickson, S. 1970. *Language and being: An analytic phenomenology*. New Haven: Yale University Press.

Erikson, E. H. 1959. Identity and the life cycle. *Psychological Issues* 1: 1–171.

———. 1962a. Reality and actuality. *J. Amer. Psychoanal. Assn.* 10: 451–74.

———. 1962b. *Young man Luther: A study in psychoanalysis and history*. New York: W. W. Norton.

———. 1963. *Childhood and society*. New York: W. W. Norton.

———. 1979. Reflections on Dr. Borg's life cycle. In *Aging, death and the completion of being*, ed. D. D. Van Tassel. Philadelphia: University of Pennsylvania Press.

Etchegoyen, R. H. 1991. *The fundamentals of psychoanalytic technique*. New York: Karnac Books.

Fairbairn, W. R. D. 1958. On the nature and aims of psychoanalytical treatment. *International Journal of Psychoanalysis* 39: 374–85.

Feffer, M. 1982. *The structure of freudian thought: The problem of immutability and discontinuity in developmental theory*. New York: International Universities Press.

Feiner, A. H. 1979. Countertransference and anxiety of influence. In *Countertransference*, ed. L. Epstein and A. H. Feiner. New York: Jason Aronson.

Felman, S. 1987. *Jacques Lacan and the adventure of insight*. Cambridge: Harvard University Press.

Feyerabend, P. K. 1975. *Against method: Outline of an anarchistic theory of knowledge*. Atlantic Highlands, N.J.: Humanities Press.

Fish, S. 1980. *Is there a text in this class?* Cambridge: Harvard University Press.

Fisher, S., and Greenberg, R. 1977. *The scientific credibility of Freud's theories and therapy*. New York: Basic Books.

Frank, J. D. 1973. *Persuasion and healing: A comparative study of psychotherapy*. Baltimore: Johns Hopkins University Press.

Freeman, A., and Greenwood, V., eds. 1987. *Cognitive therapy: Applications in psychiatric and medical settings*. New York: Human Sciences Press.

Freeman, M. 1984. History, narrative, and life-span developmental knowledge. *Human Development* 27: 1–19.

Freud, A. 1936. *The ego and the mechanisms of defense*. New York: International Universities Press, 1946.

———. 1965. *Normality and pathology in childhood: Assessments of development*. New York: International Universities Press.

Freud, S. 1900. The interpretation of dreams. *Standard edition of the complete psychological works of Sigmund Freud* 4–5: 1–627 London: Hogarth Press.

———. 1905a. Three essays on the theory of sexuality. *Standard edition.* 7: 125–245.

———. [1901] 1905b. Fragment of an analysis of a case of hysteria. *Standard edition* 7: 3–122.

———. 1907. Obsessive actions and religious practices. *Standard edition* 9: 115–27.

———. 1909a. Notes upon a case of obsessional neurosis. *Standard edition* 10: 155–318.

———. 1909b. Analysis of a phobia in a five-year-old boy. *Standard edition* 10: 3–149.

———. 1910. The future prospects of psycho-analytic therapy. *Standard edition* 11: 138–51.

———. 1911. Formulations on the two principles of mental functioning. *Standard edition* 12: 213–26.

———. 1912a. The disposition to obsessional neurosis. *Standard edition* 12: 311–26.

———. 1912b. Recommendations to physicians practicing psychoanalysis. *Standard edition* 12: 109–20.

———. 1912c. The dynamics of transference. *Standard edition* 12: 97–108.

———. 1913. The claims of psycho-analysis to scientific interest. *Standard edition* 13: 163–90.

———. 1914. Remembering, repeating and working through. *Standard edition* 12: 145–56.

———. 1915a. Instincts and their vicissitudes. *Standard edition* 14: 108–40.

———. 1915b. Repression. *Standard edition* 14: 141–58.

———. 1915c. The unconscious. *Standard edition* 14: 159–204.

———. 1917a. Mourning and melancholia. *Standard edition* 14: 237–58.

———. 1917b. A metapsychological supplement to the theory of dreams. *Standard edition* 14: 222–35.

———. 1917c. Introductory lectures on psycho-analysis, Part III. *Standard edition* 15: 241–465.

———. 1918. From the history of an infantile neurosis. *Standard edition* 17: 3–122.

———. 1920. Beyond the pleasure principle. *Standard edition* 18: 1–64.

———. 1926. The dynamics of the transference. *Standard edition* 12: 97–108.

———. 1933. New introductory lectures on psycho-analysis. *Standard edition* 22: 5–182.

———. 1937a. Analysis terminable and interminable. *Standard edition* 23: 209–53.

———. 1937b. Constructions in analysis. *Standard edition* 23: 255–69.

Furet, F. 1975. From narrative history to history as a problem. *Diogenes* Spring: 106–23.

Gadamer, H. G. 1975. *Truth and method,* trans. D. E. Linge. Berkeley and Los Angeles: University of California Press.

———. 1976. *Philosophical hermeneutics,* trans. D. E. Linge. Berkeley and Los Angeles: University of California Press.

———. 1981. Hermeneutics as a theoretical and practical task. In *Reason in the age of science,* trans. F. G. Lawrence. Cambridge: MIT Press.

Gaensbauer, T. J., and Sands, S. K. 1979. Distorted affective communications in abused/neglected infants and their potential impact on caretaker. *Journal of the American Academy of Child Psychiatry* 18: 236–50.

Gallie, W. B. 1964. *Philosophy and historical understanding.* New York: Schocken Books.

———. 1968. Philosophical analysis and historical understanding. *Review of Metaphysics* 21: 687.

Garfinkel, H. 1967. *Studies in ethnomethodology.* Englewood Cliffs, N.J.: Prentice-Hall.

Gedo, J. 1979. *Beyond interpretation: Toward a revised theory for psychoanalysis.* New York: International Universities Press.

———. 1981. Measure for measure. *Psychoanalytic Inquiry* 1: 280–318.

———. 1984. *Psychoanalysis and its discontents.* New York: International Universities Press.

———. 1986. *Conceptual issues in psychoanalysis: Essays in history and method.* Hillsdale, N.J.: Analytic Press.

———. 1988. *The mind in disorder.* Hillsdale, N.J.: Analytic Press.

Gedo, J., and Goldberg, A. 1973. *Models of the mind: A psychoanalytic theory.* Chicago: University of Chicago Press.

Geertz, C. 1973. *The interpretation of cultures.* New York: Basic Books.

———. 1983. *Local knowledge: Further essays in interpretative anthropology.* New York: Basic Books.

Gergen, K. J. 1977. Stability, change, and chance in understanding human development. In *Life-span development psychology: Dialectical perspectives in experimental research,* ed. N. Datan and W. W. Reese. New York: Academic Press.

Gergen, K. J., and Gergen, M. M. 1986. Narrative form and the construction of psychological science. In *Narrative psychology,* ed. T. R. Sarbin. New York: Praeger.

Giddens, A. 1979. *Central problems in social theory: Action, structure and contradiction in social analysis.* Berkeley and Los Angeles: University of California Press.

Gill, M. M. 1976. Metapsychology is not psychology. In *Psychology versus metapsychology: Essays in honor of George S. Klein,* ed. M. M. Gill and P. S. Holzman. New York: International Universities Press.

———. 1983. The interpersonal paradigm and the degree of the therapist's involvement. *Contemporary Psychoanalysis* 19: 200–237.

———. 1984. Psychoanalysis and psychotherapy: A revision. *International Review of Psycho-Analysis* 11: 161–79.

Gilligan, C. 1982. *In a different voice.* Cambridge: Harvard University Press.

Goldberg, A. 1987. Psychoanalysis and negotiation. *Psychoanalytic Quarterly* 56: 109–29.

Goodman, N. 1978. *Ways of worldmaking.* New York: Bobbs-Merrill.

———. 1984. Notes on the well-made world. *Partisan Review* 51: 276–88.

Goodstein, R. L. 1960. Language and experience. In *Philosophy of science,* ed. A. C. Danto and S. Morgenbesser. Cleveland: World.

Greenberg, L. S., Pinsoff, W. M., eds. 1986. *The psychotherapeutic process: A research handbook.* New York: Guilford Press.

Greenson, R. R. 1967. *The technique and practice of psychoanalysis.* New York: International Universities Press.

Greenspan, S. I. 1979. *Intelligence and adaptation.* New York: International Universities Press.

Grice, H. P. 1975. Logic and conversation. In *Syntax and semantics,* Vol. 3: *Speech acts,* ed. P. Cole and J. C. Morgan. New York: Academic Press.

Grotstein, J. S. 1981. *Splitting and projective identification.* New York: Jason Aronson.

Grunbaum, A. 1984. *The foundations of psychoanalysis: A philosophical critique.* Berkeley and Los Angeles: University of California Press.

Habermas, J. 1971. *Knowledge and human interests,* trans. J. Shapiro. Boston: Beacon Press.

———. 1980. The hermeneutic claim to universality. In *Contemporary hermeneutics: Hermeneutics as method, philosophy and critique,* ed. J. Bleicher. London: Routledge & Kegan Paul.

Hampshire, S. 1977. The explanation of thought. In *Psychiatry and the humanities,* Vol. 2, ed. J. H. Smith. New Haven: Yale University Press.

Harré, R. 1984. *Personal being: A theory for individual psychology.* Cambridge: Harvard University Press.

Hartmann, H. 1951. Technical implications of ego psychology. *Psychoanalytic Quarterly* 20: 31–43.

Havens, L. 1986. *Making contact: Uses of language in psychotherapy.* Cambridge: Harvard University Press.

———. 1989. *A safe place: Laying the groundwork of psychotherapy.* Cambridge: Harvard University Press.

Heidegger, M. 1967. *What Is a Thing?* trans. W. B. Barton, Jr., and V. Deutsch. Chicago: Henry Regnery.

———. 1968. *What Is Called Thinking?* trans. F. D. Wieck and J. G. Gray. New York: Harper and Row.

Heider, F. 1958. *The psychology of interpersonal relations.* New York: Wiley.

Hempel, C. G. 1942. The function of general laws in history. In *Theories of history,* ed. P. Gardiner. Urbana: University of Illinois Press, 1959.

Hesse, P., and Cicchetti, D. 1982. Toward an integrative theory of emotional development. *New Directions for Child Development* 16: 3–48.

Hirsch, E. D. 1967. *Validity in interpretation.* New Haven: Yale University Press.

Holt, R. R. 1972. Freud's mechanistic and humanistic images of man. In *Psychoanalysis and contemporary science,* Vol. 1, ed. R. R. Holt and E. Peterfreund. New York: Macmillan.

———. 1976. Drive or wish? A reconsideration of the psychoanalytic theory of motivation. In *Psychology versus metapsychology: Psychoanalytic essays in memory of George S. Klein,* ed. M. M. Gill and P. S. Holzman. *Psychological Issues,* Monograph 36: 159–97. New York: International Universities Press.

———. 1989. *Freud reappraised: A fresh look at psychoanalytic theory.* New York: Guilford Press.

Horowitz, M. J. 1977. Cognitive and interactive aspects of splitting. *Am. J. Psychiatry* 135: 549–53.

———. 1988. *Introduction to psychodynamics: A new synthesis.* New York: Basic Books.

Hoshmand, L. T., and Polkinghorne, D. 1992. Redefining the science-practice relationship and professional training. *American Psychologist* 47: 55–56.

Hull, C. L. 1935. The conflicting psychologies of learning: a way out. *Psychological Review* 42: 491–516.

Husserl, E. 1962. *Ideas towards a pure phenomenology and phenomenological philosophy,* trans. W. R. Boyce Gibson. New York: Collier.

———. 1964. *The idea of phenomenology,* trans. W. P. Alston and G. Nakhnikian. The Hague: Martinus Nijhoff.

James, W. [1910] 1975. *The Meaning of Truth.* Cambridge: Harvard University Press.

———. 1979. *The will to believe.* Cambridge: Harvard University Press.

Jameson, F. 1991. *Postmodernism, or The cultural logic of late capitalism.* Durham, N.C.: Duke University Press.

Kagan, J. 1984. *The nature of the child.* New York: Basic Books.

———. 1989. *Unstable ideas: Temperament, cognition and self.* Cambridge: Harvard University Press.

Kahneman, D., Slovic P., and Twersky, A. 1982. *Judgement under uncertainty: Heuristics and biases.* Cambridge: Cambridge University Press.

Kaplan, B. 1966. The study of language in psychiatry: The comparative developmental approach and its application to symbolization and language in psychopathology. In *American handbook of psychiatry,* ed. S. Arieti. New York: Basic Books.

Karon, B. F. 1984. A type of transference based on identification with an abusing parent. *Psychoanalytic Psychology* 1: 345–48.

Keat, R. 1981. *The politics of social theory: Habermas, Freud and the critique of positivism.* Chicago: University of Chicago Press.

Kernberg, O. 1975. *Borderline conditions and pathological narcissism.* New York: Jason Aronson.

Kierkegaard, S. 1959. *Either/Or,* Vol. 1, trans. D. Swenson and L. Swenson. Princeton: Princeton University Press.

Klauber, J. 1968. On the use of historical and scientific method in psychoanalysis. *International Journal of Psychoanalysis* 49: 80–88.

Klein, G. S. 1976. *Psychoanalytic theory: An exploration of essentials.* New York: International Universities Press.

Klein, M. 1975. *Envy and gratitude and other works, 1946–1963.* New York: Delacorte Press.

Kohut, H. 1971. *The analysis of the self.* New York: International Universities Press.

———. 1977. *The restoration of the self.* New York: International Universities Press.

Kovel, J. 1981. *The age of desire: Case histories of a radical psychoanalyst.* New York: Pantheon.

Kris, W. 1956. On some vicissitudes of insight in psychoanalysis. In *The selected papers of Ernst Kris.* New Haven: Yale University Press, 1975.

Krystal, H. 1979. Alexithymia and psychotherapy. *Am. J. Psychotherapy* 33: 17–31.

Kuhn, T. S. 1962. *The structure of scientific revolutions.* Chicago: University of Chicago Press.

Kukla, A. 1989. Nonempirical issues in psychology. *American Psychologist* 44: 785–94.

Kurzweil, E. 1989. *The Freudians: A comparative perspective.* New Haven: Yale University Press.

Kuzminski, A. 1986. Archetypes and paradigms: History, politics and persons. *History and Theory* 25: 225–47.

Lacan, J. 1977. *The four fundamental concepts of psycho-analysis,* trans. A. Sheridan. New York: W. W. Norton.

Lakatos, I. 1970. Falsification and the methodology of scientific research programs. In *Criticism and the growth of knowledge,* ed. I. Lakatos and A. Musgrave. Cambridge: Cambridge University Press.

Lakoff, G., and Johnson, M. C. 1980. *Metaphors we live by.* Chicago: University of Chicago Press.

Lane, R. D., and Schwartz, G. E. 1987. Levels of emotional awareness: A cognitive-developmental theory and its application to psychopathology. *Am. J. Psychiatry* 141: 133–43.

Langer, S. 1967. *Mind: An essay on human feeling,* Vol. 1. Baltimore: Johns Hopkins University Press.

Laplanche, J. 1976. *Life and death in psychoanalysis,* trans. J. Mehlman. Baltimore: Johns Hopkins University Press.

Laplanche, J., and Pontalis, J. B. 1973. *The language of psychoanalysis.* London: Hogarth Press.

Leahey, T. H. 1980. *A history of psychology: Main currents in psychological thought.* Englewood Cliffs, N.J.: Prentice-Hall.

Leavy, S. A. 1980. *The psychoanalytic dialogue.* New Haven: Yale University Press.

Levenson, E. 1983. *The ambiguity of change: An inquiry into the nature of psychoanalytic reality.* New York: Basic Books.

Lewis, C. I. 1956. *Mind and the world order.* New York: Dover.

Loevinger, J. 1976. *Ego development.* San Francisco: Jossey-Bass.

Loewald, H. W. 1960. On the therapeutic action of psycho-analysis. *International Journal and Psychoanalysis* 41: 16–33.

Louch, A. R. 1966. *Explanation and human action.* Berkeley and Los Angeles: University of California Press.

Mahler, M. 1968. *On human symbiosis and the vicissitudes of individuation,* Vol. 1. New York: International Universities Press.

Mandler, J. M. 1984. *Scripts, stories and scenes: Aspects of schema theory.* Hillsdale, N.J.: Lawrence Erlbaum.

Marcus, S. 1987. *Freud and the culture of psychoanalysis.* New York: W. W. Norton.

Marmar, L. R., and Horowitz, M. J. 1986. Phenomenological analysis of splitting. *Psychotherapy* 23: 21–29.

Marshall, R. J. 1979. Countertransference in the psychotherapy of children and adolescents. *Contemporary Psychoanalysis* 15: 595–629.

McCarthy, T. 1978. *The critical theory of Jürgen Habermas.* Cambridge: MIT Press.

McClure, B. A., and Hodge, B. W. 1987. Measuring countertransference and attitude in therapeutic relationships. *Psychotherapy* 24: 325–35.

McDougall, J. 1979. Primitive communication and the use of countertransference. In *Countertransference,* ed. L. Epstein and A. H. Feiner. New York: Jason Aronson.

———. 1985. *Theaters of the mind.* New York: Basic Books.

McDowell, J. 1978. On "the reality of the past." In *Action and Interpretation,* ed. C. Hookway and P. Pettit. New York: Cambridge University Press.

McGinn, C. 1982. *The character of mind.* New York: Oxford University Press.

McGlashan, T. 1983. Intensive individual psychotherapy of schizophrenia. *Archives of General Psychiatry* 40: 909–20.

Meissner, W. W. 1979. Methodological critique of the action language in psychoanalysis. *J. Amer. Psychoanal. Assn.* 27: 79–105.

Mink, L. O. 1970. History and fiction as modes of comprehension. *New Literary History* 1: 541–58.

———. 1978. Narrative form as a cognitive instrument. In *The writing of history: Literary form and historical understanding,* ed. R. H. Canary and H. Kozicki. Madison: University of Wisconsin Press.

Minkowski, E. 1923. Findings in a case of schizophrenic depression. In *Existence: A new dimension in psychiatry and psychology,* ed. R. May, E. Angel, and H. Ellenberger. New York: Basic Books, 1958.

Modell, A. H. 1981. Does metapsychology still exist? *International Journal of Psychoanalysis* 62: 391–401.

Munz, P. 1985. *Our knowledge of the growth of knowledge: Popper or Wittgenstein?* London: Routledge & Kegan Paul.

Nemiah, J. C. 1961. *Foundations of psychopathology.* New York: Oxford University Press.

———. 1977. Alexithymia: Theoretical consideration. *Psychother. Psychosom.* 28: 199–206.

Noy, P. 1969. A revision of the psychoanalytic theory of primary process. *International Review of Psycho-Analysis* 50: 155–78.

―――. 1977. Metapsychology as a multimodel system. *International Review of Psycho-Analysis* 4: 1–10.

―――. 1979. The psychoanalytic theory of cognitive development. In *The Psychoanalytic Study of the Child* 34: 169–216.

Oakeshott, M. 1933. *Experience and its modes.* Cambridge: Cambridge University Press.

―――. 1962. *Rationalism in politics.* New York: Basic Books.

―――. 1975. *On human conduct.* Cambridge: Cambridge University Press.

Olinick, S., and Tracy, L. 1987. Transference perspectives of storytelling. *Psychoanalytic Review* 74: 319–33.

Oremland, J. D. 1991. *Interpretation and interaction: Psychoanalysis or psychotherapy.* Hillsdale, N.J.: Analytic Press.

Orr, D. W. 1954. Transference and countertransference: A historical survey. *J. Amer. Psychoanal. Assn.* 2: 621–70.

Panel 1954. Psychoanalysis and dynamic psychotherapy—similarities and differences, rep. L. Rangell. *J. Amer. Psychoanal. Assn.* 2: 152–66.

Parisi, T. 1987. Why Freud failed: Some implications for neurophysiology and sociobiology. *American Psychologist* 42: 237–45.

Peterfreund, E. 1978. Some critical comments on psychoanalytic conceptualizations of infancy. *International Journal of Psychoanalysis* 59: 427–46.

Piaget, J. 1971. *Psychology and epistemology: Towards a theory of knowledge,* trans. A. Rosin. New York: Viking Press.

Piaget, J., and Inhelder, B. 1969. *The psychology of the child,* trans. A. Weaver. New York: Basic Books.

Pine, F. 1981. In the beginning: Contributions to a psychoanalytic developmental psychology. *International Review of Psycho-Analysis* 8: 15–33.

Polanyi, M. 1958. *Personal knowledge: Toward a post-critical philosophy.* Chicago: University of Chicago Press.

Polkinghorne, D. 1983. *Methodology for the human sciences.* Albany: State University of New York Press.

―――. 1988. *Narrative knowing and the human sciences.* Albany: State University of New York Press.

Popper, K. 1972. *Objective knowledge: An evolutionary approach.* Oxford: Clarendon Press.

―――. 1976. The myth of the framework. In *The abdication of philosophy: Philosophy and the public good. Essays in Honor of Paul Arthur Schilpp,* ed. E. Freeman. LaSalle, Ill.: Open Court.

Prince, G. 1982. *Narratology: The form and functioning of narrative.* Berlin: Mouton.

Racker, H. 1968. *Transference and countertransference.* New York: International Universities Press.

Reppen, J., ed. 1985. *Beyond Freud: A study of modern psychoanalytic theorists.* Hillsdale, N.J.: Lawrence Erlbaum.

Ricoeur, P. 1970. *Freud and philosophy: An essay on interpretation.* New Haven: Yale University Press.

Ricoeur, P. 1974. *The conflict of interpretation: Essays in hermeneutics.* Evanston, Ill.: Northwestern University Press.

———. 1976. *Interpretation theory: Discourse and the surplus of meaning.* Fort Worth: Texas Christian University Press.

———. 1983. *Time and narrative.* Chicago: University of Chicago Press.

———. 1985. *Time and narrative,* Vol. 2. Chicago: University of Chicago Press.

Rieff, P. 1968. *The triumph of the therapeutic: Uses of faith After Freud.* New York: Harper and Row.

Rockland, L. H. 1989. *Supportive therapy: A psychodynamic approach.* New York: Basic Books.

Rogoff, B. 1990. *Apprenticeship in thinking: Cognitive development in social context.* New York: Oxford University Press.

Romanyshyn, D. 1982. *Psychological life: From science to metaphor.* Austin: University of Texas Press.

Rorty, R. 1979. *Philosophy and the mirror of nature.* Princeton: Princeton University Press.

Rosch, E. H. et. al. 1976. Basic objects in natural categories. *Cognitive Psychology* 8: 382–439.

Roth, M. S. 1987. *Psycho-analysis as history: Negation and freedom in Freud.* Ithaca: Cornell University Press.

Rubenstein, B. B. 1972. On metaphor and related phenomena. *Psychoanalysis and Contemporary Science* 1: 70–108.

———. 1977. On the concept of a person and an organism. In *Science and Psychotherapy,* ed. R. Stern, L. S. Horowitz, and J. Lynes. New York: Haven.

Rumelhart, D. E. 1981. Analogical processes in learning. In *Cognitive skills and their acquisition,* ed. J. Anderson. Hillsdale, N.J.: Lawrence Erlbaum.

Russell, R. 1988. A critical interpretation of Packer's "Inquiry . . ." *American Psychologist* 43: 130–31.

Ryle, G. 1949. *The concept of mind.* London: Hutchinson.

Sabini, J., and Silver, M. 1982. *The moralities of everyday life.* London: Oxford University Press.

Salmon, W. C. 1984. *Scientific explanation and the causal structure of the world.* Princeton: Princeton University Press.

Sandler, J. 1976. Countertransference and role-responsiveness. *International Review of Psycho-Analysis* 3: 43–47.

Sarbin, T. R., ed. 1986. *Narrative psychology: The storied nature of human conduct.* New York: Praeger.

Sass, L. 1987. Introspection, schizophrenia and the fragmentation of self. *Representations* 19: 1–34.

Schafer, R. 1968. *Aspects of internalization.* New York: International Universities Press.

———. 1976. *A new language for psychoanalysis.* New Haven: Yale University Press.

———. 1978. *Language and insight.* New Haven: Yale University Press.

———. 1982. The relevance of the 'here and now' transference interpretation to the reconstruction of early development. *International Journal of Psychoanalysis* 63: 77–82.

———. 1983. *The analytic attitude.* New York: Basic Books.

———. 1984. The pursuit of failure and the idealization of unhappiness. *American Psychologist* 39: 398–405.

Scheibe, R. 1986. Self-narratives and adventure. In *Narrative psychology,* ed. T. R. Sarbin. New York: Praeger.

Schimek, J. 1975a. The interpretation of the past: Childhood trauma, psychic reality and historical truth. *J. Amer. Psychoanal. Assn.* 23: 845–65.

———. 1975b. A critical re-examination of Freud's concept of unconscious mental representations. *International Review of Psycho-Analysis* 2: 171–86.

———. 1987. Fact and fantasy in the seduction theory: An historical review. *J. Amer. Psychoanal. Assn.* 35: 937–65.

Schlesinger, H. J. 1969. Diagnosis and prescription for psychotherapy. *Bulletin of the Menninger Clinic* 41: 202–6.

———. 1981. Resistance as process. In *Resistance: Psychodynamic and behavioral approaches,* ed. P. Wachtel. New York: Plenum Press.

Schutz, A. 1966. *Collected papers III: Studies in phenomenological philosophy,* ed. I. Schutz. The Hague: Martinus Nijhoff.

Schwartz, M. A., and Wiggins, O. P. 1986. Systems and structuring of meaning: Contributions to a biopsychosocial medicine. *Am. J. Psychiatry* 143: 1213–21.

Shapiro, D. 1989. *Psychotherapy of neurotic character.* New York: Basic Books.

Shweder, R. A. 1986. Divergent rationalities. In *Metatheory in Social Science: Pluralisms and Subjectivities,* ed. D. W. Fiske and R. A. Shweder. Chicago: University of Chicago Press.

Silberschatz, G., Curtis, J. T., and Nathan, S. 1989. Using the patient's plan to assess progress in psychotherapy. *Psychotherapy* 26: 40–46.

Singer, J. R., Sincoff, J. B., and Kolligian, J. Jr. 1989. Countertransference and cognition: Studying the psychotherapist's distortions as consequences of normal information processing. *Psychotherapy* 26: 344–55.

Solms, M., and Saling M. 1986. On psychoanalysis and neuroscience: Freud's attitude towards the localizationist tradition. *International Journal of Psychoanalysis* 67: 397–416.

Spence, D. 1982. *Narrative truth and historical truth: Meaning and interpretation in psychoanalysis.* New York: W. W. Norton.

Spotnitz, H. 1969. *Modern psychoanalysis of the schizophrenic patient.* New York: Grune and Stratton.

Stannard, D. E. 1980. *Shrinking history: On Freud and the failure of psychohistory.* New York: Oxford University Press.

Stern, D. 1985. *The interpersonal world of the infant: A view from psychoanalysis and developmental psychology.* New York: Basic Books.

Sternberg, R., and Wagner, R., eds. 1986. *Practical intelligence.* New York: Cambridge University Press.

Stiles, W. B., Shapiro, D., and Elliott, R. 1986. Are all psychotherapies equivalent? *American Psychologist* 41: 165–80.

Stolorow, R. D., and Lachman, F. M. 1980. *Psychoanalysis of developmental arrests: Theory and treatment.* New York: International Universities Press.

Strawson, P. F. 1959. *Individuals: An essay in descriptive metaphysics.* London: Methuen.

Strupp, H. H. 1986. Psychotherapy: Research, practice, and public policy (How to avoid dead ends). *American Psychologist* 41: 120–30.

Sullivan, H. S. 1970. *The psychiatric interview.* New York: W. W. Norton.

Thoma, H., and Kachele, H. 1975. Problems of metascience and methodology in clinical psychoanalytic research. *Annual of Psychoanalysis* 3: 49–119.

Tucker, R. 1961. *Philosophy and myth in Karl Marx.* New York: Cambridge University Press.

Vaillant, G. 1986. *Empirical studies of ego mechanisms of defense.* Washington, D.C.: American Psychiatric Press.

Vallacher, R. R., and Wegner, D. M. 1987. What do people think they're doing? Action identification and human behavior. *Psychological Review* 24: 3–15.

Volkan, V. D. 1976. *Primitive internalized object relations.* New York: International Universities Press.

von Wright, G. H. 1971. *Explanation and understanding.* Ithaca: Cornell University Press.

Waelder, R. 1962. Psychoanalysis, scientific method, and philosophy. *J. Amer. Psychoanal. Assn.* 10: 617–37.

Waismann, F. 1965. Language-strata. In *Logic and language,* ed. A. Flew. Garden City, N.Y.: Doubleday.

Wallace, E. R. 1985. *Historiography and causation in psychoanalysis.* Hillsdale, N.J.: Analytic Press.

Wallerstein, R. S. 1973. Psychoanalytic perspectives on the problem of reality. *J. Amer. Psychoanal. Assn.* 21: 5–33.

———. 1988. One psychoanalysis or many? *International Journal of Psychoanalysis* 69: 5–21.

Wallulis, J. 1990. *The hermeneutics of life history: Personal achievement and history in Gadamer, Habermas, and Erikson.* Evanston, Ill.: Northwestern University Press.

Weber, M. 1964. *The theory of social and economic organization,* ed. T. Parsons. New York: Free Press.

Weiss, J., and Sampson, H. 1986. *The psychoanalytic process: Clinical observation and empirical research.* New York: Guilford Press.

Werner, H. 1948. *Comparative psychology of mental development.* New York: International Universities Press.

Werner, H., and Kaplan, B. 1963. *Symbol formation: An organismic-development approach to language and the expression of thought.* New York: John Wiley.

Wexler, J. 1991. Conrad's dream of a common language: Lacan and "The secret sharer." *Psychoanalytic Review* 78: 599–606.

White, H. 1981. The value of narrativity in the representation of reality. In *On narrative,* ed. W. J. T. Mitchell. Chicago: University of Chicago Press.

———. 1984. The question of narrative in contemporary historical theory. *History and Theory* 23: 1–33.

————. 1987. *The content of form*. Baltimore: Johns Hopkins University Press.

Wiesel, E. 1990. *From the kingdom of memory*. New York: Summit Books.

Williams, F. 1984–85. Translator's preface to "Dream and Existence." *Review of Existential Psychology and Psychiatry* 19: 19–28.

Wilson, A. 1986. Archaic transference and anaclitic depression: Psychoanalytic perspectives on the treatment of severely disturbed patients. *Psychoanalytic Psychology* 3: 237–56.

Winch, P. 1958. *The idea of a social science and its relation to philosophy*. London: Routledge & Kegan Paul.

————. 1964. Understanding a primitive society. *American Philosophical Quarterly* 1: 307–24.

Winnicott, D. W. 1947. Hate in the countertransference. In *Through paediatrics to psycho-analysis*. London: Hogarth.

————. 1965. *The maturational processes and the facilitating environment*. New York: International Universities Press.

Wittgenstein, L. 1968. *Philosophical investigations,* trans. G. E. M. Anscombe. New York: Macmillan.

Wollheim, R. 1974. *Freud: A collection of critical essays*. New York: Anchor.

————. 1984. *The thread of life*. Cambridge: Harvard University Press.

Zaner, R. M. 1981. *The context of self: A phenomenological inquiry using medicine as a clue*. Athens, Ohio: Ohio University Press.

Zukier, H. 1985. Freud and development: The developmental dimensions of psychoanalytic theory. *Social Research* 52: 3–41.

Zukier, H., and Pepitone, A. 1984. Social roles and strategies in prediction: Some determinants of the use of base rate information. *Journal of Personality and Social Psychology* 47: 349–60.

Name Index

289

Subject Index

Abstraction, 28; modes of, 256; scientific, 142. *See also* Analytic abstraction

Abstraction from experience, 95, 99 n. 20; in history, 91, 92; in phenomenology, 93; in science, 89, 92

Abstractive transformation, 201

Academic psychology, 69, 263; methodological circle in, 14–16

Action(s), 123, 124; and agency, 122–28; conceptualization of, 120, 122–23, 125–26, 127, 128, 146, 151–52; narrated, 153; objective framework of, 171 n. 25; problems of identification of, 169 n. 17

Action language, 27, 28, 118–21, 122–28, 170 n. 23, 183, 250 n. 68; recontextualized as narrative discourse, 128–29

Action theory, 120, 121

Actual past, 142, 143

"Advent of the intentional," 175 n. 51

Affect(s), 53, 167 n. 4, 195, 196, 197; and cognition, 198–201, 209; as derivative of development, 205; as developmental process, 198; differentiation of, 190; hierarchical organization of, 211–12; variable distribution of, 199

Affective arousal, 205; management of, 191, 192, 197

Affective-cognitive development, 196–97

Affective-cognitive interaction, 193–95

Affective communication, 197, 198, 199, 246 n. 47; distorted, 212–13, 245 n. 40; maturational level of, 216

Affective development: discontinuity in, 198–99

Affective experience, 164, 192, 193–94, 202; and cognitive structures, 193–94, 195–204, 205, 206, 213, 217–18; as derivative of development, 209; development of, 191

Affective information: double processed, 206; primary process of, 204, 205

Affective meaning: as presentational symbolism, 202

Affective states: maladaptive, 199; primitive, 204

Affective structures: development of, 213–14

Affirmative orientation (analyst), 130, 134

Agency: and action, 122–28

Aggression, 196

Ahistorical discourse, 88

Alexithymia, 62 n. 15, 244 n. 28

American psychoanalysis, xv, xvi, 105, 165 n. 1, 184, 191; conceptualization in, 229; conceptualization of past in, 3–4, 33; controversy in, 183, 257; core controversy in, 5, 9–11, 12, 23–27, 33, 41, 242 n. 18; historical understanding of, 152; past in, 76, 253–54; scientific and hermeneutic trends in, 57; scientific conceptualization of, 209

Anaclitic depressive affect, 240 n. 8, 245 n. 40

Analogical rationale, 184–85, 214–20

Analysand: relationship to past, 136–37. *See also* Patient(s)

Analysis: empirical/psychological, 73; in history, 70, 71; past in, 52. *See also* Psychoanalysis

293

Identity(ies), 62 n. 12, 160; constrained by reality, 151; in difference, 157; in narrative development, 267; narrative of, 160
Infancy/infant, 189, 190, 192; affect in, 198; clinical/observed, 48, 52–53, 54–55, 56, 57; inner world of, 194
Infant-caretaker relationship, 22
Infantile prototype, 194–95
Infantile sexuality, 47
Information processing, 117; double, 206, 207; empathic understanding as, 243 n. 23; hermeneutics as model of, 110; in primary process, 204, 205; transformations in schemata for, 198
Inquiry(ies), 13, 16, 105, 149, 181, 260; empirical-analytic/hermeneutic conceptions of, 58; historical-hermeneutic, 152 (*see also* Historical inquiry); history as, 65–66, 67–68; hypothesis-driven, 184; mixed, 95; model of, 59; narrative as, 73–74; new avenues of, 31–33, 262, 265, 266–69; past in, 46–47; plurality of modes of, 16–17; traditions of, 259. *See also* Unity of inquiry
Insight-oriented therapies, 195, 242 n. 17
Instinct, 196, 221–22; in/and body-mind, 163; Freud's theory of, 45, 60 n. 3, 224–25
Instinct-driven theory, 197, 205, 222, 249 n. 63
Instinctual discharge, 183, 197
Intentional theory, 227–28
Intentionality, 138, 140, 149, 172 n. 35, 240 n. 9, 249 n. 62; continuum of, 229; in patient, 241 n. 14; relation to biological finalities, 22; of repetition, 227; symbolic transformation of experience of, 219
Interpersonal interaction: in clinical situation, 85
Interpersonal matrix, 215
Interpersonal relations, 145; evolution in, 212
Interpersonal Theory, 4
Interpretation(s), 109, 134, 183, 192, 195, 203, 241 n. 13; in action language, 127–28; conflict of, 57–58; of countertransference, 110; distinct from interven-

tion, 169 n. 15; in Dora case, 82; historical, 25–26, 153; historicity of, 162; knowledge of past through, 218; meaning accessible through, 125; narrative versus historical truth in, 257; objectivity in, 111; and pluralism in psychoanalysis, 234; of prelinguistic dispositions, 177 n. 56; true/false, 36 n. 11; truth and efficacy in, 36 n. 11, 263
Interpretation of Dreams (Freud), 163
Interpretative communities, 151
Interpretative function of analyst, 195
Interpretative interventions, 218, 219, 242 n. 15, 247 n. 48
Interpreter: historically situated, 123
Intervention(s), 22, 29, 247 n. 48; choice of, 216, 217, 241 n. 14; classes of, 218–20; developmental level and, 192; effectiveness of, 27, 31, 36 n. 11, 37 n. 14, 59 n. 1, 97 n. 8, 234; interpretation distinct from, 169 n. 15; narrative interpretations as, 25; presentational symbolism in, 202–3; psychoanalysis as theory of, 268
Intrapsychic Self, The (Arieti), 211
Intrinsic reference, 137–38, 139
Irrational processes, 35 n. 1
Isolation, 213, 246 n. 44

Knowledge, 46; clinically relevant, 232; derived from psychoanalytic practice, 262; effective history and, 114; empirical-analytic historical-retrospective developmental, 157–58; engendered by history, 165; in fallacy of hermeneutic universality, 162; historically structured, 73, 132; objectivity of, 112; organization of reality as, 206; of the past, 52, 75, 86, 87; past as object of, 142; psychoanalytic, 117–18, 140; as relational, 12, 13, 89; scientific, 168 n. 11, 250 n. 67; secondary process represents world as, 175 n. 52; as self-constituting or socially constituted, 12–13, 90, 126; science as paradigm of, 91; technical/practical, 29, 30; two propositions regarding, 12–14, 16–17, 32, 57, 58
Knowledge-in-practice, 269